Jesus
the Terrorist

First published by O Books, 2010
O Books is an imprint of John Hunt Publishing Ltd., The Bothy, Deershot Lodge, Park Lane, Ropley,
Hants, SO24 0BE, UK
office1@o-books.net
www.o-books.net

Distribution in:	South Africa
	Alternative Books
UK and Europe	altbook@peterhyde.co.za
Orca Book Services	Tel: 021 555 4027 Fax: 021 447 1430
orders@orcabookservices.co.uk	
Tel: 01202 665432 Fax: 01202 666219	Text copyright Peter Cresswell 2009
Int. code (44)	
	Design: Stuart Davies
USA and Canada	
NBN	ISBN: 978 1 84694 274 7
custserv@nbnbooks.com	
Tel: 1 800 462 6420 Fax: 1 800 338 4550	All rights reserved. Except for brief quotations
	in critical articles or reviews, no part of this
Australia and New Zealand	book may be reproduced in any manner without
Brumby Books	prior written permission from the publishers.
sales@brumbybooks.com.au	
Tel: 61 3 9761 5535 Fax: 61 3 9761 7095	The rights of Peter Cresswell as author have
	been asserted in accordance with the
Far East (offices in Singapore, Thailand,	Copyright, Designs and Patents Act 1988.
Hong Kong, Taiwan)	
Pansing Distribution Pte Ltd	
kemal@pansing.com	A CIP catalogue record for this book is available
Tel: 65 6319 9939 Fax: 65 6462 5761	from the British Library.

Printed by Digital Book Print

O Books operates a distinctive and ethical publishing philosophy in
all areas of its business, from its global network of authors to
production and worldwide distribution.

Jesus
the Terrorist

Peter Cresswell

BOOKS

Winchester, UK
Washington, USA

CONTENTS

Acknowledgements

I am indebted to my partner Julia and to my publisher John Hunt for supporting me in what has been a rewarding and exacting venture. Special thanks to family – Fiona and Jon, David and Eloise – for help with design and technology and to Bill for reading the manuscript and making many helpful suggestions.

Introduction

Let everyone who is zealous for the law and supports the covenants come out with me!
Maccabee 2, 26-27

Think not that I have come to abolish the law and the prophets; I have come not to abolish them but to fulfil them. For truly, I say to you, till heaven and earth pass away, not an iota, not a dot, will pass from the law until all is accomplished. Whoever then relaxes one of the least of these commandments and teaches men so, shall be called least in the kingdom of heaven; but he who does them and teaches them shall be called great in the kingdom of heaven.
Matthew 5, 17-19

For whoever keeps the whole law but fails in one point has become guilty of all of it.
The Letter of James 2, 10

Interpreted [from Isaiah], these are the three nets of Belial with which Levi son of Jacob said that he catches Israel by setting them up as three kinds of righteousness. The first is riches, the second is fornication, and the third is profanation of the Temple. Whoever escapes from the first is caught in the second, and whoever saves himself from the second is caught in the third.
The Damascus Rule, Qumran

If you would be perfect, go, sell what you possess and give to the poor. ... It is easier for a camel to go through the eye of a needle than for a rich man to enter the kingdom of God. ... Come now, you rich, weep and howl for the miseries that are coming to you. ...You have lived on the earth in luxury and in pleasure; you have fattened your hearts in a day of slaughter.
Matthew 19, 21. Mark 10, 25. The Letter of James 5, 1,5

Whoever divorces his wife and marries another, commits adultery against her; and if she divorces her husband and marries another, she commits adultery.

Mark 10, 11-12

In the temple he found those who were selling oxen and sheep and pigeons, and the money changers at their business. And making a whip of cords, he drove them all, with the sheep and oxen, out of the temple; and he poured out the coins of the money changers and overturned their tables. And he told those who sold the pigeons, 'Take these things away; you shall not make my Father's house a house of trade.' His disciples remembered that it was written, 'Zeal for thy house will consume me.'

John 2, 14-18

And if your hand causes you to sin, cut it off ... And if your eye causes you to sin, pluck it out...

Mark 9, 43, 47

Do not think that I have come to bring peace on earth; I have not come to bring peace, but a sword. For I have come to set a man against his father, and a daughter against her mother, and a daughter-in-law against her mother-in-law; and a man's foes will be those of his own household.

Matthew 10, 34-36

The Romans dismissively described those who resisted them as 'lestai', which can be roughly translated as robbers or bandits. But, except for a few who may have been motivated simply by gain, Jews in first century Palestine who took up arms against the Romans were seeking to restore their independence. They saw themselves as zealous for the Law of their forefathers and often described themselves as 'zealots'.

As labels, these are relative, with their meaning depending on who used them and with what perspective. The equivalent modern terms would be terrorist and freedom fighter which are also relative. In many emerging nations, yesterday's terrorists have become today's respected statesmen, part of the political process. In Palestine now, with two states jostling together in one territory, there are two sets of people fighting for their freedom and survival, each describing the other as terrorist.

Another term 'sicarii' derives from short 'sicae' daggers used as weapons. People described in this way by the Jewish historian Josephus supported messianic leaders against the Romans and collaborating Sadducee high priests.

I have described Jesus in the title as the Romans would have perceived him, rather than use an archaic term such as 'zealot' with little modern resonance. I hope this draws attention to what was, at the time, a very brutal and shocking conflict. It does not mean that I personally share the Romans' perspective! It does mean that I take the view that the history of the period has been masked by subsequent writers with differing agendas.

The subject of this book is the person Christians call Jesus, his companions and adversaries in the first century and the people who came after him. There are a number of sources available including the New Testament gospels and several other non-canonical gospels. There are substantial accounts by Josephus and references by other historians. Letters exist which were purportedly written by the self-proclaimed apostle Paul. Events in the years following the crucifixion are described in the Acts of the Apostles and in accounts by follower of Jesus' brother James.

The problem is that these stories do not always agree, sometimes in the details and sometimes in significant respects. To disentangle conflicting accounts, it is necessary to look at the motivations and credentials of their authors and their later editors. But this cannot be done without first telling the story of which these people are a part. Since each part of the exercise depends on the other, this presents a major dilemma.

To break out of the circle, I will sometimes have to adopt assumptions which are only later clarified. I may sometimes then have to revisit and revise arguments in a new context. Progress may thus not always be entirely linear.

It is worth holding to the fact that there was one reality in first century Palestine, one set of events and one set of characters, though of course experienced in different ways by those involved at the time. The Jewish historian Josephus describes a tumultuous period of rebellion and resistance to the Romans, but says little or nothing about Jesus. The gospels make Jesus a major player, but give little indication of the conflicts taking place all around him, during his lifetime. The Dead Sea scrolls, stowed away in caves just a few miles from Jerusalem, appear to give no information which relates to the gospels. The gospels apparently have nothing to say about the Essenes, presumed authors of the scrolls, even though this group was in Judea at the same time as Jesus and did play a significant role in the life of the Jewish community.

What is certainly not true is that the events described in various sources were independent of each other, operating as parallel universes. There were no reality bubbles keeping people apart so that they played parts in markedly different dramas taking place in the same geographical space and at the same time. It is the challenge of this book to try and reconstruct what was happening from accounts which are varying and undoubtedly biased by the authors' own perspectives.

There are also difficulties in presenting and understanding the material available because of the way various characters interlock. It is for example very hard to investigate Paul, possible author of some of the epistles, without also straying into a discussion of the role of James, the brother of Jesus. An understanding of James would similarly be incomplete without consideration of his interaction with Paul. So there is bound to be a degree of recapitulation and repetition, references backwards and forwards, in sections on these and other characters.

It will not alas be possible for me just to tell it how it is, without qualification, from page one. The scale of the task is illustrated by the difficulty in deciding just who was involved. There are, for example several characters called 'Simon' in the New Testament. Three of those making an appearance are, I suggest, manifestations of the same person, Simon who was another of Jesus' brothers. But none of them was, as indicated by the gospel text, a leper or the son of someone called Jonah or the father of Judas the betrayer or a Cananite. There are likewise three or four Josephs. But one may be an invention, with his role really taken by someone else. A second may also be fictional, the product of a mistranslated reference to Jesus. A third has had some very important information about him disguised. And there is a fourth character not named as Joseph but who, it can be deduced, was actually called Joseph.

This should all become clearer as the book progresses. I can only invite patience and suggest that the journey will be worth while.

That there were far fewer fore names in New Testament times than there are now is a potential source of confusion. A plethora of zealots and others are called Eleazar/Lazarus. The names Ananus and Ananias crop up frequently among priestly Sadducee families. Herod 'the Great' passed his name down to many in succeeding generations of the Herodian family. At the end of the book, there is a list of characters and some family charts which may be of help.

The problem with names is compounded by the fact that the authors sometimes made mistakes and sometimes deliberately changed names to suit their purposes. This is hard to sort out, the source of another level of confusion and obfuscation.

One strange aspect is the number of key characters who exhibit qualities or take actions that are completely discordant. The classic example is provided by Simon, nicknamed Peter, 'the Rock' on which Jesus will build his church. His vacillation is usually explained away as the product of competing human strengths and weaknesses. He is the one portrayed as perceiving Jesus' divinity, while at the same time failing to comprehend his leader's ultimate destiny and fate. From being the strong foundation stone of the movement, he goes to the low point of denying his leader, not once but three times.

Simon, brave enough to take a swipe at the servant of the High Priest, at first cowers outside the court room door during the trial of Jesus. He is later sent by James as an emissary to check up on the apostle Paul. But he apparently cannot make up his mind whether to accept Paul's view that eating restrictions dividing Jews and Gentiles should be abolished.

The strong and fiery side of Simon's character finds echoes in other sources, where he continues the dialogue and confrontation with Paul and ultimately goes voluntarily to Rome, embracing martyrdom. There is also a reflection of the militant Simon, hunted down and imprisoned by King Agrippa, in another character of that same name who outfaces the King and secures a ransom or bribe.

The character of Judas is apparently more straightforward. But Judas moves seamlessly from being the group's treasurer to Jesus' betrayer, apparently at his own leader's behest. There is also another Judas who was one of Jesus' brothers, depicted in the gospels as seeking to obstruct his preaching mission. But this Judas was, like the group's treasurer and presumed betrayer, also an apostle.

Both the treasurer Judas and the brother Judas have nicknames indicating membership of violent, messianic anti-Roman groups. There is, as it happens, a separate record of several such revolutionary characters of this name in the first century Judea, including one living at precisely the same time.

So, are there three co-existing characters named Judas? Or, two? Or, just one?

Another brother, James, is demeaned in the New Testament, sometimes subtly and sometimes more directly as, for example, in his given title, James-the-less. It must be presumed that he was among the brothers who unhelpfully sought to interrupt Jesus during his preaching and haul him back home.

But James is also clearly described as a key apostle. He next became leader after Jesus of the community of followers in Jerusalem. He is described, in one of the non-canonical gospels, as the first person Jesus went to see after the crucifixion.

These are here alternative perceptions which are hard to reconcile. Has there been a transformation of character? Or is it a case of two different takes on essentially the same character?

In the case of Saul (or Paul), the split in personality is pushed to the fore. The thoroughly evil Saul relentlessly pursues those of 'the way', and participates in the murder of Stephen. But then he becomes the saintly Paul, enduring countless beatings and privations, all in the service of a saviour he never met.

But Paul comes into conflict with James and Simon, conducting his campaign with a degree of venom, vitriol and guile that would more befit his alter ego, Saul. There are other accounts suggesting that Saul/Paul never stopped being 'the enemy'.

So, is there one character with a changed or split personality? Or a bad Saul and a separate good Paul? Or an evil Saul who feigned his sainthood, or had it manufactured for him?

There are even whole groups characterised in conflicting

ways. In the gospels, Pharisees are denounced by Jesus but they are also his helpers, providing some of his key supporters.

Then, there are 'the Jews' as a whole. In a mass movement, they are by definition Jesus' followers. Yet they are blamed in the gospels for his death and crucifixion. So, who was it who captured, tried, convicted and executed him? While Jesus may have had enemies among his own people, those who killed him were the Romans.

It is part of the purpose of this book to try to sort out the competing definitions and accounts and see which are more original and more plausible.

Jesus himself is portrayed in more than one way in the gospels. The main theme is of a man out of his time, with a mission directed not just to the Jews but the world as a whole. He is a man with a mission to give his message and then go meekly to his death. But there are counter indications within the gospels which suggest that his character was much more violent and confrontational, that his religious message was thoroughly Jewish and fundamentalist and that his mission as a messiah or liberator was only to the Jews.

The story line is of a woman impregnated by God and a godman sacrificed to save mankind. But that story was there in the literature as pagan myth long before the days in which Jesus is presumed to have lived. The tales of Osiris and Dionysus and other similar godmen were used extensively in converting a Jewish rebel into a Gentile Christ.

The sayings attributed to Jesus also have antecedents. The twin principles of loving God and one's neighbour are core parts of Pharisaic Judaism. Ideas such as finding the kingdom of God within oneself and securing salvation through self-knowledge originated with the gnostics, who formed a branch of Christianity persecuted out of existence by the Roman Church. They in turn derived such concepts from pagan belief.

Ideas of obedience, self-sacrifice and of forgiveness may

provide good principles for living. But these may have had their origin, more than anything else, in the need to create a Church that would accept the directions of its leaders and be no threat to Rome.

The 'sayings of Jesus' incorporated in Matthew and Luke, as well as the non-canonical gnostic gospel of Thomas, may originally have been one whole collection, gathered together some years after the event. But it requires detective work and guesswork to decide which sayings are original and which were later added in. Even then, there is no certainty whether these sayings originated with one man, or were the collective wisdom passed down through a group of people, his contemporaries and possibly followers.

Even if, in an original form that cannot now be accurately recreated, they are the work of one man, there is no certainty who this man was. It may have been Jesus, or his father, also a 'master', or his brother James who took over from him, or his cousin John the Baptist, or another brother Simon or someone else.

There is a lot that can be deduced about Jesus from what is known of Jewish society at the time, from other contemporary records, from dissecting the gospels and from the subsequent development of events. The character and actions of his brothers and followers throw light on the sort of person that Jesus may really have been.

As will be seen, this evidence does not support the somewhat contradictory ideas in the gospels that Jesus was an otherworldly person, uninvolved with the daily realities of Roman injustice and repression, or a wine bibbing bonviveur who consorted with dubious characters and paid scant regard to the details of religious observance. These depictions may have their origin in the twin Christian imperatives: to make a Church fit for Rome and to distance this Church from its real origins within Judaism.

The evidence supports the idea that Jesus was more like his

brother James, 'zealous' for the Law and perhaps even like Mattathias, the first of the Maccabeans, who took his followers out into the desert to fight a guerilla war rather than submit to having Jewish Law abolished and overturned.

There are gospel sayings and parts of the narrative that resonate with this. Though it is being equally selective, some have been reproduced here (pps vii-viii).

Those sayings and reported actions of Jesus that go against the picture, which the gospels have been fashioned to present, have an added authenticity. These may well be the shreds of the original that later editors neglected to modify or eliminate, surviving despite rather than because of their attentions.

According to the gospel record, Jesus went to Jerusalem and confronted the collaborating Jewish authorities. He was charged, according to Luke, with a treasonable offence, claiming to be king. He was crucified by the Romans.

He was by these indications a major figure in the resistance to Roman occupation. But, again according to the script, he did not himself attempt to mount an insurrection.

So, what happened to his followers who urged him on, and survived him? Did they simply abandon their own hopes of re-establishing an independent Jewish kingdom? There is evidence, sensationally, that some of them were there to fight in the war against Rome that took place 30 years later, that it was the same messianic line involved in this uprising, and that it may have been a descendant of Jesus who stepped forward as the next son of David.

Jesus, like his fellow Jews, would have resented the daily humiliations forced on his people by the Roman occupiers. As a nationalist, messianic contender, he would have looked towards the day when the Jewish kingdom would be restored. The picture which I will therefore suggest is more valid is not that of gentle Jesus, a sacrificial world redeemer, but of Jesus who claimed the throne of David.

Note that the following time references are used throughout: BCE (before the Common Era) for BC and CE (Common Era) for AD.

Note also that following the first chapter 'Yeshua' is used predominantly where other writers might refer to 'Jesus'. There are two reasons. Firstly, 'Yeshua' more accurately reflects the name that would have been spoken and recognised at the time (see ch 1). Secondly, using this name helps to create some distance from the person adopted by Christianity and the possibly ingrained perceptions associated with him.

There is no pressing need to do this with other characters in the New Testament. So, for the sake of simplicity, the usual English versions of Hebrew and Aramaic names have otherwise been followed. 'Mary' for example is retained in preference to 'Miriam' and 'James', following the precedent set by the King James version of the bible, is used instead of 'Yacob' or 'Jacob'.

Chapter 1: A story told in names

Imagine being transported in a time machine to the streets of Capernaum or a bustling market place in Jerusalem, around CE 35. You are now in an improbably privileged position, within the territory of the New Testament, able to see for yourself and sort out some of the questions which for subsequent centuries have bothered historians and theologians.

The question you might well want to ask a passer-by (in the Aramaic or Hebrew you have carefully cultivated for the trip) would be, 'Where might I find Jesus Christ?'

But, alas, you would almost certainly be greeted with mute incomprehension. The reason is that, whatever one's religious position now, it has to be accepted that there was simply no one of that name in first century Palestine. No one who might answer to a call in the street or a roll call in class. There was no Jesus Christ.

There are two parts to the explanation why. Firstly, the word 'Christ' is our word, an anglicised version of the Greek word 'Christos'. This in turn is a literal translation of a Hebrew word, 'masioch' which means anointed, and relates to anyone anointed in Jewish ritual to a position of high office, as for example a king or a high priest.

The word masioch has come through as messiah in English, carrying a further meaning: the Jews at this time were longing for and expecting a warrior king to arise and liberate them from their oppressors. The messiah would ideally be descended from David, one of the first of the old kings of Israel, although this line over the centuries including two periods of enforced exile had become tenuous, lost in the mists of time.

The Jews had been dominated by a succession of powers: Philistines, Assyrians, Babylonians, Persians, Macedonians and Seleucids or Syrian Greeks. But, in the first century CE, the oppressors who had once again reduced the Jews to the status of a subject people were the Romans.

The Roman rulers would have been very much resented by the majority of Jews. Next on the hate list was Herod who had manoeuvred himself into the position of being a Roman client king. In the process, he supplanted Jewish Maccabean kings who had, for a brief period, clawed power back and presided over an independent state of Israel. As an Indumean, he was from a group which had in the past been conquered and forcibly converted to Judaism – but he would not have been seen by many people as a Jew.

Then there was the vast extended Herodian family, springing from Herod's many wives, who inherited and ruled over different parts of Israel after the despot's death. One son, Herod Antipas (Herod the Tetrarch, in the gospel stories), ruled over Galilee and Perea for more than forty years. The Romans made another descendant, a grandson of Herod called Agrippa, king of Judea, after Pontius Pilate had been recalled from being governor.

Against all of these – Herod, Herodian kings and princes and the Romans themselves – a variety of people came forward as self-professed 'messiahs', deliverers of their people. Like the Maccabees, their claims to genealogical descent from David were often slim or even non-existent. They were united, however, in their determination to remove foreign rule and the worship of foreign gods (idols) and restore Jewish faith in all its purity. The rebellions failed and there were often mass reprisals; thousands were crucified throughout Palestine when three separate rebellions were put down after the death of Herod.

So there were not one, but many messiahs at this time. Even if the passer-by, by a leap of imagination and familiarity with Greek, understood the import of your question, he might very well not have understood how to answer it.

'Christ' might just have meant something, but 'Jesus'?

This is once again our version of a Greek word, 'Iesous'. Since the gospels are written in Greek, we do not know for certain what the original Hebrew or Aramaic word was. But the probability, supported by Matthew's version of the annunciation story (1, 21 – see below), is that it was 'Yeshua' or 'Yoshua' which in Hebrew is derived from 'Salvation' (hoshua) or 'God is help/salvation' (Yah hoshua). In Greek, there are are no 'y' or 'sh' sounds, so 'i' and 's' were substituted in transliterating the Hebrew original. Since 'a' or 'ua' represented a feminine ending in Greek, this was replaced with a masculine ending, 'ous'.

In this way, 'Yeshua' became 'Iesous' in Greek and 'Iesus' in Latin.

The letter J was only added to the modern Latin alphabet about 500 years ago and was for a time used interchangeably with 'I' for several different sounds. Used in place of 'I', as in 'Jesus', it was then retained when 'J' became associated with the distinct, hard 'jeh' consonant sound. So, ultimately, even the soft 'yeh' sound of Yeshua was lost.

Rendered in transliteration in the Old Testament as 'Joshua', and in the New Testament and works by the historian Josephus as 'Jesus', 'Yeshua' was a fairly common Jewish name. In first century Israel, there was a tradition of names running in families, with a son often called by the name of his father or grandfather. In the case of Joseph and Mary, the gospel stories have it that the parents were told by an angel in a dream to call their child Jesus (Yeshua). The justification for the name, according to Matthew, is that the child will 'save his people from their sins'.

People did not have surnames, one reason why it became hard to trace lines of descent. They were usually known by a given name and as 'son of' (in Hebrew 'ben' or sometimes 'bar', as in Aramaic) or 'daughter of' (in Hebrew and Aramaic, 'bat') of a father, specified by his given name. Nicknames also abounded. Jesus, the gospels tell us, was born of Mary who was husband (or betrothed partner) of Joseph. So, the next try is therefore to ask for Jesus, the son of Joseph, using the correct words in Hebrew.

But disappointingly, asking for Yeshua ben Yusuf might also fail to elicit the information you want. These are both fairly common names, but that is not the only reason passers-by may be unable to help. It is time, before continuing the quest, to step back into the time machine and reexamine the gospel text.

The earliest of the canonical gospels, Mark, omits any reference to a father. The gospel of John has two references which could be taken as indicating that Jesus was of the tribe of Joseph, but had a differently-named father (John 1.46 and 6.42). The latter reads 'Is not this Jesus, the son of Joseph, whose father and mother we know?'

Matthew and Luke introduce nativity tales in which Mary is the mother, Joseph the husband of Mary, and Jesus the product of a union between God and Mary, echoing pagan myths. The story is not developed to include brothers and sisters, even when Luke gives an account of the boy Jesus staying behind in Jerusalem twelve years later on. But there *are* brothers and sisters. In parallel passages, the gospels of Mark and Matthew refer to unnamed sisters and four named brothers of Yeshua/Jesus: James, Simon, Judas and Joseph/Joses. Joseph, Mary's supposed husband, disappears from the story line after the nativity and (in Matthew) flight to Egypt. After this point, there is no reference in either Luke or Matthew to Joseph by name.

This apparent reluctance to describe Jesus' family as a whole stems from the discordance, which early gospel authors must have recognised, between a holy family embracing Mary, God and Jesus on the one hand and a natural family on the other embracing Mary, her husband and natural children, both male and female. Furthermore Mary, as God's consort, must (it was argued) be deemed perfect and virginal. So, a doctrine developed in which Mary was not only a virgin at the time of Jesus' conception – but remained a 'perpetual' virgin!

Such implausibilities were hard to uphold in view of the

points where Jesus' brothers are unambiguously described, not only in the gospels but in the Acts of the Apostles and other early sources. But the text of the gospels was as far as possible moulded to fit doctrinal preconceptions. In situations where Mary was, at the time of the crucifixion, defined by reference to her children either or both of James and Joses were mentioned. But Jesus was left out. This left the way open for a presumption, even though the situation defines this Mary as the mother of Jesus, that it was really some other Mary who just happened to have children with the same names!

Mary's husband was made into a shadowy figure and references to the family as a whole were cut out. It was argued, notwithstanding the evidence, that the brothers were really only 'cousins'. Mary could not after all have had any natural children, if she had been a virgin all her life.

A remarkable piece of text in John's gospel (John 19, 25) is, I will argue, a survival of this process, retained because it seemed to support the hypothesis of the brothers of Jesus as cousins. It is, however, the product of a mistranslation and would, if correctly rendered, counter this view. Because it is a survival from an earlier version of the gospels or an early source, it also provides a crucial clue as to the original family of Jesus.

In this, Joseph does not figure. He has been invented to serve as a distraction. The real husband of Mary and father of Jesus was someone else.

The passage in John's gospel (Revised Standard Version) describes a group of women, closely linked to Jesus, standing by the cross after the crucifixion:

> But standing by the cross of Jesus were his mother, and his mother's sister, Mary the wife of Clopas, and Mary Magdalene.

Among the synoptic gospels, Luke mentions only some

unnamed women. Mark (15, 40) describes the same scene as follows:

> There were also women looking on from afar, among whom were Mary Magdalene, and Mary the mother of James the younger (less) and of Joses, and Salome who, when he was in Galilee, followed him, and ministered to him;

In quoting Mark, Matthew (27, 56) follows the same wording and adds further detail. Salome appears as the wife of Zebedee:

> There were also many women there, looking on from afar, who had followed Jesus from Galilee, ministering to him; among whom were Mary Magdalene, and Mary the mother of James and Joseph, and the mother of the sons of Zebedee.

Comparing these passages, the fourth century Church apologist Jerome decided that Jesus' 'mother's sister, Mary (the wife) of Clopas' was the same person as 'Mary (the mother) of James and Joseph/Joses'. He then further concluded that the brothers of Jesus mentioned in Mark and Matthew, who included James and Joseph/Joses, must really have been cousins since they were children of a sister of Jesus' mother. Jerome recognised that Mary would thus have been married to Alphaeus, the father of James; he appeared to see 'Clopas' as just a surname or title.

The thesis appeared later to gain strength when it was recognised that 'Clopas' and another word 'Alphaeus' are alternative renderings in Greek of an Aramaic word 'Chalphai'. In all the gospel lists of apostles, James is described as the son of Alphaeus. He is thus also, by virtue of the passage in John as it is rendered, the son of Jesus' mother's sister.

There are fundamental flaws, even on the surface, with this account. No family, then as now, would have created the confusion of having two children with the same forename: Mary the mother of Jesus and a sister Mary, wife of Clopas and mother of those otherwise described as Jesus' brothers.

Furthermore, the stories in the gospels, even if not actual accounts, are idealised accounts of the crucifixion. They described the woman who would have been present at the cross, and these would have been significant women in Jesus' life including his mother. In John's version, Jesus' mother is still there. But what the proposition by Jerome and others does is remove Jesus' mother from the scene in the accounts in the synoptic gospels, Mark and Matthew. Already, in these gospels, she is referred to by a circumlocution (as the mother of two of her other children) because of the difficulty, previously noted, these authors had in reconciling the natural family of Jesus with his theoretical family based on Christian doctrine.

The proposition also fails to deal with another discrepancy. Salome/the mother of the sons of Zebedee is among the three women according to Mark and Matthew, but not apparently listed by John.

All these difficulties vanish once it is recognised that the passage in John's gospel is only there because it appears to support the 'brothers as cousins' hypothesis. It was retained as it is in the Greek original, over a long period during which the gospels were edited, for that very reason.

But an examination of the Greek text shows that it has been misinterpreted and then mistranslated. The error arose either because of lack of care, or because of a preconception, in interpreting the Greek word ordering. Adjectives or phrases were often displaced to a position later in the sentence, away from the words they qualified. The word for word translation of the crucial passage in John is as follows:

But there had stood beside the cross of Jesus the mother of him, and the sister of the mother of him, Mary (the wife) of Clopas, and Mary Magdalene.

It can be seen that the phrase 'the mother of him' occurs twice and the writer has placed 'Mary (the wife) of Clopas' for convenience after the second of these which it then qualifies, along with the first reference. The passage should be rendered in English as follows:

> But standing by the cross of Jesus were his mother, Mary the wife of Clopas, and his mother's sister, and Mary Magdalene.

The three gospel accounts of the woman standing by the cross are now perfectly reconciled. They all have three women present including Mary Magdalene and Jesus' mother Mary. The same third woman is present in the three acounts. She is Salome, who is 'the mother of the sons of Zebedee' and also the sister of Jesus' mother Mary.

The accounts accord with descriptions in the gospels and elsewhere which list James in particular as one of Jesus' brothers. There is no longer the cumbersome fiction of two sisters, both called Mary. Salome is back in all three accounts. The information provided in John fills a gap in explaining why the third woman is significant enough to be placed at the cross. As Mary's sister, she is also Jesus' aunt.

But Mary now has a husband called Clopas/Alphaeus. There is no place or need for her putative husband, Joseph. By misreading the passage in John's gospel, however, the relationship between Mary (Yehua's mother) and Clopas was instead taken as that of sister-in-law and brother-in-law. Then, I suggest the synoptic gospels were modified in the light of this. Clopas was excised from their record, leaving only traces in the form of a character Jesus meets on the road to Emmaus (Luke 24, 18) and references to Alphaeus as the father of James and Matthew/Levi. Joseph was introduced at the nativity as a stand-in for Mary's real husband.

Armed with this understanding, you may now be more

confident of getting the information you want. Having drawn a blank with 'Jesus Christ' and then with Yeshua the son of Joseph, Yeshua ben Yusuf, you step once more from your time machine on to the streets of Jerusalem and ask for 'Yeshua ben Clopas'. Now, you might well get a most definite response. Depending on when you asked and who you asked – possibly either a Herodian informer or a zealot sympathiser – you could well be arrested and taken before the Sadducee High Priest or, alternatively, hurried away to a safe hiding place. There was, the evidence suggests, someone with that name with a place in the history of the time.

There are, as it happens, other names which you could have tried, given that people then often had one or more nicknames. Jesus/Yeshua is also described in the gospels as 'the master' or 'teacher' (in Aramaic 'abba'), a title suggesting a person with a degree of learning and deserving respect. It might also have been accorded to his father who the gospels indicate was a builder (as opposed to a carpenter), from the Greek 'tectonis'. This suggests a startling reappraisal of traditionally understood gospel narrative, given that 'son of the master' translates in Aramaic as 'bar abbas'. And that's the name of the person, Barabbas or Jesus/Yeshua Barabbas according to early sources, whose release the Jews are described in the gospels as seeking instead of Yeshua!

The crowds in Jerusalem were more plausibly demanding, not the death of their messiah but his own immediate release. Gospel editors and writers sometimes divided up individual characters so as to repress particular attributes. So the 'bad' 'bandit' Jesus who affected to lead a revolt against the Romans ended up in prison, while the 'good' Jesus was crucified to save mankind! Simon Peter is similarly treated (see ch 2 p 51).

The Romans, who controlled much of the known world at the time the gospels were being written, are not portrayed as responsible for Yeshua's death. They are instead depicted as being pressured into it by a baying Jewish mob.

Indeed some texts, such as the gospel of Peter, actually have the Jews carrying out the execution. Such circumspection and evasion has to be seen in the light of the fact that the Romans were the masters and the gospels were being written for a non-Jewish, Roman world.

Another possibility is that the imprisoned robber or rebel Jesus Barabbas was not Yeshua himself but his son. Such a person could well have taken the same name and been described as a son of 'the master'. Though there were exceptional circumstances, which may for example have applied to Jesus' brother James, as a normal man in Jewish society Jesus would have been married. He would, unless he or his wife were infertile, have had children. But these, if they existed, have been eradicated more thoroughly than his siblings from the text. The surviving evidence for children is slim, apart from this one, very curious name. The evidence for Jesus' married state on the other hand, which will be considered, is quite strong.

Following the original line of thought (you are still just disembarked from your time machine), there would probably have been no clear response had you asked to speak to 'the master'. This was a fairly general term of respect and many people besides Yeshua might have been known by that name.

But there is another title besides Yeshua ben Clopas that might well have invoked a definite response from your passer-by.

Jesus is described in the Greek of the earliest canonical gospel Mark (and in the Jewish Talmud), as 'the Nazarene' – erroneously identified in translation with Nazareth, a place which did not appear even to have existed at the time. The Nazarenes or Nazoreans (from Hebrew 'nozrim' meaning 'keepers' or 'observers' of the covenant) were a Jewish group concerned, under the subsequent leadership of James the brother of Jesus, with matters of purity and strict observance of Jewish law. Their manner of organisation has very strong parallels with the people who wrote the Dead Sea scrolls, described as Essenes. Both groups were messianic in their outlook. So it is likely that, in the gospels, 'the Nazarene' with its anti-Roman, revolutionary, messianic overtones was deliberately mistranslated.

Asking for 'Yeshua the Nazarene' should certainly have indicated, to the cautious and suspicious passer-by, that you had some allegiance to an alternative counter group to the Roman occupiers and/or Sadducee High Priest collaborators.

Curiously, as will be seen, a request for 'Yeshua the Egyptian' or even simply 'the Egyptian' might also have provoked a very nervous response.

What I am suggesting then is that there was no person specifically called 'Jesus Christ' at the time to which the gospel stories relate. But there may well have been a historical character, with a real name and possibly several nicknames, known to many of his contemporaries. This person was not an isolated figure but someone who was part of a messianic movement, who was arrested and subjected to execution by crucifixion, like many other Jewish resistance fighters (or terrorists as the Romans would have perceived it) around that time. He had brothers and sisters and a father named Clopas/Alphaeus. What makes this person so different, however, is that his story was adapted and transformed into a wider religion for the Gentile (non Jewish) world.

But this, you might argue, is the real point. Regardless of what Jesus/Yeshua was known as or called, the gospels tell us that he was born from a mystical union between God and a woman (Mary) and that his mission was to redeem people's sins by his own self-sacrifice and that, by his crucifixion at the hands of the Romans, he achieved just that. Surely that's what is important. The gospels are, after all, the word of God?

The first and overriding problem with this argument is the gospels are all too evidently the work of man. They are full of mistakes: Mark for example finds it hard to get his first century Palestine geography right, locating Sidon in the wrong place and moving Gerasa thirty miles or so up to the Sea of Galilee. They contradict themselves and each other on matters like the sequence of events in the passion story, the details of Yeshua's travels and his supposed sayings.

The gospels clearly also have a historical context and are about someone who was expected as a Jewish liberator, a warrior king who would drive out the latest in a succession of foreign occupiers. Just analysing the name that has come to us in translation, 'Jesus Christ' tells us that.

He was supposed in the gospel story that we now have to be the Son of God – and could not therefore have been in the genealogical (father to son) line of David, as the Jew's expected messianic liberator. But the gospels of Matthew and Luke spell out complicated family trees that link Yeshua back to David in a direct line of male descent. These, unsurprisingly, contradict each other.

His mother Mary was supposed to have been a virgin, but in the gospel stories she had a betrothed partner or husband, Joseph. A passage in John's gospel, which has survived for the very reason that it was misinterpreted, indicates that she had a husband named Clopas. A further fragmentary reference to Clopas exists in Luke (see p 76).

Mary went on to have several other children – Yeshua's brothers and sisters, named or described in the gospels and elsewhere.

Yeshua is portrayed as a popular figure, attracting large crowds, yet the same gospels depict him as hostile to Jews – who were of course his supporters and his own people! He is quoted as attacking mainstream groups – scribes, 'hypocrites' and Pharisees – but there are also several instances where Yeshua is described as being helped by or on friendly terms with Pharisees.

There would appear then to be a parallel story line which runs counter to the main themes in the text. But what is original and what has been added on? How much of the story can be identified as pure invention, embroidery by people short on details writing many years after the event? How much is deliberate falsification?

If a Jewish messianic liberator, a 'masioch', was expected – and the circumstances demanded it – then this is what the Jewish people will have got. Just as they had other messiahs responding to other situations of oppression at other times. The worldwide mission to save people from their sins was then added, in the later development of Christianity.

There is certainly strong evidence to support such a thesis, which will be considered. For the moment, it will be profitable to look at some of the other incongruities in the text. Names of people, rather like place names, as we have seen often give a lot of information. Kept for the sake of continuity, or because they are already there in popular culture and imagination, they can remain as fossils from an original truth, eroded and distorted by the attentions of censors and editors down the years.

The names of some of Jesus' followers are redolent of the violent and frightening world that was first century Palestine, a world that is scarcely touched upon in the authorised and revised story line of the gospels.

Chapter 2: Band of brothers

Names are the bricks and mortar of any tale and, however a story is embellished, they tend to be retained in retelling over time. This is partly so that the narrator can identify with the existing framework of the reader or listener – which he may then be going to embellish or modify. It is partly also that names may be remembered fairly accurately long after an event, and long after other details have become hazy in an individual's memory or through being passed down orally from generation to generation. In any new version of a story, the names are thus hard to deny and need to be incorporated.

It is also much easier to use what one has – and a storyteller may not realise that the names he uses may be conveying something quite different from what he is now trying to relate.

As has been seen, the name 'Jesus Christ', which could not have been the actual name of anyone at the time, does encapsulate information about a character that goes contrary to the reworked story line: a Jewish liberator of Jewish people from foreign domination, rather than a world redeemer. As might be expected, there are bits of the text which, having escaped the attentions of later editors, support what was probably the original story line (eg Mark 7, 24-27 and Matthew 15, 21-24). These passages tell the story of a woman, Greek or Cananite, who asked Yeshua to help her sick daughter. Yeshua is portrayed as disinclined to help her because she was not a Jew:

And Jesus went away from there and withdrew to the district of Tyre and Sidon. And behold, a Canaanite woman from that region came out and cried, 'Have mercy on me, O Lord, Son of David; my daughter is severely possessed by a demon.' But he did not answer her a word. And his disciples came and begged him, saying, 'Send her away, for she is crying after us.'

He answered, 'I was sent only to the lost sheep of the house of Israel.' But she came and knelt before him, saying, 'Lord help me.' And he answered, 'It is not fair to take the children's bread and throw it to the dogs.' She said, 'Yes, Lord, yet even the dogs eat the crumbs that fall from their master's table.' Then Jesus answered her, 'O woman, great is your faith! Be it done for you as you desire.' And her daughter was healed instantly.

(Matthew 15, 21-28)

Yeshua, according to the Matthew, saw himself as concerned *only* with 'the lost sheep of the house of Israel'. It is a message which is repeated earlier in Matthew in precisely the same form, when Yeshua is sending out his disciples to preach and heal – to Jews, certainly, but specifically not to Samaritans and Gentiles (Matthew 10, 5-6).

In the story quoted above, his followers took a similar view, asking him to send the woman away. Though in the end, in the story, Yeshua relented and healed the woman's sick daughter, the point is made. Yeshua was a Jewish messiah. He was not embarked on the physical or spiritual liberation of the wider, Gentile world.

In looking at names, embedded in the text like ancient artefacts, let us start with one of the most famous of Yeshua's followers, Simon who is also called Peter. He first appears in Mark as a fisherman with his brother Andrew, as also were James and John, the sons of Zebedee, by the Sea of Galilee. The latter are described as owning their own boat, so these early recruits to Yeshua's following could have been people with resources and some wealth. Not so much humble labourers as entrepreneurs, with standing and status in their community. They were, it should be noted, not random recruits but people who were part of Yeshua's close circle of friends and family. James and John, the sons of Zebedee and Mary's sister Salome, were Yeshua's cousins and Simon and Andrew were their working companions.

Later in Mark, Simon is most memorably depicted as denying Yeshua three times, after Yeshua had been arrested. But it may be this element was introduced to make Simon appear vacillatory and weak, just as he is in Paul's letter to the Galatians over the question of sharing food with Gentiles (Galatians 2, 12). In Acts, Simon is made to affirm Paul's position that the distinction between food regarded as clean or unclean, according to Jewish Law, is henceforth to be disregarded (Acts 11, 2-10).

Yeshua's brother James, who became leader of the Nazorean community in Jerusalem, is treated in similar fashion in the gospels. For the most part, he is relegated, along with the other brothers, to the position of a carping bystander. In Mark, he is described dismissively as 'James the less' (Mark 15, 40). The objective, I suggest, was to diminish the role of those who had been key followers of a Jewish messiah. Simon, however, needed as a bridge and figurehead for the emerging Christian Church, would be recreated and rehabilitated.

Simon has a nickname. In Aramaic, it is 'Cephas' and in Greek it is 'Petros', meaning rock. From this derivation and point in time comes 'Peter', commonly used as a forename today.

But it certainly wasn't a usual name around CE 35. It was then a surname or nickname and it had, as such names do, some reference or meaning. In Mark, the earliest of the canonical gospels, Yeshua simply assigns Simon his nickname when assembling his core band of twelve close followers or apostles. There is no explanation given for it.

Matthew, later in time and later in interpretation, fills the gap with an elaborate scenario.

Yeshua asks his followers who people think he 'really' is. And he then asks who they think he is. Simon replies 'You are the Christ, the Son of the living God', for which response he is rewarded with the title 'Petros' or Peter because 'on this rock I will build my church' (Matthew 16, 13-20).

No matter that Simon's reply here is contradictory: the expected 'masioch' or 'Christos' was to be a mortal warrior, to liberate the Jews from Roman rule, and not a God or Son of God!

Rock could certainly be a metaphor for a strong place on which to build. But it also signifies, if substantial enough, a place that is easy to defend or a vantage point from which to harry an enemy. If handy enough, a rock makes a convenient missile to hurl down at the enemy from a place of ambush or from fortifications. It indicates hardness, toughness, unwillingness to budge or compromise.

So, 'rock' as a nickname has some aggressive or warlike connotations.

Before bestowing the title, Yeshua refers to Simon by what appears, in the New Testament translation, to be his full name, Simon Bar-Jona. From this, the reader is supposed to gather that Simon is the son of Jona or Jonah.

This depends, however, on the assumption that the author of Matthew used an Aramaic or Hebrew form 'bar' meaning 'son of' in combination with a Greek genitive, 'Jona' meaning 'of Jonah'. Such a construction would have been both clumsy and at variance with usage elsewhere. Matthew and the other gospel authors, who wrote in Greek, consistently used the Greek word 'uios' for 'son of', as in son of David (Matthew 1,1).

If the Greek text is examined, before translation into the Revised Standard Version, the problem can be resolved. The name reads simply (and without a hyphen) as 'bariona'. While this word has no resonance in Greek, it does have a precise meaning in Aramaic. 'Bariona' means fugitive from justice, or outlaw. This appears to be an instance of the gospels authors leaving an Aramaic or Hebrew word in its original form, where a translation would have awkward implications. The process of mystification is taken further, as in this case, when the Greek is translated into another language according to Christian preconceptions.

The author of John's gospel, who would have had the text of Matthew available to him, could also make no sense (or chose to make no sense) of 'bariona'. In the Old Syriac version of this gospel, Yeshua refers to 'Simon bar Jonah' and then later to 'Simon bar Yonan' (John 1, 42 and John 21, 15-17). This may follow a formulation in Greek where consonants have been added to avoid a feminine ending. In the Greek New Testament, 'Yonan' was then interpreted to be a shortened form of Yohanan, which means John, and so these readings in both instances became 'son of John'.

Simon's other nickname is therefore likely to have been 'Simon the Outlaw'. In the Talmud (Jewish compendium of civil law) the word bariona (plural birionim) is used to describe zealots who fought against Rome. This is not an aspect of Simon's character or life that the gospel editors for the Roman church would have wanted to convey. So the title was left in Matthew, in its original form, to be subsequently misconstrued.

Matthew, or the subsequent editors of Matthew, associated the giving of the name Peter (Petros or Cephas) to Simon with the doctrine of Yeshua as the 'Son of God'. He then goes on to link it with something else that is apparently known about Simon 'The Rock'. That something, as presented, is very curious.

Yeshua rewards Simon by saying he will give him 'the keys of the kingdom of heaven' with the proviso that 'whatever you bind on earth shall be bound in heaven, and whatever you loose on earth shall be loosed in heaven'.

Now is this all purely symbolic? Is Simon Peter being appointed spiritual leader of the Nazarenes or Nazoreans? Hardly likely, since James, one of the brothers Yeshua, next filled that office.

There's equally an element of temporal power, to bind or loose on earth, so it is not just a spiritual office. What, as possibly the core of the matter, does the phrase 'the keys of the kingdom' mean?

In effect, in giving Simon the symbolic keys, Yeshua is assigning him the practical role of chief minister in his 'ecclesia' or church, someone who would have both military and judicial power.

The terms 'bind' and 'loose' were also used at the time in respect of the powers of the Sanhedrin. So Yeshua apparently expected that, in the worldly kingdom that would come about, his followers would have supreme religious and judicial power.

The phraseology used in Matthew is far from accidental: it parallels that used in the Old Testament book Isaiah, in predicting that King Hezekiah's chief minister Shebna will be replaced by Eliakim. The prophet describes how this will be carried out by divine will:

> And I will place on his shoulder the key of the house of David; he shall open, and none shall shut; and he shall shut, and none shall open. And I will fasten him like a peg in a sure place, and he will become a throne of honour to his father's house.
> (Isaiah 22, 22-23)

However we interpret the words Yeshua is credited with using now, it is clear that the source for this story in Matthew had in mind a role assigned to Simon Peter which had real political power.

But is the story based on an early source or is it a later Christian embellishment?

As the gospels and Acts record, Yeshua and his followers were Torah-observing Jews who went to their local synagogues and the temple in Jerusalem. They may have been part of a sect, fully within Judaism, but they were not engaged in setting up an alternative church. This is something which was accomplished a little later by Paul and his followers (see ch 5).

It is significant that the reference to 'my church', attributed to Yeshua in Matthew, occurs nowhere else in the gospels. It does appear therefore that this was something that was introduced, after the Catholic Church had become established, as a justification for the authority it was beginning to claim in both civil and religious matters. It might have been original to Matthew, given that the gospel was written some time after the crucifixion and the separation of Christianity from its Jewish roots. But it could also have been inserted even later, as the gospel was rewritten in the light of the Church's evolving structure and doctrine.

Simon Peter was certainly central to this. He was redefined as a key figure in the early Christian Church and transported figuratively to Rome to become its first Bishop, even though there is no evidence in the gospels that he had ever been there. Nor, for that matter, is there any reference in Acts which, if Simon Peter had gone to Rome, would certainly have mentioned it.

The story in Matthew, in which Yeshua grants Simon the keys to the kingdom, is thus designed to provide the basis for a transformation. Simon is, however, by no means a random choice among Yeshua's followers. Other material in the gospels suggests that he was close to Yeshua and militant, wielding a sword when an attempt was made to arrest his leader. His nicknames suggest a warlike character.

It may be that the Church borrowed a character who did have a position with some military or political power within the nationalist, messianic Nazoreans.

There is an intriguing reference, in the pages of the Jewish historian Josephus, to someone also called Simon carrying out the very functions in Jerusalem that Yeshua had so recently bestowed. It is around CE 40, four years after the crucifixion of Yeshua, and the Romans have abandoned direct rule and appointed a Herodian, Herod Agrippa I, grandson of the despot King Herod, as King of Judea. The problem at the outset for Herod Agrippa is that he might well not have had the power base and armed forces to enforce his rule.

The Romans had strategically-placed trained troops and could use the threat of action from other imperial forces elsewhere to induce order. But they never had enough troops to carry out detailed day-to-day administration in Judea, or for that matter, similar provinces. To do this, they relied in Judea on a collaborating group of Sadducees around the High Priest, whom they appointed.

When King Herod died in BCE 4, this sparked three separate rebellions which were quickly and brutally quashed. The Romans then appointed sons of Herod to rule over different parts of Israel. In Judea and Samaria, Herod's son Archelaus was so callous and incompetent that a deputation of his subjects went to Augustus Caesar to plead for his replacement. Caesar obliged and installed a governor or procurator instead.

The Romans subsequently decided to restore a client king in Judea, it may well be to counter the growing influence of messianic nationalism. At the forefront of this in Jerusalem was the Nazarene/Nazorean community, reputed to number many thousands, led by James after Yeshua's crucifixion.

The person chosen, Herod Agrippa, was a grandson of King Herod and someone with a degree of Jewish royal blood. As one of his wives, King Herod had married Mariamme, who was a Maccabean princess – only as it transpired a temporary diversion from his policy of exterminating the Maccabeans. Herod had her uncle Antigonus II executed, killed her mother and grandfather Hyrcanus II and had her brother Jonathan drowned. Unable to brook any form of rivalry, even within his own family, he executed Mariamme and finally her two sons. But their children, including Herod Agrippa, survived.

Herod Agrippa, grandson of King Herod and Mariamme, came then with a mixed pedigree. On the one hand, he was inextricably associated with the Herodians as a direct descendant of the despot Herod, foisted on the Jews by the Romans. On the other hand, he was descended from the Maccabeans who had ruled Israel as independent Jewish kings. He would potentially have had a degree of popular support.

On his appointment in CE 37, Herod Agrippa was careful, as the historian Josephus relates, to cultivate the religious nationalists, by funding the ritual observances of a 'considerable number of Nazirites' (that is, Nazarenes/Nazoreans). He then introduced what must have been a popular innovation, a tax rebate for householders in Jerusalem. He also deposed the current High Priest, Theophilus, who came from an extended family which had been consistently hostile to the Nazoreans, replacing him with Simon Cantheras from a separate priestly lineage.

After a short time, however, the situation had changed. Reading between the lines of Josephus, it appears that Herod Agrippa had nonetheless failed to placate the fundamentalism of Jewish opposition leaders, which evidently found support with the masses. It was a religious view that demanded strict adherence to purity laws especially in regard to the temple. James and his followers objected to temple sacrifices made on behalf of the Roman Emperor and to the presence of foreigners of any kind in the temple itself. Agrippa's ancestry as has been noted was not wholly Jewish; it was in part Idumean, from Antipas, the grandfather of King Herod.

Josephus relates that a certain Simon, 'with a reputation for religious scrupulousness' and able to gather a religious meeting (in Greek 'ecclesia' or church), had the 'audacity' to denounce Herod as 'unclean' and therefore to be excluded from the temple. Josephus has it that Simon then, rather surprisingly, apologises. But he also records that, confronted by Simon in Caesarea, Herod Agrippa presented Simon with a gift.

This incident sheds light on what would have been the true state of affairs at the time. While ultimate power lay with the Romans, through certain retribution from its largely distant armies, at local level there were a variety of sources of influence. The mere fact of having been appointed did not give Herod Agrippa the capacity or the resources to rule. He would have needed substantial funds to pay for his troops and also people willing to fight for him. In the person of Simon, he met with a powerful rival leader with popular support. It would seem that, faced with Simon and his religious army, he simply bought him off with a ransom or bribe.

The situation was not helped by the fact that Agrippa had sacked his new High Priest and reverted to one from the old dynasty of Ananus, which had a history of persecuting the Nazoreans. In a sea of factions and counter factions, Agrippa still did not have the authority to impose his own will. Simon had the confidence to confront him.

So who was this man, with such strong and fundamental religious opinions? He had an ecclesia or church, just as Yeshua had assigned Simon 'Petros' to preside over a church. He had power, was of the same thinking as the Nazoreans and was in Jerusalem at precisely the same time as the gospel Simon, following the crucifixion. Josephus makes his Simon a 'native of Jerusalem' whereas Mark describes Simon as a Galilean fisherman.

Allowing for some character rewriting by gospel editors, it is conceivable that the texts are presenting separate perspectives on the same person.

At one point in the gospels, the real Simon – the man with the audacity to confront a king – emerges. This is when, at the time of Yeshua's arrest, Simon takes his sword to the High Priest's slave, slicing off his ear (John 18, 10).

As added confirmation that Josephus and the gospels are writing about the same character, the Acts of the Apostles (12, 1-5) continues with the story. Herod Agrippa (or possibly his brother Herod King of Chalcis who ruled in his place for a time after Agrippa's death) subsequently switched from a policy of dialogue to one of persecution. He imprisoned Simon Peter, who managed to escape, and had John's brother James beheaded, that is killed 'with the sword'.

Yeshua's fiery right-hand man, chief minister or commander, certainly lived up to his reputation and nicknames as 'Simon the Rock' and 'Simon the Outlaw'.

As the Nazoreans' religious leader, however, James the brother of Yeshua managed to maintain and expand his following, apparently without conflict for twenty more years. James may have remained untouchable for so long, both because of his popularity and his lack of ostensible political involvement.

The death of the other James, the brother of John and son of Zebedee, brings the story back to the two other followers that Yeshua also assigned strange nicknames. It is recorded in Mark that, gathering the twelve together, Jesus named these two 'Boanerges', or 'Sons of Thunder'.

It appears this may have been a reflection of their disposition to violence, as in the gospel of Luke (9, 52-56) when the pair asked Yeshua whether he would like them to call fire down from heaven to consume a Samaritan village that had failed to receive him. Thunderbolts and lightning were, of course, the weapons of the Roman God Jupiter, giver of victory. Was Yeshua having a dig at the Romans, in choosing this particular name – sons of *their* God of victory – for two of *his* own followers?

Victory was certainly what these two were expecting on the march south from Galilee to Jerusalem, before the feast of the Passover, as they argued about their place in the coming Jewish kingdom. They wanted key positions, at Yeshua's right and left hand in his 'glory' (Mark 10, 37). In Matthew's gospel, it is their scheming mother Salome who instigates the request (Matthew 20, 21). The subsequent indignation of the other disciples at this preemptive move makes it clear what this was all about. The sons of Zebedee, and their mother on their behalf, were not talking about a heavenly paradise but an earthly kingdom in which they were expecting to take positions of prime importance!

James and John were seen, if their nicknames are an indication, as warriors in the cause. Not unreasonably, they expected to be rewarded with a share of power, when that cause came to triumph. Moreover, they were putting in their bids because it seemed to them at least that the moment was imminent. An assault on Jerusalem, as a prelude to a war of liberation, provides the reason they appeared to believe they were marching south. There is then a fit between the names and the actions and characters of these two cousins of Yeshua, as described in the narrative – which in turn throws light on Yeshua's motivation for taking his followers to Jerusalem.

It also helps solve the problem provided by Christian interpretation of the text, that Yeshua was going to Jerusalem simply in order to be crucified. That is implausible both in its own terms and in the context of various other messianic rebellions directed against Rome at the time. It is also inconsistent with surviving elements in the story, including the comments by the sons of Zebedee, that suggest a militant intent.

James and John, like Simon, were given nicknames that reflected their character and the way they behaved. This is certainly thought-provoking, as an indication of a possible agenda that is now disguised in the gospels. But these labels are as nothing compared to the awesome names taken by some other disciples. Mark (3, 19) lists one of the twelve disciples as 'Simon the Cananean'. Simon from the village of Cana in Galilee?

The author of Mark could not bring himself to translate the Hebrew word cana – which means zealot! But Luke (6, 16) does, with no trace of embarrassment, in naming this particular disciple as 'Simon who was called the zealot'. In another list, in a document called 'The Letter of the Apostles', there's an apostle listed in the place taken by Simon in Matthew and Mark. His name, in a text written this time in Latin, is 'Judas Zealotes' or 'Judas the Zealot'.

There are so far, with Simon the Outlaw, three possible references so far to 'zealots' among the close followers of Yeshua. What, it must be wondered, are they doing among disciples, portrayed in the gospels as peacably engaged in preaching and healing?

'Zealot' was the name given to the fiery followers of Mattathias who refused to sacrifice to idols, at the behest of the Persian King Antiochus, slew the king's messenger at the altar and then took his followers out into the desert to fight an ultimately successful guerilla war. Mattathias roused his supporters with the words, "Let everyone who is zealous for the law and supports the covenants come out with me!" and he did successfully instigate an, albeit short-lived, dynasty (the Maccabeans) of independent Jewish kings.

Subsequently, the word was applied to Jewish fundamentalists who refused to compromise their principles. The historian Josephus identifies a 'fourth' such philosophy after Sadducee, Pharisee and Essene – different only from the Pharisees in their willingness to suffer torture and death rather than compromise their beliefs.

Josephus describes as zealots those actively prosecuting the war with Rome, following the uprising in CE 66. So, if there were really zealots in the key listed followers of Yeshua, then it strongly suggests that his mission was very different from the one presented in the familiar gospel story line.

Another disciple, Judas Iscariot, who is presumed to have betrayed Yeshua, also has an intriguing name. Various efforts have been made to identity his surname/nickname with a place, such as Kerioth, but not at all convincingly. The most obvious and plausible, and very closely-corresponding name tag, for this particular follower is 'Judas Sicarios', after the anti-establishment resistance group of sicarii described by Josephus, whose speciality was assassinating political opponents using their curved daggers or 'sicae'. These included, in the run up to the war with Rome, Jonathan who was part of the family of High Priests implicated in the crucifixion of Yeshua and the extra-judicial stoning of his brother James.

So here was another follower of Yeshua with a robust and warlike name, Judas 'sicarios' – a Greek term for which the closest modern equivalent would be 'Judas the assassin'.

The sicarii were acting against what they perceived as collab-orators, possibly revenging themselves against the murderers of James. But, rather than being another group arising later, and performing this role, the strong possibility is that this was just a few years later on the *same group* as could be counted among Yeshua's followers.

Among the named twelve disciples of Yeshua, there are five only with nicknames, all with highly aggressive overtones: a rock which could be a weapon or an impregnable place of defence, alternatively an outlaw, two sons of thunder (possibly sons of the Roman god Jupiter), one or possibly two zealots/religious fundamentalists and one assassin. In contrast, the picture presented in the gospels, by writers later than and split away from the original Nazorean followers of Yeshua, is of a world redeeming saviour looking for a heavenly, not an earthly, Jewish kingdom, and not at all antagonistic to the empire of Rome.

These writers could not and would not have deliberately inserted the names in order to counter what they were trying to convey! The names had to have been there all the time, from original source material, and accidentally or incidentally retained. As I have suggested, some names were probably already familiar to the initial gospel audience through oral tradition and would have been kept in the gospel accounts to add a ring of truth, even though much of the other detail was altered.

The question that now arises is what is the underlying reality to which all this relates? As a start, it is helpful to look at those who – in the gospels once decoded – were the real core followers of Yeshua. In following chapters, I will then look at some of the things in the story that cannot be right and see in a historical context what could be right.

Numbers had enormous mathematical and magical significance in the world which, for the early gospel writers, was still dominated by pagan beliefs. There had to be twelve first followers of Yeshua, no matter how many followers there actually were, because this was of a figure of real importance. There were twelve signs of the zodiac in the Babylonian astrological calendar, which the Jews had adopted while in exile. So there were twelve tribes of Israel, twelve apostles and a central council of twelve for the group at Qumran, called by others Essenes and related in many ways to the Nazoreans.

Mark and the two other synoptic gospels, Matthew and Luke, give detailed lists of the twelve apostles. The author of Luke is believed also to have been the author of Acts, where a list appears identical to that in Luke, except that the positions of James & John and Andrew, brother of Simon Peter, have been exchanged and Thomas has been moved further up the order.

There is a further list written later, this time in Latin rather than Greek, in a document entitled 'Epistula Apostolorum' or Letter of the Apostles.

These lists are set out for comparison in the chart on p 45. The nearest the author of John gets to a list is in describing a 'post resurrection' appearance, in which Yeshua meets his disciples by the Sea of Tiberias (Galilee). Those present were Simon Peter, Thomas called the twin, Nathanael of Cana in Galilee, the sons of Zebedee (James and John) and 'two others of his disciples' who were unnamed.

Thomas as a character is a mystery. The name derives from the Aramaic (Thauma) for twin. The author of John repeats this with the Greek word for twin, Didymus. Hence Thomas (Aramaic, twin) called Didymus (Greek, twin). The elaboration is not helpful. We are not told the character's real name or, just as importantly, whose twin or relative he is.

Bartholomew as a name is also simply descriptive, a Greek transliteration of an original title, clearly 'bar' (son of) somebody. Usually, it is is taken to derive from 'bar Talmai', the latter meaning a furrow or mound in Hebrew or Aramaic – which is an odd name or nickname for this character's father.

Once again, there is only a descriptive title or phrase, so we do not know this person's given name. In four of the lists, however, he follows Philip who is described in John's gospel as the person who leads Nathanael to Yeshua. While Philip and Bartholomew are linked and Nathanael is absent in the synoptic gospels, in John's gospel Philip and Nathanael are linked and there is no mention of Bartholomew. So it may be that there is only one character, described at different points as Nathanael and Bartholomew. While his given name would have been Nathanael, he might also have been defined by reference to his parentage as 'bar Talmai'.

The list in the later 'Letter of the Apostles' is very different from the others and appears to split some characters, including Nathanael/Bartholomew, confusing the picture still further.

Another identification that can probably be made is between 'Levi the son of Alphaeus' and 'Matthew', whom Yeshua found sitting in the tax office. Yeshua called 'Levi' to follow him (Mark 2, 14) and, in precisely the same words, did the same to 'Matthew' (Matthew 9, 9), also on the way out of Yeshua's 'own city', Capernaum. These could sensibly be alternative descriptions of a character, Matthew who was of the tribe of Levi (or a Levite) and a son of Alphaeus.

A comparison of these various lists of apostles is very enlightening. One of the most striking points is the high degree of correspondence between them. While this may be the result of all the lists depending on the earliest of the gospels, Mark, it does stand in contrast with the supposed genealogies of Yeshua in Matthew and Luke. These certainly do not agree.

The other striking observation is that the lists in the synoptic gospels (and Acts) have two separate groups with another group, possibly linked to the first, sandwiched between.

In the first group, there are the companions of Yeshua who were part of the fishing community in Galilee: Simon Peter and his brother Andrew as well as James and John, who were the sons of Zebedee and also Yeshua's cousins. Linked to these may be Philip, described in John (1.44) as being from the same place Bethsaida as Simon Peter and Andrew, and Bartholomew (possibly Nathanael) who were among Yeshua's early followers. So too may have been Thomas, sometimes described as Didymus, the twin. There is incidental confirmation of these disciples, including two of Yeshua's cousins, being part of a working group of fishermen in the story of a post crucifixion appearance in John (21, 1-3). Simon Peter decides to go fishing and takes with him Thomas, James and John the sons of Zebedee, Nathanael (Bartholomew) and two other unnamed disciples – possibly Andrew and Philip.

The final group of disciples consists, as listed in Matthew's gospel, of Matthew the tax collector (Levi son of Alphaeus in Mark), James the son of Alphaeus, Lebbaeus who was surnamed Thaddeus and Simon the Cananite or Cananean. These are followed by the twelfth disciple, Judas Iscariot, described in the gospels as having betrayed Yeshua.

It needs to be appreciated that the order in which names are given in the gospels is rarely accidental. So, for example, the list of women described as helping Yeshua or being present at the crucifixion reflects an order of precedence, or the order of importance in which the writer regarded these personages. Judas Iscariot, the betrayer, is always listed last in the gospel lists. Simon Peter by contrast, given 'the keys of the kingdom' and regarded by Catholics (wrongly) as their first pope or bishop, is listed first both in Acts and the synoptic gospels.

In the lists given in the 'Letter of the Apostles' and Acts, only eleven apostles are given because Judas Iscariot, having committed suicide or been killed, is eliminated. The 'Letter of the Apostles' list is also very jumbled; it appears that something strange is going on.

Taking the order given in the main lists to begin with, the final group of four comes after Simon Peter and the other fishermen followers of Yeshua. It was thereby portrayed by the synoptic gospel writers as being of less significance, of lower status – ranking in importance only above the traitor Judas Iscariot. So, who are these four disciples?

James is described in each case as being the son of Alphaeus. Matthew the tax collector, who can be identified with Levi in Mark, is also the son of Alphaeus. So he and James are brothers.

The name 'Alphaeus' derives from the Aramaic 'Chalphai', as does another variant 'Clopas' or, as sometimes rendered in translation, 'Cleophas'. The wife of Clopas/Alphaeus, Mary, is described in John's gospel as one of the three key women being present at the cross after Yeshua's crucifixion. By comparison of this text with similar passages in Mark and Matthew, it has been shown that this Mary must have been the same person as Mary, the mother of Jesus.

Among her children, as the passages in Mark and Matthew describe it, were James and Joses/Joseph. These are among the brothers of Yeshua listed elsewhere in these gospels as James, Joses/Joseph, Simon and Judas.

In Luke's list Thaddeus, also called Lebbaeus in Matthew, appears to have disappeared. But in his place is Simon 'who was called the Zealot', a character who can be identified with Simon the 'Cananite' or 'Cananean'. As has been noted, the derivation of these is from the Hebrew word 'cana' meaning 'zealot' which Mark was clearly loth to translate. In Simon's place is Judas 'of James'. Assuming that two of the disciples have simply been swapped about, this would make Judas 'of James', the equivalent of Thaddeus in Mark and Matthew.

'Thaddeus' is not only a possible derivation from Judas. The historical evidence indicates that it was in this instance. A second or third century document, entitled 'The Apostolic Constitutions' refers to 'Thaddeus also called Lebbaeus and surnamed Judas the Zealot', thus identifying the two. An eleventh century writer Papias compiled a lexicon in which 'Mary the wife of Cleophas or Alphaeus' was also described as 'the mother of James the bishop and apostle, and of Simon and Thaddeus and a certain Joseph'. Here clearly, in making Mary the mother of the four children described as brothers of Yeshua in the gospels, 'Thaddeus' was used as synonymous with 'Judas'.

The last two of the group of four are thus Judas/Thaddeus and Simon who can be presumed, as Papias did, to have been among those described as Yeshua's brothers. It needs to be said that Papias was probably following Jerome who, in the fourth century, attempted to argue that these brothers were really only Yeshua's 'cousins'

In Luke and in Acts, the familial reference is omitted in describing 'Judas [ ] of James'. In the Greek, the omitted reference would often be 'son'. But it makes much more sense, especially having identified the disciple James (who remained celibate) as the brother of Yeshua, for the originally intended description to have been 'Judas the brother of James'.

The most compelling and powerful explanation for the cluster of four characters, who come before Judas Iscariot in the Apostles' lists, is that they are a group who are *all* Yeshua's brothers.

Simon, the last of the four, can be identified with the brother of that name, described in the gospels of Mark and Matthew. He can be identified with the remaining brother named by Papias as one of the sons of Mary and Alphaeus/Cleophas. And, finally, he can be identified with Simon/Simeon, the son of Alphaeus, who went on to lead the Nazorean community after Yeshua and then James.

Joses/Joseph, one of the brothers described in Mark and

Matthew, is rather an insubstantial character. He gets no further reference in the gospels and is not included in any the apostles lists. Unlike James, Simon and Judas, he lacks historical backing outside of the gospels. It seems that either he died young, or he is misidentified in the gospels.

The group of four in the Apostles lists – Matthew, James, Judas and Simon – are however all sons of Alphaeus/Cleophas and as such brothers of Yeshua/Jesus. But why all the obfuscation and why, just as importantly, are the brothers put so far down the list in order of precedence, only just above Judas Iscariot?

Some of the lack of clarity may well have come from lack of knowledge. That cannot however be the whole of the story. If the true place of these 'apostles' can be worked out now from the clues left many centuries later, then it could and would have been known by the original writers, with access to sources since lost and only a relatively few years after the event. The role of the brothers of Yeshua has been deliberately obscured by the way they have been treated in the apostles' lists.

The process of denigration of the brothers and close followers of Yeshua can also be seen elsewhere in the gospels. James was head of the Nazorean community as successor to Yeshua, had a huge following and was a popular, revered figure known as James 'the Just' or 'Righteous One'. But in the gospel of Mark, he is referred to disparagingly as 'James the less' (Mark 15, 40) and elsewhere, as has been seen, simply as 'James the son of Alphaeus'.

LISTS OF THE APOSTLES

MARK (3, 14-19)

Simon Peter 'the rock'	James & John sons of Zebedee 'sons of thunder'	Andrew	Philip	Bartholomew	Matthew	Thomas	James son of Alphaeus	Thaddeus	Simon the Cananean	Judas Iscariot

MATTHEW (10, 1-4)

Simon Peter	Andrew his brother	James & John sons of Zebedee	Philip	Bartholomew	Thomas	Matthew the tax collector	James son of Alphaeus	Lebbaeus who was surnamed Thaddeus	Simon the Cananean	Judas Iscariot

LUKE/ACTS (6, 13-16/1, 13)

(Luke's list as below; Acts exchanges positions of 'James and John' and 'Andrew his brother', promotes Thomas to Bartholomew's position and omits the deceased Judas Iscariot)

Simon Peter	Andrew his brother	James & John	Philip	Bartholomew	Matthew	Thomas	James son of Alphaeus	Simon who was called the Zealot	Judas (brother) of James	Judas Iscariot

EPISTULA APOSTOLORUM

John	Thomas	Peter	Andrew	James	Philip	Bartholomew	Matthew	Nathanael	Judas Zelotes	Cephas

Yeshua's brothers are made to appear in the text in Mark as unhelpful, trying to obstruct his mission. Thus, in Mark 3, 31, his mother and brothers seek to call Yeshua away at the start of his teaching ministry but he repudiates them, looking around at the crowd, with the words, 'Here are my mother and my brothers!'

In contrast with this presented picture, the other evidence from the gospels and other sources is that Yeshua's brothers were among his closest supporters. Four are present, in some cases only thinly disguised, in the apostles' lists. Two, James and then Simon (the zealot), succeeded him as leader of the Jewish Nazorean community in Jerusalem.

Judas, it will be argued, also went on to play an active role. Like James, he has a letter in the New Testament attributed to him (Jude 1, 1).

What then was the motivation of the gospel writers, or their later editors and rewriters? We do not, of course, know who they really were since the gospels were simply ascribed to people with the names Mark, Matthew, Luke and John. It may be, as suggested by an early authority, that the original version of Mark was written by John Mark who travelled with and interpreted for Simon Peter, who spoke only Aramaic. It is possible that the gospel of John was in part sourced from the long-lived 'disciple whom Jesus loved', known for convenience as John the priest. It then appears to have been substantially modified, with added anti-Jewish polemic, by a character known as John the Elder from Ephesus.

The awkward fact is that all of the canonical gospels were written some years after there had been a split between followers of Paul and the Nazoreans, who included among them the family and original followers of Yeshua. They were written by those who supported Paul, a self-appointed apostle who wanted to establish a breakaway church appealing to a wider audience including Gentiles and without regard to Jewish Law including purity rules, dietary restrictions and the practice of circumcision.

This partly explains why the brothers of Jesus, like James and Simon, who were Torah-upholding Jews and leaders of the Nazorean community, were diminished and placed at the bottom of the heap in the apostles' lists.

A second factor is that, as the story of Yeshua/Jesus was elaborated, it took on very widespread attributes of pagan mythology (as in the tales for example of Osiris and Dionysus) in which God inseminates a mortal woman to produce a godman or demigod who is killed and then resurrected. Mary became that mortal woman, a virgin, and Yeshua/Jesus her and God's 'only begotten' son. The gospels were subsequently edited and reedited to reflect this orthodoxy – and that meant disguising the role of Yeshua's brothers. That process had begun, before any of the gospels were written, when Paul was writing letters to churches that he had established outside Judea, often in or linked to displaced Jewish communities. 'Christ' was no longer a Jewish warrior liberator but, as Jesus Christ, a mystical resurrected godlike figure, Son of God, though as Paul also states (Romans 1, 4) still seen as born 'according to the flesh'.

It is now clear why Yeshua's brothers and sisters were such an embarrassment, creating so much difficulty for emerging Christian theology. They could hardly have been eliminated since they formed a large part of the story and there was other evidence of their existence, including the parts played by James and Simon in the Jerusalem community, Yeshua's first and only real church. But the story was rewritten and names were modified or obscured in such a way as to reduce or diminish their importance.

Not only was it widely recognised that 'James the Bishop' was the brother of Yeshua, but this recognition was extended in other sources to the continuing role of the other brothers. Eusebius, for example, quotes Hegesippus, a source from shortly after the time of Yeshua, that 'Judas called the brother of the Lord according to the flesh' went on to have children of his own. He also refers to

Simon/Simeon as son of Mary and Cleophas, though only as a 'cousin' or 'relative' of Yeshua.

Church authorities have over the centuries tried to argue that Yeshua's brothers and sisters were really not siblings but all of them his cousins. Eusebius maintained that Alphaeus was the brother of Joseph, so that James and his siblings would in this way have been cousins of Yeshua. Jerome generated a second route by creating two sisters, both called Mary, one the husband of Joseph and the other the husband of Alphaeus. A third route was invented still later. It was argued that the supposed second Mary, married to Cleophas/Alphaues, was really the sister of Joseph and that the writer of John had meant to say his mother's 'sister-in-law' in describing the women present at the cross! There is no basis for such speculation, although the motivation for it is clear.

In Hebrew, the word 'akim' can mean either siblings or cousins. This, it was maintained, was how a misunderstanding arose in the gospels that Yeshua had brothers and sisters rather than cousins.

The chief flaw with this argument is that the gospels are written in Greek, which has words that clearly differentiate cousin from brother or sister. There is no reason to suppose for example that Simon and Andrew or James and John were not brothers, but cousins. Even if they were using some Hebrew sources, it appears that Greek gospel authors had enough information to make these distinctions.

It is also likely that Yeshua, as a normal Jewish man, born 'according to the flesh', as Paul states, would have had brothers and sisters: that is the reality which the gospels reflect. Paul, also writing in Greek, described James as the 'brother of the Lord'. He made a clear distinction between himself and the 'other apostles' and the 'brothers of the Lord' (Corinthians I, 9, 5). Taken together, the evidence suggests that, rather than Yeshua having cousins as opposed to brothers and sisters, relationships were deduced or invented in order to make the assertion possible! If Yeshua was to become a godlike saviour of the world, then he needed to be distanced from his Jewish family and roots. He needed as the Son of God a virgin mother and therefore to have no brothers.

In terms of the Apostles' lists, the final phase of reediting can be seen in the later Latin version, in the 'Letter of the Apostles'. The two successors of Yeshua as leaders of the Jewish Nazorean community, James and Simon, do not appear. They have been eliminated entirely. Simon Peter, assigned 'the keys of the kingdom' as Yeshua's commander in chief in Matthew's gospel, has been downgraded to third place after John and Thomas. In this way, the Nazoreans, the real followers of Yeshua who formed the Jerusalem church, have been almost entirely wiped from the pages of history.

Judas/Thaddeus, the brother of Yeshua, is however still there as 'Judas Zelotes', following the description given in the Apostolic Constitutions, and in the same place as Judas (the brother) of James in the lists in the gospel of Luke and Acts.

Judas Iscariot, the betrayer and presumed to have died by his own hand, is not included in a list now of eleven, not twelve apostles.

To make up numbers, the place of James the son of Alphaeus is taken by Nathanael. However, Bartholomew, possibly 'son of Talmai', whom the author does not appear to recognise as Nathanael, is retained as well as Nathanael. The place of Simon the zealot is taken by Cephas, while Peter/Petros is also retained – even though these two names are Aramaic and Greek versions of the nickname, 'The Rock', for the same character Simon in the gospels.

There is a degree of confusion here, but how much of it is inadvertent? There is at least an unconscious severing of the character of Simon, nicknamed Peter, into two parts. The bad Cephas, bad because according to Paul (Galatians 2, 11-14) he drew back from efforts to abolish rules which separated Jews and Gentiles, is relegated to the bottom of the list where the much maligned character Judas Iscariot had been. But the rather better Petros, though weak for supposedly in the gospels denying Yeshua three times, is kept in third place.

It can be seen that the editor of Paul's letter to the Galatians is following the same practice or principle as the writers/editors of the gospels: when the accurate rendering of a word in Greek would reveal an inconvenient truth, then it is very often left untranslated in its original, Aramaic form. This happened with the name Judas barabbas (son of the master) in all four canonical gospels, with the misrendered Simon bariona (the outlaw) in Matthew and with Simon 'the Cananite' in Mark, nevertheless rendered precisely as Simon Cana, Simon the zealot, in Luke.

The editor of Galatians had a problem in that Paul is describing a fundamental clash between himself and his followers on the one hand and James, Peter and the Nazorean followers of Yeshua on the other over the position of Gentiles and, indeed, Paul's whole conduct and representation of the message of Nazorean Judaism. Paul describes his adversaries with venom, spite and ill-concealed contempt, these 'reputed pillars' who sent 'false brethren' to 'spy' on him. The problem, of course, was that the emerging Christian church needed as founders these real followers of Yeshua to give it credibility.

The solution came about in several ways. James was to an extent written out of the record, his role diminished and his contribution disparaged (hence 'James the less'). Paul was made into an apostle by divine revelation (something he appeared to have been seeking to be, in any case) and then somewhat unconvincingly brought into dialogue with the Jerusalem community, in Acts.

Peter 'the Rock' was, I have suggested, as a character divided into two parts. In Greek translation (Petros), he is made to support Paul in a speech to the Jerusalem assembly (Acts 15, 7-11). In Galatians, Peter appears in Greek translation as the apostle entrusted, as Paul maintains, with the gospel to Jews, the circumcised (Galatians 2, 8). But, when a few lines later Paul attacks him of drawing back from eating with Gentiles, for fear of the 'circumcision party', it can be presumed because of the prohibition on food sacrificed to idols, his name is left in Aramaic as Cephas, likewise meaning 'the Rock'.

Peter, one of the twin founders fashioned by the Church, could not have been shown to be in such open conflict with Paul. Hence, the cynical device (but usual given the other examples) of leaving his name in its Aramaic form in parts of Galatians to create two characters, one good one supporting Paul and the other bad, opposing Paul.

It is worth noting that the description in Acts, though in many parts a fictional tale, does appear here to have some solid basis. And in Acts Peter is described as having a mission to the uncircumcised! This would explain why, as a representative of James, he went quite properly to see what Paul was doing in Antioch and no doubt elsewhere in the diaspora, among communities of Jews and Gentile god fearers.

Ironically it was Saul, the persecutor of the Nazoreans, who sought to reinvent himself (and possibly disguise his origins) by giving himself another name and calling himself Paul. Simon Peter, however, has here had this same sort of character/name split retrospectively forced on him. Not only that, but as Cephas and also in many instances as Petros, his character has become a gross distortion of the real person made Yeshua's chief minister, fiery leader of a religious militia and possibly a man with the confidence successfully to confront King Agrippa.

As a final note, it would appear that John's gospel, like the 'Letter of the Apostles', comprises a later stage in the editing out of the brothers of Yeshua from their true place in the story. The description of those seven present in the post-crucifixion appearance by the Sea of Tiberias (Galilee) is a list excluding a core part of the Nazorean movement.

Included are 'Simon Peter, Thomas called the Twin, Nathanael of Cana in Galilee, the sons of Zebedee and two others of his disciples'. This list omits Judas Iscariot, by then presumably dead, and any mention of the four brothers of Yeshua, and sons of Alphaeus, that have here been identified. It is effectively also an apostles' list, but minus the religiously zealous or militant brothers of Yeshua and minus Judas Iscariot (sicarios or assassin).

The 'two others' could have been Andrew and Philip or two of the militants that the writer could not bring himself, or did not wish, to mention. The ultimate author of John, presumed to be John of Ephesus, coming later than the authors of the other canonical gospels was, if anything, even more antipathetic to the Nazorean Jews, the direct inheritors of Yeshua's legacy.

It is extraordinary and enlightening how much information can be gleaned from the names which have survived into the very much edited and sanitised accounts of the life and deeds of Yeshua. The derivations of words have revealed the militancy and warlike character of some of Yeshua's family and followers. Comparative analysis of various sources have brought the brothers of Yeshua back to their place as supporters at the centre of the movement rather than, as they have deliberately portrayed, as confused, carping and doubtful bystanders. It has been possible to demonstrate both the process and the ways in which central figures like James have been denigrated and displaced and ultimately, even, eliminated from the record

The study of names has in this way provided some sense of the archaeology of the gospels. The names of characters, with a basis in historical reality, are highly enduring fragments that can often survive, even when the story line is entirely changed.

Yeshua's brothers and brothers have reemerged from the obscurity into which they have been deliberately placed. The survival of their graphically violent names and nicknames, though at first puzzling, suggests that something other than the fiction we now have from the main story line of the gospels was going on in first century Palestine. What that was, and how that may relate to what is now in the gospel story, will be considered in the next chapter.

Chapter 3: Violent times

It is now estimated that Yeshua was born a few years before the date to which his birth is traditionally assigned. The likely date, which fits well with the account in Matthew's gospel and other evidence, was probably around BCE 6. This was during the last years of the reign of King Herod, an Idumean who had become the client king of Israel under Roman patronage.

It was a point in time that marked the closing of a dynasty of independent Jewish kings, the Maccabeans, which lasted little more than 100 years following generations of rule by foreign powers.

Herod's father, Antipater who was governor of Judea, had intervened in a fratricidal civil war between Jewish Maccabean princes Aristobulus II and John Hyrcanus II. By virtue of Roman support, Antipater's candidate John Hyrcanus triumphed, though to be reinstated only as High Priest with the largely honorary title of 'ethnarch' – no longer a king of Israel. Real power passed to Antipater as procurator, with his sons Phasael administering Judea and Perea and Herod taking control over Galilee.

The Maccabeans subsequently staged a short-lived comeback. With the help of a Parthian army, Antigonus, the son of Aristobulus II, managed to get himself installed as High Priest in place of John Hyrcanus and also as King of Judea.

Herod was forced to take refuge in his palace and fortress atop Masada, before going to seek help from Rome. The Roman senate responded by appointing him as the King of Judea. All Herod had to do was make this a reality.

With Roman military support, it took three years of war with Antigonus, culminating in a final and successful battle for Jerusalem. Antigonus was captured and taken to Rome in chains, and then beheaded by the Romans at Herod's request. Such summary justice was very much a portent of things to come.

Herod then ruled as a client king under the Romans from BCE 37 to BCE 4. Although he had the backing of Rome, there were at the outset limitations to his power. He had to relate both to the Jewish supreme council of elders, the Sanhedrin, and the High Priest John Hyrcanus II.

A huge row erupted when he took action against a group the Jewish historian Josephus describes as 'bandits', summarily executing their leader Hezekiah and many of his followers. John Hyrcanus indicted Herod before the supreme legal authority, the Sanhedrin. But Herod managed to brazen the matter out, relying on his support from Rome.

The response from Hyrcanus suggests that Hezekiah was possibly more than a minor brigand chief. He had a son Judas who later on led another ill-fated rebellion against Rome. So it may be Herod was dealing with messianic contenders who wanted to restore an independent, Jewish throne.

Herod gradually eliminated all those he could with such pretensions, murdering the aged High Priest John Hyrcanus, his daughter Alexandra and her son Jonathan. He married John Hyrcanus' granddaughter Mariamme, one of several of his wives, presumably at least partly in an effort to ingratiate himself with the people – through the promise of Maccabean blood in the next generation of Herodian kings. But he tired of this plan, had Mariamme executed too and then ordered the deaths of her two sons.

Herod had become more and more paranoid. He had spies everywhere and no one was safe who ventured to criticise.

Having removed restrictions on his power by eliminating many of his actual or potential opponents, Herod was able to operate as an absolute monarch. He embarked on vast building projects including the rebuilding of the temple in Jerusalem and the reconstruction of a Mediterranean seaport, which he named Caesarea after his patron, the Roman Emperor Augustus Caesar.

These projects kept the populace occupied, perhaps too busy to think up plans of rebellion. But they laboured under the imposition of a huge burden of taxation required to provide the necessary funding.

Herod was unpopular because of his cruel treatment of many of his subjects, his repression of the Maccabeans, his collaboration with the Romans and the fact that he was a non-Jewish king imposed by outsiders. The gospel story of his alleged murder of all the male children in Bethlehem under two years old (Matthew 2, 16), in an effort to eradicate an expected messiah, is probably no more than a reflection of the Old Testament story of Moses. But it does at least give an idea of Herod's reputation.

When Herod died in BCE 4, those yearning for liberation saw potential relief after years of suffering. Not one but three rebellions broke out in Palestine, under the leadership of three separate messiahs, or would-be Jewish kings and liberators. In Galilee, the son of the supposed bandit Hezekiah whom Herod had executed, Judas, took over the capital Sepphoris and armed his followers from the Roman armoury there. Simon, a former slave of Herod's, operating from Perea east of the river Jordan, moved in with an armed band to plunder the royal palace at Jericho and proclaimed himself king. In Judea, Athronges waged an initially successful campaign with his brothers and announced that he was king. It took the intervention of three Roman legions and numerous auxiliary troops to quell these rebellions. But the revolt was ultimately completely and cruelly put down. Besides many hundreds killed in battle, around 2000 prisoners taken alive were crucified by the Romans throughout Palestine.

After Herod's death, three of his sons were appointed by the Romans as rulers in different areas of Palestine. Herod Antipas in Galilee and Philip in Northern Palestine remained in their positions for many years. The third son, Archelaus, ruler of Judea and Samaria, was so utterly incompetent and brutal that a deputation of his subjects went to Augustus Caesar to demand his replacement. Caesar responded by banishing Archelaus and instigating direct rule under a Roman procurator.

So, for many years afterwards, and throughout the whole of Yeshua's adult life, a Roman governor or procurator was in overall charge of Judea. The Jewish council (Sanhedrin) was left with jurisdiction in everyday matters and minor criminal offences. But the power to impose and implement the death penalty was retained in Roman hands.

So too was the power to levy taxes. Following the instigation of direct rule under a procurator, Coponius, a census was instigated around CE 6 by the Syrian legate Quirinius for the purpose of tax assessment. This led to a tax revolt under the leadership of another Judas, described by the historian Josephus as a Galilean, priest and leader of a nationalist sect fighting for religious freedom and political independence. Judas conducted his campaign under the slogan 'No Lord but God'. But the rebellion ultimately came to nothing. According to Acts (5, 37), Judas perished in the attempt and his followers were scattered.

These various revolts, and the harsh treatment meted out under Herod and then under direct Roman rule, would have been fresh in the memory of many Jewish people in the years that Yeshua and his followers were growing up.

The next Emperor Tiberius liked to keep his procurators or governors in place for long periods. So, for a long time, including the years leading up and the crucifixion of Yeshua, Pontius Pilate was procurator in Judea. Now, while Herod as a Roman client king was heartily disliked by many of his subjects, he did at least have the guile or common sense to respect Jewish religious beliefs and customs.

One central issue was the purity of the temple in Jerusalem, the centre for Jewish religious observance. Gentiles were barred and so were pagan images. This is probably why Roman coins, with the image of Caesar on them, had to be exchanged for temple coinage in purchasing doves for sacrifice. Herod intervened only minimally in temple affairs, contenting himself with the erection of a single golden eagle, the symbol of Roman authority, over the temple gate. Even this, however, was eventually pulled down by objectors, many of whom were subsequently caught and executed, when Herod appeared to be on the brink of death.

The insistence on, and even extension of, an area of religious practice where Roman writ did not run may well have been a subtle form of subversion, a way of a carving out some degree of religious freedom and independence in the face of Roman imperial power. Whether the Romans were aware of a disguised agenda and determined to quash it, whether they were less sensitive to Jewish feelings or whether even they simply felt that they had the power, and did not have to bother with the religious sensitivities of their subjects, is unclear. But there were, during the time of Roman direct rule, a number of incidents that generated conflict. Several occurred while Pontius Pilate was procurator, from about CE 26 to CE 37.

Shortly after taking up his post, Pilate posted soldiers with their standards, carrying embossed images of the Emperor, into Jerusalem. This generated a mass protest since the 'graven' images were considered idolatrous. A crowd, gathering strength as it went, walked to Caesarea and besieged Pilate in his palace for five days and nights. Pilate summoned the protestors, surrounded them with soldiers and threatened them all with death. The protestors responded by offering to die en masse, rather than back down. This left the procurator with the awkward prospect of having to justify massacring so many people for so little apparent justification. So instead he conceded the point and had the offending standards removed from Jerusalem.

Another incident occurred when Pilate raided temple funds,

without Jewish consent, to build an aqueduct taking water into Jerusalem. This led to a substantial popular protest in the city which Pilate put down by mixing soldiers with the crowd, disguised in civilian clothes. At a prearranged signal, the soldiers took out clubs and beat the protestors. As the Jewish historian Josephus describes it, the blows inflicted were harder than Pilate had sanctioned or anticipated and many people were killed on the spot or trampled to death in the rush to escape.

At this point in Josephus' history of the Jewish people, *Antiquities*, there is a description of Jesus who 'was the messiah' and who was executed under Pilate. However, most scholars agree that this is something that has either been inserted, breaking the continuity of the text, or greatly modified by later Christian editors. Josephus' apparent confession of Christian belief would certainly have run against his background as a Pharisee priest, his zealot past and his aristocratic pedigree, through family connections with the Maccabeans, as well as the general tone of his writings. Apart from which, identifying himself with the Christians, who were a growing sect, often troubling the empire, might very well have put him at risk from his Roman patrons. As will be seen, Josephus was a great survivor and adept at covering his tracks.

However, the insertion of text or the possible existence of original text relating to Yeshua at this particular point indicates that the trouble over funds for the aqueduct into Jerusalem came before, possibly even just before, problems that Pilate had with the Jewish leader Yeshua as described in the gospels. There is support for this in the descriptions in the gospels relating to an uprising. In Luke, Yeshua was told while on his way to Jerusalem of 'Galileans whose blood Pilate had mingled with their sacrifices'. Mark describes, after Yeshua has been captured, a certain Barabbas 'among the rebels in prison, who had committed murder in the insurrection'.

While it is possible that Josephus has missed out on an

incident of major proportions, alluded to in the gospels, it is far more likely that the references in Mark and Luke are both to consequences of the temple funds/aqueduct uprising. In which case, this can be dated to CE 36, just before Yeshua's campaign and towards the very end of Pilate's term as Roman procurator in Judea.

Josephus makes no reference to Yeshua in his *Jewish War* produced around CE 75, though there are references of disputed authenticity in a Slavonic version that appears to have been translated from a Greek original. His later work, *Antiquities*, completed in CE 93, has some obscure tales whose significance will be explored and the direct, though highly dubious, references to Jesus outlined above.

Luke, who was also something of an historian, delved into the Roman archives and appears to have quoted directly the charges levelled against Yeshua, that he was 'perverting the nation, forbidding (the Jews) to give tribute to Caesar, and saying that he himself is (the messiah) a king'(Luke 23.2). It should be noted that the charge of forbidding tribute goes directly contrary to the gospel tale in which Yeshua told his listeners to 'render to Caesar the things that are Caesar's'. Either the charge was incorrect or incorrectly quoted by Luke or alternatively Yeshua's message was edited, as in other instances, for a pro-Roman, conformist Christian church.

The gospels report that Yeshua embarked on a preaching mission shortly after the death of John the Baptist. This sequence indicates in turn that Yeshua was crucified in the spring of CE 36, following an incident in which the blood of his fellow Galileans had been spilled. I have argued that this was likely to have been the temple funds uprising, as described by the Jewish historian Josephus.

The final incident in Pilate's rule as procurator came towards the end of the same year and led to his downfall. In adjacent Samaria, where people of Semitic origins observed their own form of temple worship, a man came forward as the Taheb (restorer), pledging to find the sacred temple vessels which it was believed Moses had hidden on Mount Gerizim.

Presumably seeing another possible messianic uprising, Pilate blocked the way up the mountain with cavalry and heavily-armed infantry. Many of the Taheb's followers were killed on the mountain. Some of the leaders were captured and executed.

A delegation from the Samaritan community went to complain vociferously to Vitellius, Roman governor of Syria, that this had been a slaughter of innocents, people who were in fact refugees from persecution initiated by Pilate. Vitellius decided in favour of the protestors. He recalled the procurator to Rome and put in a temporary replacement. Pilate lost his job, probably not just for one miscalculation, but a succession of misjudgements over a period culminating in the massacre beside Mount Gerizim.

The mid first century was certainly a turbulent period for Palestine. There were a number of incidents, leading up to a general uprising which resulted in the destruction of Jerusalem in CE 70. Josephus describes the clash between John the Baptist and Herod Antipas, which led to John's execution most probably in CE 35. He outlines the confrontation that took place six years later in CE 41 when the Emperor Caligula ordered the Syrian legate Petronius to place a statue of himself as the god Zeus incarnate in the temple at Jerusalem. Petronius managed to avert a major Jewish rebellion by stalling, in the hope of a change of circumstances. There was, in the nick of time. The Emperor died and the provocative demand for a statue became superfluous.

Another character called 'Theudas' was captured around CE 46, while apparently fleeing from the Romans, before he could cross the river Jordan to safety. He was beheaded and many of his supporters were also killed. A year or so later, two other rebels, James and Simon, whom Josephus describes as sons of the tax rebel Judas the Galilean, were crucified. As will be seen, these incidents may well have been connected.

Around CE 50, a clash between Jews and Samaritans was so inadequately mishandled by the Roman governor Cumanus that it turned into a serious rebellion.

The Roman governor Felix (CE 51 – 60) dealt with what Josephus describes as a 'bandit' chief Eleazar, crucifying him and many of his men. He also reportedly repelled an 'Egyptian false prophet' who encamped on the Mount of Olives with a small army, ready to overwhelm the Roman garrison in Jerusalem.

This story, recounted in *Antiquities* and in the *Jewish War*, eerily echoes gospel narrative. In both versions, the Egyptian escapes and it seems the Romans went on looking for him. So much so, that the captain of the Roman garrison in Jerusalem Claudius Lysias is reported as asking Paul in Acts whether Paul was not himself the Egyptian! This happened after Paul had been arrested, for his own safety, after having been set upon by a crowd of 'Asian Jews'. It was alleged that Paul was teaching against Jewish Law and that he had been bringing Gentiles into the temple.

In the years leading up to the Jewish revolt, Josephus describes Judea as being overrun with 'brigands', the sicarii who used their curved daggers to assassinate opponents, mingling with the crowds and melting away in the subsequent confusion. One prominent victim was the High Priest Jonathan, though rather strangely Josephus implicates the Roman governor Felix in this.

In CE 62, Josephus reports that the High Priest Ananus took advantage of a gap, after the governor Festus had died and his successor Albinus was not in place, to convene a council to accuse Yeshua's brother James of transgressing Jewish law. James was condemned and stoned to death, illegally since the death penalty could only be imposed by Roman sanction. Other sources, besides Josephus, indicate that James had attained substantial popular support as leader of the Nazoreans and represented an alternative focus of at least religious authority.

From this moment on, conflict between the forces described as sicarii and those of the High Priest grew. The sicarii undertook a series of kidnappings in order to secure, by exchange, the release of their own people held prisoner.

The situation was further inflamed when the Emperor Nero sent a governor Gessius Florus who seemed bent on provoking the Jewish population. Several early church authorities, including Origen and Eusebius, report Josephus as saying that James was a person of such great standing and virtue that his death led to the destruction of Jerusalem. The implication was that the disastrous outcome of the war was a form of divine retribution. But the passage, if it ever existed, is no longer present in current-day versions of Josephus.

Curiously, in the *Jewish War*, there is such an association – but it is between the fall of Jerusalem and the death of the former High Priest Ananus at the hands of Idumeans. After the war, there was both persecution of the new Christian sect, started under Paul, and a clampdown on the Jewish Nazoreans. The Romans may not always have made the distinction between worldwide messianists and Jewish messianists, both representing a challenge and both possibly spreading disaffection and dissent.

The Roman general Vespasian, who quashed the Jewish revolt and became emperor, ordered a purge of all the descendants of 'Sons of David', which would have included the family and followers of Yeshua and James. His sons Titus and Domitian, who succeeded him, pursued the same policy. Those believed to be descendants of David, including the grandsons of Yeshua's brother Judas, Zoker and James, were rounded up and questioned.

The next emperor Trajan had Simon/Simeon bar Cleophas, the third brother of Yeshua, crucified around CE 98. Simeon would by then have been very old. According to Eusebius, the descendants of Judas, who would have included Zoker and James, were executed too.

Of the four brothers of Yeshua identified, it appears that only Matthew lived to die a natural death.

These details of what took place around the lifetime of Yeshua, mainly from Josephus, demonstrate how brutal the times were and particularly how brutal the Romans really were. There were almost continuous purges against active Jewish nationalists and messianists. The Nazorean followers of Yeshua and James were under constant pressure.

There is no doubt that Roman rule was in general deeply resented, as were Jewish collaborators. It is interesting that, in describing the moment when the Jewish uprising is about to break out, Josephus puts into the mouth of the Herodian King Agrippa II, a personal friend of the historian, an impossibly long oration in which the king urged the citizens of Jerusalem not to embark on war. The reasons that Herod Agrippa advances are, however, practical ones. Rome was too powerful. Other stronger nations had been forced to submit to Rome. It was also too late: the moment to have made a supreme effort was in the face of Pompey's invasion, when the Romans were weaker and Israel, under the Maccabeans, was stronger. The Jews didn't have the allies, men, weapons, ships and funds. There is however no argument that the Jews should stay loyal subjects because the Romans were such good rulers or because, as subjects, they enjoyed such great benefits in being part of the empire!

Having been captured by the Romans, Josephus had become their interpreter and propagandist, with a brief to write material that would both glorify Roman military achievements and also deter others who might also consider rebellion. But the views attributed to Agrippa might also have been the ex Jewish commander and historian's own. Josephus had been to Rome and had seen at first hand the forces the Romans could muster. As he describes it, he advocated coming to terms before and during his time as commander of the Jewish forces in Galilee.

The reasons the Jews went to war were however religious

rather than practical. Their religion was inextricably intertwined with their very idea of nationhood – and they were finally goaded into rebellion when this religion and their religious leaders were threatened.

Josephus was thus ambivalent (as he portrays himself) about the enterprise, even though he was one of the key military figures on the Jewish side. He was born in CE 37, just after the crucifixion of Yeshua. He was a member of a priestly family and could trace his ancestry back to the Maccabeans. By his own admission, he had explored all the main Jewish positions including that held by an ascetic and possibly anti-establishment group, before finally (as he claims) settling on being a Pharisee priest. Given this background, it is difficult to evaluate the motivations that Josephus ascribes to various individuals and groups. He may have been writing as much to protect himself and others as to please his new patrons.

In his later work, *Antiquities*, Josephus described the adherents of three philosophies: Essenes, Sadducees and Pharisees, together with a fourth philosophy set up by Judas the Galilean. The followers of Judas' way were identical with the pious Pharisees, except for an unquenchable passion for liberty and readiness to uphold their principles even in the face of torture and death.

Rather than being a distinct school of thought, it would seem then that these people are those that are elsewhere described as either as 'sicarii' or zealots, motivated however in their resort to violence by religious conviction.

Both before and after the time that Yeshua lived, Jews were bound together by their religion, by the covenant they believed that their God had set up with his chosen people. They were united by a determination to preserve their religious freedom.

The dominant philosophy at this time was that of the Pharisees. This was the group that respected not only the written law of the Hebrew bible, but also a considerable amount of oral law that had been passed down and interpretations of the law that were made according to new circumstances. The Pharisees were involved with teaching and adjudication of disputes. Becoming a Pharisee sage, or later rabbi, involved years of patient study. Far from being rigid and oppressive, as some of the gospel text suggests, the Pharisees were tolerant of dissent, allowing different views on philosophical issues. By contrast, the Sadducees were more rigid, acknowledging only the written law and allowing no deviation from it.

It may be that doctrinal differences, such as belief in the immortality of the soul and an afterlife – held by Pharisees though not by Sadducees – were what originally distinguished the two groups. But for some time the Sadducees had been compromised by the fact that foreign rulers had appointed Sadducee High Priests, with powers of enforcement, as a practical means of administration. The priests came from families or tribes who, it was believed, could trace their descent back to original priests at the time of King David – and were thus Zaddokites or Sons of Zadok. In Hebrew, the cluster of letters 'zdk' means righteousness. Zadduki or, as transliterated into Greek, a Sadducee literally means a person who is righteous.

The Sadducee priests had ceremonial powers in the temple and were concerned with correct observance of ritual and performance of temple sacrifices.

On the central council or Sanhedrin, the Pharisees were in the majority. But because of delegated power, directly from the Romans at the time of Yeshua, the High Priest's faction was able to exert considerable influence. It was, indeed, the High Priest's police enforcers (including Saul) who were sent out to round up messianic activists considered to be a threat to the status quo and to Rome.

Few Jews were happy in a situation of occupation. For the most part, however, the strategy adopted by the main religious group, the Pharisees, was to wait and see, in the expectation that the promised messiah would deliver them from their enemies. This is illustrated in the position taken by the Pharisee leader Gamaliel, as described in Acts (5, 27-42), when Simon Peter and other followers were brought before the council for teaching about Yeshua, having been forbidden to do so.

The underlying structure of the incident is enlightening. The reason the apostles were forbidden was that they could 'bring this man's blood upon us'. In other words, the followers of Yeshua were recognised as subversive of Roman rule, likely to bring retribution on everyone. Simon Peter's response, 'We must obey God rather than men', echoed the 'No Lord, but God' position taken by the tax rebel Judas when the census was instigated for tax purposes. Josephus, it should be recalled, regarded this person as the founder of the militant, freedom-seeking, fourth philosophy.

Gamaliel advised his colleagues to steer clear and leave the apostles alone, 'for if this plan or undertaking is of men, it will fail; but if it is of God, you will not be able to overthrow them'. The Sanhedrin followed his advice and freed them.

If the main religious groups were not openly advocating the overthrow of Roman rule, why then was there so much violent unrest at the time and what was the source of it? While devoting only a little space to the Sadducees and Pharisees, Josephus went on at some length in the *Jewish War* about a third philosophy, that of the Essenes. This was a smaller group, living in scattered communities, which had withdrawn from temple worship at Jerusalem. Members pooled their property, had strict rules for religious observance, maintained a hierarchical structure and operated a long, three year process of initiation for those who wanted to join. Although marriage was possible, celibacy was seen as the ideal.

This description has so much in common with the practices of people who lived at Qumran, and who produced the Dead Sea scrolls, that archaeologists have described these people as

Essenes. The scroll authors however described themselves in their writings as 'the poor' and as 'Sons of Zadok'. Religiously strict and ascetic, in the manner of the Essenes described by Josephus and other contemporary commentators, the Dead Sea community came to be regarded by some scroll analysts as an eccentric and extreme but also inward-looking and pacifist sect.

There was indeed a strongly Christian group controlling the scrolls' translation and dissemination, who wanted to deny the group's militancy and possible connections with Yeshua's followers. As is now beginning to be recognised, this could only be done by ignoring or regarding as purely allegorical much of what 'the poor' wrote about themselves – as well as some of what others wrote about them.

Josephus, for example, wrote that 'in the war with the Romans' they were subjected though without success 'to every torture yet invented in order to make them blaspheme the Lawgiver or eat some forbidden food.' He otherwise goes into no detail about their participation in the war but does mention in passing that one of their number, 'John the Essene', was made a military commander at the outset of the Jewish revolt.

It appears that the Roman general Vespasian took time out to destroy the settlement at Qumran, while preparing his siege of Jerusalem. Was he aware that, in their writings, the community looked forward to a final battle between 'the sons of darkness' and 'the sons of light' when 'the kittim' (the Romans) would be finally defeated? Their war scroll set out how this battle would be conducted and they also had a copper scroll, giving details of hidden treasure, quite possibly funds for the war that was envisaged. None of the treasure was found; so it may have been used for the purpose of supporting an army against the Romans.

Not necessarily all those who belonged to the community became freedom fighters. But the religious philosophy of 'the poor' was intertwined with messianic nationalism.

The Nazarene or Nazorean sect, linked to Yeshua and his

brother James, had many similarities with 'the poor' at Qumran, even to the extent of sharing the same self-description! As Paul stated (Galatians 2, 10), what James and the other Nazorean leaders demanded of him was to 'remember the poor', meaning raise funds for the Jerusalem church from among 'god fearing' Gentile and Jewish communities abroad.

To be a Nazarene was to be seen to be subversive by definition, an agitator. Luke, the historian and author of Acts, recorded the charge against Saul/Paul when he was brought by the High Priest Ananias before the Roman Governor Felix, just as he did the charge brought against Yeshua. It was that Paul was 'an agitator among all the Jews throughout the world, and a ringleader of the sect of the Nazarenes' (Acts 24, 5).

Paul was here being accused of being an anti-Roman militant. But the terms used imply that the Nazoreans as a whole could be described as that – and this would have included James and Yeshua, who was described as the 'the Nazarene' in the earliest of the canonical gospels, Mark.

Not all the Nazoreans would necessarily have ended up fighting the Romans and it appears the movement may have had religious and militant wings. But some would have done. And what more prime candidate than Yeshua's man given 'the keys of the kingdom', hard as rock and with a fiery temper, Simon Peter? Very possibly, this was the same Simon (in Josephus) with a 'reputation for religious scrupulousness' who confronted King Agrippa I and demanded that he should be barred from the temple as unclean.

It is time then to look in more detail at James, the brother of Yeshua, leader of the Nazoreans, at his character and views. This should throw light both on the people he led and those who came before him, including Yeshua.

This will lead subsequently to further questions. Was Yeshua a pacifist world-redeemer, as the gospels have it, or a practical revolutionary as active as the nicknames ascribed to his close followers suggest? Was he a rebellious zealot or a cautious and careful Pharisee?

If he was a rebel leader, what became of the revolution that, according to our available history, never happened?

If Yeshua claimed to be King of the Jews, in the mould of the Maccabeans and as charged by the Romans, why wasn't the mantle of kingship passed on, as happened with the Maccabeans? What happened to his brothers now revealed, notwithstanding the gospel rewrite, as active partners in an earthly project?

Chapter 4: Nazorean leaders: James and Yeshua

Around the time that Yeshua lived, a community existed at Qumran by the shores of the Dead Sea of religious, ascetic and fiercely nationalistic Jews who had withdrawn from the everyday life and orthodox temple worship because, as they saw it, Israel had been led into evil ways. Their concern seemed to encompass a number of issues, including the character of the priests, defilement by 'riches', 'profanation' of the temple and 'fornication'. A number of perceived misdemeanours were grouped under this latter term, including some forms of remarriage and relations between certain categories of relative such as uncle and niece. The community believed that purity rules, under which sacrifices were carried out and temple sacrifices conducted in Jerusalem, were not sufficiently stringent. They objected to the use of the orthodox liturgical calendar in determining the Sabbath, feast days and days of fasting and instead used their own more rigid version.

The community at Qumran produced extensive literature, including commentary on existing biblical text which they related to recent or contemporary events. It seems, as they themselves described it, to have been a nerve centre for a number of similar communities, 'assemblies of the camps' and 'assemblies of the towns' throughout Israel. Because there is so much correspondence in detail, it also appears that this is the same group that others, including the Jewish historian Josephus, described as Essenes. Josephus devoted far more space to the practices and beliefs of the Essenes than to the majority group among the Jews, the Pharisees, or the Sadducees from which the High Priests were chosen. According to his estimate, the Essenes numbered about four thousand and could be found scattered throughout Israel in small colonies. They would certainly have had a presence in the nearby capital, Jerusalem, where there was indeed a 'gate of the Essenes'.

How strange it is then that, in the whole of the New Testament gospels, there is no mention whatsoever of this group.

It is strange, until it is remembered that 'Essenes' is not what this group called themselves. They described themselves in a number of ways, as 'keepers of the covenant' and as 'sons of Zadok' (which derives from 'righteous').

They also called themselves the 'poor' – and the poor are certainly everywhere in the New Testament. They are there among the groups that are blessed in the beatitudes; they are there as the people that James asked Paul especially to remember. They were James' followers and they would have been Yeshua the Nazarene's too.

The evidence supports a conclusion which may be surprising to us now. But that is only because of the false picture edited into the gospels and now ingrained in our consciousness.

The gospels are not about the poor or Essenes and do not comment on them. But the poor are an invisible presence, vested in the very characters of the gospel stories, a link running through every line.

The parallels are extensive and, in some instances, startling. Yeshua told those who wanted to follow him to sell their goods and give their money to the poor. He and his disciples pooled their funds which were then administered by a treasurer, Judas Iscariot. Acts describes the early followers of Yeshua, following the crucifixion, selling their land and houses to put the money into a common fund to be distributed according to need.

In the same way, the Essenes' 'men of the council' held their property and income in common, looked after by a 'bursar'. Lower in the hierarchy, the 'men of the covenant' could live with their fellow Jews and own property but gave two days earnings every month in order to support widows, the sick and others among them in need.

The Nazorean followers of James had a central council of twelve with, as Paul described it (Galatians 3, 9) three 'pillars' who were James, John and Cephas (Simon Peter). This was probably not the same as the first group of family and followers around Yeshua, which gospel writers made up to twelve (regardless of however many there actually were) because this was a significant number.

In the ruling group, James, John and Cephas are at a higher level, and outside the twelve. Thus, as Paul also wrote (Corinthians I, 15, 5), Yeshua appeared, following the crucifixion to Cephas and *then* to the twelve. As Paul describes it, Yeshua appeared still later to James whose importance Paul, like the gospel writers after him, was seeking to minimise. The non-canonical gospel of the Hebrews, however, has Yeshua appearing first to James:

> But the Lord, after he had given his linen clothes to the Servant of the Priest [that is, High Priest], went to James and appeared to him. For James had sworn that he would not eat bread from the hour in which he drank the Cup of the Lord until he should see him rising again from those that sleep.

It seems that this gospel, like the gospels of the Nazoreans and Essenes, originated from followers of James (Ebionites) and was based on a source or sources independent of the canonical gospels. Subsequently suppressed by the Church, these gospels also have in common the fact that they now only survive in fragmentary quotations. As I will argue later, it is quite likely that the canonical gospel writers made use of a common Nazorean account of the passion, as did the writer of the gospel of the Hebrews. This would have recognised (what is also common sense) that, after the ordeal of crucifixion, Yeshua would have made contact with those most important to him: his brother James who took over the leadership of the Nazorean community, his brother Simon/Simeon who next became leader and his chief minister/commander Simon (Peter).

The author of Luke must have been aware of the relative importance of these characters. Yet he, or subsequent editors of his gospel, continued the policy, already expressed by Paul in Corinthians, of denigrating James. This significant brother of Jesus, next leader of the Nazoreans, was cut from the story.

However, as has already been amply illustrated, names or fragments of names have a tendency of sticking in the text as evidence of an earlier (possibly truer) version of events. In Luke, Yeshua makes a first appearance after the discovery of the empty tomb on the road to Emmaus to two of his followers, an unnamed person and someone called Cleopas! There has clearly been some nifty editing here since Cleophas, it will be recalled, is one of the alternative names, the other being Alphaeus, of the father of Yeshua's brothers and thus of Yeshua himself. Furthermore, when the two return to Jerusalem and tell the other disciples, this causes a general acclamation, 'The Lord has risen indeed, and has appeared to Simon!'

Piecing the evidence together, it seems that what Luke was not allowed to say was that Yeshua appeared first to his brothers 'James and Simon bar Cleopas' (or possibly James bar Cleopas and Simon Peter), this being cut to 'Cleopas' and 'Simon' at different parts of the text.

Judas Iscariot appears from Acts to have been a member of the council, because there was an election by lot to replace him. It is also possible that the entire story of Judas Iscariot, together with his death and the election to replace him, was an invention. That would have been why Paul, whose letters predate the gospels and Acts, wrote of twelve apostles when there should have been eleven, with Judas dead, at the time of the immediate post-Crucifixion appearances.

The Nazoreans had a council of twelve and it seems that early Christian authors borrowed this idea in writing their gospels.

The 'poor' or Essenes were organised in precisely the same way as the Nazoreans, with a supreme council of twelve laymen and three priests. It is also relevant that the three people, James, John and Cephas (Simon Peter), described as 'pillars' by Paul are the three disciples on which there is some evidence of a priestly connection. Simon may well have been the religiously scrupulous person Josephus described as able to gather a congregation or 'ecclesia'. John can be identified with the disciple 'whom Jesus loved' (not the same person as John, son of Zebedee), who provided a safe house for the Passover meal and who held back from going into the tomb, for fear of defilement. So, he too may well have been a priest. James was certainly a priest for the Nazoreans. He is described by early church sources as connected to the priesthood and carrying out priestly functions.

The Nazoreans appear to have adopted an approach where marriage was generally allowed, but celibacy practised by some key figures. Among their leaders, both James and his successor Simon/Simeon are described as having remained celibate. But one of the brothers, Judas, is described in several sources as being married and there are also references to his grandchildren. The evidence of the gospels, surviving the efforts of censors, indicates that Yeshua had a partner, Mary Magdalene, and that they too were married.

It appears that, though marriage was permitted, celibacy was an ideal for those in the higher levels of the Essenes, the men of the council. So here again, in terms of policy and practice, the two groups mirror one another.

The Nazoreans took communal meals together, which had special significance as an expression of solidarity, just like the Essenes.

Early church sources on James indicate that he engaged in ritual cold bathing. The *Pseudoclementine Homilies* contain texts originating from the Ebionites (literally, 'poor ones'), who followed after and revered James. At several points in *Homilies*, there are also references to Simon Peter bathing. That the writer thought it important enough to include this information indicates that it was a form of ritual practice.

Taking cold baths, as a means of purification, was also part of the ritual of the Essenes. There are references in the texts and there are even the remains of bath houses in the ruins of their settlement at Khirbet Qumran, close to the caves where the Dead Sea scrolls were hidden.

All four gospels have the disciples and Yeshua celebrating their Passover meal in the run-up of events leading to the crucifixion. The Passover in the orthodox Jewish calendar fell on a different day each year, but this year it was on the Saturday, the Sabbath. Thus, in all the gospels, the Passover was celebrated by Yeshua and his disciples a few days *before* everyone else. The synoptic gospels have a description of events which indicates that this might have been on the Thursday night. But these gospels, derived largely from the same source, conflate events for dramatic effect in an impossibly tight schedule.

Only John's gospel has a timetable that provides sufficient scope for all the events described to happen: the final meal in Jerusalem, return to the Mount of Olives, arrest of Yeshua, interrogation before the Sanhedrin, trial by the Roman authorities, sentence and execution. In this sequence, the Passover meal would have been celebrated on the Wednesday night. This was when the Essenes, who divided the year into a fixed number of weeks, also celebrated their Passover. Not just for one year, but every year.

No group would have held its Passover on a different night from the rest of the community without good reason. The only available reason is the obvious one: that Yeshua and his followers were connected to or part of the same tradition as the Essenes. It will be recalled that Yeshua sent his disciples to locate the safe house, in which the meal would be celebrated (Mark 14, 13), with orders to find and follow a man carrying a jar of water. Such a person would certainly have stood out (because fetching water was woman's work) as a member probably of an all-male community, for which there are few candidates besides the Nazoreans/Essenes.

There's a glimpse of another such character, the young man dressed in a white robe (Mark 16, 5) telling the women at the tomb that Yeshua had gone. This was another one of the invisible helpers, members of the community of which Yeshua and his brothers and his followers were a part. In the gospel of Peter, two young men of radiant appearance help Yeshua from the tomb.

The fourth century writer Epiphanius noted that all Christians were once called Nazoreans, which indicates a degree of primacy for James and his followers over and above the church at Antioch established by Paul where, according to Acts, believers were first known as 'Christians'. But Epiphanius went further. He also observed that they were once called Jessaeans or Essenes!

So is the link between Yeshua, abstracting his character as far as possible from gospel myth, and the Essenes proven? It is a case of there being such strong parallels between the Nazoreans, later led by James, and the Essenes that this has to be far more than pure coincidence. The Nazoreans and Essenes, who both called themselves 'the poor', were either the same group, called by others by different names. Or the Nazorean movement grew from the Essenes, the original 'keepers of the covenant', in strength and popularity by virtue of the messianic family that it harboured.

Yeshua is described as 'the Nazarene' in Mark and in the Jewish Talmud. This is often incorrectly translated to indicate that he was 'of Nazareth'. But the word Nazarene is so close as to be almost identical with Nazorean, given that vowels would have had to be deduced in original written Hebrew or Aramaic text. It is not so close to Nazareth, the name of a place which may not even have existed at the time Yeshua lived.

Paul was accused in Acts of being a member of this messianic, nationalist group using the same term as used in Mark, that is as 'a pestilent fellow, an agitator among the Jews throughout the world, and a ringleader of the sect of the Nazarenes' (Acts 24, 5). The term 'Nazarene' here clearly refers to a religious sect or movement rather than to a place. This should therefore also apply to the references to Yeshua as a Nazarene in Mark.

The general picture presented in the gospels suggests that Yeshua was a leader, rather than just a member of the group. His advice and opinions are often sought on various weighty matters, he is respectfully addressed as 'teacher' or 'master' and he has a substantial following. In the introduced story in John's gospel of the woman caught in adultery, it seems as if Yeshua is being asked to make a judgement or ruling. I will suggest (see ch 11) that this was even clearer in an original version taken out of the text, edited and then reinstated.

There are indeed aspects of the portrayal of Yeshua's character in the gospels that may be a clear and deliberate distortion. Luke, for example, makes Yeshua into a worldly figure, with disciples who ate and drank instead of praying and fasting (Luke 5, 33). Yeshua is even charged with consorting with the hated tax collectors and 'sinners'.

The picture that is so painted may have been part of the effort by gospel writers and editors to distance Yeshua from mainstream Judaism – becoming as, Christians would have it, someone looking to a wider audience.

Yeshua took his message to the people. On the evidence, his aspiration was to be a Jewish king or ruler of a kingdom on earth, perhaps even in parallel with Roman occupation. He was described as a master or teacher but not specifically as a priest.

But, that aside, he would in many respects have been in the same mould as his brother James. Sources agree that James was the first leader of the Nazoreans, at least after Yeshua. He was a fierce upholder of Jewish Law, including dietary restrictions and the requirement for circumcision, both for those born into Judaism or converting to it. He was a strict vegetarian, celibate and ascetic, disavowing such earthly pleasures as wine or other strong drink and the Roman hot baths. He was known as James 'the Just' or 'the Righteous One' and was renowned for his devotion, to the extent that his knees were hardened through constant praying.

Several early church writers described James in these terms. The earliest commentary comes from Hegesippus, quoted by Eusebius, writing in the second century, sixty or so years after James:

> He alone was allowed to enter the Place of Holiness, for he did not wear wool, but linen, and he used to enter the temple alone, and was often found upon his bended knees, interceding for the forgiveness of the people, so that his knees became as callused as a camel's, because of the constant importuning he did before God and asking forgiveness for the people.

As he is described here, and in similar sources, James is first of all portrayed as a priest, interceding before God on behalf of the people. Is that possible?

James was the leader of the Nazoreans who constituted a branch within Judaism, differing from the mainstream according to later Ebionite sources only in the belief that the messiah had come in the form of Yeshua, who had been one of their number. He was one of the three 'pillars', described by Paul, who would seem to have been priests, along the lines of the central council of three priests and twelve laymen that had supreme authority among the Essenes.

James came from a family that had priestly connections. Mary, mother of Yeshua, wife of Alphaeus/Cleophas and his mother also, had a 'kinswoman' Elizabeth whose husband Zachariah was a priest serving in the temple at Jerusalem.

So James could have been and probably was a priest, as part of his role as a leader of a group within Judaism. But it was almost certainly not as part of one of the traditional Sadducee priestly lineages. It would seem that, as part of an overall position in which the Essenes and Nazoreans were involved, James placed himself in opposition to the Sadducee temple elite.

He took this, as the passage quoted above and others like it indicate, to the extent of arrogating for himself the role of not just a priest but that of the High Priest of the people of Israel in the temple at Jerusalem!

The references are quite clear and unambiguous. They relate to the Day of Atonement (Yom Kippur) when, once a year, the High Priest was permitted to enter the Holy of Holies to supplicate God for forgiveness for the sins of the Jewish people. On that special day, purity requirements were stricter than usual and animal products were barred. So the High Priest wore white, coarse linen instead of a mixture of wool and linen.

But what was James doing acting as High Priest? He certainly was not the official High Priest, appointed by King Agrippa II on behalf of the Romans. The incumbents during this period are recorded successively as Jonathan, Ishmael, Joseph, Ananus and Joshua. If James were leader of a group related to, or identical with, the Essenes, then his entry into the Holy of Holies might well have been on a different day from the official Day of Atonement. The Essenes were, as has been noted, using a different calendar. This would have avoided a direct clash with the official High Priest performing his duties, making it at least possible that James did attempt to carry out a role of de facto religious leader of his people.

The High Priest and his faction among the Sadducees would probably not have welcomed an intrusion into what they may have perceived as their sole responsibilities. James had a substantial following, numbering many thousands according to Acts, and so could not perhaps have been lightly challenged. So the Sadducees bided their time and then struck at a moment when they could eliminate James without securing, as they should have done, proper Roman authority. At this time, only the Roman authorities in the person of the governor could confirm or pass a sentence of death.

The moment to strike came in CE 62 when the Roman governor Festus had died and the new person Albinus, appointed by the Emperor Nero, was still on his way to take up his position. As reported in *Antiquities*, the High Priest Ananus hastily convened the 'judges of the Sanhedrin', that is not even a full Sanhedrin, and had James and some other supporters accused of transgressing the law and stoned to death.

Deputations of 'those of the inhabitants of the city who were considered the most fair minded and who were strict in observance of the law', went to King Agrippa and to Albinus, still on his way to take up his new job, to complain. The outcome was that the High Priest Ananus was deposed.

But a struggle which began, even before James' death, between the 'high priests, on the one hand, and the priests and leaders of the populace of Jerusalem, on the other', that is between the Sadducee elite opposed by Pharisees and Nazoreans, continued to gain momentum. The death of James, who was a very much revered and popular leader, must certainly have heightened discontent and exacerbated the conflict. From that moment on, until the actual outbreak of war four years later, a civil conflict smouldered on. Josephus reports that the servants, that is police force, of the High Priest took by force income due to lower ranking priests. There was fighting between rival Sadducee factions. Members of the Herodian family, Saul and Costobar, took the opportunity to plunder the property of their opponents, 'those weaker than themselves'. The opposition in turn, described as 'sicarii' by Josephus, began to engage in guerilla war, taking hostages for exchange with some of their own people who had been captured. A few years beforehand this group, or another such group described as sicarii, had assassinated Jonathan, the High Priest at the time and brother of Ananus.

Several sources, the canonical gospels, early church authorities, the Acts of the Apostles and writings attributed to the Ebionites attest to the importance of James as the leader of the Nazoreans, indeed as the first leader of the group of Yeshua's followers after his crucifixion by the Romans.

Acts, written by the author of Luke's gospel, records a dispute between the followers of Yeshua under James (the 'Jerusalem Church') and Paul and his followers. The issue at stake was ostensibly the level to which Gentiles, who wished to become followers, should have to conform to Jewish practices in respect of circumcision and dietary restrictions. There was already a class of Gentile 'god fearers' who were attached to Jewish communities and synagogues. They were required to keep laws, believed to have been handed down by God to Noah after the flood, for mankind in general to follow. The Jews, God's chosen people, had to adhere to much stricter rules.

The verdict given by James was essentially a recapitulation of this position, that Gentiles had to abstain from idol worship, from 'blood' (that is, bloodshed or murder), from 'fornication' (that is, sexual offences including incest and adultery) and from meat that had not been killed in the Jewish manner, in which the blood had been drained away. By these means, they would not of course have become full Jews. To do that would have required circumcision, adherence to all the dietary restrictions and other requirements of the Torah. But, as James observed (Acts 15, 21), they were not actively looking for converts since they were not at all short of practising Jews following the Law of Moses in the synagogues.

Acts has to admit that the dispute between the Jewish

followers of Yeshua and Paul and his party took place and describe it, because it really did happen. But the seriousness of the dissension is played down and Simon Peter is given an unlikely bridging role, somewhere between the opposing positions of Paul and James. Thus in Acts, he is described as having a vision of a 'heavenly tablecloth' spread with all kinds of animals, reptiles and birds, clean and unclean, which God commands him to kill and eat (Acts 10, 9-16). Having then shared a table with Gentiles, he is described as going back to Jerusalem to 'the circumcision party' and convincing them of the need to admit Gentiles, without bothering about purity rules and effectively therefore on Paul's terms. However, this event comes earlier in Acts than Paul's summons to Jerusalem and the judgement given by James (Acts 15, 13-21) which restated the Noahide rules for god fearers. Prohibitions on food sacrificed to idols and meat from animals that had not been killed in the kosher manner, with the blood drained away, still were to be maintained.

James' authoritative statement of the Nazoreans' position indicates that they had not moved at all towards Paul's position. It was rather a reaffirmation and an admonishment intended to clarify and prevent any deviation in future from the position taken by Judaism towards Gentile god fearers.

So there was actually no conversion to Paul's view, despite the representation given by the clumsily introduced device of Peter's 'heavenly tablecloth' vision.

Paul's own letters, especially Galatians, which were written earlier that Acts, give a clearer impression of the animosity and discord between the two groups.

Paul went away from the meeting, with James and his followers in Jerusalem, believing that he had a dispensation to preach to the Gentiles very much how he liked. And he went on telling his followers and potential converts that circumcision was unnecessary, that the Torah was a dead letter, that salvation could only come by faith in a 'risen' Jesus Christ and that the distinction between Jews and Gentiles had henceforth been abolished by God!

Eventually, evidence of Paul's counter-teaching came back to the Nazorean community in Jerusalem and Paul was summoned for a second time. This time, however, the tone is more serious and there is an underlying menace which even the author of Acts cannot entirely disguise. This is James's rebuke, directed at Paul:

> You see, brother, how many thousands there are among the Jews of those who have believed; they are all zealous for the law, and they have been told about you that you teach all the Jews who are among the Gentiles to forsake Moses, telling them not to circumcise their children or observe the customs. What then is to be done? They will certainly hear that you have come.
> (Acts 21, 20-22)

Paul was then made to undergo a humiliating seven day penance in the temple, with his head shaved as a gesture of compliance, to demonstrate 'that there is nothing in what they have been told about you but that you yourself live in observance of the law.'

'The Jews' certainly did know that Paul had come. A rioting crowd tried to drag him from the temple and kill him and then, after he had been arrested by the Romans and subsequently brought before the Sanhedrin, there was a plot to kill him. This was based on a typical zealot-style 'oath neither to eat nor drink till they had killed Paul' (similar in form it will be recalled to James' oath in the gospel of the Hebrews not to eat bread until he had seen Yeshua again).

Paul was finally saved – from 'the circumcision party', those whom Acts earlier portrayed as having come via Peter into amicable agreement with him! – by being taken into protective Roman custody.

James comes across in these passages in Acts as a figure of prime importance. He is the leader of the Nazoreans and one of the triumvirate of three priestly 'pillars'. He is a firm upholder of the Law for Jews, while willing to accept a less strict regime for Gentile god fearers. He is popular, with many thousands of followers.

What I believe has so far been insufficiently appreciated is that James appears to have been acting and speaking, not just for a faction among Jews, *but for the Jewish people as a whole*. So it is that he can pronounce on the rules that should be applied to Gentile 'god fearers', attracted to synagogues in the Jewish diaspora. He is able to send a message to them by letter, setting out what rules of diet and behaviour they should and should not obey. It should be remembered that these were the synagogues for all Jews, not just outposts for the Nazoreans. It would surely not have been possible for James to have acted in this way had not the Pharisees consented.

This assumption of a more general authority is in accordance with the role that James is described by early church authorities as taking, that of seeking to atone for the sins of the Jewish nation as a whole.

James became a threat, at least to the Sadducee elite, because of his very popularity. As an Ebionite source (*Pseudoclementine Recognitions*) described it, 'we who had been very few became in the course of a few days, by the help of God, far more than they. So that the priests at one time were afraid, lest haply, by the providence of God, to their confusion, the whole of the people should come over to our faith.'

The same source indicated that the *only* difference at issue was belief in Yeshua/Jesus. In other words, there was at this point, a doctrinal conflict between Jews (albeit stirred up by Paul who, according to *Recognitions*, intervened in the debate and caused a riot and assault on James). Both sides still recognised the same Torah, and the same rules of behaviour. The only difference was that James' followers maintained that one of their number was the expected Jewish messiah (latest in a long line) who, though crucified by the Roman authorities, was still alive and able to return again.

To have had so many followers, the Nazoreans under James must have made inroads into the main body of belief in Judaism, that of the Pharisees. But this was not really an issue, since in almost every respect their beliefs were the same. However, as the source quoted above suggests, it was the Sadducee elite which was alarmed for it was 'their priests' who saw their support draining away.

The gospels had an agenda to make it appear that Yeshua was at odds with his fellow Jews. Hence, the hostile anti-Jewish comments in Matthew and John, and ritual denunciations of Pharisees and others. However, the underlying text, as the writer Maccoby has demonstrated, shows a degree of cooperation and friendliness between Yeshua and many Pharisees. Yeshua is described in the gospels as dining with and having discussions with key members of this group. Pharisees came and warned him that Herod Antipas, Roman appointed ruler of Galilee, and his soldiers were looking for him. Prominent Pharisees, such as Nicodemus, a member of the Sanhedrin, were numbered among his supporters.

There was also a congruence of belief: Yeshua upheld the twin Pharisaic principles, both derived from the Old Testament (Deuteronomy and Leviticus), of loving God and one's neighbour as oneself. His view of the Law (Matthew 5, 17-48), was in the Pharisaic tradition, strict but requiring extrapolation and interpretation, as opposed to the Sadducee approach which had a rigid framework determined solely by existing written law.

So it might well have been possible for supporters of the Pharisees to come across to the approach of Yeshua and then James, without compromising their core beliefs. They were all Jews believing in the same covenant with God and the same requirements for circumcision, dietary restrictions and limitations on sexual relations. Effectively, James may have come to be an authority figure not only for his own Nazorean supporters but for a much wider following within Judaism, including many who were nominally Pharisees. The Jewish historian Josephus indicated that, before settling on becoming a Pharisee, he had tried all the main schools of thought – Sadducee, Pharisee and Essene. There must therefore have been a degree of fluidity in the boundaries between these groups. He even conceded having spent time studying a fourth, perhaps more anti-establishment, philosophy under a character to whom he gives the pseudonym 'Banus'.

Josephus had good reason however, as a captured Jewish commander who had gone over to the Romans, to play down his zealot past. He may thus have distorted and also oversimplified the situation. The Sadducee priestly families secured their position by descent. So it may not have been possible to become a member of the Sadducee elite without having the right family background.

Also, the term 'zealot' was not really applied by Josephus in a consistent or coherent fashion. It was not so much indicative of a distinct group as a label that could be applied to anyone (or adopted by anyone) who took opposition to rule by foreign powers (which almost all Jews felt) and unwillingness to compromise on religious principle to the point of actual rebellion. Like the word 'bandit', it was applied fairly widely and in a somewhat denigratory fashion. Josephus may have wanted to make the opposition appear less deeply rooted, and less coordinated, than it must have been to conduct a longstanding and initially very successful rebellion against Roman occupation.

As already outlined, the Pharisee leaders were adopting a 'wait and see' approach, which is why Gamaliel advised the Sanhedrin to steer clear of and set free Simon Peter and the other arrested followers of Yeshua. If these activists were not from God, then this would show up in due time. If, however, it transpired that they were from God, then it would be better not to have opposed them!

Given a degree of fluidity between religious groups, it may have been possible to have been a Pharisee or supporter of the Pharisees and a Nazorean at the same time. Ordinary people who followed Pharisee beliefs and the Pharisee sages (later rabbis), who applied the law and taught in the synagogues after years of training, were thus able to give their support to James without a sense of contradiction. They were all Jews who supported the same Law. While leading Pharisee Jews were cautious in their approach to those, like Simon Peter, who may have able to summon a sizeable and effective church militia, they would have been warmer to people like James, pious and ascetic, a firm upholder of the Law. These people, in contrast with the militants, could at least for a time have been safe to associate with. They were left alone, in the years after the crucifixion, in the purge against more active messianists (Acts 8, 1-3).

There might appear to be a contradiction between ordinary Pharisees becoming followers of James and the association, in structure and belief, between the Nazoreans under James and the 'poor' or Essenes at Qumran. The latter, it will be recalled, were most probably a group that had broken away from mainstream Judaism, believing themselves to be God's elect and the Sadducee priests and temple worship to be corrupt.

However, the opposition of the poor or Essenes to the Sadducee High Priests mirrors the tension between Pharisees and the Sadducees over such matters as the relevance of oral tradition and the place of ritual in worship. The Essenes too developed their own rules, adapted to circumstances.

The key difference would have been the Essenes' withdrawal from temple sacrifices which the Pharisees still supported. This was not a problem perhaps for the bulk of members of the poor, 'men of the covenant' who lived like their fellow Jews except that they were bound by stricter obligations. But it may well have been something that occupied key figures, priests like James and 'men of the council'.

James might well have objected to the official temple sacrifices and made his own offerings. Church sources suggest that he separately celebrated the key festival of Yom Kippur, the Day of Atonement, on behalf of the people – and it could have been this that brought about his downfall.

If, as I have suggested, the Nazoreans were either identical with, or derivative from, 'the poor' or Essenes at Qumran, then James would certainly have objected to the official temple sacrifices. Epiphanius reports that, according to a now-lost Ebionite text *The Ascents of James*, he did indeed do this.

James' brother and predecessor Yeshua, in 'cleansing' the temple in Jerusalem, overturned not only the tables of the money changers but the seats of those who sold pigeons for sacrifice. This could have been an attack as much on the idea of blood sacrifice as its commercial exploitation.

The Ebionites, or 'poor' ones, followers of James in later times, are reported to have been hostile to the ritual practices of the Jerusalem temple. Epiphanius also quotes a gospel of the Ebionites, repressed by the Church and since lost, as claiming that Jesus had come to abolish sacrifices. It appears likely that, even if it did not go this far back, a tradition developed among the Nazoreans/Ebionities that was more in line with the approach of the Essenes to temple sacrifice.

Josephus described the number of Essenes in their various settlements throughout Israel as about four thousand. But James' followers in Jerusalem alone appeared to have numbered more than this. It is therefore possible that the Nazorean movement grew out from and then outgrew the original Essene community in Jerusalem.

The Essenes did practice adoption, which would have helped

to ensure than any bias towards celibacy did not cause the group to dwindle into oblivion. There would have been an advantage in placing Yeshua and his brothers, including James, in this way as children in the group, making them for the time invisible and saving them from the attentions of the Herodians. This is what I suggest is behind the Luke's story (2, 41-52) of the visit by Yeshua's family to celebrate Passover in Jerusalem. The boy Jesus 'stayed behind' in the city, but it may be that this was a lot longer than three days! No wonder, when he returned much later to Galilee, years later as an adult, people wondered that someone so learned could have been Joseph's son (see ch 11 p 380).

The addition of a group of brothers, claiming to be 'Sons of David', a messianic and potentially monarchical group, would have changed the complexion of the 'poor' in Jerusalem. There would have been more edge, an added element of danger. As the brothers in their adulthood impacted on wider Jewish society, preaching and rallying support, they would have touched on a deep longing. Here were the very people who could bring about the kingdom on earth, and with it their freedom. They and their message would have had immense popular appeal, and that is why the numbers of the Nazorean followers grew so rapidly, in just a few years.

A further factor that needs to be considered is this. It was not just the question of the application of Jewish Law that divided Paul and his associates from the followers of Yeshua. There was a profound difference in the way these two groups described their founder.

For the followers of James, and the Ebionites or 'poor' ones who came after him, Yeshua was a person who like many others claimed to be the expected warrior leader, king (or messiah from 'masioch' meaning anointed) and liberator of the Jewish people from oppression. He had been crucified by the Romans but was regarded at the time as being still alive, and able one day to return.

There are a number of possible bases on which this belief might have been held. One is that Yeshua had been saved by a miracle and called up to heaven directly by God while still alive, like Methuselah and Elijah and other figures in Jewish legend and scripture. Another is that Yeshua survived the crucifixion and was alive and in exile. These ideas will be explored further in chapter 8.

None of this, however, required the beliefs that Yeshua was a supernatural being, a literal 'Son of God', and that accepting this was a prerequisite (indeed the only route) for salvation. Paul, by contrast, while conceding in his letter to the Romans that Yeshua was 'born according to the flesh', taught that believers could aspire to a form of 'gnosis' or mystical union with God through him, as the 'Christ'. Moreover, borrowing from pagan beliefs, he advanced the idea that Jesus Christ (Yeshua), as Son of God, had sacrificed himself to save mankind.

These ideas would have been regarded as idolatrous and repugnant by Jews and were not part of Nazorean beliefs. If they had been, the Nazoreans would not have been able to draw such widespread support or participate in daily synagogue and temple worship, as described in Acts. They would not even have been able to function, as they did effectively, within the framework of the Judaism that James so fiercely defended. But when it comes to the disagreements described in Acts and reflected in Paul's letters, which led to Paul being twice summoned to account for himself in Jerusalem, there is no mention of this fundamental division over the nature of Yeshua: Jewish messiah for the Nazoreans – world saviour and Son of God for Paul. Why is that?

It may be that Paul had not at that time fully formulated his doctrine. It may even be that some aspects, as Christian belief developed, were written by later editors into his letters. But there is also another possible explanation.

The time of the first summons was around CE 48, only a

few years after the crucifixion and following the first wave of persecution of the activist followers of Yeshua. Paul's proselytising by this point would have been limited and his letters to the various 'Christian' communities that he had set up, or was about to set up, had not been written. The difference at this point was about what should be done in respect of the observance of Jewish law by Gentiles.

James gave his ruling. This was essentially a recapitulation of the Noahide rules for 'god fearers'. While Jews would continue to observe the whole of the Torah, Gentile converts would only be required, as previously, to observe certain rules including a prohibition against idolatry and the requirement to eat only meat from which the blood had first been drained. There would thus be two classes of follower within the same movement.

It would appear that Paul instead chose to teach and put into practice the line that all such distinctions should be abolished. When Paul was summoned to Jerusalem a second time, several years later, the situation had moved on. James had heard reports indicating correctly that Paul had been teaching that circumcision and the observance of the Torah were no longer necessary and should be abandoned, not just by Gentiles but by Jews in the diaspora living among Gentiles. For this, Paul was made to undergo a week-long, purification ritual as a graphic public demonstration that he was still subject to Jewish Law.

There was, however, no mention in the charges that Paul had been teaching the sacrilegious belief that Yeshua was literally the Son of God. It is possible that differences were masked by the use of the same language, though with subtly different meanings. Jews saw themselves as 'sons of the father' and prayed to God their father every day. The Lord's prayer (Luke 11, 1-4) in which Christians similarly pray to 'our father' is in its origins a typically Jewish prayer and one which Yeshua might have used. In the Old Testament (Samuel II, 7, 12-14), God is described as making a promise to treat David's offspring and successors as his own sons. So 'Son of God/the father' would have been an appropriate messianic title. It might not have been apparent that Paul was, in the way that he was using the term, inventing a new and heretical doctrine.

In the story line, as reported in Acts, there is also no mention of any differences over the eucharist meal. First mentioned in Paul's first letter to the Corinthians, this seems to have parallels with the normal Jewish practice of saying a blessing, breaking bread and then passing it round at the start of a meal. In the Gentile communities that Paul founded, however, this ritual was supplanted or transformed. A pagan ceremonial meal was introduced, in which the body and blood of the sacrificed mangod was symbolically consumed – something that would have been anathema to Jews.

It is probable that the Christian eucharist was a relatively late transformation (see ch 6) and not widely established by the time that Paul was summoned to Jerusalem for a second time. It is also possible that the form, similar to that used for a Jewish meal, may have masked the difference of meaning.

Whether recognised or not, these issues would have been subservient to what centrally concerned Judean Jews led by James – which was Paul's attempt to wean other Jews away from their religion. Yeshua was important as a messiah with, as they believed, a valid claim to the kingship. But he was not fundamental to Jewish belief, any more than other messiahs who had arisen over the years had been. Moreover, he had brothers, nephews and possibly even sons who would have been well able to carry on the monarchical line!

James and other core Nazorean leaders probably did not know all that Paul was doing, in their name, but they knew enough. They were aware that they had a problem.

Chapter 5: The enemy: Paul

In many respects, there is a more substantial body of information to draw on in investigating the character and life of Paul than there is available for Yeshua. Not only is there a source, the Acts of the Apostles, which purports to describe what Paul did, but there is a collection of writings in the New Testament, letters to newly formed Christian churches, attributed to Paul himself.

There are in addition some traces left of an alternative version of events from people who opposed Paul. The authors were followers of James and his Nazorean community, whose traditions they were seeking to maintain. These people, the Ebionites or 'poor ones', were persecuted by the Roman Church and had their writings suppressed. They were eventually also ostracised and declared heretical by mainstream Judaism because of their continued belief in Yeshua, as prophet and messiah, despite the failure of the prediction that he would return.

The banning and burning of Ebionite literature, though extensive, was not completely effective. A core reflecting their beliefs and their view of Paul has survived in a long and romantic tale. This describes the travels of the apostle Peter and Clement, who became a convert and a bishop. The plot, the framework for the story, is Clement's fortuitous recognition of and reunion with his parents after a long separation. On this is hung a treatise of theological and philosophical preaching and theorising attributed to Peter, often in the form of a dialogue with a real or imaginary foe, the Samaritan magician Simon Magus.

There are two works dealing with the story which have a substantial amount of material in common. The titles by which they are known, *Pseudoclementine* (because fictitiously attributed to Clement) *Homilies* and *Recognitions*, reflect their content. Within *Recognitions*, an alternative description is preserved of the conflict between Paul on the one hand and James and the Jerusalem community on the other. Contained in the discourse with Simon Magus in *Homilies*, there is a section which seems to reflect the clash between Peter, together with other apostles who had personally known Yeshua, and Paul whose inspiration had come in the form of a vision. These works appear to relate to a source which was also used by the author of Acts.

That this core of writing does reflect an Ebionite source is confirmed by the correspondences with what early church authorities describe. The fourth century writer Epiphanius for example, in denouncing the Ebionites, refers to their beliefs as outlined in a now-lost gospel. It is ironic that this gospel of the Ebionites, having been suppressed by the Church, is actually preserved in fragmentary form as a result of such quotations.

Epiphanius quotes the Ebionites as calling Yeshua the 'true prophet', his status being an altogether human person given prophetic powers by God. He reports that the Ebionites believed that Yeshua opposed animal sacrifice but otherwise observed the Torah. This corresponds in detail with the presentation of belief in the *Pseudoclementine Homilies* and *Recognitions*. Their authors are generally against animal sacrifice and positive towards vegetarianism. They advocate, as in a letter supposedly from Peter to James, full adherence to the Jewish law.

The canonical gospels bear the marks of having been extensively edited. So it is possible that the letters attributed to Paul may also have been altered in copying. Clear motivations can be identified for the gospel editing – to sever Yeshua from his Jewish roots, minimise or deny altogether his family, expunge the true Jewish messianic meaning and exonerate the Romans, while blaming the Jews for Yeshua's death. But it is hard to envisage what compelling reason there might have been for making significant changes to Paul's letters. The picture of Paul presented therein, of a man preaching obedience rather than revolution and widening the message to cover the Gentile world, while at the same time incorporating pagan and gnostic themes, accords with other available evidence and may well have been true. There was no need for the Church to censor Paul since the Church was essentially Paul's own creation!

However, the possibly fair portrayal of Paul that emerges from the letters presents a problem for Christian apologists. Though supposedly transformed from his former evil self after his vision on the road to Damascus, Paul comes across in his letters as deceitful and scheming, malicious and vindictive. His own ego is matched only by a massive inferiority complex; having been rejected by the followers who actually knew Yeshua, he assumes a false mantle of humility as the least of the 'Lord's servants' while at the same time claiming to be better than them! It is Paul, desperate and perhaps even deranged, who first blames the Jews as a whole for Yeshua's death.

There are fourteen letters in the New Testament attributed to Paul, but scholars agree that some of the letters are later and from the pen of different authors. A core of just five letters is generally believed to have been written by Paul. There are various grounds for rejecting others as not even originally authentic.

There is, for example, no reason to attribute the letter to the Hebrews to Paul, since the letter is anonymous and in a very different style. It contains arguments that are not expressed elsewhere, for example that Jesus/Yeshua should be considered to be in the role of High Priest. Nominally addressed to 'the Hebrews', it appears as a later Christian claim for precedence as a religion over Judaism.

Three letters, two addressed to 'Timothy' and one to 'Titus', who are described in other letters as followers of Paul, are pastoral in character, dealing with such matters as rules of behaviour and the qualities that should be expected of elders, deacons and bishops. These presuppose a level of organisation that would not yet have been present when Paul was reputedly conducting his missionary activity, in mid first century, and therefore can be regarded as later additions.

There are four letters (Philemon, Ephesians, Philippians and Colossians) which, from their content, give the impression of having been written while Paul was in Rome, held either in imprisonment or protective custody. This would make them relatively late in date, following a sequence of events in which Paul undertook missionary activity, came into conflict with the Nazorean community under James, was attacked, prosecuted by the High Priest/Sanhedrin and then removed to Rome. However, there is no mention of Rome in the letters or any indication of real, physical captivity: Paul refers to himself as a 'prisoner for Christ'. It may however be that Paul, rather than being in prison, was in some form of benign house arrest, for his own protection as much as anything else. His description of his situation would be consistent with that.

Although the tone of these later letters is generally moderate, there are still references to the differences between Paul and the Jerusalem followers of Yeshua over circumcision, dietary restrictions and the necessity for observing Jewish law. In the sharpest of these, the writer adjures, 'Look out for the dogs, look out for the evil-workers, look out for those who mutilate the flesh' (Philippians 3, 2). 'For we are the true circumcision, who worship God in spirit', the writer adds. A similar argument is made in Colossians (2, 8-14).

The prison letters are consistent with what will be found in the core letters attributed to Paul. They lack details of his biography and any clear references to interaction with James' followers. These letters may or may not have been written by the writer of the core letters, in which the issues and interactions with the Jerusalem church are more extensively covered.

There remain five core letters – Thessalonians I, Corinthians I and II, Galatians and Romans – which bear the hallmarks in content, tone and style of having been written by the same author, someone crucially involved in the creation of the early Christian church and in conflict with the followers of Yeshua. That person as far as can be ascertained was Saul, who took on the persona of Paul, and was a main character in the Acts of the Apostles written by the author of Luke. One further letter, Thessalonians II, was written to correct the impression in Thessalonians I that the Second Coming was immediately at hand. Some of the converts, it would appear, had given up work (Thessalonians II, 3, 6-13) on the grounds that they were about to be called up to heaven with the hosts of resurrected dead and living fellow believers! This second letter may have been written by Paul, or added later as an embellishment to the first by someone in his following.

All of the core letters, on the assumption that they are genuine, need to be located in some form of historical context and also, with care, related to the later narrative provided by Acts.

The first letter to the Thessalonians, like the second, has as one of its concerns the predicted Second Coming of Yeshua. Possibly the earliest of the five core letters, it was written after Paul and two companions had been to Thessalonica in northern Greece and founded a church there.

This was as part of a missionary journey around CE 50 following a meeting in Jerusalem between Paul and James in which the rules for Gentile converts (god fearers) were decided and sent as a letter from James (Acts 15, 22-29). Two of James' followers, Judas Barsabbas and Silas, took the letter, while accompanying Paul and Barnabas back to Antioch.

The letter or decree from James, the leader of the Nazorean community – possibly at that time the dominant influence within Judaism – would have had great authority and would likely have been copied and widely distributed. It is probable that Paul and his companions Barnabas and Sylvanus carried it with them, as their authority, on a missionary journey which took them to

Thessalonica only months later.

There are similarities in the prescriptions in the letter as described in Acts, to 'abstain from what has been sacrificed to idols and from blood and from what is strangled and from unchastity' and what is written in the *Didache*, an instruction book carried by early Christians. This states (6, 3) that 'concerning food, bear what you can, but abstain strictly from food offered to idols, for it is worship of dead gods.'

Like Paul's letters and Acts, the *Didache* appears to have been added to and altered. However, if it was in its original form a copy of the apostolic decree sent out by James, this could explain the concerns of the Thessalonians, which Paul seeks to meet, over what might happen in the last days. In the *Didache* (16, 2-9), it is stated that 'you shall assemble frequently, seeking what your souls need, for the whole time of your faith will be of no profit to you unless you are perfected at the final hour'. Then, when 'the world shall see the Lord coming upon the clouds of heaven ... to reward each according to his deeds ... the evil shall go away into eternal punishment but the righteous shall enter into life eternal.'

The Thessalonians were apparently worried that this meant that some of their number who had already died before being 'perfected' (that is, fully observing all the requirements placed on god fearers) would be denied the reward of eternal life, especially as – according to the apparent sequence in *Didache* – the righteous who were alive would join the Lord and all his saints *before* the resurrection of the dead.

Paul's first letter to the Thessalonians was intended to give reassurance that, notwithstanding the wording of the *Didache*, those who had died would not be left out: 'the dead in Christ will rise first; then we who are alive, who are left, shall be caught up together with them in the clouds to meet the Lord in the air' (Thessalonians I, 4, 16-18).

His second letter extends the time scale, again with very clear reference to the *Didache* which indicated that, before the final coming, there would be a great time of testing. The *Didache* describes how 'false prophets' would arise and there would be an 'increase of lawlessness', heralding the appearance of the 'world deceiver as a son of God and he shall do signs and wonders and the earth shall be betrayed into his hands' (*Didache* 16, 3-4). Paul's version borrows the same wording: 'that day will not come, unless the rebellion comes first, and the man of lawlessness is revealed, the son of perdition ... proclaiming himself to be God'. 'The coming of the lawless one by the activity of Satan will be with all power and with pretended signs and wonders' making those who 'refused to love the truth'...'believe what is false' (Thessalonians II, 2, 3-12).

Two important conclusions can be drawn: firstly that the *Didache* almost certainly embodies the conditions and teachings sent out in a letter by James, following the 'Jerusalem council', and secondly that Paul subsequently took these with him on his early missionary journeys.

The next letter in the core sequence is directed to the Galatians, living in the region of modern day Turkey. The situation has changed in that Paul is now having to defend himself and try to negate the efforts of others preaching 'another gospel'. It transpires that what Paul is apparently referring to is the 'circumcision party', that is James and the followers of James who sent 'false brethren ... to spy out our freedom which we have in Christ Jesus'! He complains that, though Peter had been eating with the Gentiles, that is abandoning dietary restrictions as now advocated by Paul, when 'certain men came from James ... he drew back and separated himself, fearing the circumcision party' (Galatians 2, 4 –12).

Paul also attacks the requirement for circumcision, suggesting at one point that those who advocate it should go and castrate themselves! He attacks the Jewish Law and even the need for it, on the grounds that 'if you are led by the spirit you are not under the law'. He maintains that there should no longer be any boundaries 'neither Jew nor Greek... for you are all one in Christ Jesus' (Galatians 5, 12; 5, 18 and 3, 28).

This is not merely radically different but a radical repudiation of the Judaism of Yeshua's Nazorean followers and the accommodation that they, under the authority of James, had set out for Gentile god fearers following the old Noahide laws.

Paul shows his contempt and disdain for the central three members of the Nazorean council 'James and Cephas and John, who were reputed to be pillars' and particularly for Cephas (Peter) whom he opposed 'to his face, because he stood condemned' (Galatians 2, 9-12),

Paul provides as self-justification an account of his past life, which is full of his sense of self importance: how the gospel had come to him by 'a revelation', how he had 'persecuted' the church and then 'advanced in Judaism beyond many of my own age among my people, so extremely zealous was I for the traditions of my fathers' (Galatians 1, 12-14). He describes how, by means of revelation God had revealed his Son not merely 'to' but 'in' him, with a mission to preach to the Gentiles and that – far from consulting with or seeking authority from the apostles – he then started off on his own self-appointed mission. He is keen to suggest that he went to the meeting in Jerusalem, at which the Nazorean community decided the rules for Gentile god fearers, 'by revelation', whereas as will be seen it appears from Acts that he was summoned. And he suggests that he was more than their equal, that those 'who were of repute added nothing to me; but on the contrary when they saw that I had been entrusted with the gospel to the uncircumcised ... [they] gave to me and Barnabas the right hand of fellowship, that we should go to the Gentiles and they to the circumcised' (Galatians 2, 2-10).

Paul's account of his credentials and his relationships with the Nazorean community will certainly need to be examined both for coherence and against the story in Acts, as well as against what remains of the Ebionites' testimony.

The first letter to the Corinthians, who lived in southern Greece, continues with many of the themes present in Galatians. Paul defends himself from accusations which have been made that he is not a real apostle, presumably on the grounds that he never met Yeshua and is now acting without the direction of those who did know him: 'Have I not seen Jesus our Lord? Are you not my workmanship in the Lord? If to others I am not an apostle, at least I am to you; for you are the seal of my apostleship in the Lord' (Corinthians I, 9, 1-2).

Paul also has to defend himself from charges that he is doing rather well out of his ministry. He maintains his right to have food and drink, pointing out that the other apostles and Yeshua's brothers are quite happy not to work and depend on the community: 'Do we not have the right to be accompanied by a sister as wife (possibly meaning female co-worker), as the other apostles and the brothers of the Lord and Cephas? Or is it only Barnabas and I who have no right to refrain from working for a living?' (Corinthians I, 9, 5-6). It appears, however, that Paul is doing rather more than just gaining a subsistence living: 'If we have sown spiritual good among you, is is too much if we reap your material benefits?' (ibid, verse 11). This is a point which I will come back to.

Like the Galatians, the Corinthians are apparently being led astray, but in this case by internal dissension. Paul sets out his writ on a variety of subjects, including the excessive use of speaking in tongues. Quite in character, he claims to be better at this than anyone else! He also takes pride in his deceitfulness, in being 'all things to all men', as he claims in order to win converts. But it is not converts to Judaism, or the Judaism for Gentiles of James and the Nazorean community, but converts to a new religion that Paul himself is rapidly manufacturing. This is a religion which rejects Jewish law, circumcision even for Jews and dietary rules: 'To the Jews I became as a Jew, in order to win Jews; to those under the law, I became as one under the law –

though not myself under the law – that I might win those under the law' (Corinthians I, 9, 20).

The unscrupulous Paul is not merely preaching an alien doctrine but hiding and misrepresenting what he does from James and the others. He can scarcely conceal his vanity and pride in this: 'Well, I do not run aimlessly, I do not box as one beating the air; but I pommel my body and subdue it' (Corinthians I, 9, 26-27).

In this letter, Paul sets out instructions for a 'Lord's supper', the basis of which he claims came to him personally in a vision from the risen Jesus! (Corinthians I, 11, 23-26). Paul therefore appears as the prime generator of this ritual, which was then copied into the canonical gospels. These were created after the letters, and draw from the wording in the letter to the Corinthians, which is why the source for the ritual of the eucharist has to be Paul himself. After the crucifixion, Yeshua's followers carried on as practising Jews (see next chapter).

He also claimed that Yeshua was buried and 'raised on the third day in accordance with the scriptures' (Corinthians I, 15, 4). This is testimony earlier than the canonical gospels, but not that of an eyewitness and not, despite the claim, based on any specific biblical prophecy.

In his second letter to the Corinthians, Paul returns to the theme of countering rivals preaching a gospel which varies with his. One of his targets is 'unbelievers' but the main thrust of his attack is directed to people who preach 'another Jesus than the one we preached' (Corinthians II, 11, 4). Who can these be? As becomes clear a line or two later, they are evidently apostles from the Nazorean church, doubtless sent to keep a check on Paul's activities.

Paul contends that 'I think that I am not in the least inferior to these superlative apostles' (Corinthians II, 11, 5). But this is just the point. He has been accused (on the good grounds that he had had nothing to do with Yeshua) of not being a real apostle, and so he does have a real sense of inferiority! This is manifested in his sarcastic tone and his constant need to assert that he really is just as good as them (as, for example, again in Corinthians II, 12, 11).

There are even darker depths to Paul's hostility; he likens his rival apostles to servants of Satan masquerading as servants of righteousness and he predicts for them a dire fate:

> And what I do I will continue to do, in order to undermine the claim of those who would like to claim that in their boasted mission they work on the same terms as we do. For such men are false apostles, deceitful workmen, disguising themselves as apostles of Christ. And, no wonder, for even Satan disguises himself as an angel of light. So it is not strange if his servants also disguise themselves as servants of righteousness. Their end will correspond with their deeds. (Corinthians II, 11, 12-15)

Apologists for Paul are quite desperate to suggest that these rival apostles had some other origin than the Jewish Nazorean community under James. But there is no evidence of any other such group and the description in the letters of Paul's hostility to James and his followers is consistent and coherent, running right through the narrative. At points, as in the letter to the Galatians, they are directly identified.

Paul is not just predicting but relishing the fate awaiting his rivals. In the same manner, in his first letter to the Thessalonians, he gloats over misfortune suffered by those who had hindered him from 'speaking to the Gentiles', who I suggest would have been the most 'zealous' element within the Nazoreans:

> For you, brethren, became imitators of the churches of God in Christ Jesus which are in Judea; for you suffered the same things from your own countrymen as they did from the Jews, who killed both the Lord Jesus and the prophets, and drove

us out, and displease God and oppose all men by hindering us from speaking to the Gentiles that they may be saved – so as always to fill up the measure of their sins. But God's wrath has come upon them at last!
(Thessalonians I, 2, 14-16)

This passage has puzzled some analysts, given that the letter is dated to around CE 50 and the assumption that the 'wrath of God' visited upon the Jews must have been the destruction of the temple in Jerusalem at the end of the Jewish revolt in CE 70. It was therefore suggested that the passage as quoted above was not part of the original letter, but interpolated later.

There is however a better and simpler explanation, one which does not depend on the tortuous device of material being added later without any apparent motivation. This is that the text in question is original and refers to what at the time were recent events. There were undoubtedly many misfortunes which befell the Jews, besides the failure of the war with Rome. The late forties were marked by a period of dissident unrest and persecution by the Romans, during which Theudas was executed in CE 46 and the brothers James and Simon around CE 47 or 48.

If Paul's schadenfreude is directed to this, then it would imply that Theudas, James and Simon were part of the Nazorean movement which indeed, I will argue, they were! (see ch 10).

It is hard to put aside Paul's charge of deicide against the Jews as a whole (that they 'killed both the Lord Jesus and the prophets'), as the result of a meddling insertion by a later editor. It is repeated in Galatians where he says, 'It is those who want to make a good showing in the flesh that would compel you to be circumcised, and only in order that they may not be persecuted for the cross of Christ' (Galatians 6, 12). Even from a distance of almost two thousand years, it is abundantly clear that it was the Romans who cracked down on and executed Jewish messianic leaders and who, even according to the very muddied gospel record, also convicted and crucified Yeshua. It would have been even clearer still to Paul, coming on the scene only a few years after the event and able to talk to some of those who were witnesses or who had taken part.

So why did he repeat, indeed it would seem originate, this outrageous and venomous accusation? He was certainly under pressure from the Jerusalem community, who were sending out their own people, the 'some men who came down from Judea' of Acts 15, 1, to check up on him. They were beginning to find evidence and accuse him, as becomes clear later (Acts 21, 21) when Paul is summoned for a second time to Jerusalem, of preaching to Jews against the Torah and circumcision.

As has been noted, he was also accused, again it would seem with justification, of abusing his position in relation to Jewish communities in the diaspora and their attachments of Gentile god fearers to obtain funds for his own use.

Paul was highly sensitive to criticism of his poor face-to-face communication skills: 'Even if I am unskilled in speaking, I am not in knowledge' (Corinthians II, 11, 6); 'For they say, "His letters are weighty and strong, but his bodily presence is weak, and his speech of no account"' (Corinthians II 10, 10).

He was also under attack for his lack of credentials:

Are they Hebrews? So am I. Are they Israelites? So am I. Are they descendants of Abraham? So am I. Are they servants of Christ? I am a better one – I am talking like a madman – with far greater labours, far more imprisonments, with countless beatings, and often near death.
(Corinthians II, 11, 22-23)

Paul was at least a master of written rhetoric. What he does say may well have impressed his mostly untutored Gentile audience in Corinth. But what he doesn't quite say, here as elsewhere, though he says almost everything else, is 'Are they Jews? So am

I'. The reason is that Paul, though he may have been of Idumean stock and circumcised, was actually not a Jew. He admitted however to masquerading as a Jew (see Corinthians 1, 9, 20 quoted above) in order to try to convert Jews to Christianity.

He also was not, as appears to be claimed in the letter to the Philippians (3, 6) and is suggested in Acts (22, 3), a Pharisee scholar, though he may have had the aspiration to be. Paul states that he was 'as to the law a Pharisee', a carefully qualified description on a par with his claim that he had 'advanced in Judaism beyond many of my own age among my people' (Galatians 1, 14). However, as any careful analysis of Paul's writing shows, he could not have been been a Pharisee scholar. None of his Old Testament quotes are from the Hebrew original, but from the Greek translation which often introduced errors. A Pharisee sage would have gone back to source. Paul did not because he was not a Pharisee; it is probable his Hebrew was simply not good enough. Also, as Maccoby points out (*The Myth Maker: Paul and the invention of Christianity*), whenever Paul in his letters attempts a form of legal argument, it lacks the precision of someone who had Pharisee training.

Furthermore, the Pharisees are shown as generally sympathetic to the Nazoreans and Yeshua, as for example in the passage where Gamaliel advocated a lenient and tolerant approach to Simon Peter and the other disciples (Acts 5, 34-39). On several occasions in the gospel accounts, prominent Pharisees are shown in meetings and discussion with Yeshua, on one occasion warning him of danger from the soldiers of Herod Antipas. Paul could hardly then have been pursuing the early Nazoreans as a Pharisee – more likely as an associate of the Sadducee High Priest's faction. And that's *exactly* how it is described, in that Saul 'went to the High Priest and asked him for letters to the synagogues at Damascus, so that if he found any belonging to the Way, men or women, he might bring them bound to Jerusalem' (Acts 9, 1). The Sadducees and Pharisees were opposed on matters of religion and on collaboration with the Romans. So, if Paul was acting with the Sadducees, he could not therefore have been a Pharisee even, as his letters imply, by aspiration.

Paul was an outsider to messianic, nationalist Jews, for what I will argue was a very special reason. He was at first treated with acute suspicion, and then finally rejected by the Nazoreans. His sense of injustice, his wounded pride, his burning ambition, his recognition of his own shortcomings, his frustration, he turned outwards in bile and invective against those who had not accepted and recognised him. This explains how his hostility became so pathological and unhinged, to the point of making what was in fact a preposterous libel, that it was in fact the Jews and specifically the 'circumcision party', that is the Nazoreans, who had actually killed Yeshua!

The evidence is that Paul himself was the source for this. His letters (Thessalonians and Galatians) predate Acts which – falsely – attributes similar sentiments to Simon Peter (Acts 2.23 and 4.10) who really was a Jew and a key follower of Yeshua.

Paul's libel was also unfortunately repeated in the gospels, where the Jews are reported as demanding Yeshua's execution with the crowd baying (Matthew 27, 25), 'his blood be on us and on our children!'

Untrue, because Yeshua was a Jewish messiah killed not by his fellows but by the Romans, this false accusation has nonetheless been used down the centuries as an excuse for persecuting Jews. Paul, motivated perhaps equally by spite against the Nazoreans and the need not to upset the Romans, has a lot to answer for.

The last of the core epistles, Romans, appears to have been written in the period running up to the Jewish revolt or possibly even during it, given the elliptical note about the 'sufferings of this present time' (Romans 8, 18). The hostile references to his opponents have all but gone: the Nazoreans may well have had more than enough on their hands to spend time worrying about

Paul, as society in Jerusalem began to dissolve in a battle between the collaborating Sadducee elite and the 'sicarii'.

Much of the letter is devoted to a long consideration of the place of law, meaning Jewish law, and faith, with the somewhat curious conclusion that 'Israel who pursued the righteousness which is based on law did not succeed in fulfilling that law ... because they did not pursue it through faith, but as if it were based on works' (Romans 9, 32). This can be seen as a counter to the Nazorean view, as expressed by James or by one of his followers, that deeds are what matter:

> What does it profit, my brethren, if a man says he has faith but has not works? Can his faith save him? If a brother or sister is ill-clad and in lack of daily food, and one of you says to them, "Go in peace, be warmed and filled," without giving them the things needed for the body, what does it profit? So faith by itself, if it has no works, is dead.
> (The Letter of James 2, 14-17)

Paul however considers that 'Gentiles who did not pursue righteousness have attained it', that is through his ministry! Faith is used interchangeably in the discourse as a quality, belief in God and specifically belief in Yeshua.

The letter attributed to James is one surviving fragment of the other half of a dialogue or conflict, which for the most part has to be deduced from what Paul says. The Church suppressed the Nazorean record.

As Paul wrote the last of the core letters, around CE 55 or 56, Jews were suffering at the hands of the Romans and so their power to influence him may in consequence have diminished. But in any case Paul recognised that they were not going to be part of the new order which he sought to create. In opposing him, they were to be seen as 'disobedient' to Paul's God-given message: 'As regards the gospel they are enemies of God, for your sake; but as regards election they are beloved for the sake of their forefathers' (Romans 11, 28). Paul needed the Jews to provide a respectable pedigree for Christianity; hence the references in the latter part of his statement. In his analogy, the Jews provided the stock of the tree, on which the new Gentile branch had been grafted, rather ominously replacing branches which had been 'broken off because of their unbelief' (Romans 11, 20).

It is is hard to escape one underlying message in this analogy, and it could hardly have escaped Paul's readers. In Roman and Jewish society, a patrilineal principle operated. The Roman client-King Herod had eliminated males in the Maccabean line of claimed Davidic descent, grafting on his own line through his marriage to a Maccabean princess. These murdered Maccabeans were branches of the Davidic tree which had been ruthlessly 'broken off'. Other more recent messianic claimants, not necessarily with any Maccabean links, such as Theudas and the brothers James and Simon (see ch 10) had also been similarly extirpated.

More generally, Paul appears to be presenting the plight of the Jews during a period of conflict (which culminated in actual rebellion) as being a consequence of their rejection of his reworked version of Yeshua's message! The Jewish historian Josephus, as reported by early church authorities, by contrast saw the disaster of the war with Rome and destruction of the temple as the result of the death of James.

Examination of the core letters attributed to Paul has offered some very clear insights into the character and motivations of the self-styled apostle, Paul. These are corroborated by what was later written in Acts by a writer who is believed also to have written the gospel of Luke.

The Acts of the Apostles, in a similar vein as the *Pseudoclementines*, presents a Hellenistic style romance detailing deeds of some of the apostles, most notably the supposed missionary journeys of Paul in the years following the crucifixion. While a central plot is lacking, there is a central concern with the relationship between Paul and the Jerusalem church, that is the Nazoreans under James.

Unlike the letters, the core of which I have presumed were originally written by Paul during the first century, Acts dates from the second century, possibly after the failure of the second Jewish revolt which lasted from from CE 132 to 135. By this time, a small but flourishing Christian church had been established outside Palestine in the communities first evangelised by Paul and his followers. Judaism, deeply damaged by conflicts with Rome, was no longer a threat.

However, the church still needed the historicity provided by the link with Judaism, with the books of the 'Old' Testament used as a respectable pedigree and to herald the new order embracing the worship of 'Jesus' as Son of the deity. One of the purposes of Acts was to minimise and disguise the conflict between Paul and the Jerusalem community or church under James, so evident in Paul's letters, in particular Galatians. Another was to integrate Paul and his theology within the authority of the church, with its hierarchical structure of bishops and deacons. Paul had been a charismatic individual, deriving his authority by claimed personal divine revelation. The church, however, wanted contact with the divine to be controlled and mediated by it and had therefore to counter the idea of revelation by personal 'gnosis'.

So Paul, in the story, was brought under the authority of the 'church', though at the time to which the narrative relates it wasn't in fact the Christian church (which Paul instigated and invented) but the Nazorean community! It will be recalled that they differed from other Jews only in their belief that their Yeshua was the long-awaited Jewish national liberator or messiah.

The slant in the narrative is aided by the fact that, in actuality, James was a figure of authority who *did* have precedence over Paul and his followers. It needs to be recognised, however, that the relationship portrayed in Acts is coloured by the myth retrojected into the story of there being 'one church', when in fact there was one movement within Judaism and one schismatic sect, that is Christianity, in the making. The picture, as presented in the letters, of a much greater degree of friction is likely to have been more accurate.

Why, it might be wondered, if it was so important to minimise the conflict between Paul and James, was it not written out altogether? The problem may have been that there was then other available evidence. Even now, it would require many alterations to Paul's letters and to the surviving testimony of the Ebionites – not possible to be effective of course since the information is already disseminated! In the second century, there would have been a strong oral tradition and other Nazorean and Ebionite writings in existence, even though these have in whole or in part subsequently disappeared. It would not have appeared feasible at the time to deny the conflict, but it was possible to attempt to rewrite and reinterpret it.

In examining Acts, it should also be borne in mind that it was, at the time of writing, in large part a fanciful tale, a composite of sources, moulded together for a purpose and since subjected to considerable embroidery.

Paul emerges in the narrative of Acts as Saul, a persecutor of the 'church in Jerusalem', that is the Nazorean followers of James. He is first portrayed as consenting to and officiating at the murder by stoning of Stephen, a character who may have his real origins in a servant of the Emperor Claudius called Stephen (described by Josephus) who was attacked and robbed by zealots around CE 49.

According to Acts, Saul was 'ravaging the church, and entering house after house, he dragged off men and women and committed them to prison' (Acts 8, 3). This was apparently under the authority of, and possibly in the employment of, the Sadducee High Priest, from whom he shortly afterwards obtained letters of authority to pursue members of the community who had fled to Damascus, part of the territory of the Arab King Aretas. On his way to Damascus, Saul is reported to have had a vision of Yeshua who reprimanded Saul for persecuting him. This accords with the claim of divine revelation in the letters (Galatians 1, 12).

As a result, Saul goes over to the side of those whom he had previously been persecuting, proclaiming in synagogues in Damascus Yeshua as the Son of God. He then has to escape the city, lowered over the wall in a basket, because of Jews plotting to kill him (Acts 9, 23-25). It is unclear who these 'Jews' might have been, and more likely that Saul was trying to escape from Aretas, angry at Saul's infringement of his sovereignty – as described in an alternative version of the incident by Paul himself (Corinthians II, 11, 32-33).

It is also unlikely that Saul at this stage was preaching Yeshua as the Son of God, because this was a doctrine that he had yet to formulate and because this was not what the Nazoreans themselves believed. What is clear, from the evidence of Acts and Corinthians, is that Saul's mission to Damascus went wrong. He then sought to change sides and join the Nazoreans in Jerusalem. Acts describes what happened next:

> And when he had come to Jerusalem he attempted to join the disciples; and they were all afraid of him, for they did not believe that he was a disciple. But Barnabas took him, and brought him to the apostles, and described to them how on the road he had seen the Lord, who spoke to him, and how at Damascus he had preached boldly in the name of Jesus. So he went in and out among them at Jerusalem, preaching boldly in the name of the Lord. And he spoke and disputed against the Hellenists; but they were seeking to kill him. And when the brethren knew it, they brought him down to Caesarea, and sent him off to Tarsus.
>
> (Acts 9, 26-30)

This is a passage which is full of ambiguities. It is not clear that Saul even succeeded in joining the disciples; the picture presented in the passage is that they are frozen in immobility as he moved 'in and out among them', neither embracing him nor repelling him. They had reason to believe that Saul was dangerous.

The 'Hellenists' who sought to kill Saul are a puzzle. But the High Priest's Sadducee clique was subject to Hellenising influences and had good cause for hostility towards someone they had supported, quite possibly employed, but who was now seeking to join their Nazorean opponents.

What to do with Saul was undoubtedly a problem, solved at least temporarily by the disciples shipping him back to his home town of Tarsus, in what today is Turkey.

Then, with Saul conveniently on the sidelines, Peter is described as having his vision of a vast heavenly tablecloth full of all kinds of birds and animals which he is commanded to eat, whether or not unclean. This is interpreted by Peter as a dispensation to eat with Gentiles, even food forbidden to Jews.

Barnabas then goes to fetch to Saul, who thereafter becomes Paul, from Tarsus to go to Antioch in Syria. The two stay for a year, teaching a large number of people, and it is from this time that followers in Antioch first become known as 'Christians'. They next take famine relief to Jerusalem, return to Antioch and set sail on a preaching mission to Cyprus and what is now southern Turkey.

This account differs markedly from what Paul himself says, not surprisingly given that the objective in Acts is to minimise from the outset the conflict between Paul and the Jerusalem church.

Paul claims in Galatians that he didn't consult with the apostles at all! He didn't need to because he had received his mission to preach to the Gentiles directly from God in a vision and he therefore had no need of their authority:

> But when he who had set me apart before I was born, and had
> called me through his grace, was pleased to reveal his Son in
> me, in order that I might preach him among the Gentiles, I did
> not confer with flesh and blood, nor did I go up to Jerusalem
> to those who were apostles before me, but I went into Arabia;
> and again I returned to Damascus.
> (Galatians 1, 15-17)

It seems clear that Paul saw himself as acting on his own
authority based on divine revelation, owing nothing to anyone,
certainly not 'those who were apostles' before him. But equally
very clearly he is sensitive to suggestions as to the priority of the
apostles or that he had deferred to them. He may be protesting
rather too much:

> Then after three years I went up to Jerusalem to visit Cephas,
> and remained with him fifteen days. But I saw none of the
> other apostles except James the Lord's brother. (In what I am
> writing to you, before God, I do not lie!)
> (Galatians 1, 18-20)

Paul is sensitive about something and that something, I suggest,
is that he was, as Acts suggests, in some way rebuffed by the
Nazoreans.

There are echoes of this in what their successors, the Ebionites,
believed about Paul. According to the fourth century writer
Epiphanius, the Ebionites described Paul as a discontented Greek
(that is, Gentile) who converted to Judaism and underwent
circumcision because he wanted to marry the High Priest's
daughter. Paul flew into a rage when he was rejected and then
started writing against the Jewish law.

This is an account with some obscure allusions and
undoubtedly distorted by Epiphanius' dislike for the Ebionites
and their dislike in turn for Paul. But it does support the position

that Paul, having been thwarted in his ambitions within Judaism, turned like a disappointed suitor against the religion he had formerly sought to embrace. Another source, an Arabic document believed to incorporate early Ebionite beliefs, contains a similar accusation, that Paul abandoned observance of the Torah because of his personal ambitions and to gain the backing of Rome.

It should also be noted that Herod twice married a High Priest's daughter or grand daughter, partly as a means of consolidating his political power. One of the two was a Maccabean princess and it may be that Herod hoped thereby to defuse Jewish nationalist aspirations. In this context, the accusation directed against Paul is that he had overweening political ambition. Whether this could really have been accomplished through marrying the High Priest's daughter, or whether this was simply a metaphor, cannot now be determined – though some more light will shortly be shed on the matter.

The other part of the account in Acts which does not ring true is Simon Peter's sudden cosmic realisation that henceforth all foods were to be permitted to Gentiles and Jews alike. A truer reflection of the position is that described in Galatians, 'For before certain men came from James, he ate with the Gentiles; but when they came he drew back and separated himself, fearing the circumcision party' (Galatians 3, 12).

It was, of course, acceptable for Jews to eat at the table of Gentile god fearers, providing that they were only offered food permitted to Jews. But Paul was maintaining that the distinction between Jews and Gentiles in the new order had been abolished (Galatians 3, 28). Furthermore, while he opposed sacrifices to idols, he also argued that, since idols 'have no real existence', it was of no consequence if one ate food which had been offered to idols (forbidden to both Jews and Gentile god fearers). The only proviso was if this might induce someone 'weaker' and with less knowledge to eat the food as if offered to idols, and therefore as if the idol really did exist! (Corinthians I, 8, 4-13; 10, 27-30; Romans 14, 20-23).

The point is that Peter could well have inadvertently ended up eating forbidden food, just as a consequence of the position taken, by the providers of the food, that it did not really matter. That is what had almost certainly come to the ear of James and what his emissaries had come to inform Peter about. This is a more likely scenario than the alternative, that Peter suddenly decided to abrogate the Torah on dietary restrictions and then, just as suddenly, revert back.

The first missionary activity that Paul together with Barnabas conducts is from a community of 'Christians' in Antioch that, I suggest, had already begun to deviate from the Judaism of the Nazoreans. Despite maintaining that he had a God-given mandate to convert Gentiles, Paul is actually described from the very first as preaching his message to Jews in Jewish synagogues; thus 'they proclaimed the word of God in the synagogues of the Jews' (Acts 13, 5, 16 ff). Paul's mission to the Gentiles is then portrayed as a consequence of the refusal of Jews to listen to him, 'it was necessary that the word of God should be spoken first to you. Since you thrust it from you, and judge yourselves unworthy of eternal life, behold, we turn to the Gentiles' (Acts 13, 46). No matter that this is completely at variance with the position earlier in Acts, and also in Paul's letters, that Paul had received his commission, specifically to the Gentiles, in a vision! Moreover, if the representation in Acts is anything like accurate, it is no wonder that Jews turned against him because he repeats, albeit in muted form, the accusation of deicide, 'though they could charge him (Yeshua) with nothing deserving death, yet they asked Pilate to have him killed' (Acts 13, 28).

Paul and Barnabas in this way stir up the Jews in Pisidia and they are driven out of the district. They then enter a synagogue at Iconium and speak to an audience of Jews and Gentiles, presumably god fearers, but have to flee when there is an attempt to stone them. Then at Derbe, Paul is actually stoned, dragged out of the city and left for dead, before being rescued by his followers. The narrative continues with Paul undertaking more preaching and returning by sea to Antioch in Syria.

At which point, as Acts has it, Paul and Barnabas are appointed to go to Jerusalem to discuss the issue of the dispensation for Jews and Gentile god fearers over adherence to the Torah and circumcision.

From Paul's perspective, the issue was the claim by 'some men' who had come down from Judea, that 'unless you are circumcised according to the custom of Moses, you cannot be saved' (Acts 15, 1). In fact, what Pharisee Jews believed was that, once the messiah had come, full converts to Judaism would no longer be accepted – because it would then be to everyone's advantage to be converted. So god fearers, who were only required to adhere to some of the Law, would although saved effectively be second-class citizens in the messianic kingdom.

The Nazoreans differed from mainstream Pharisees in just the fact that they believed that they had had the messiah in the form of Yeshua. They were awaiting his imminent Second Coming. Indeed, as I will argue, they may have believed that he had survived crucifixion and was physically in exile, ready to return and liberate his people. On either view, there was an obligation to offer Gentiles the advantages of not just status as god fearers but full conversion.

This was a central issue in the discussions at Jerusalem around CE 49. Another must have been, though it is not treated at this point in Acts, the discord caused by Paul preaching his message at Jews.

Overlying this is the writer's attempt to paste on to Peter the view of Paul that God had abolished distinctions between Jews and Gentiles (Acts 15, 9). It is hardly likely that Simon Peter subscribed to this position, since even Paul at this stage was keeping the explosive doctrine to himself. In addition, according to Galatians, there was a split between Paul and Peter over the issue of dietary restrictions.

James' judgement was that the Gentiles should only be required to fulfil the basic Noahide laws: to abstain from worship of or sacrifice to idols, from unchastity/fornication (that is sexual offences such as incest and adultery), from meat that had not been killed in the Jewish way with the blood drained away and from 'blood' (meaning bloodshed or murder). They would thereby attain the status of god fearers and, by this dispensation, also be accepted within the Jewish messianic movement. James added the observation that 'from early generations Moses has had in every city those who preach him, for he is read every Sabbath in the synagogues' (Acts, 15, 21). In other words, there was no need to evangelise too strongly for full converts from among the Gentiles since Judaism had no shortage of followers.

By implication, therefore, the pressure was going to be lifted on Gentiles to go for full conversion. On the other hand, it must have been expected, or at least hoped, that Paul would be more diplomatic in his future dealings with diasporan Jews. Just to make sure, the conclusions of James were put in the form of a letter (the Apostolic decree) to be sent to these communities, and Paul was accompanied back with a delegation of 'leading men among the brethren', including Judas Barsabbas and Silas. They, rather than Paul and Barnabas, took the letter with them.

It is clear that what had taken place was a meeting of the Nazorean Council to which Paul had been summoned and which made a ruling in respect of Paul's proselytising. This is not apparently how Paul saw it. His view, expressed in his letter to the Galatians, was that he was at least an equal partner and that he had been given – or simply had – the right to deal how he liked with Gentiles.

It was, of course, a recipe for conflict. As Paul's subsequent letters to the Galatians and Corinthians indicate, he had to contend with a number of visits from representatives of the

Nazoreans in Jerusalem seeking to counter his teaching that the Torah was abrogated. Not only that, but Paul also continued to argue in synagogues and stir up trouble among Jews. After one such confrontation in Corinth, the writer of Acts reports Paul as once again saying that from then on he would preach to Gentiles (Acts 18, 6). Lip service it would seem to the idea of Paul having a special mission to Gentiles, because just a few lines later he is reported as again arguing in the synagogue at Ephesus!

Following a third missionary journey, Paul is once more summoned to Jerusalem. It is now around CE 57. This time, the situation is much more serious. James and the other Nazorean elders have had reports of Paul teaching Jews in the diaspora that they should no longer observe the Torah; indeed the elders have spent a considerable effort over a period of years to counter this message.

Despite an introduction in the narrative which attempts to convey an impression of harmony, the writer of Acts, in simply reporting what happened, cannot avoid conveying the very real and bitter conflict. The introduction to the passage is in fact, in tone and content, completely at odds with the subsequent text.

Paul is reprimanded and made to undergo a penance which would demonstrate to his converts that, whatever Paul had previously said, he and therefore they were still bound by the Torah:

When we had come to Jerusalem, the brethren received us gladly. On the following day Paul went in with us to James; and all the elders were present. After greeting them, he related one by one the things that God had done among the Gentiles through his ministry. And when they heard it, they glorified God.

And they said to him [Paul], 'You see, brother, how many thousands [myriades – 'tens of thousands'] there are among the Jews of those who have believed; they are all zealous for the law, and they have been told about you that you teach all the Jews who are among the Gentiles to forsake Moses, telling them not to circumcise their children or observe the customs. What then is to be done? They will certainly hear that you have come. Do therefore what we tell you. We have four men who are under a vow; take these men and purify yourself along with them and pay their expenses, so that they may shave their heads. Thus all will know that there is nothing in what has been told about you but that you yourself live in observance of the law. But as for the Gentiles who have believed, we have sent a letter with our judgement that they should abstain from what has been sacrificed to idols and from blood and from what is strangled and from unchastity.' Then Paul took the men, and the next day he purified himself with them and went into the temple, to give notice when the days of purification would be fulfilled and the offering presented for every one of them.

(Acts 21, 17-26)

Even in translation, there is no mistaking the menace in James' statements to Paul. Zealous Jews would certainly come to know and, as events proved, were already aware that Paul had arrived. As Hyam Maccoby points out in his excellent analysis of Paul (*The Mythmaker*), some early manuscripts have additional wording, 'the multitude must needs come together for they will hear that you have come'.

Events then follow fairly swiftly. Even before he has finished his penance, Paul is dragged from the temple and set upon by a crowd of 'Asian Jews', possibly some of those who had been antagonised by Paul's teaching on his missionary journeys and who were now in Jerusalem. He is charged by the crowd of both teaching against the Torah and polluting the temple by bringing non-Jews into it. Paul is then rescued by soldiers and escapes being scourged by claiming Roman citizenship. Certainly better timed since, on his missionary travels at Philippi, he apparently only mentioned his Roman citizenship *after* having been beaten and imprisoned!

It seems that this citizenship may have pointed up something about Paul that he was at times not keen to stress. When the Roman tribune said that he had paid a large sum for his citizenship, Paul – though a native of Tarsus – replied that he was born a Roman citizen (Acts 22, 29). Paul's adventures (and it has to be remembered that Acts is, like the *Pseudoclementines*, an adventure story) continue thick and fast. The Romans put Paul before the Sanhedrin, perilous for Paul because as it will be remembered Paul had previously been on a mission for the Sadducee High Priest to persecute Yeshua's followers and had changed sides.

The High Priest and his following would not have been at all pleased with someone who had deserted to the opposition. But Paul, with his renowned ability to be 'all things to all men' claimed to be a Pharisee and (improbably) induced the Sanhedrin to engage in a violent and divisive debate over the question of the resurrection of the dead. This was an issue which divided the Pharisees and Sadducees.

Paul is again rescued by the Romans, pulled out from the ensuing fracas and taken to their barracks. There is next a plot by a group who, in typical zealot fashion, vow neither to eat nor drink until they have killed Paul. These are described as having conspired with the 'chief priests and elders', that is the Sadducees on the Sanhedrin, to get Paul out of the Roman barracks and into the open on the pretext of seeking to try Paul's case 'more exactly'. It seems an unlikely alliance, although both these groups according to the story had reason to treat Paul with hostility.

Paul is tipped off by his nephew, his sister's son, and once again the Romans save Paul. The danger would appear to have been acute, requiring a trip at the dead of night with an escort of 'nearly two hundred soldiers with seventy horsemen and two hundred spearsmen' to take him safely to appear before the Roman Governor at Caesarea.

Once there, Paul is depicted as making the same case as he did before the Sanhedrin. This was that that he was really being attacked because of his belief in the resurrection of the dead, which he shared with Pharisees but not the collaborating Sadducees. He is charged however by a spokesmen for the former High Priest Ananias and other elders with the mere fact of his association with the Nazoreans, 'We have found this man a pestilent fellow, an agitator among all the Jews throughout the world, and a ringleader of the sect of the Nazarenes' (Acts 24, 5). The formula has a similar ring to the charge brought against Yeshua, as reported in Luke (23, 2). It may be that the common author of Luke and Acts had access to some official records.

The context in which this action took place should be recalled. The Sadducee elite and dissident 'sicarii' were embroiled in a gathering conflict involving kidnapping and assassinations. Roman writ probably only ran in Jerusalem and other major towns. Paul, according to the storyline, was being identified with militants whom the collaborating Sadducees perceived as a threat.

The Governor Felix temporised. He kept Paul confined for two years, seeking to obtain money from him and conversing with him frequently. So, how had Paul suddenly become rich enough to warrant this attention? Was the money some or all of the funds that Paul had been collecting for the Jerusalem community but failed to hand over in its entirety? And what was the aim of such a lengthy debriefing; was it perhaps to try to obtain information about zealot activists with whom Paul had been associating?

Then, when Felix was succeeded by Festus, another attempt was made by 'the chief priests and the principal men of the Jews' to get an agreement for Paul to go back and stand trial in Jerusalem, the object being to ambush and murder Paul on the way. The Roman governor is shown as minded to free Paul, with the Jewish Sadducee authorities objecting and demanding Paul's execution, which only the Roman authorities could sanction. Paul appealed to have his case determined by the Emperor Nero, rather than be put back into the hands of his enemies.

So Paul was sent to Rome where he arrived after a shipwreck, a story colourfully described and quite likely plundered from the life of Josephus. Nothing is said of what the Emperor thought or did, only that Paul lived there 'two whole years', wording which suggests that Paul then went somewhere else, possibly even back to Jerusalem.

The narrative of Acts ends there abruptly and it is about CE 62, the year in which Paul's fierce rival James was stoned to death. It may be that there is an ending to Acts that was lost. Alternatively, it may be that things happened in the relationship between Paul and the Nazoreans that simply could not be said. Or it may be that these things were said and were later cut out.

Acts provides the framework, as has been noted, for an attempt to integrate Paul with the early followers of Yeshua and also with the structure of the emerging Roman Church. But the material for that framework, especially in the latter part where there is little or nothing to go on in Paul's letters, is sparse. It is, after all, a story in which the author has invented or embroidered details to make up for gaps.

One obvious fiction is the supposed alliance between the Sadducee chief priests and sicarii assassins in a plot to kill Paul! By that time, according to the record provided by Josephus, these groups were engaged in a murderous sequence of killings and kidnappings. They are therefore most unlikely as co-conspirators. It could not furthermore have been just the Sadducees who were prosecuting a case against Paul because they were in a minority on the Sanhedrin. It had to be the Jewish leadership as a whole, and more particularly the Pharisee majority. Indeed the Pharisees and Nazoreans, who I have argued were not at all opposed, were very concerned over Paul's activities in stirring up conflict with diasporan Jews. The Pharisees wanted Jews outside Palestine to remain in coexistence and not be subject to persecution by Rome. Paul's influence was unhelpful, he was disrupting the balance.

The writer of Acts gives Paul a spurious claim that he was being persecuted for his belief in resurrection (life after death), a nice touch to disguise the true situation as evidenced by the sequence of events. Paul had offended the Jewish community as a whole and was the object of attack by its militant elements. He was rescued from this by the Romans, not once but three times if the narrative is to be believed.

Furthermore, the Romans do not even charge Paul. He is held at Caesarea in what amounts to protective custody with the very strong presumption, given all the plots described, that this was for Paul's own safety. He is then transferred to Rome where he remains in that state, and again there is no indication that he was ever charged with anything. Paul's letters, supposed to have been written while he was in prison, do not mention being held by the Romans or in Rome, just that he was a 'prisoner for Christ'. He may very well have felt like this, if he was being held against the possibility that he could be attacked or killed.

Why would the Romans have bothered to do this? Why, indeed, did they go to the trouble of taking Paul to Caesarea with a truly immense escort of two hundred foot soldiers, two hundred spearsmen and seventy horsemen, at a time when their resources were stretched? He may, as Acts describes, have been a Roman citizen. But he had somehow acquired that status; he was not by birth a Roman. The size of the escort suggests a person of great importance, a leader or a general perhaps, someone the Romans could not afford to lose. But Paul was apparently not such a person, just a humble tentmaker (Acts 18, 3) from Tarsus, albeit a man with very great ambitions. It could, of course, be that the detail of the escort is simply part of the elaboration of the story in Acts, another piece of fiction. But it sits oddly with the rest of the text and the apparent aim of the writer to cut Paul to size, bringing him within the structure of the Church.

I suggest the possibility that the size of the escort, perhaps not precisely as described but in general terms, is one of the circumstantial details in this part of the narrative that is true. It will have been remembered, perhaps written down and passed on, because of its exceptional nature, because it was a striking fact. It became part of the material collected and incorporated into the writer's tale which was part fiction and part fact, part justification for a particular position and part a record of events.

If the Romans wanted to transport and keep someone, then they would at that time have had to provide a considerable force. The High Priest Jonathan had recently been assassinated. The Sadducee elite were in conflict with zealots and sicarii and there would have been large areas of 'bandit country', outside of strongholds of the Romans and King Agrippa II, where Roman writ did not run.

They wanted to keep Paul because he must have been, despite the evidence so far, in their eyes someone of importance.

He was of course, or would come to be, important as an early leader within the breakaway 'Christian' church and he was equally important as a figure of opposition to the Nazoreans and their successors, as followers of James, the 'Ebionites' or 'poor ones'. Their writings were, however, systematically suppressed by the Church. So, while references suggest that there were accounts as extensive as the canonical gospels, what survive are mere fragments, often in quotations by their critics.

There are fortunately some passages within a piece of writing, a fictitious account of the travels of Clement with the apostle Simon Peter, while in dialogue with a character called Simon Magus, Simon the Magician. The *Pseudoclementine Recognitions* and *Homilies*, two separate texts with a considerable degree of overlap, have the framework of a romantic tale in which ultimately Clement and his long-lost parents and brothers are all reunited with each other. Upon this framework is hung the discourse in which points of theology and philosophy are elaborated. And, as precursor to this, there is an account in *Recognitions* in the form of instruction by Peter to Clement, covering the whole history of Judaism and their messiah, Yeshua. This section presents a core of Ebionite, and by extension, Nazorean belief.

It has survived the attentions of early Christian censors presumably because of its appearance within something else, a combined pseudohistorical romance and philosophical discourse. Set out baldly as what it was, it would most likely have been burned like all the other Ebionite texts.

The references are made generally to Yeshua as the 'True Prophet', which suggests that the document predates the Council of Nicea in CE 325 when the Church voted by a majority to decide that Yeshua was the Son of God and reworked the gospels accordingly. The early Church authority Origen (around CE 185-254) quotes part of *Recognitions*, which therefore dates the work as a whole at least to the early third century. It may be that the passage setting out Ebionite/Nazorean belief is second century, around the same time as Acts, though of course still written many years after the events to which the texts relate.

At the time described in *Recognitions*, seven years after the crucifixion, it is claimed that Yeshua's followers had increased to such an extent that they outnumbered those of 'the priests':

> When he had suffered, and darkness had overwhelmed the world from the sixth even to the ninth hour, as soon as the sun shone out again, and things were returned to their usual course, even wicked men returned to themselves and their former practices, their fear having abated. For some of them, watching the place with all care, when they could not prevent his rising again, said that he was a magician; others pretended that he was stolen away.

Nevertheless, the truth everywhere prevailed; for, in proof that these things were done by divine power, we who had been very few became in the course of a few days, by the help of God, far more than they. So that the priests at one time were afraid, lest haply, by the providence of God, to their confusion, the whole of the people should come over to our faith. Therefore they often sent to us, and asked us to discourse to them concerning Jesus, whether he were the Prophet whom Moses foretold, who is the eternal Christ. For on this point only does there seem to be any difference between us who believe in Jesus, and the unbelieving Jews. But while they often made such requests to us, and we sought for a fitting opportunity, a week of years was completed from the passion of the Lord, the Church of the Lord which was constituted in Jerusalem was most plentifully multiplied and grew, being governed with most righteous ordinances by James, who was ordained bishop in it by the Lord.

The debate is arranged between the High Priest Caiaphas and others on the one hand and James and his followers on the other. The positions taken by Pharisees, Sadducees, Samaritans, the followers of John the Baptist and others are successively refuted, until the point is reached in the tale when everyone is on the point of converting to the Nazorean position. But then an 'enemy' intervenes ...

But when [James] had spoken some things also concerning baptism, through seven successive days he persuaded all the people and the high priest that they should hasten straightway to receive baptism.

And when matters were at that point that they should come and be baptized, some one of our enemies, entering the temple with a few men, began to cry out, and to say, 'What mean ye, O men of Israel? Why are you so easily hurried on?

Why are ye led headlong by most miserable men, who are deceived by Simon, a magician?' While he was thus speaking, and adding more to the same effect, and while James the bishop was refuting him, he began to excite the people and to raise a tumult so that the people might not be able to hear what was said. Therefore he began to drive all into confusion with shouting, and to undo what had been arranged with much labour, and at the same time to reproach the priests, and to enrage them with revilings and abuse, and, like a madman, to excite every one to murder, saying, 'What do ye? Why do ye hesitate? Oh sluggish and inert, why do we not lay hands upon them, and pull all these fellows to pieces?' When he had said this, he first, seizing a strong brand from the altar, set the example of smiting. Then others also, seeing him, were carried away with like readiness. Then ensued a tumult on either side, of the beating and the beaten. Much blood is shed; there is a confused flight, in the midst of which that enemy attacked James, and threw him headlong from the top of the steps; and supposing him to be dead, he cared not to inflict further violence upon him.

But our friends lifted him up, for they were both more numerous and more powerful than the others; but, from their fear of God, they rather suffered themselves to be killed by an inferior force, than they would kill others. But when the evening came the priests shut up the temple, and we returned to the house of James, and spent the night there in prayer. Then before daylight we went down to Jericho, to the number of 5000 men. Then after three days one of the brethren came to us from Gamaliel, whom we mentioned before, bringing to us secret tidings that that enemy had received a commission from Caiaphas, the chief priest, that he should arrest all who believed in Jesus, and should go to Damascus with his letters, and that there also, employing the help of the unbelievers, he should make havoc among the faithful; and that he was hastening to Damascus chiefly on this account, because he believed that Peter had fled thither.

It is clear both from the general context and from the commission sought from Caiaphas, to persecute followers in Damascus, exactly as in Acts, that the enemy is meant to be Paul/Saul. Indeed, a marginal note in one manuscript actually states as much.

Now, this is a fictionalised account just as much as Acts and it also contains inconsistencies. For example, the rule of Caiaphas as High Priest ended in CE 36, but the events described are supposed to have taken seven years (a week of years) after the crucifixion. But this has been dated to CE 36, in the light of some fairly firm dates provided by John the Baptist's confrontation with Herod Antipas over his divorce with the daughter of King Aretas and marriage to his brother's wife, who was also his niece.

Either the date of the crucifixion calculated on this basis is wrong or the great debate, if it took place, was with a High Priest later in time than Caiaphas.

The structure of the event seems to have been built around the early persecution of Simon Peter and other followers of Yeshua, in the years immediately following the crucifixion. It includes a similar speech by Gamaliel to the one made in Acts, when Peter was brought before the Sanhedrin. But there is no parallel in Acts or elsewhere to the intervention by Paul/Saul and an actual physical assault on James.

It seems certain that, had this taken place as described, then the whole sequence outlined in Acts, and reflected in Paul's letters – when Paul sought to join, was initially rebuffed, set up his own ministry, was summoned, sent away and then summoned to Jerusalem again – could not have happened. At least, it could not have happened after the physical assault on James. After that, no interaction would have been possible between Paul and the Jerusalem community.

There would also not have been time, especially with all the missionary journeys, for it all to have happened in the seven years following the passion.

So, it is in some measure a fiction. There is also just a possibility that it is a coded or garbled record of something else that did really happen. This is an account which may have survived despite being mixed up, or perhaps because of being mixed up, with other events.

This early Ebionite account may have survived by chance, while others were lost, because it became incorporated in a fictional tale. It could also be that someone put it in the tale of Clement in order for it to survive, at a time when Nazorean writings were being systematically destroyed. What they inserted in a story of a great debate, embroidered and probably notional, was a key assertion, that Paul assaulted James in the temple. James is described, circumstantially, later in the text as still limping a week after the attack.

The assault in the temple, like the detail of the huge Roman escort for Paul or the execution of Simon Peter upside down, was something that would have stuck in the memory and might have been passed down a generation or two until it was finally written down, maybe as much as a hundred years after the event. By which time, of course, much or all of the original context would have been lost.

I have suggested it is unlikely that the attack on James, if it happened, took place when the story suggests, in the early years of the development of the Jerusalem community. The likely context would have been the time when relations had utterly broken down, after Paul had been summoned a second time to Jerusalem and made to undertake a humiliating penance, when James and the others had become aware of the contempt in which Paul held them (as evinced in Galatians) and when they knew for certain that Paul had been teaching against the Torah and totally disregarding their instructions. In this atmosphere of evident hostility, such a physical attack is plausible.

At the time in question, however, Paul was supposed to be languishing many miles away under house arrest in Rome and therefore unable to stir up discord in Jerusalem. But that is when the narrative in Acts ends and possibly why it ends, just before the death of James. Could Paul have come back at a moment when James was suddenly vulnerable, as some of his more militant sympathisers were stepping up their attacks on the Sadducee establishment? Could Paul have thereby assisted in pushing James over the brink?

There is in *Homilies*, which broadly follows *Recognitions* on the tale of Clement and its philosophical discourse, an additional section believed to be Ebionite in origin setting out a discourse between Simon Peter and Paul, this time in the guise of Simon Magus, the Magician. The central question is Paul's claim to be an apostle, having never met Yeshua, by virtue of divine revelation through a vision. Simon Magus (aka Paul) contends:

He who hears any one with his own ears is not altogether fully assured of the truth of what is said; for his mind has to consider whether he is wrong or not, inasmuch as he is a man as far as appearance goes. But apparition not merely presents an object to view, but inspires him who sees it with confidence, for it comes from God.

Simon Peter, however, replies:

But can any one be rendered fit for instruction through apparitions? And if you will say, 'It is possible,' then I ask, 'Why did our teacher abide and discourse a whole year to those who were awake?' And how are we to believe your word, when you tell us that he appeared to you? And how did he appear to you, when you entertain opinions contrary to his teaching?

But if you were seen and taught by him, and became his apostle for a single hour, proclaim his utterances, interpret his sayings, love his apostles, contend not with me who companied with him. For in direct opposition to me, who am a firm rock, the foundation of the Church, you now stand. If you were not opposed to me, you would not accuse me, and revile the truth proclaimed by me, in order that I may not be believed when I state what I myself have heard with my own ears from the Lord, as if I were evidently a person that was condemned and in bad repute.

This early Ebionite and anti-Pauline text gets to the nub of the issues. Why should Paul be given any credence when he was preaching against the experience, knowledge and instruction of those who and actually known Yeshua? Of course, the words are no more those of Simon Peter than are the utterances ascribed to Saul/Paul when before the Sanhedrin in Acts. They were written post the letters of Paul and post the gospels, to which at various points both *Recognitions* and *Homilies* relate.

So, for example, the last line of the passage quoted above resonates with the words of Paul who 'opposed [Cephas/Peter] face to face, because he stood condemned' (Galatians 2, 11). Even more pertinent is the introductory part of *Homilies*, an epistle supposedly from Peter to James, where it is stated that:

For some from among the Gentiles have rejected my legal preaching, attaching themselves to certain lawless and trifling preaching of the man who is my enemy. And these things some have attempted while I am still alive, to transform my words by certain various interpretations, in order to the dissolution of the law; as though I also myself were of such a mind, but did not freely proclaim it, which God forbid! For such a thing were to act in opposition to the law of God which was spoken by Moses, and was borne witness to by our Lord in respect of its eternal continuance; for thus he spoke: 'The heavens and the earth shall pass away, but one jot or one tittle shall in no wise pass from the law.' And this he has said, that all things might come to pass.

This would appear to refer to the portrayal in Acts of Simon Peter acquiescing in the abolition of the Torah's distinction between clean and unclean foods and foods permitted to Gentiles/god fearers and food permitted to Jews (Acts 11, 1-18). These again would not have been the words of Peter, but the understanding of people very early on that Peter had, notwithstanding some of the account in Acts, remained a Torah-abiding Jew. The 'enemy' is once more evidently Paul.

What is really significant is the evidence this gives of the existence of a group of people who followed Yeshua and James, who did not believe that Jewish Law had been overturned by Yeshua and who, on the contrary, still followed that Law.

These were the Jewish followers of Yeshua in the second century, or at the latest the third century, since after that they were driven out of existence. If anyone, then these, rather than Paul's 'Christ'ians of Antioch, were the proponents of the doctrines and inheritors of the traditions of the Jewish messiah Yeshua.

Paul, the 'enemy' of the Nazoreans and Ebionites, was clearly someone of stature. He had a great impact, both on their future and the development of a breakaway Christian church, appealing to the wider Gentile world. He was considered so important that the Romans gave him an enormous armed escort for the journey from Jerusalem to Caesarea, despite their need to conserve forces in the face of a growing sicarii insurrection. He was able almost single-handedly to intervene in a temple debate and transform it into chaos. He alone, it would seem, had the prime commission to pursue Jewish messianic, nationalist dissidents. All this, despite the supposition that he was just a tent maker with the lucky attribute of Roman citizenship.

For the Nazoreans and their Ebionite successors, he was by definition 'the enemy'. And who could the enemy have been, if not someone closely associated with the Romans? As others have noted, there are some curious coincidences in that names of prominent characters, described by the historian Josephus, are also the namesakes of people closely associated with Paul as his co-workers and travelling companions in Acts and the letters.

Silas, for example, is described in Acts as going with Paul and Barnabas to Antioch with the decision of James in respect of rules to be observed by god fearers. Silas is also depicted as travelling with Paul on his missionary journeys. In Josephus' *Antiquities*, his namesake is a 'general' in Agrippa I's forces.

'Simeon called Niger' is described as a prophet or teacher in the early church at Antioch in Acts, while Josephus has a character Niger as courageous leader of a group of Idumeans against the Romans. Cornelius in Acts is the Roman centurion who became a convert. In Josephus, there is a Cornelius who bears a letter from the Emperor Claudius to the Roman governor Cumanus. Philip who preached and healed at Samaria (Acts) is paralleled by Philip, a commander in the army, or more likely and less grandly the militia, of King Agrippa II.

It may be just coincidence or it may be that the author of Acts, short of material, used the names of characters he was familiar with in reading Josephus to pad out his narrative. As such, characters like this in Acts may be pure inventions.

Except that some of them, for example Silvanus possibly as a Roman version of Silas, also appear in Paul's letters which unlike Acts originated and were circulated *before* Josephus wrote the first of his books, the *Jewish War* in CE 75. There are certainly a number of references in the letters which suggest that Paul was moving in very rarefied circles.

One character Ephaphroditus is mentioned twice in Paul's letter to the Philippians, supposedly written while Paul was being held in Rome around CE 60. Ephaphroditus appears as a messenger or go-between, who has recently been very ill. He is close to Paul, his 'brother and fellow worker and fellow soldier'; bringing gifts to Paul from Paul's followers in the Roman colony of Philippi in what is now eastern Greece.

Paul ends his letter with a revealing salutation, 'All the saints greet you, especially those of Caesar's household'.

This suggests that Paul had when he was being held, having appealed to the Emperor Nero and been taken to Rome, sympathisers in the Emperor's household. Is that feasible? A few years later, in CE 64, Nero instituted a great persecution against Christians, as scapegoats for a fire that swept Rome. However, at the time that Paul was first held, his breakaway Jewish sect may not have been seen as a particular threat. Indeed, as I will suggest, Paul may have been regarded as potentially useful, given his dramatic fall-out with the nationalist, messianic and essentially anti-foreigner and anti-Roman Nazoreans.

Ephaphroditus is a very uncommon name. It so happens that there was someone of that name in Nero's household, acting as the Emperor's secretary, at the very time that Paul/Saul was writing his letter.

A few more years later and Josephus is now in Rome in exile, having been taken prisoner, cooperated with his captors during the siege of Jerusalem and then set upon the task of writing a history of the Jewish war, which would flatter the Roman victors and demonstrate to others the futility of revolt. Someone would have been needed to organise and supervise Josephus. That someone was none other than Ephaphroditus, to whom Josephus actually dedicates several of his books. In *Antiquities*, Josephus describes him as 'a lover of all kinds of learning, but principally delighted by the study of history'. Clearly, this person was Josephus' publisher and patron.

Ephaphroditus apparently survived a long time and eventually became the Emperor Domitian's secretary. He was ultimately executed by Domitian, ostensibly for assisting in the death of Nero, which might have been either murder or suicide. If Ephaphroditus had been an overt Christian, as Paul seems to suggest, it seems hardly likely that he could have survived Nero's purge of Christians following the Great Fire of Rome. On the other hand, it is plausible that Ephaphroditus was assigned to look after Paul, in the words of the letter to the Philippians to 'minister to [Paul's] need' (Philippians 2, 25), given that Paul was in some respect an important prisoner or a useful informer. Ephaphroditus certainly did perform a similar role in respect of Josephus, maybe eight or ten years later. Given that Paul misrepresented the position of Simon Peter, reworked and obstructed the rulings of James and the other Nazorean leaders in Jerusalem and gave untrue or misleading information about his own status, it would not be surprising if – to impress the Philippians – he had put a gloss on the role of the Emperor's youthful, intelligent and learned secretary. Not his keeper, but in Paul's eyes his equal: 'brother and fellow worker and fellow soldier'. Possibly even, a 'saint' in 'Caesar's household'!

If Paul was initially looked after in the same way as Josephus was later, and by the same person, then he was regarded as someone important by the Romans. Just how important he might have been becomes clear in the light of a revealing comment that Paul lets slip in his letter to the Romans, the significance of which must have escaped later gospel censors. The customary list of greetings at the end include, 'Greet those who belong to the family of Aristobulus' immediately followed by 'Greet my kinsman Herodion'. Except for its context, there is arguably nothing particularly significant about the former; there might have been any number of candidates for the head of household, Aristobulus. But the import of the latter is unmistakeable. Paul is admitting to be a member of the Herodian family, a relative of 'Herodion' which means 'little Herod'! And there quite definitely was a little Herod living at the time that Paul was writing, a child named Herod of one Aristobulus and Salome, the same Salome who in the gospel story demanded the head of John the Baptist (see Herodian family tree, Appendix IV).

In the light of this, the greeting to Aristobulus, a name common in the family trees of Herod and the Maccabeans, also appears significant. He may well have been the father of Herodian (little Herod). Or he may have another member of the family with the same name who was alive at that time.

The evidence in Paul's letters is important, because it comes from sources earlier than the gospels. It is backed up, however, by a significant statement in Acts that 'in the church at Antioch there were prophets and teachers, Barnabas, Simeon who was called Niger, Lucius of Cyrene, Manaen the foster brother of Herod the Tetrarch [Herod Antipas], and Saul' (Acts, 13, 1). Thus, included in the core members of very first assembly or church (ecclesia), where Jewish and Gentile followers were known as 'Christians', is someone who as foster brother of Herod the Tetrarch was a prominent member of the Herodian family. That would be surprising if Paul were, as he tried to represent himself, a 'Hebrew' learned in Pharisee law. Not at all surprising if Paul were himself, as now seems evident, a member of the Herodian family!

Accepting the evidence, that Paul was a member of the Herodian family, suddenly makes a lot of what had previously appeared confusing suddenly, startlingly clear. The Nazoreans were afraid of Paul just because he was a Herodian, someone the Romans supported and who beyond a certain point they could not touch. It explains why, as Acts vividly portrays it, they remained almost frozen as Paul, whom they had tried to rebuff, moved freely in and out of them. It explains why he was known as 'the enemy', because that is what Roman client Herodian rulers were to the Nazoreans/Essenes and Ebionites. What was a mystery, the question of Paul's Roman citizenship, is now simply explained. King Herod and his descendants were granted hereditary citizenship by the Roman Senate, grateful for Herod's success in restoring Palestine to Roman rule. Paul, or rather Saul as he really was, was a member of the Herodian family and so he qualified. That is why, as Paul is given to claim in Acts, he had his citizenship 'by birth'.

It also explains the force of the Ebionite accusation that Paul 'wanted to marry the High Priest's daughter' – just like Herod. He wanted to do that, or he might have wanted to do that, because he was a Herodian, just like Herod. It was a way in which Herod extended and consolidated power, just as the ambitious Paul might well have wanted to do.

The reasoning behind, and justification for, Paul's circumlocutions in regard to his own status are now also clearly apparent. King Herod's father Antipater and grandfather Antipas were Idumeans, a neighbouring people of similar Semitic origin to the Jews, whose ancestors were conquered and forcibly converted. So Paul could presume to claim to be a descendant of Abraham, a Hebrew, of the tribe of Benjamin – all vague generalities that might be applied to an Idumean. Many of the Herodians indeed saw themselves as Jewish, and there was Jewish blood in some lines (not Paul's, it will transpire) through King Herod's marriage to Mariamme, a Maccabean princess. Paul was nearly, almost, not quite, a Jew.

It is no longer so surprising that the characters, who appear as Paul's companions in Acts, have namesakes who are Idumeans, Herodians and Romans in the accounts by Josephus. It is also now stunningly evident why the Romans took the trouble to rescue Paul and why they deployed the very large force necessary to get him safely back to Caesarea and from there to Rome. Paul was not merely a citizen; he was a member of a family that was important to Rome, whose members had been given jobs ruling different part of Palestine, including Judea. Moreover, Paul had come into contact and conflict with the Nazoreans, who were religiously uncompromising messianists (thus 'zealous'). It

appears that he had then become the target of a militant nationalist group (sicarii or political 'zealots'). Quite possibly this
group had taken its inspiration, if not its direction, from the
Nazoreans.

The Romans would have wanted to learn more about these
groups. This is probably why, in Acts, while Paul was kept in safe
custody for two years in Caesarea, the Roman governor Felix
'sent for him often and conversed with him'(Acts 24, 26). It was
thus a very lengthy debriefing. As Acts has it, Felix also hoped to
secure money, perhaps part of the funds that Paul had collected
with the ostensible objective of supporting the Jerusalem
community – but which may not have been delivered.

As well as the references in Corinthians, described earlier,
there is other evidence that Paul was making fairly free use of the
money he was supposedly collecting for James and the others in
Jerusalem. There's an oblique allusion, which may be suggesting
this, in a tale recounted by Josephus in *Antiquities* (see p 275).
There is also a curious story in the *Acts of Peter* where Simon
Peter battles with Simon Magus who, as in Homilies, may be a
stand in for Paul. Simon Magus is staying with a wealthy woman
Eubula and repays her hospitality by stealing all her valuables.
Simon Peter uncovers the plot and forces his opponent to flee
Judea, as indeed the 'other' Saul, brother of Costobar, did at the
beginning of the Jewish War.

Peter may also have been collecting money, in the guise of
Simon 'with a reputation for religious scrupulousness'. This is
the person who is described by Josephus as extorting a ransom
from King Agrippa I. Taking money from a Herodian, who
was by definition a fornicator because of practices like uncle-
niece marriage, would have concerned Peter's followers. His
justification for this appears to have survived in a tale in the *Acts
of Peter*, in which Peter is criticised for receiving a large gift from
a woman, a notorious fornicator, with the nickname Chryse (the
golden). Peter argues that she brought the money as a debtor to

Christ (originally, Yeshua) who was thereby providing for his followers.

The sword-wielding Simon Peter, it should be remembered, had been appointed by Yeshua as his chief minister, commander of the church (ecclesia) militant. It is not unreasonable to think that Peter was not only collecting for the immediate needs of the Nazoreans but to help fund a fighting force for an inevitable clash with the Romans. However, as is clear from both Acts (eg Acts 15, 7) and Paul's letters, Peter was like Paul also going to diasporan Jews and Gentile god fearers. These communities would have felt the pressure from these competing demands, faced with the invidious choice (according to a very ancient phrase) of 'robbing Peter to pay Paul'.

The theory that Paul was a Herodian is supported by evidence, in Paul's letters and Acts, for the presence of which there is no other satisfactory explanation. It is a better theory than others, for example that Paul's family were tent makers, hypothetically to the Roman army, and for this service were rewarded with citizenship, which was rather surprisingly passed on. The reason is that this latter theory, as with others like it, explains one fact and nothing else, while the argument I have put forward causes a whole range of otherwise incongruous detail to fall into place.

It has been suggested that Paul could not have been a Herodian because, in his interview with King Agrippa II in Caesarea, after being taken there by the Romans, there is no sign on either side of recognition. They would have known each other, as fellow Herodians.

The answer to that, of course, is that the interview with Agrippa as conducted is just so much embroidery by the author of Luke, as for example is the fanciful and spurious case supposedly put forward by Paul to the Sanhedrin and to Felix that he was being persecuted because, unlike the Sadducees, he believed in resurrection. Putting words into the mouths of characters (pseudepigraphic: not so much what they said but what they might have said) was at the time an accepted convention.

Reliance can be placed only on what are probably the core facts: that Paul was under attack, that he was rescued by the Romans, transported to Caesarea with a considerable armed escort and then taken to Rome.

It is interesting, however, that Acts has Agrippa come with his sister Bernice to Caesarea to interview Paul. Acts (26, 30-32) makes it clear that the King supported Paul, to the extent of arguing that he could have been set free had he not appealed to the Roman Emperor Nero. Evidently, Paul appealed because he needed to get out of Palestine. His life was at risk: he had been subject to several attacks and his enemies at that point were actively planning to kill him.

One reason for Agrippa's support would have been the fact that Paul was then at odds with the very people, militant Jewish religious nationalists, with whom he and his father before him had been engaged in a long and bitter civil conflict. The Judean King Agrippa I had killed James, the brother of John and cousin of Yeshua, and imprisoned Simon Peter. Agrippa II, client King of Galilee, would soon be assisting the Romans in putting down the Jewish revolt instigated by zealots. Like Festus, he would have wanted to find out what Paul knew.

Agrippa may also have sided with Paul simply because he was part, even if distantly related, of the Herodian extended family. So if, as I have argued, Paul (aka Saul) was a Herodian, is there any evidence as to precisely who he was? As it happens, there is good information on many members of the Herodian family tree provided largely, though not exclusively, by the Jewish historian Josephus.

One such person named Saul, not a particularly usual name at the time, was descended from the sister of Herod the Great through her marriage to another Idumean, Costobarus.

Saul and his brother, also named Costobarus, are important characters, described by Josephus as playing a central role in the events leading up to the outbreak of the Jewish revolt (see Herodian family tree, Appendix IV).

At the point at which sacrifices to the Emperor and Rome have been suspended and the Roman garrison at Masada overrun, delegations were sent from those against the war (Herodians and the High Priest's faction) to the Roman procurator Gessius Florus and King Agrippa II, asking them to quash the insurrection before it got out of hand. It would seem, as Josephus cynically notes, that it was already too late and the chief motivation was to establish their innocence before the reckoning that was to come! Among the delegation sent to Agrippa were 'Saul, Antipas and Costobar, kinsmen of the king'.

After the first phase of the War, when the rebels inflicted a crushing defeat on the twelfth legion led by Cestius Gallus, Saul together with his brother Costobar and others who had identified themselves with Rome, went over to Cestius and were then sent 'at their own wish' to the Emperor Nero. The reason for this was, according to Josephus, 'to acquaint him with their own plight and to lay the blame for the war on Florus (the Roman Governor)' (*Jewish War*, II, 566). The Temple Treasurer Antipas, who stayed behind, was with many others killed by the rebels.

Philip, son of Jacimus and commander of King Agrippa II's army, was one of those who 'slipped away' with Saul. He originated from a colony of 'Babylonian Jews' near Bethsaida, home territory to his namesake among the disciples. He was evidently a friend of Saul, just like the evangelist Philip with whom Paul/Saul stayed in Caesarea (Acts 21, 8). He did sufficiently badly in defending the Romans garrison, massacred at the outset of the Jewish revolt, to be accused later of deliberately betraying it.

The son of Jacimus may, like Agrippa himself, have had divided loyalties. From a community of Jews reintroduced from the diaspora, he would have had links with the Greek-speaking Gentile world. In John's gospel, Philip appears as an intermediary, introducing Nathanael to Yeshua and then later brokering a meeting between Yeshua and some 'Greeks' at Passover, just when an armed clash seemed inevitable (John 1, 45 and 12, 20-21). In Acts, he was one of seven appointed by the Nazoreans to administer the distribution of food during famine to the Greek community. Also in Acts, Philip is credited with converting Simon Magus (Simon the magician) who then became his companion (Acts 6, 5 and 8, 9-13). But, as can be seen from the passage above (p 135) in the *Pseudoclementine Homilies*, which appears to have a source common to Acts, Simon Magus is often used as a stand-in for Paul. The detail of the evidence indicates one character, seen through the distorting lenses of various story tellers with different agendas. Philip the disciple/evangelist and Philip the commander, companion of Paul/Saul, may be one and the same (see Appendix II).

In his later book, *Antiquities*, Josephus fills in some more detail about Saul and his brother Costobar who 'were of the royal lineage and found favour because of their kinship with Agrippa'. In the period of growing anarchy, following the stoning to death of James in CE 62, these two abused their privileged position and 'were lawless and quick to plunder the property of those weaker than themselves' (*Antiquities* XX, 214). If the case that I have advanced that Paul/Saul of the Letters and Acts was a Herodian, and of sufficient prominence to have thereby attained Roman citizenship, then the Saul described by Josephus provides a remarkable match.

There is in fact no other Saul to provide a match, since it was not among the Herodians a common name. Furthermore, this particular Saul was living at the right time and would have been about the right age. He was, moreover, on the Roman side against the messianic nationalists – like Paul. He seems to have had some of the characteristics which can be seen in Paul, a degree of arrogance and ruthlessness and a predilection for taking possessions not his own. Paul, I suggest, may have changed his name from Saul, not to mark a change of character but to distract from and disguise his origins.

An examination of the Herodian family tree (Appendix IV) provides some indications as to why the Saul or Saulus described by Josephus may have been impelled to seek wealth by plundering the property of zealot nationalists who were victims of the civil conflict. Saulus was the grandson of the sister of King Herod (the Great). Via this link, Herod King of Chalcis and Agrippa I would have been, in current kinship terms, his second cousins.

But his aunt Bernice had married her cousin Aristobolus, son of King Herod by Mariamme, a Maccabean princess. So Herod King of Chalcis was in addition his first cousin by this latter route. Not only that, but Saulus' father Antipater had married his cousin Cypros, daughter of King Herod by Mariamme. With brother and sister marrying sister and brother, Herod King of Chalcis was thus his first cousin twice over. Aristobulus, the Kings's son, and his son Herod (possibly Herodion or 'little Herod') were by two routes his first cousins, respectively once and twice removed. They were certainly close enough to be the kinsfolk described in Paul's letter to the Romans.

Saulus was closely tied in by kinship to the Herodian family tree. But because his primary link, Salome the sister of King Herod, was female, he was out of the patrilineal line of descent and therefore without any real power and most probably wealth by virtue of his position. The Herodians, as can be seen, concentrated power and wealth in the male line, reinforcing it through a conscious strategy of marrying close female relatives, either nieces or cousins. Herodias, sister of King Agrippa I and Herod King of Chalcis, was considered such a desirable match that she was married successively to two of her uncles! The second, Herod Antipas, had her at the price of antagonising upholders of Jewish Law, spilling the blood of John the Baptist and fighting a war with the father of the wife he divorced, the Arab King Aretas.

After a time, the lines of kinship became more tangled and the close kin who married were often related in several ways. For the sake of clarity, some of the links are not shown in the family chart in Appendix IV. Agrippa I for example married his first cousin Cypros. She was the daughter of his aunt, who had done the same, so that she was his second cousin also. The marriage of Herod King of Chalcis and Mariamme was not, as it appears from the chart, an exception to the rule. They were in fact distantly related and in more than one way.

Saulus, and for that matter his brother Costobarus, were almost structured by the accident of their birth to feel resentful, denied positions of influence they believed should rightfully be theirs. They were closely related through the Herodian web of intermarriage to people who had real power, but they were outside the male line and so not part of it. So, they took steps to remedy the situation, according to Josephus plundering the property of 'those weaker than themselves'.

This is an appraisal which also perfectly fits Paul who slots, from the clues that there are available in Acts, into the position held by Saulus in the Herodian family tree. Paul (as Saul) pursued those of 'the Way', like Saulus, and may well have had their goods as his reward.

The defensive posture taken in some of his letters suggests that he was accused by his opponents of misusing, for his own purposes, funds ostensibly collected for the Nazoreans (the 'Saints') in Jerusalem. This is reinforced by the suggestion in Acts that the Roman governor Festus hoped to secure money from Paul. There are also oblique tales in *Antiquities* and the *Acts of Peter* which indicate a belief that Paul was stealing some of the funds entrusted to him.

It appears, if his Ebionite critics are to be believed, that Paul may have tried other strategies to secure the power denied to him, actually or symbolically seeking to marry the High Priest's daughter. Herod (his great uncle, if this analysis is correct) did do just this, marrying the daughter of the High Priest Boethus and grand daughter the High Priest John Hyrcanus II, both of whom were named Mariamme.

By origin an Idumean, a group conquered and forcibly converted, Paul was only nominally a Jew. He may, as his letters seem to indicate, have initially harboured ambitions to be a great Pharisee sage like Gamaliel. He claimed to be a Pharisee, having advanced in the study of Judaism beyond many of his peers. But he was not recognised as a Pharisee scholar and he does not appear as having the necessary training, mastery of legal argument or even familiarity with Hebrew.

Paul claimed to be a Roman citizen, but he may not even have been entirely secure in that. If it were as Saulus, then his claim was by membership of the Herodian family. Although closely related, and descended from King Herod's sister, he was not however directly linked in the male line. This could explain why he used his claim to Roman citizenship as a last resort, when he was threatened with a beating and the possibility of being handed back to a lynch mob.

Acts records how Paul, under the authority of the Sadducee High Priest, began by persecuting the Nazoreans. He then sought to ingratiate himself with them but was treated with fear and suspicion. He became progressively more alienated, and drawn into conflict, as a result of his refusal to accept their jurisdiction and authority.

If the evidence from Paul's letters is considered with Acts, a picture emerges of Paul failing to achieve the influence within Judaism he needed to compensate for his inability to exercise real power as a Herodian. So he created his own field of influence, among god-fearers and other potential Gentile converts, for a religion creatively combining elements of pagan Mithraism, gnostic belief and Nazorean propaganda or myth. As Herod had commandeered the Maccabean line of descent, so Paul took over and subverted for his own purposes Jewish messianism.

What Paul tried to attach himself to was a dominant and growing force in Judaism, its religious fundamentalism gaining strength in the face of Roman rule. The gospels, ultimately products of Paul's endeavours, attempt to portray something different. Yeshua is shown as a charismatic individual, though without a following within Judaism and opposed (with the Nazoreans/Essenes excluded) to all of its major groups: Sadducees, scribes and Pharisees. This has been shown to be false on several counts. Yeshua was a Nazorean leader, with a following which grew under his brother James to the point at which James could claim to act and speak for Jews as a whole. Moreover, on points of essential doctrine and in terms of cooperation the Nazoreans and Pharisees were not opposed.

It is consistent that Paul would have attempted to join a dominant group. Why would he have bothered with something less, if his aim were to gain influence and power? The gospels downplayed the messianic movement, once Paul had broken from it, because they were then selling not the religion of Yeshua and James who believed in the Law, but Paul's own Church.

Paul first tried to infiltrate the Nazoreans, it can be presumed with the aim of gaining a position of authority. Then, when that strategy apparently failed, he sought to create an alternative power base. This he did by seeking to attract Jews and attached god-fearers in the diaspora, while under the guise of still remaining within the Nazorean fold. In the face of a hostile reaction among Jews and then a breakdown of relations with the leaders in Jerusalem, Paul reached a point where his message was aimed at Gentiles in general and his prospectus divorced from Judaism.

Though he eventually succeeded in gaining some standing in his lifetime, it was nevertheless only as the initiator and leader of what was then a relatively small splinter group. It appears that to begin with some of the cult's prime instigators, for example the foster brother of Herod Antipas at Antioch, were fellow Herodians.

Paul did create what would become an attractive package for the Gentile market, remixing the Nazorean message with elements of pagan and gnostic belief. But the substantial inroads made by Christianity came later, after the failure of the Jewish rebellion. The Nazoreans and other zealot groups were defeated and dispersed, leaving Judaism in no state to counter the religion promulgated by followers of Paul.

There is however a remaining problem in identifying Paul with the Herodian Saulus. Josephus describes Costabarus and Saulus in Jerusalem plundering the property of 'those weaker than themselves', around CE 64 in the turmoil leading up to the Jewish rebellion. So, if Paul was being held in Rome at the time, he cannot have been the same character as Saul.

This is however based on a presumption, given that the narrative in Acts ends around CE 61 or 62, before the death of James, with Paul in Rome. He appears to have been in a form of protective custody, to safeguard him from the Jewish zealots who, according to Acts, had already hatched several plots to kill him. The Romans had laid no charges against him and, it seems from Acts, were unwilling to do so. The early church authority Eusebius, however, stated that Paul did not remain in Roman custody.

There is a plausible scenario which takes into account that Paul, aka Saul and as argued here a Herodian, was also the Herodian Saul, brother of Costobar, whom Josephus describes. It is around CE 60 or 61. As both Acts and the *Pseudoclementine Recognitions* describe it, there has been an enormous growth in numbers of the Jewish Nazorean followers of James. This sect follows a Jewish messiah they claim to be still alive, although the Romans claim to have executed him. Many former Pharisees have transferred allegiance to a group whose other core beliefs are essentially their own, but with a more nationalist and less compromising approach to religious and political affairs. It appears to be on the point of becoming the accepted, majority force in Judaism. This is alarming to both the Sadducee elite and the Roman authorities, aware that militant, messianic groups they call 'bandits' or 'sicarii' may be taking their inspiration from Nazorean and other religious nationalists.

So it is decided to send Paul/Saul back to Jerusalem with a brief to disrupt if possible the expansion of this movement. Paul is keen to go anyway, as he's still smarting from the humiliation received the last time he came before the Nazorean elders. He also sees a possible opportunity to bolster the fortunes of the splinter 'Christian' group that he has been fostering. It is a risky mission, though Paul has the support of the Romans and he is a member of the Herodian family.

Then comes the climactic clash in the temple, which the writer of *Recognitions*, however, erroneously puts much earlier. This is possibly because he links the narrative with Paul's journey to Damascus which would have taken place in the early years following the crucifixion. I have argued that it makes more sense to place the physical confrontation in Jerusalem as an event later in time, after relations between Paul and the Nazoreans have irrevocably broken down.

Paul enters the temple with a group of followers, incites people to attack James, instigates a physical assault on James and causes a riot. James is thrown down the temple steps and injured, his followers are at least temporarily dispersed and the Sadducee elite seize the moment to move against the Nazoreans. James is taken, condemned by a hastily convened group of some of the Sanhedrin and – taking advantage of the absence of the Roman governor – stoned to death.

Paul (aka Saul), whether or not he metaphorically held the coats of the executioners (as in the story of the murder of

Stephen), takes advantage of the situation by plundering the property of Nazoreans who have been imprisoned, killed or forced to flee following the death of James. He stays in Jerusalem as a rumbling civil conflict gathers pace between the messianic nationalists and the Sadducee elite. Josephus describes it in *Antiquities* as 'class warfare between the high priests on the one hand and the priests and the leaders of the populace of Jerusalem on the other'.

It is now CE 64 and back in Rome a disastrous fire sweeps the city. The Emperor Nero blames Paul's Christian followers as scapegoats, and instigates a vicious purge against them.

This is very bad news for Paul and worse is to come. War breaks out between the Jews and Romans and there is a breakdown of civil jurisdiction in Jerusalem. Cestius Gallus at the head of the twelfth legion is sent to crush the revolt but is instead heavily defeated. Facing certain death as a collaborator at the hand of the rebels, Paul and some others defect to Cestius. One of Paul's kinsmen, the city treasurer Antipas, stays behind and is killed.

But now, with Christians actively being persecuted in Rome, Paul has nowhere safe to go. He is sent to Nero and where he is imprisoned as a leading Christian agitator and then later beheaded. His Roman citizenship, granted to him as a member of the Herodian family, preserves him from the arguably much worse fates of either being burned or crucified.

So Paul, having made enemies in all directions, finally runs out of luck. He becomes a victim of his own conspiracies.

I have set out the evidence which indicates that Paul was a member of the Herodian family. This in turn explains how he secured the Roman citizenship that in Acts he is given to admit he did not buy. I have suggested that there is a strong case that Paul/Saul was also the character Saulus in the pages of Josephus. He was someone of importance and influence, given protection by the Romans.

This explains why the apostles, when approached, would have been fearful and would not have taken Paul fully into their confidence. It might even have suited them that he had, were they even were aware of it, a curious and distorted view of who Yeshua was or had been. Their messiah was a real person, a potential liberator, a focus for opposition to authority, someone possibly still at large. Paul was preaching about someone who was other-worldly, offering mystical knowledge of God, and not a threat to Rome.

Paul's message might paradoxically have made them safer. But it became apparent that he was agitating against their beliefs, undermining the fundamentals of Judaism. At which point, he became not just someone who was dangerous and to be treated with caution, but the enemy.

Paul was, however, a key figure in creating a religion for the wider Roman world. This new religion made use of Jewish history and pagan myth and ritual, while converting Yeshua into an other-worldly figure, someone would have been unrecognisable to those who had known him. Paul wrote before the gospels were compiled and influenced their composition, so that for example the sacrificial meal which he had invented was incorporated into their description of contemporary events. Later editors completed the process by which a mortal man, Yeshua, a would-be Jewish liberator and claimant for the throne of Israel, became a divine saviour, sacrificed to atone for the sins of the world, half God and half man.

The gospels, whose original derivation is 'good news', became synonymous with unimpeachable truth. But is it a case of gospel truth … or gospel lies?

Chapter 6: Gospel lies

There were not just one or two but dozens of different gospels and similar works circulating in the first two hundred years or so after the time when Yeshua lived. The Ebionites, or 'poor ones', revered James and maintained a form of Judaism in which Yeshua was a central figure. There were many gnostic sects, preaching a religion depending on a personal relationship between the individual and God and a Yeshua who was more spirit than man, in some cases clearly not even a historical figure at all. During this time, Christianity gained ground alongside a variety of popular pagan cults but its followers were in a very small minority.

At the beginning of the fourth century, the Emperor Constantine adopted Christianity and the situation radically changed. From being a minority sect, it became increasingly the official state religion. Pagan beliefs were over a period of years suppressed, as were varieties of Christianity that conflicted with the officially adopted religion of the Roman Catholic Church. The number of recognised, canonical gospels was reduced to just four. Many others were treated as heretical: outlawed and, wherever found, burned. A few gnostic texts survived, all that remained until a whole library of gnostic works was discovered buried in the desert in Egypt at Nag Hammadi in a large pottery jar. Another gnostic text, the gospel of Judas, discovered in a grave, was left by a dealer to rot for years in a safe deposit box and was only recently deciphered and transcribed.

The writings of the Ebionites, such as the lost gospel of the Hebrews, now survive only in fragments quoted by other authors or in sections hidden, by accident or by design, in other documents.

The four gospels that were retained – Matthew, Mark, Luke and John - all contain some attempt at a biography of Yeshua, largely concentrating on the period of his adult life leading up to and including his crucifixion.

Of these, Mark is the earliest, written most scholars agree around CE 70. It appears to derive from a collection of material, though relying on one source for the passion narrative.

In this, it is similar to the non-canonical gospel of Peter, leading some to suggest an original common source for both, which can be called the 'Cross gospel'.

The gospels of Matthew and Luke were written later still, with additional material on the birth and early life of Yeshua and sayings attributed to him. There are similar sayings in the gnostic gospel of Thomas suggesting, as with the passion story, a common source for the Sayings of Jesus. This is sometimes referred to as Q, from the German 'Quelle' for source.

John's gospel comes last of all, probably written around CE 100, with additional material including the full story of Lazarus and further details for the passion narrative.

The gospel texts were written and circulated and then acquired the names of putative authors. In the case of Mark, it was believed that the gospel was written by John Mark. This person, mentioned in Acts, was reputed to have travelled with Simon Peter and acted as his Greek-speaking interpreter – so acquiring the information needed to write the gospel account.

The gospel of John is supposedly the witness of the 'disciple whom Jesus loved' (John 21, 20-24), conveyed in great old age to the actual author of the gospel. The author was possibly John the Elder who lived in Ephesus at the beginning of the second century.

All of these gospels were written by Christian authors, after a fundamental split had developed between them and the Jewish Nazorean followers of Yeshua under James and then Simon/Simeon in Jerusalem. They were created after Paul had begun to develop the theology of a church with worldwide appeal, different and distinct from the Judaism to which Yeshua subscribed. They were produced after the disastrous Jewish revolt, which ended with the obliteration of the temple and the city of Jerusalem and with it the much of the Nazorean community, along with hundreds of thousands of other Jews.

These accounts are thus not those of the followers of Yeshua but rather those of a rival sect, small then and arguably at that time of marginal significance. But they are seen now through the distorting lens of almost two thousand years of history, during which time Christianity grew to become a dominant force in Western culture and society.

Though providing most of the available evidence on Yeshua's life, the canonical gospels need to be treated with caution. Though the title of this chapter may seem harsh, it is intended as a corrective to the idea, embodied in the phrase 'gospel truth', that the bible is inerrant, the standard for absolute veracity. As will be seen, the gospels contain many contradictions, mistakes and misrepresentations. A clear example of a consciously introduced falsehood is given by Luke's story of how Yeshua came to be born in Bethlehem.

Luke saw that there was a problem in that it was generally believed that a future messiah would come from the city where King David grew up, Bethlehem in Judea, as prophesised in the Old Testament (Micah 5, 2). But Yeshua and his family had grown up in Galilee, where Capernaum was described as his 'own city'. So Luke invented a story in which a census, undertaken under the Roman governor Quirinius, required families to go back to their ancestral homes. For Yeshua's parents, this was to be seen as the city of David. Mary is heavily pregnant when she travels (over 70 miles on foot) and Yeshua is born in Bethlehem.

The story is false for a number of reasons. The census under Quirinius was conducted in CE 6 whereas Yeshua was born about BCE 5, during the reign of King Herod. So Yeshua was born earlier, where his parents lived in Galilee, and at the time of the

the census would have been about 11 years old.

The device of having to enrol where one's ancestors lived is clearly a fiction. Such ancestral homes, going back generations, would have been impossible to establish objectively. Many people would not have known the origin of their ancestors, going back twelve or more generations. There was also no good administrative reason for requiring people to travel great distances to be counted. The ensuing chaos and dislocation is not something that the Romans would have willingly brought on themselves. Finally, there is frequent mention of Yeshua's Galilean origins in other gospel passages. It is certainly made clear in John's gospel that Yeshua was from Galilee, in contradiction to scriptural prophesy (John 7, 40-52).

Details which were not true, such as the census story in Luke, were introduced in an effort to make the text consistent with doctrine. But there is also a more pervasive source of error. The gospels that we have now are the product of hundreds of years of copying and editing. By carelessness or by design, scribes have over the years introduced many hundreds of variations. It becomes difficult to evaluate which if any of several versions of the same text in different manuscripts may be original. Even when versions agree, there is no guarantee that the agreement is not based on changes from an earlier version replicated in making additional copies. These issues were acknowledged as early as the third century by the Christian philosopher Origen and pointed out even earlier by the pagan critic of Christianity, Celsus.

Only fragments of manuscripts survive dating from earlier than the fourth century. So it is hard to decide what had been modified or altered, and when, in the three hundred years or so leading up to this time. Over such a long period there will have been considerable scope for both creative rewriting and haphazard change. In the fourth century, under Constantine, there was an effort to disseminate a uniform text. Even that seems to have involved a degree of reconstruction to make the story fit with the prevailing theology.

Anti-Jewish, and specifically anti-Pharisee, sentiments appear to have been introduced fairly early on, together with efforts to downplay the significance of Yeshua's brothers, especially James. This reflects the split of Paul and his followers away from the Nazorean Jews, which had happened by the time the first versions of the canonical gospels were written. It also reflects the effort by Paul to dissociate Yeshua and his teaching from the Jewish practice and Law to which Yeshua had in reality subscribed.

The beginnings of a second level of distortion can be seen in the nativity stories in the later gospels of Matthew and Luke. Paul had stated that Yeshua was born according to the flesh. It would seem he meant by this that Yeshua was born though a natural process of conception. But the stories in these later gospels propagated a myth that Yeshua had been born from a union between a mortal woman Mary, who was a virgin, and God (in the form of the Holy Ghost) himself!

There are many strong precedents for such stories. Myths of a similar godman had existed in pagan societies for many hundreds of years before the birth of Yeshua. The earliest known is the Egyptian legend of Osiris, which became linked with the Greek story of Dionysus. The basic story was the same, grafted on to existing mythology and beliefs. So, for example, the legendary godman became known as Mithras in Persia (now Iran) and Attis in Asia Minor (Turkey).

It is very difficult to believe that these tales, well known to the authors of the gospels, were not the source for the Christian nativity story. Just as God (Jehovah) was reported to have mystically impregnated Mary, so it was related that Zeus impregnated Semele, also a virgin, with one of his thunderbolts, to conceive Dionysus, the 'Son of Zeus'. Attis and Adonis were also characterised as the products of unions between mortal virgin women and gods.

As well as borrowing the theme, Christianity also copied the details of pagan myths and ceremonies. Dionysus was, like Yeshua, depicted as having been born in an ox stall. The 'wise men' who came to the birth of Yeshua are described as 'magi', the name given to followers of the Persian godman Mithras. His birth, on December 25th like Yeshua's, was said to have been witnessed by three shepherds.

In another version, the birth of the godman Aion was celebrated on January 6th, a date which some Christian groups have recognised as Yeshua's birthday.

These dates, around the turn of year, reflect the fact that what is being celebrated is a pagan festival of the winter solstice, the point when the earth in the northern hemisphere begins to turn back towards the sun. That happens now on December 21st but the date was once, according to the old Julian calendar, December 25th.

Other details of pagan myth were also adopted into the biography of Yeshua. Dionysus, for example, is often pictured astride a donkey, such symbolism indicating a triumph over lust or the lower self. The gospel story also has Yeshua riding on a donkey on his way into Jerusalem. This links with the pagan myth and it fulfils the Old Testament prophecy of Zechariah, that a victorious King of the Jews would enter the city in this way.

In the pagan myths, the godman is often killed and like Yeshua miraculously reborn. Dionysus like Yeshua was hung on a tree. Osiris was said to have descended into hell, before rising on the third day and ascending into heaven – following precisely the letter of the Christian creeds adopted many hundreds of years later!

The idea of divine communion by eating the sacrificed god was practised in pagan cults. Followers of Mithras, for example, were offered a sacrament of consecrated bread and water mixed with wine. Writers Freke and Gandy have, in *The Jesus Mysteries*, pointed out the similarities between an inscription quoting

Mithras and a passage in John's gospel attributed to Yeshua.

Here is the pagan godman Mithras speaking first:

> He who will not eat of my body and drink of my blood, so that he will be made one with me and I with him, the same shall not know salvation.

And now, Yeshua:

> ...unless you eat of the flesh of the Son of Man and drink his blood, you have no life in you... He who eats my flesh and drinks my blood abides in me, and I in him.
> (John 6, 53-56)

Not just the sentiment but the wording of these two passages is remarkably similar. The Mithraic rituals came first, and the simple fact is that the early Christians borrowed from them.

As Paul reports it, in his letter to the Corinthians, dated around CE 54, he gained the inspiration from Yeshua. Since Paul never met Yeshua, he must have meant some visionary or mystical experience, similar to his conversion on the way to Damascus:

> For I received from the Lord what I also delivered to you, that the Lord Jesus on the night when he was betrayed took bread, and when he had given thanks, he broke it, and said, 'This is my body which is for you. Do this in remembrance of me.' In the same way also the cup, after supper, saying, 'This cup is the new covenant in my blood. Do this, as often as you drink it, in remembrance of me.' For as often as you eat this bread and drink the cup, you proclaim the Lord's death until he comes.
> (Corinthians I, 11, 23-26)

What Paul did was link the pagan ritual with both the special Passover meal, which Yeshua and his followers had celebrated, and the normal Jewish practice of blessing bread, breaking it, and handing it round with wine at the start of a meal. The 'new covenant', it should be noted, in which this ritual played a central part, was the sacrifice of the godman Yeshua to atone for the sins of the world. As Paul would have it, the new covenant was there to replace the defunct old covenant of Jewish Law.

However, Jews would have regarded and did regard the idea of eating the body of their sacrificed god as abhorrent and blasphemous. This was one reason that Paul made little headway amongst Jews in gaining converts for his new religion, while succeeding in attracting Gentiles. Paul and his followers initiated the eucharist, leaving gospel authors writing later to incorporate a prototype ceremony into the 'last supper' officiated over by Yeshua. But the words that are put into Yeshua's mouth in the synoptic gospels were, as Paul had stated, those revealed to Paul in a claimed vision or dream years after the crucifixion.

It can be safely assumed that these gospel writers do not have a source for the eucharist ritual other than Paul. If they had, then Paul would have known about it and would not have needed to rely on his device of a heavenly vision. In addition, they have borrowed the wording from Paul's letter to the Corinthians which would have been available to them. Here, for example, is Mark's version:

> And as they were eating, he took bread, and blessed, and broke it, and gave it to them, and said, 'Take; this is my body.' And he took a cup, and when he had given thanks he gave it to them, and they all drank of it. And he said to them, 'This is my blood of the covenant, which is poured out for many'. (Mark 14, 22-24)

Paul's letters are earlier than the synoptics and this careful copying indicates that Paul, rather than anything else that might have been available, was the source. Paul, furthermore, is clear that he himself is the source through some form of mystical revelation. Thus, by his own admission, it was his invention.

Since Paul's first letter to the Corinthians can be dated to around CE 54, this gives an idea of when the Christian eucharist meal came into being. If it had long been adopted by Yeshua's Nazorean followers, then Paul's claim as the originator would have been seen, and could have been shown to be, demonstrably false.

The source for John's gospel, the long-lived disciple 'whom Jesus loved', had no recollection of such a ceremony. This is what he would have conveyed to the gospel's author. However, by the time this author was writing early in the second century CE, the practice had become widespread among Christian communities. He had to reconcile the evidence of his source with both the assertions in Paul's letter to the Corinthians and current practice. The gospel writer resolved the problem by inserting the idea as a saying by Yeshua:

> unless you eat the flesh of the Son of man and drink his blood, you have no life in you; he who eats my flesh and drinks my blood has eternal life, and I will raise him up at the last day. (John 6, 53-54)

He must have been aware, not least from his source, that this was not a concept that would have been entertained by Jews. So he portrays some of Yeshua's follower deserting him, in response to this teaching.

As Acts records it (Acts 2, 46), the followers of Yeshua continued in the early years after the crucifixion to attend the temple together and break bread at meals, entirely in the manner of ordinary Jews! There is no intimation of a separate ritual as described by Paul and then, I have suggested, retrospectively inserted into the story by the authors of Mark and the other gospels. There is no description of a break, as indicated by the author of John, within the Jewish, Nazorean fold. Around CE 40, there was no distinct communion meal ordained by Yeshua. The evidence indicates quite the opposite, that it was created later by Paul. Instructions to perform such a ritual are also missing from what James, as described in Acts, decided should be required from Gentile god fearers, in CE 48 (Acts 15, 19-21; 21, 25).

The letter shortly afterwards written to them, on the authority of James, may form the basis of the *Didache*, a brief document which early believers carried with them, incorporating 'The Teaching of the Lord by the Twelve Apostles to the Gentiles'. This has clearly been added to over time, but it nonetheless contains the core of James' ruling:

> If you are able to bear the whole yoke of the Lord, you will be perfect, but if you cannot, do what you can. Concerning food, bear what you can, but abstain strictly from food offered to idols, for it is worship of dead gods.
> (*Didache* 6, 2-3)

The phrasing not only echoes what James says in the account in Acts of the 'Jerusalem council', to which Paul was summoned, but it also encapsulates the view taken on circumcision and the observance of the whole of the Torah (Law). The proposition was that 'it is necessary to circumcise them, and to charge them to keep the Law of Moses.' To which the response was made, in the mouth of Simon Peter, 'Now therefore why do you make trial of God by putting a yoke upon the neck of the disciples (Gentile god fearers) that neither our fathers nor we have been able to bear?' (Acts 15, 5-10). Like other Jews, the Nazoreans believed that circumcision was required of Jews in order to be 'perfect'. Thus it was necessary for Jews to be saved, but would not be a requirement for Gentiles.

Comparative analysis by Alan Garrow has indicated that the *Didache* was composed before Paul's letter to the Thessalonians in CE 50 and his first letter to the Corinthians in CE 54. Ideas and wording used indicate that these letters were dependent on the *Didache*, rather than vice versa. If that is so, it means that the original for the *Didache* fits well in both composition and timing as the decree which James authorised to be sent out to Gentile converts to the Nazorean movement.

The *Didache* sets out prayers for a communal meal, but there is no statement about bread and wine symbolising Yeshua's body and blood, no reference to the sacrifice of Yeshua for mankind or his death, no mention even of a last Passover meal celebrated by Yeshua and his disciples. This was still to come in what Paul initiated and first set down in his first letter to the Corinthians.

Where did Paul get his ideas from? The pagan cult which prevailed in his native Tarsus was that of Mithraism, in which there *was* a special celebratory meal of wine and bread, with the hosts marked with the sign of a cross! The Christian act of communion today, even after so many years, faithfully reflects this earlier and original pagan ritual.

Mithras was worshiped as a sun god, the god of light, and indeed Sunday was the holy day observed by his followers and then by Christians.

One of the cultic symbols was a divine bull, symbol of spring or rebirth. Mithras is often depicted in sculptures and drawings in the act of killing the bull, surrounded by several other animals – a dog, snake, raven and scorpion. These animals are among those in the signs of the zodiac, representing constellations of stars, and this suggests that the tauroctony, the depiction of the slaying of the bull, had astrological significance.

Initiates were sometimes placed in a pit below a grid over which a bull was sacrificed, drenching them with blood. This washing in the blood of the sacrificed animal was seen as a necessary form of cleansing, preparation for salvation and eternal life. Following the sacrifice, the flesh of the bull was then consumed.

Worshippers believed that by participating in the ceremonial meal, eating the flesh and drinking the blood of the sacrificed bull, they would be born again. It was seen as a way of ensuring that after death, going before the Mithras for judgement, they would be granted a place in Paradise and eternal life. Possibly because of the cost involved, bread or fish was used in routine celebration in place of the flesh of the sacrificed bull and wine to symbolise the blood.

The eucharist meal which Paul introduced creatively recombined elements of the cult: bread and wine, blood and sacrifice for salvation, the washing away of sins, identification with and consuming the sacrificed god. The idea of consuming the body and drinking the blood of the god comes directly from Mithraism (see inscription quoted above, p 163). Paul in fact took over wholesale the physical elements of the Mithraic ceremonial meal. In Tarsus, and later at Antioch, Paul was able to gain converts to his new version of Judaism by offering pagan worshippers the comfort of keeping their existing rituals, with 'Jesus' substituted as the symbolic sacrifice guaranteeing eternal life.

Moreover, what had been adopted as a ritual of necessity (since bulls could not routinely be sacrificed) became the preferred form – and animal sacrifice was done away with. This would have increased the appeal of the new, recombined religion among the majority who could not afford expensive sacrifices. A seven-stage Mithraic ranking system, representing enlightenment or spiritual progress, was also discarded. With the sect freed of these requirements, it became easier to belong.

In drawing elements from Judaism, Paul removed another barrier, the requirement for circumcision. Indeed, all that was required of followers was that they participate in the ritual and affirm their belief.

In the process, the connection with the historical Yeshua, a mortal potential Jewish liberator was lost. So too was the emphasis which he and his brother James and their Nazorean followers had placed on deeds, rather than empty ritual and belief or 'faith'.

Though Christianity dominates now as one of the world's major religions, it was in the balance which of the competing mystery cults the Romans would adopt as the Empire's official religion. Mithraism was tried first of all. In CE 304, Mithras was declared Protector of the Roman Empire. But, just a few years later, the Roman Emperor Constantine opted instead for Christianity. It may indeed be that Constantine recognised the elements that the two religions had in common, thanks in large part to the creative efforts of Paul, and saw this as an advantage, in potentially drawing on a larger pool of existing devotees. The Emperor apparently saw no contradiction in supporting either or both of the cults. After converting to Christianity, he retained for himself the title, 'Pontificus Maximus', high priest in the cult of Mithraism.

The adoption of Christianity nonetheless marked the beginning of the end of the old world order. Under Constantine, the old religion lost its preeminence and some of its support. The shift continued over the years, culminating in more active prohibition under Theodosius towards the end of the fourth century. Pagan worship was banned and blood sacrifice prohibited. Temples were pulled down and Christian churches built on their foundations. Paganism was persecuted out of existence and many pagan writings, encompassing science and philosophy as well as religion, were destroyed.

In this way, the myths and ritual which predated Christianity, and from which Christianity borrowed, came to be disregarded or forgotten. At the time, however, the compelling similarities between Christianity and pagan theology and myth were only too apparent.

This was no problem for pagan philosophers who saw their tales as allegories, fictional devices to convey essential truths. But Christians now had a religion with a stamp of authority, the official religion of empire, and the story of the killed and resurrecting godman, born of a union between a mortal virgin and an immortal god, was taken as the literal truth.

This created enormous problems for early church writers, given the fact that the details surrounding the birth of Yeshua and other biographical details in the gospels were clearly and evidently derived from preexisting pagan myth. There was really no answer to this (other than eventually to suppress critics out of existence). Catholic apologists had to resort to ludicrous and lame explanations such as 'diabolical mimicry'. This was that the devil, knowing that the saviour of the world would eventually be born, invented all these exactly parallel stories beforehand solely in order to confuse would-be believers! As the second century Pagan critic Celsus caustically pointed out, what was so special about Christians and their myth that they should insist that it was true, while maintaining that all the other divine birth myths were false – simple allegories as Celsus himself readily admitted?

Among the advantages that Christianity had for its successful dissemination was that it was based, or claimed to be based, on an historical character. It had from the fourth century the powerful backing of Rome, through a coincidence of interests between an authoritarian church structure and the centralised power of the Roman state, derived from the Emperor. It appeared to have an ancient pedigree, through the Jewish Old Testament, and it incorporated the essentials of existing, popular mystery religions. It offered salvation for the individual by faith alone, without the trappings of detailed Jewish ritual observance and practices such as circumcision.

That it was based on myths and deliberate falsifications counted for little against this powerful combination of forces. The Emperor Constantine convened a council in Nicaea in CE 325 to decide and codify the religion's beliefs in a fixed creed to which all followers had to adhere. He appointed Eusebius, bishop of Caesarea, to write a history of Christianity.

Eusebius carried out the task – more of a rewrite than a write – assiduously. As he readily admitted, he included only that which 'might rebound to the glory of the church' while suppressing that which might disgrace it! Old copies of the gospels were recalled and scribes were appointed, under Eusebius, to make new copies for distribution throughout Christendom. These copies would incorporate into the gospel text the results of the deliberations of the council, which for example decided by a majority that Jesus (Yeshua) was the Son of God. This was the culminating phase in a process by which the gospel stories had been progressively altered to fit the Church's evolving doctrine.

In this way, Mary was made into a virgin, even though she was either married to or betrothed to the father of Yeshua at the time of his conception and then birth – and even though she went on to have several other children. She was made into the consort of God, just as in the pagan myths, despite having a mortal husband.

Yeshua was made into the literal Son of God, despite the fact that he was regarded by his followers as a Jewish messiah, reputedly tracing his ancestry as a son of David back to the old kings of Israel. If his ancestor had been David, he must therefore have had a human father!

As has been noted, Jews saw themselves as sons of the Father. The progeny of the line of David was believed to have been promised by God to be treated as his sons. So 'Son of God', if applied to Yeshua at the time, could well have carried this messianic, though not literal, meaning. The other title of respect that Yeshua took on, Son of Man, was also one which would have been attributed to a Jewish national liberator (Daniel 7, 13). It is a form which was also often used as an elaborate way of saying 'man', as in mankind, or just 'a man'.

It is significant that, in the gospel sayings attributed to Yeshua, he sometimes refers to himself as the 'Son of Man' but never as the 'Son of God'. This latter phrase crops up in two ways. It is either put on the lips of someone else, such as Nathanael in John's gospel or Simon Peter in Matthew. Or it is put forward as a pitch by the gospel author or more often a later editor, as in some versions of the opening statement in Mark's gospel.

As already noted, the proposition that Yeshua was literally the Son of God appears very clearly to have its origins in pagan myth. It is also at odds with an understanding of a coherent universe, governed by laws which do not change randomly or at the whim of a divine creator. But, quite apart from such considerations, the idea is also denied by the detail of the gospel evidence. In the earliest of the canonical gospels, Mark, a rich man comes up to Yeshua and addresses him as 'good teacher'. Yeshua replies, 'Why do you call me good? No one is good but God alone' (Mark 10, 17-22). This early author, or his source, thus conveys a view that Yeshua saw himself as, and was, simply a man. Not God or a Son of God, who can be presumed by virtue of his divinity to be both perfect and good.

It is hardly likely that, as church doctrine accumulated into a full-blown cult of Yeshua as the Son of God, this contradictory detail was inserted into the text. It is far more probable that it is a surviving piece of the original tale. By the time Matthew was writing, the cult had become well established. And Matthew, who used Mark as a source, was acutely aware that this source material did not fit in with the new orthodoxy.

So, he altered the words around a bit! In the original version in Mark, the rich young man asks, 'Good teacher, what must I do to inherit eternal life?' In Matthew (19, 16-22), the accolade is deflected from Yeshua to the action required. Now the young man asks, 'Teacher, what good deed must I do, to have eternal life?' The reply, in order to conform with the alteration, loses its meaning: 'Why do you ask me about what is good? One there is who is good.'

But, why should he not ask? Yeshua is after all a Nazorean leader, a teacher, and can quite well tell the man what is good behaviour. Indeed, Yeshua immediately goes on to cite the commandments! Matthew might just as well have cut out the now garbled response.

In the *Didache*, in origin I have argued a Jewish Nazorean document, Jesus/Yeshua is referred to not as the Son of God but as God's servant/child. This is a title which has overtones of the idea of God's suffering servant in the Old Testament (Isaiah 52 13-15; 53, 1-12).

Doctrines such as Yeshua as the Son of God, as they evolved, were written in to the gospels. Some ideas, like that of the Trinity or Yeshua's presumed identity with God (being of one substance with the father) were adopted, without any basis provided in the text. The creation of self-standing creeds represents a further level in the process of editing source material.

Yeshua was deliberately made to appear in the gospels as estranged from his immediate family, even though his brothers were his helpers and his successors, inextricably involved with the same project. His own personal details were suppressed, in making him into an odd, asexual person in a Jewish world where there was an obligation for most to marry and have children. But traces remain in the text which indicate what the real situation might have been.

As many scholars agree, the characters Mary Magdalene and Mary, the sister of Martha and Lazarus, were probably based on the same person. Bearing the same first name, they fulfil the role of Yeshua's companion in different parts of the gospel text. But they never appear together in the same scene, as they might well have done had two different women been involved. There is just one moment when the two characters overlap and merge into one.

All the gospels have the story of a women anointing Yeshua with precious ointment, in the manner a Jewish king, prior to his final journey into Jerusalem. The oil is identified in two of the gospels as spikenard, and described in three as contained in an alabaster jar.

Matthew and Mark place the incident in Bethany, at the house of Simon the leper (Aramaic grb 'garba'). This is possibly a mistranslation in Greek of the name of someone known by his trade as a jar maker. In Aramaic, this is spelt the same, grb, but pronounced 'garaba'. In these gospels, the stories are virtually identical, and in each case the woman anoints Yeshua's head with the precious oil. Luke adds the detail that Simon, whose house it is, is a Pharisee.

In John's gospel, the location is also Bethany and it is Mary, sister of Martha and Lazarus, who anoints Yeshua. Both Luke and John agree on significant detail: the woman anoints Yeshua's feet and wipes his feet with her hair.

So it is clearly the same incident that is being described in these two gospels. But in Luke, the action is performed by 'a woman of the city who was a sinner'. Yeshua cures her, that is reforms her, by forgiving her sins. Then, a few lines later, Mary Magdalene 'from whom seven demons had gone out' is listed among female followers of Yeshua who had been cured of evil spirits. The seven demons were of course the seven vices or deadly sins, and so it would seem that the woman who was a sinner was Mary Magdalene. This makes it possible for the accounts in John and Luke's gospels, which agree in other respects, to agree also on this – providing Mary sister of Martha and Mary Magdalene are one and the same.

In this incident, in which Yeshua lays claim to the throne of David, the two characters named Mary are thus interchangeable, fulfilling one historical role.

Mary was among a number of women who provided Yeshua and the disciples with financial support. Yeshua is described in the non canonical gospels of Mary and of Philip as Mary's partner, in the latter kissing her often and loving her more than all the disciples. It is also hardly credible, given the strict rules of behaviour at the time, that Yeshua could have stayed with Mary at her family's house in Bethany, without being married to her. In addition to this, there are several instances in the gospels where behaviour indicates that she was his partner and married to him.

In the story of Lazarus for example, in John's gospel, Yeshua was summoned to help Lazarus who was sick but delayed coming to his aid (John 11, 1-44). When Yeshua arrived, Lazarus had apparently died and was entombed. Martha came out of the house to meet Yeshua and criticised him for arriving too late. In the meantime, Mary remained inside until called out by Yeshua. Both women had lost a brother and both had equal cause to be angry. But, while Martha felt free to confront Yeshua, Mary behaved as a Jewish wife would have done, meekly waiting to be summoned.

In the gospel of Luke, when Yeshua returned to Bethany, Mary sat his feet while Martha was left to do the cooking and serving (Luke 10, 38-42). Martha then complained at the lack of assistance. But instead of making her complaint directly to her sister, she directed it through Yeshua which indicates that Mary was under his authority. This she certainly would have been, as his wife.

There is also an evocative story in John's gospel of Mary outside the empty tomb encountering Yeshua, whom she at first mistakenly believed to be the gardener. Yeshua cannot contain himself and calls out her name. She replies 'teacher' (or master). In New Testament translations, Yeshua's reply is usually given as 'do not touch me'. But a more accurate translation of the original Greek would be 'do not *hold on to* me'. The part relieved, part grief stricken, Mary was clearly clinging for dear life to her man, who was then very much a solid object and very much alive. This is notwithstanding the qualification, no doubt added in editing the story, 'for I have not yet ascended to the Father'.

It is also indicative that, where the central female characters are mentioned in the gospels, in nearly every instance Mary Magdalene is mentioned first, before Mary the mother of Yeshua and Salome, the wife of Zebedee. As the sister of his mother Mary, Salome was also Yeshua's aunt. Order of listing was taken very seriously at the time and indicated order of ranking – and the *only* person who would have ranked above Yeshua's mother in order of importance would have been his wife!

There is thus both presumptive evidence and strong circumstantial evidence to support the idea that Mary Magdalene was indeed the wife of Yeshua. In the story of the marriage at Cana, described in John's gospel, the names of the bridegroom and bride are omitted. But the fact that Yeshua went to the wedding feast with his disciples, his mothers and his brothers suggests that he was not merely a guest but an integral part of the proceedings. This is confirmed by the detail that, in dealing with the problem of a shortage of wine, the problem was first referred to Yeshua's mother as the host. So it was therefore one of her children who was getting married.

Since the situation was then dealt with by Yeshua, it can be presumed that he was the bridegroom. Indeed, the master of ceremonies immediately offers his compliments to the bride-groom for sorting out the problem! So this was, on the evidence, Yeshua's own wedding.

Yeshua could have remained celibate like his brother James, as one of the senior members, the men of the council, in the ranks of the Nazoreans/Essenes. What information there is, however, indicates that he was was married, like Simon Peter and like the vast majority of Jews.

Indeed, if he were a claimant to the throne of Israel, as the gospels suggest he claimed to be and Pilate believed him to be, then he would have needed heirs to carry on the royal line. As the oldest of the brothers, it may have been incumbent on him to marry and if possible have sons.

It is ironic that the only support for Christians who claim that Yeshua was not married lies in the possibility that he was a member of an exclusive Jewish inner order, utterly strict and uncompromising in its adherence to the Torah. This would be indicative of a man who wanted to reinforce the existing covenant and not, like Paul a few years later, create an entirely new one.

The lie that misrepresents Yeshua's marital status in the gospels is one of deliberate omission. It adds to other lies, that he was at odds with his brothers, that he was hostile to most of his fellow Jews, that he was the product of a union involving God impregnating a mortal woman, that his mother was a virgin and that he was, like other mythical pagan godmen, raised miraculously to life again. The gospel writers elaborated, excised and edited.

The authors of Matthew and Luke even found support for the 'virgin Mary' thesis in a prediction by the Old Testament prophet Isaiah who apparently wrote, 'Behold a virgin shall conceive and bear a son and shall call his name Immanuel' (Isaiah 7, 14). This was however based on a mistranslation. Hebrew had two words for virgin, one of which simply meant a young woman. But in the Greek translation of the Old Testament Septuagint, undertaken for Jews who had no Hebrew, there was only one meaning, that of a woman who was physically intact because she had not had sex.

In the original Hebrew, Isaiah had simply predicted that a young woman would conceive and bear a child who would become a person of importance. Not a virgin, and not a virginal Mary whose biography was manipulated to fit her into this role. There were not enough words in Greek and as a consequence the original prophecy of Isaiah was mistranslated.

The Catholic Church simply ignores the errors and misrepresentations that, for the most part, its own people introduced. The literalist version of Christianity is a sad travesty of pagan myths and of the Nazorean Jews' beliefs.

But when the distortions, the fanciful embroidery and imaginative padding, are stripped away, what is left? Some writers say that the answer is that there is nothing at all. There is no historical Yeshua, or alternatively none that can be reliably ascertained. So, is there anything at all in the text that can be relied upon, as real first-century gospel truth?

What might help in deciding what traces there may be in the gospels of an original story is some unaltered and genuine document from the period. Something that would give an idea of contemporary style and convention, as well as the writer's concerns and preoccupations. Ideally, it would have been written in Judea, by Jews about the time that Yeshua lived. It is a lot to ask.

Chapter 7: Hidden text

The irony is that, for Christians, the whole of Jewish history is perceived through one moment frozen in time and everything happening before or afterwards is related to it. For the people who lived through it, and Jews now, their history is and was a continuous flow, a flux with events and circumstances interdependent. However, when it comes to evidence of what happened, what Christians have now in the gospels is flux reintroduced: layer upon layer of centuries-long editing and interpolation, inserted prophecies, links to earlier writings, people invented or omitted, names and places changed, characters distorted or merged.

What would it be like to have a genuine snapshot of events, perceived through Jewish eyes, an authentic commentary from the first century? It would obviously be only one view, not necessarily objective and not necessarily with any sense of historical perspective. Just a snapshot, from one point of view.

It seems evident that we do not have this. But let's imagine that a scroll has just been found, miraculously preserved where it had many centuries ago been hastily hidden in the foundations of the temple in Jerusalem. The date when the document was deposited, and so also the latest date when it might have been written, is CE 68, a short while before the Romans razed the temple to the ground at the end of the Jewish uprising. It was written during the siege by a zealous Jew belonging to the Nazorean movement, a member of the so-called Church at Jerusalem. It sets down the Nazoreans' concerns, their take on what has been happening.

Some allowance must be made for contemporary convention: so we will assume that the writer gave his views via a series of commentaries on an Old Testament prophetic book, relating it verse by verse to what had been happening at the time. What might the resulting text have looked like?

For a start, I am going to make a reasonable assumption that a central figure will be their own leader James – only a few years previously put to death at the hands of the Sadducee elite.

The text will contain line after line describing and condemning the Romans, 'quick and valiant in war', causing many to perish, 'plundering the cities of the earth', with 'their evil plotting' inspiring 'all the nations with fear and dread'. It will describe how the Romans encircled the 'fortresses of the people' 'with a mighty host', picking them off one by one, until only Jerusalem remained. That is the reality which, at the time of writing, the scroll author will have faced.

But what caused the successive defeats in the writer's view is really the judgement of God on the 'sins of the inhabitants' of these cities (a common theme of the Old Testament prophets in explaining Jewish misfortunes and also one used by Josephus in explaining the Jewish rebellion's disastrous outcome). God will, however, ultimately reward the virtuous who 'keep his commandments' and keep their faith in his word.

However, in the meantime, one particular sin has brought God's judgement on the people. This is the behaviour of those members of the 'council' (Sanhedrin) and the Jewish community who kept silent and gave no help when Paul, 'who flouted the Law', came and stirred up an attack on James.

For the writer, the author of this hypothetical text, Paul will be described simply as the 'liar'. He will be depicted as 'raising a congregation on deceit', causing many 'to perform a service of vanity for the sake of its glory'. But these people will ultimately labour in vain and be punished by God.

The text will also attack the Sadducee High Priest Ananus, who under Roman patronage 'ruled over Israel', forsaking God and his precepts 'for the sake of riches'. Ananus, the author will charge, accumulated wealth by confiscating the goods of 'men of violence who rebelled against God', and also by exploiting ordinary people, robbing 'the poor'. And, perhaps even worse, the writer will maintain that Ananus failed to maintain purity laws and observe sexual prohibitions, living 'in ways of abominations amidst every unclean defilement.'

Ananus will be condemned most particularly for the 'iniquity committed' against James (according to Josephus, stoned to death at his instigation as High Priest) and also against 'the men of his Council', that is the Council of the Nazoreans under the triumvirate of three, including James. The crucial conflict will be described (as in other sources) as having taken place on the Day of Atonement, as celebrated by the Nazoreans/Essenes. On this day, 'their Sabbath of repose', Ananus pursued James to consume him with his 'venomous fury' to (or in) 'the house of his exile.'

For this crime, and for his offences generally against 'the poor', God will deliver Ananus 'into the hands of his enemies' who will inflict 'horrors of evil diseases/defilements' on him and take 'vengeance upon his body of flesh.'

The Romans will prevail, securing tribute from 'all the peoples' but ultimately 'on the Day of Judgement, God will destroy from the earth all idolatrous and wicked men' including the Romans who 'sacrifice to their standards and worship their weapons of war'. It is a fair if obvious prediction: like all others, the Roman Empire would ultimately collapse.

Such a scroll would provide a plausible (but hypothetical) story or prospectus from the point of view of one group: supporters of James, opposed to the Romans and collaborating Sadducee High Priests, contemptuous of Paul as the would-be infiltrator, the 'liar' who seeks to subvert and misrepresent Jewish Law. It offers a likely shocking view of Paul for Christians, who have subsequently elevated him to the status of sainthood while ignoring the many apparent defects of his character. Aside from the malice and vanity expressed in his letters, these failings include his admitted participation in a pogrom and at least one recorded murder, that of Stephen!

But the prospectus, as I have presented it, does not exist. There was no such scroll hastily written and buried for posterity in the temple foundations at Jerusalem, at least none that has been found.

But I have not imagined the text. It is unedited, authentic, first century. It is real.

We do have *precisely* the description as I have given it in a genuine scroll, a contemporary document, tallying with details in Josephus and with what is known from several sources about James, *except* that all the main characters are referred to by pseudonyms, rather than by their own names. The text in the document, word for word in translation, is real. The quotes are all as I have given them.

But the names the author uses are the 'Teacher of Righteousness', the 'Wicked Priest' and the 'Liar' or 'Spouter of Lies'. For the sake of the present argument, these pseudonyms have been translated respectively as James, the brother of Yeshua, for the 'Teacher of Righteousness', the High Priest Ananus for the 'Wicked Priest' and Paul (or Saul) for the 'Liar' or 'Spouter of Lies'. The text as quoted is from a Dead Sea Scroll, a Commentary on the Book of Habakkuk, hidden in a cave at Qumran probably in CE 68 when it appears Vespasian took time off from the siege of Jerusalem to destroy the Essenes' settlement.

The Commentary on Habakkuk is within a tradition of the 'pesher' in which old biblical texts were analysed and then used as an explanation for contemporary events. While in this case one text has been scrutinised line by line, quotations were sometimes taken from a number of sources.

There are a number of fragments of such texts among the recovered Dead Sea scrolls, eighteen or so in all. But each of these is an original commentary on an Old Testament source. Unlike many other documents found at Qumran, there are no copies. This is significant in that it suggests that the peshers may have been fairly ephemeral; in each case the writer analysed past prophecy in an effort to make sense of current events. When the situation had moved on, and the old prophecy seemed less relevant to a changed situation, the analysis might not have been deemed worth keeping. At least, the motivation for disseminating it by copying would have diminished. So the pesher would then have been destroyed or put to one side.

The commentary on Habakkuk was found in a cave where it had been placed with other documents, including a copy of the community's code of conduct and a War Rule which described how the Sons of Light would ultimately defeat the army of the Sons of Darkness. It appears that this pesher was not a discarded and accidentally preserved document, something no longer of any great importance. It must have been seen as still crucially relevant by whoever placed it in the cave. There is a strong case that this was done when the community at Qumran faced Roman attack, that is in or just before CE 68, and that the events to which it relates involving the Teacher of Righteousness and the Wicked Priest were in the relatively recent past.

The Book of Habakkuk itself dates from the period about BCE 600 when Judah's desire for freedom and independence, as Assyrian power declined, was cut short by the rise of the Babylonians (Chaldeans) whose King Nebuchadnezzar took Jerusalem and forced many of its people into exile. How could their righteous and loving God let this happen, the prophet wondered? The answer was the consolation that, as in the past, good would ultimately triumph and the evildoers would be overthrown.

The writer of the Commentary on Habakkuk was trying to draw lessons for his own people's predicament, in some ways parallel to that described by Habakkuk.

Another pesher, a commentary on psalm 37 from the Old Testament Book of Psalms and similar in its style of writing, was found in a different cave. This too refers to the conflict between the Wicked Priest and the community's Teacher of

Righteousness, also a Priest. The Wicked Priest is described as plotting to have the Teacher put to death and then laying hands on him. But, apparently, at the point of writing this pesher, the Teacher was still alive and the writer concludes, in the words of the psalm, that God 'will not abandon him to his [that is, the Wicked Priest's] power or let him be condemned when he is brought to trial.'

The team of academics who first pieced together and translated the scrolls from the early nineteen fifties onwards were for the most part western scholars with Christian belief or a Christian background. Archaeological evidence from artifacts left behind at the settlement at Qumran, particularly coins, indicated that it was occupied for about two hundred years from BCE 130 up to the point when it was destroyed by the Romans during the Jewish uprising. There is a gap in the record when the settlement was apparently ruined and abandoned for some years in the latter part of the first century BCE.

It is possible to envisage different points of time at which the commentaries on Habakkuk and psalm 37 may have been written, during the 200 year period when the settlement at Qumran was occupied. But the international team were predisposed to believe that these, and other documents expressing the messianic expectations of the group, were created early on. The community's teaching arose, according to this view, from the common ground out of which which Christianity and Rabbinic Judaism also sprang. But it could be safely consigned as an evolutionary dead-end.

Accepting a much later date, in the first century CE, would have made that safe presumption much less feasible. A messianic group from the same time, the same area, and with many of the same ideas, organisation and practices as the early Nazorean followers of Yeshua could be a parallel or linked movement. It could even be, in effect, the same movement. And, since the gospels are known to have been subjected to centuries of alteration and addition, the scrolls – pristine from their nineteen centuries old time-capsule – would be the more authentic voice of Yeshua's movement. In the scrolls, however, there is no virgin birth, no person who is half-God half-man, no miraculous resurrection from the dead, none of these trappings introduced by later Christianity. The messiah the community expected to rescue the Jewish people and defeat their foes would be a man, a Davidic King. Possibly even two messiahs (literally persons anointed to power) might arise, a High Priest and a King.

Such an interpretation was something that Christian academics, treating their beliefs as absolutes, simply could not contemplate. Their rigid and blinkered perspective can be summed up in the dismissive comment by one of the team, Dr Geza Vermes, that 'no properly Judeo-Christian characteristic emerges from the scrolls and unless we are much mistaken, the zealots were scarcely a company of ascetics' (*The Dead Sea Scrolls in English*).

On both counts, in this extraordinarily complacent statement, Vermes is profoundly mistaken. The community of the 'poor' who wrote the scrolls pooled their property, practised baptism by immersion, participated in solemn communal meals, had a central council of twelve with a ruling triumvirate of three priests and advocated strict adherence to the Law – just like the contemporaneous Nazorean community under James. Their senior members were celibate, or aspired to celibacy, like Simeon and James. They engaged in ritual cold bathing, like Simon Peter and James.

They described themselves as 'the poor', followers of 'the Way', men of the 'New Covenant', in exactly the terminology applied to or used by the early followers of Yeshua and James.

Some of the documents they produced have uncanny parallels with sections of the gospels, for example the 'Messianic Apocalypse', which speaks of the messiah who will 'release the captives, make the blind see and raise the downtrodden', as in exactly the same sequence in the gospels of both Luke and Matthew. Another scroll fragment looks forward to the messiah who will be 'named son of God and they shall call him son of the Most High', precisely the terms that the author of Luke's gospel has the angel Gabriel use in describing the child who will be born to Mary (Luke 1, 32-35). So what then did Luke, writing much later, use as a source or template for his story? The similarities suggest that the gospel authors knew about and used the Essenes' material. Or they may, alternatively, have been working from a common source.

There is indeed a case from the scroll documents for an early 'Essene'-Nazorean link or, in Vermes' terminology, a Judeo-Christian characteristic and origin.

Vermes' comment that 'zealots were scarcely a company of ascetics' carries all sorts of mistaken implications. Asceticism, meaning the practice of austerity and self-denial, has been a characteristic of groups both peaceful and violent (for example, the samurai) right down to the present day. If he meant to say 'pacifists', which zealots unless purely religious were not, then he is also mistaken in implying this as an attribute of the Essenes. The evidence from the scrolls points to the community being prepared to envisage violence to achieve its ends. It produced an elaborate plan for a final apocalyptic battle with the 'kittim' (Romans) in which the community, as the Sons of Light, would overcome the company of darkness. It called on God's vengeance against its enemies: the Romans, 'scoffers', the Wicked Priest, the spouter of lies.

The settlement at Qumran, shows some evidence, moreover, of having been fortified. If the scroll authors can in any way be described as Essenes, then they were at least militant Essenes.

Which may perhaps not be such a contradiction. Although Josephus, in his *Jewish War*, describes the Essenes as living a rigorous, religiously strict and simple life, he also reveals that during the War, the Romans 'racked and twisted, burnt and broke them, subjecting them to every torture yet invented in order to make them blaspheme the Lawgiver or eat some forbidden food, but could not make them do either...'. It would seem that Josephus is being just a trifle disingenuous. If this were just a band of mild ascetics, why would the Romans have bothered to go to such lengths when they had a lot else to do putting down an insurrection and dealing with genuine militant zealots?

A little illumination is cast on the situation with Josephus' later description in *Antiquities* of a 'fourth' or zealot philosophy whose adherents 'have a passion for liberty that is almost unconquerable, since they are convinced that God alone is their leader and master'. Furthermore, 'they think little of submitting to death in unusual forms and permitting vengeance to fall on kinsman and friends if only they may avoid calling any man master.'

This has echoes of the similar resolution Josephus describes as being shown by the Essenes. It may be, as I have suggested in *Censored Messiah,* that the lines between groups were not so sharply drawn. From the religiously extremely zealous often come the politically extremely zealous, especially in societies where religious belief and political identity are intertwined. As Josephus records, one of the Jewish commanders in the war against Rome is named as 'John the Essene', so here at least was one Essene who was not at all pacifist!

There is in fact no direct evidence that the scroll writers would have described themselves, as 'Essenes', militant or otherwise. It is better to regard them in their own terms as religiously strict, exclusive, zealous for the Law, messianic nationalists, prepared to suffer for their beliefs, prepared if necessary to fight.

That certainly makes possible a first century CE date of origin for key scrolls such as the Habakkuk and psalm 37 commentaries, when the concerns of the scroll writers would have reflected the events and circumstances around them. The international team dismissed this possibility, not for any reasons to do with evidence, but purely because of their preconceptions. So, what credence can be placed on their theory of a first or even second century BCE origin for the scrolls and the key characters with which these are concerned?

The interpretation by Vermes is that the Teacher of Righteousness and his followers objected to Hasmonean (Maccabean) kings also taking on the position of High Priest, when these roles should have been separate and when the Hasmoneans lacked the proper priestly credentials. The Teacher and his community regarded themselves as the elect of Israel, the only ones still following God's holy Law. So they took themselves off into exile at Qumran, to wait for the day of reckoning when the transgressors (as they saw it) would be overthrown.

Jonathan, one of the sons of Mattathias, was the first to take on the combined role of High Priest and client King under the Seleucids (Syrian Greeks) in BCE 152. A few years later, his brother Simon succeeded him and the combined roles were made hereditary. According to Vermes, Jonathan (though it could equally, according to this theory, have been Simon) is the 'Wicked Priest' whose rule the Teacher of Righteousness objected to and caused him to go with his followers into exile. The Wicked Priest then pursued the Teacher and killed him.

There are some very major flaws with such a theory. In the first place, the Romans did not appear until much later on when they intervened, as Seleucid power crumbled, in a civil war between contenders for the Hasmonean throne. In BCE 63, the Roman general Pompey toppled the Hasmonean King Aristobulus II. Judea then became a Roman dominion indirectly administered at first through a Hasmonean High Priest, stripped of any royal title, and then by Herod, an Idumean client King.

It has to be presumed, by Vermes' theory, that the author of the commentary on Habakkuk was writing with passion some time in the second half of the first century BCE about the Romans, only recently on the scene, and simultaneously about the crimes of long-dead Hasmoneans a century before! This must be very unlikely. The form of the commentary, with attention switching verse by verse back and forth between the 'kittim' or Romans and the Teacher, the Wicked Priest and the Spouter of Lies, strongly suggests on the contrary that the author was dealing with what to him were contemporaneous subjects.

Another difficulty is that the Romans were at this time largely absent rulers, governing their province through local adminis-trators. They were not tramping through Judea, encircling and taking city after city, destroying all in their path. At least, they were not doing that until much later, at the time of the Jewish uprising well into the first century CE. This most definitely provides a much better context for the Habakkuk pesher, when the Romans were acting precisely as the pesher describes.

The destruction of the Qumran settlement some time during the latter part of the first century BCE, its abandonment for a number of years and then its reoccupation about the time of the imposition of Roman direct rule in CE 6 is put down by one of the international team, Roland De Vaux, to the effects of an earthquake (in *Archaeology and the Dead Sea Scrolls*). But, had that happened, it would not have been too difficult for the inhabitants swiftly to rebuild their relatively uncomplicated mud brick buildings. Longer abandonment suggests a political event, a crisis, something which turned out the inhabitants and prevented them from coming back. This in turn suggests that the people eventually reoccupying Qumran may not have been the same as those who were there before.

As Neil Silberman suggests (in *The Hidden Scrolls*), a Hasmonean settlement beside the Dead Sea might well have been cleared when Herod came to power. Then later, at the beginning of the first century CE, it could have become a refuge for zealots, angry at the excesses of powerful Herodians and the occupation by Rome. That is much more likely than an earthquake, for which there is no real evidence and which would not have had the consequences that de Vaux claims.

It is astonishing how glibly an 'official' theory can have been promoted that leaves so much unexplained. The team's hypothesis leaves two of the key characters, the Teacher of Righteousness and the Liar unidentified. It does not explain why the scroll authors felt it necessary to use pseudonyms. It makes inexplicable, if the alternative explanation for key scrolls of first century CE origin is rejected, why the community preserved scrolls from the past but then failed to comment on the horrors of the War with Rome, the schism and conflict going on all around them. It offers no reason why the Romans took the trouble, if the Essenes were merely harmless religious eccentrics, to obliterate the community at Qumran.

It is certainly relevant that the international team's *own* palaeographical analysis of the scrolls' script identified the style of both the Habakkuk and psalm 37 peshers as Hasmonean, within a time frame from BCE 30 to CE 70, that is well after the initial Roman intervention and into the period of nationalist messianism of the early Christian period.

It is a much better theory that the characters and people the scroll writers were describing were all from their very troublesome present, in the first century CE, when the Romans were rampaging throughout the land, when the temple was defiled by sacrifices to the Emperor and when many of the priestly caste were collaborators, tax gatherers and enforcers, beneficiaries of their subservience to Rome. This was also a time when Herodian rulers amassed wealth, engaged in such practices forbidden by the community as niece marriage and polluted the temple by their very presence. They were in fact from the community's perspective the very embodiment of evil, the three 'nets of belial', as described in the scrolls, set to catch Israel: riches, fornication and profanation of the temple. The theory of first century CE origins, on the evidence, offers a more comprehensive and coherent coverage of the facts.

There are now good candidates for the roles of Wicked Priest, Liar and Teacher of Righteousness whose interrelation accords well with what the scroll author attests. There's Paul who came into conflict with James and who *did* raise a congregation based on deceit, deceiving the Nazoreans as to what he was doing and deceiving his followers as to what the Nazoreans required of them. Paul was, as the analysis of his letters and Acts has shown, expert in deceit, seeking by his own admission to be 'all things to all men' to further his aims. There are instances in the letters which show that Paul was sensitive to criticisms made of him, for example that he had been spending on himself money collected for the Jerusalem community. He appears to have been aware of and stung by his epithet as the 'Liar' or 'Spouter of Lies', feeling the need to include the adjuration 'I do not lie!' when making significant statements about himself.

This happened when he claimed that, after having had his divine revelation, he did not consult with or even meet the apostles for several years (Galatians 1, 16-20). Paul asserts, 'In what I am writing to you, before God, I do not lie!' His claim, however, conflicts both with the account in Acts (9, 26) that he was initially rebuffed and also with common sense. His very first move, after receiving his wonderful vision, would surely have been to connect with those who had known Yeshua and find out more.

Paul also felt the need to protest that he wasn't lying, after making a whole litany of claims. At one point he claimed that he was a Hebrew, an Israelite and a descendant of Abraham (perhaps generally true for people of Semitic descent in Palestine, but *not true* in implying that Paul was a Jew). He also maintained that he was 'better' than them – 'these superlative apostles', 'false apostles, deceitful workmen, disguising themselves as apostles of Christ' (outrageous in contemporary terms, since Paul appears to be referring to the Nazorean followers who had actually worked with and known Yeshua, and certainly arguable from our perspective now). He adduced a whole list of sufferings that he could boast of, including receiving 39 lashes five times, being beaten with rods three times, shipwrecked three times, stoned once (a small wonder that he was still alive!) (Corinthians II, 11, 24-31). He protests that 'God ... knows that I do not lie!'

In one of the pastoral letters, presumed to have been written after Paul's time, the same formulation is used. Paul is given to claim that he was 'appointed a preacher and apostle... a teacher of the Gentiles' (*not true* against Paul's own assertions that he had received a visionary commission, though consistent with his own interpretation of the outcome of the 'Jerusalem Council'), adding that 'I am telling the truth, I am not lying' (Timothy, I, 2, 7). So *was* Paul aware that his opponents had dubbed him, 'The Liar'? It certainly does appear so.

As for a possible 'Wicked Priest', the High Priest Ananus was a contemporary of Paul and, as Josephus reports, responsible for James being stoned to death. There is evidence from other sources that this had something to do with a conflict on or over the Day of Atonement, when James went into the holy inner sanctum, as only a High Priest should, to intercede on behalf of his people. Ananus is therefore a plausible candidate, though it could also have been the former High Priest Ananias (see ch 10, p 291).

The scroll commentary on psalm 37, similar in form to the Habakkuk pesher, has the Wicked Priest seeking to have the Teacher of Righteousness put to death because he served the Law. As is clear from Acts and the Letter of James, what James stood for in opposition to Paul, the putative Spouter of Lies, was full adherence to the Jewish Law.

Once the Romans took direct control of Judea, after removing Herod's brutal and inept son Archelaus from the position of client king, the Roman-appointed High Priests were, as Josephus records (*Antiquities* XX 251), leaders of the nation. This is just as the Habakkuk commentary has it: the Wicked Priest (Ananus) 'ruled over Israel.' Ananus was indeed subsequently appointed to have administrative control over Jerusalem, and by extension Israel, after the outbreak of the uprising against Rome.

As Robert Eisenman has pointed out (in *The New Testament Code*), when the first century contemporary identifications are accepted, other pieces of the jigsaw fall into place. It had, for example, previously been surmised that the confrontation between the Wicked Priest and the Teacher of Righteousness indicates that the former (whoever that was) pursued the latter (whoever that was!) to Qumran and had the Teacher killed there:

> *Woe to him who causes his neighbours to drink; who pours out his venom to make them drunk that he may gaze on their feasts!* [*Hab 2, 15*]
>
> Interpreted, this concerns the Wicked Priest who pursued the Teacher of Righteousness to the house of his exile that he might confuse him with his venomous fury. And at the time appointed for rest, for the Day of Atonement, he appeared before them to confuse them, and to cause them to stumble on the Day of Fasting, their Sabbath of repose.
> *(Commentary on Habakkuk)*

However, as in English, Hebrew sentences with a series of pronouns have to be interpreted with care. Thus, 'the house of his exile' could equally well have applied to the Wicked Priest – a place of his exile, rather than that of James. At the time, the Sanhedrin was actually in exile, sitting outside of its normal place in the Temple Mount. So, the phrase used could have been applied to proceedings of the Sanhedrin which Ananus convened, at 'the house of his exile' against James.

James, known as 'James the Just', contemporary with Paul

and Ananus and victim of the latter, fits in better than any other figure as the Teacher of Righteousness. His concerns with matters of purity and Law and works, rather than faith, are in line with those of the scrolls' authors. His position, as one of three 'pillars' in a community with a council of twelve, accords with the organisation of the Dead Sea community.

This interpretation allows for the possibility that Yeshua and at least some of his brothers were taken in to a closed community of the 'poor', in or near Jerusalem, at least partly for their own safety (see also ch 4 p 92 and ch 11 p 381). Given that Yeshua is at various points described as a Nazarene or the Nazarene in the gospels, this could well have been a community of Nazoreans. The community was in turn linked with, or can be identified with, the Essenes, with whom it has many parallels and similarities.

John the Baptist, cousin and messianic predecessor of James and Yeshua, expressed similar concerns and may also have been brought up in such a community. He perished, according to the gospels, for arguing that the marriage of Herod Antipas to Herodias was 'unlawful'. For the 'poor' at Qumran, it was fornication on several grounds: that Herodias had divorced her first husband and she was marrying (for the second time) an uncle.

The addition of a family claiming Davidic descent to the community would have provided a powerful boost. The appeal of the community widened and it grew in strength and numbers. James became leader of the Nazoreans and as such, I suggest, also the figure described in the scrolls as the Teacher of Righteousness.

The description of the fate inflicted on the Wicked Priest, for which there is otherwise no historical parallel, accords in uncannily precise detail with what happened to Ananus as described by Josephus in the *Jewish War*. The pesher, as it has been translated, states that 'they inflicted horrors of evil diseases and took vengeance upon his body of flesh'. But a better equivalent for the Hebrew word 'mahalim' in the context is defilement or pollution, rather than diseases, which it is much more possible for someone to inflict.

Similarly, the English rendering 'his body of flesh' for the original Hebrew is an empty tautology, whereas the better translation 'the flesh of his corpse' actually makes sense.

It will be recalled from the Josephus that Idumeans, supporting the zealots during the siege of Jerusalem, killed Ananus and then stood on his corpse while 'ridiculing' him before tossing his naked body over the city wall to be devoured by wild animals and dogs. A fair rendering of this is that 'they inflicted horrors of evil defilements (such mutilation or other bodily desecration is hinted at by Josephus and would have been quite likely in the circumstances) and took vengeance upon 'the flesh of his corpse' (the outrage of denying the body proper burial and effectively feeding it to dogs).

Who 'they' may have been, to have been motivated to take such revenge, is indicated in the previous paragraph of the Habakkuk pesher which described 'the men of violence who rebelled against God' whose riches the Wicked Priest had stolen and amassed. The Idumeans were certainly men of violence, as described by Josephus, and might well have had cause to resent Ananus who used or abused his position, again according to Josephus, to create personal wealth.

It should finally be noted that there is strong evidence (see ch 4) that the Nazoreans and Essenes were one and the same movement, or that the former evolved from the latter. In which case, James as leader of 'the poor' at Jerusalem was also necessarily leader of his other 'poor' followers, also keepers of the covenant and followers of the Way, a few miles away at Qumran.

It would be hard to overestimate the importance of the Habakkuk pesher. What scholars would like to have is solid documentary evidence from the first century CE, relating to

Yeshua and his followers, untainted by centuries of amendments and additions. What few seem to have picked up on is that there is a problem of recognition: it can sometimes be hard to see what is already there.

Because the gospels are so familiar, it might be expected that an original would be at least a bit like them. But, because the gospels have been so much moulded and altered, there is every possibility that such an original document would be almost *nothing* like them. Moreover, such a document would, unlike the gospels, reflect the conventions of the time, such as making commentary on contemporary events by reference back to ancient biblical texts.

The Habakkuk commentary appears as a contemporary document from the first century of the Common Era. It is what solid documentary evidence from the period *would* look like. It really *is*, I suggest, that evidence!

The commentary was written by people whose organisation and lifestyle paralleled that of the Nazoreans, and who were just a few miles away. It is more than highly likely that there were links; it is plausible that the writer was really talking about Ananus, Paul and James. Perhaps surprisingly to us, the story as analogy leaves out Yeshua. But that is because Yeshua as a focus of attention is a Christian concern deriving, not from contemporary history, but from the later historical development of that religion and its ideas. The Nazoreans/Essenes were at this point primarily concerned with their leader James the Righteous, only recently hounded to death.

A century of so later, after two failed uprisings, the heart had been torn out of the messianic movement. There was a group which persisted, still venerating James. These were the Ebionites, or 'poor ones', who also laid claim to Yeshua though as a Jewish, rather than a Christian, messiah.

The wrathful, militant nationalists, calling for the final battle, in which the 'Sons of Light' would defeat the 'Sons of Darkness', had been crushed. But they left behind a written record which has astonishingly survived. The Habakkuk pesher is probably a better reflection of first century Jewish messianism than any gospel text that we now have or are ever likely to find.

Why, it will be wondered, did the writer of the scroll use pseudonyms instead of people's real names? The answer has to be that he was indeed living in dangerous times and it would have been both risky directly to criticise establishment figures or to identify with anti-Roman, anti-Herodian, messianic or nationalist leaders. The circumlocution was used, just in case the documents ever fell into the wrong hands.

Similar discretion was exhibited for the same reasons by gospel sources writing at this time. In an early version of the first synoptic gospel (Secret Mark), the story is told of a young man who had died and was raised by Yeshua after being entombed. It corresponds in detail with the tale of Lazarus in John's gospel, but in Secret Mark it is an anonymous youth who is brought back to life. As a key supporter and witness, Lazarus was in real danger (John 12, 10) and that may be why in the earlier gospel he is unnamed.

When the source for John came to be incorporated in a gospel account years later, Lazarus was presumably dead and beyond the reach of any further retribution from the Romans or Sadducee chief priests. The same could well apply to Nicodemus, a Pharisee leader and secret supporter of Yeshua, who features in John's gospel but not in the earlier synoptics.

Scroll authors were also circumspect, though in a different way, using pseudonyms that their closed circle of followers but not outsiders would understand. It is an indication that they too were writing about contemporaries, people who it was either dangerous to criticise or who might have been at risk if identified.

So this is another reason why the author of the Habakkuk commentary was writing about real people in his time, rather than long-dead, forgotten villains and heroes. Who would have cared among the establishment, which was in any case Herodian and thus formally anti-Maccabean, if he had named and criticised King Jonathan who had lived 100 years or more before? Who would have cared if he had named their group's presumed original founder, once again long since dead? Neither the unlikely first century BCE author postulated by Vermes, nor the far more probable first century CE author would then have needed to use pseudonyms.

Putting the argument another way, there is no absolute proof as to the identities of key characters in the Habakkuk commentary. But the identifications given above, following the analysis given by Robert Eisenman, are on the evidence the most plausible.

But this cannot be said about arguments put forward by the original experts who examined and translated the Dead Sea scrolls. These were, for the most part, Christian academics, meaning not merely people from a Christian cultural background but, as core believers, committed a priori to a Christian interpretation of the evidence. They needed to believe that the 'Essenes' were an extreme, though largely harmless, cult locked away in the desert, isolated from the real world around them – and thus insulated from the developments that were taking place as they wrote, *less than fifteen miles away* in Jerusalem. They could not conceive that the people who wrote the scrolls were militant, nationalistic zealots, part of a network of opposition, which included the Nazoreans, that raged and schemed and plotted and did actually generate rebellions against the occupying Romans. They could not even begin to countenance what was staring them in the face, that this could be the authentic voice of first century, messianic Jewish nationalism – while the gospels were merely a faint refraction, overlain with centuries of textual editing, falsification and rewriting to serve quite different purposes.

They could not even consider the very plausible hypothesis

that the authors of the scrolls were connected with the same Jewish people centred around the person we identify as Jesus or Yeshua and his family and followers. That is despite being his immediate neighbours, linked by ties of religion, nationality and opposition to Rome, in a relatively small and densely networked community.

The international team restoring and translating the scrolls kept control so tight that only a privileged inner circle were allowed access for some 45 years from the first discoveries in the caves at Qumran in 1946 and 47. This meant that important texts were withheld for many years and the team's interpretation, released simultaneously with the publication of any document, enjoyed an enormous edge in terms of prominence and timing. It became instantly, though emanating from one small group with its own narrow view, an official, authorised version. Eventually, as a result of a challenge instituted by Robert Eisenman and others, copies were made of the material assembled so far for independent scholars to make their own translations and draw their own conclusions.

Just prior to this, again in response to the same pressure, the team began to undertake radio carbon dating tests on some of the scrolls, though once again without allowing independent scrutiny or the involvement of anyone with a differing view into the process. The initial results were then produced, along with claims that the crucial sectarian scrolls, the ones which related to the Teacher of Righteousness and the Wicked Priest, could not have been written after BCE 40, thus ruling out a connection between the militant Essenes at Qumran and the origin of early Christianity.

As with the team's theories of before-Christ origins, this rapidly became the academic orthodoxy (and used to attack Eisenman), even though control of the process rather than the merit of the data or results was what determined this outcome. Subsequent analysis has shown that the data supports the theories of Eisenman and others as well as, or better than, the international team's version.

Crucially, the margins of confidence for dating are so wide, sampling so limited and possibilities of contamination so great that it is impossible to draw absolute conclusions. The basis for the establishment position appears to be that the Habakkuk pesher was radio carbon dated to the first century BCE, between BCE 104 and 43. But this date was based on an inaccurate dating curve, and the revised dating was subsequently updated to between BCE 88 and 2. This itself is on a 'first sigma', the span that radio carbon dating theory posits would contain the actual date 68 per cent of the time. Taking a second sigma span, with 98 per cent confidence, the pesher could have been written at any time between about BCE 180 and CE 180! Required for a confident prediction, the information becomes so general as to be almost useless.

Not only that, but the psalm 37 pesher was by the same method dated to well into the first century CE, a first sigma span of between CE 22 and CE 78 on the recalibrated curve. Since this document is very similar to the Habakkuk pesher in form and content, and identical from the point of view of palaeography (the analysis of script), it gives confidence that the latter dates from about the same time, that is the first century CE. There is even a little added weight from the fact that the psalm 37 pesher talks about the Teacher of Righteousness as under attack from the Wicked Priest, but still alive, while the Habakkuk pesher has him already slain – and so the latter must in theory have been a slightly later document.

In the case of the Habakkuk text, the fact that only one sample was taken for radio carbon dating further reduces reliability. In addition, the scroll had been handled and cleaned so often over the years, as to make the impact of contamination on radio-carbon dating a real possibility.

It is tragic that the concerns of the scroll custodians appear to have been to protect their reputations and establish ascendency, rather than engage in discourse and dialogue in pursuit of a better appreciation of the circumstances described by and surrounding the generation of the scrolls. Crucial documents, including the commentaries on Habakkuk and psalm 37, could well have been written in the first century CE, allowing for the range of probability of the dating, possible errors, incomplete sampling and other factors. These include the possibility that some of the scrolls may have been written on old parchment.

Having reanalysed the data, Joseph Atwill and Steve Braunheim concluded that the group which put out press releases claiming first century BCE provenance 'was simply biased ab initio and was confirming its own theories with its interpretations of the results' (*Redating the radiocarbon dating of the Dead Sea Scrolls*). The establishment scholars wanted quickly to establish a version which was based on their own preconceptions, and rubbish their opponents.

The point is that it is quite a hopeless enterprise to take on board all the baggage of Church dogma and then seek to look at the period when Christianity originated in an academic or dispassionate fashion. In the same way, Christian writers are not equipped to cope with the overwhelming evidence that most of their core beliefs are fictions: borrowed from pagan myths, invented to deal with doctrinal disputes, inserted to provide a pedigree or to deny Jewish origins.

For the most part, their response to the arguments raised in the previous chapter has been stony silence. A few have conceded that while, yes, some aspects of the Christian creed can be seen as symbolic, the core of belief remains. It has to be asked: what core? That Mary was *really* a virgin? That Yeshua, rather than a Jewish would-be messiah, was *really* the Son of God? Or that Yeshua (if he wasn't born of a virgin or the Son of God) was *really* miraculously brought back to life, after being stone-cold dead?

As the second century critic Celsus pointed out, pagans understood perfectly well that their stories of gods consorting with mortal women and of a dying and resurrecting god-man were allegories. But Christians, who borrowed them, misrepresented these fictions as fact.

The question that now needs answering is this. Is there anything in the gospel stories themselves that could be regarded as true, or reflecting some real aspect of first century Palestinian life and a drama that took place within it?

What is left when the dogma is cut away?

Chapter 8: Gospel Truth

The approach of simply asserting as true propositions, which can be demonstrated to be false, has become increasingly difficult. At least, it has for independent-minded individuals. Church leaders can continue blithely to ignore reasoned criticism because they know that millions will believe whatever they are told to believe, however unreasonable or preposterous. But genuine Christian scholars face a challenge, provided by the mounting weight of analysis and evidence, that many of their cherished beliefs are simply false.

Retreating to a core of beliefs that can be defended is, as I suggested at the end of the last chapter, not a viable option. Once reason is admitted, very little is left and the believer is left with the options of rejecting the doctrine as a whole, fudging the issues or mouthing words that he knows are false.

Another approach has been to accept not merely that the evidence is flawed but that it is *all* entirely contrived or unreliable. This prepares the way for a last ditch defence: this is that there is no reliable written evidence but, in the absence of such, Christianity is 'proved' by the witness of its followers or by the tradition handed down from generation to generation or by revelation or by inspiration or by something else equally intangible. The case against this rests on two bases. The first is that the evidence with its limitations, far from proving nothing, demonstrates that Yeshua was something other than what Christians claim him to be. The second is that 'witness', in whatever form, is merely another way of putting forward assertions and then making evidence and facts fit in with them.

While some Christian writers concede that there are elements in the passion story that are fictional, Crossan (in *The Historical Jesus*) goes further, arguing that it is entirely a work of fiction. In this way, he must hope to disarm his sceptic critics.

Taking the gospel of Peter (see Appendix III) as his base, Crossan provides a demonstration of how the story could have been derived from interwoven Old Testament prophetic texts (one of the types of Hebrew pesher previously described). It would have been constructed by the bewildered and demoralised followers of Yeshua as a way of drawing comfort in the face of adversity.

The calamity which first century followers of Yeshua faced was the capture, execution and death of their leader. Crossan accepts the crucifixion of Yeshua as an historical event, as recorded by the Roman writer Tacitus and also as apparently noted by the Jewish historian Josephus. The first account of the passion was then written some years after the event as a means of making sense of it and, Crossan argues, on the basis of Old Testament prophecy rather than any direct evidence.

Crossan postulates an original core story, the 'Cross gospel', reflected in the narrative in the gospels of Mark and Peter. The other passion accounts are in turn primarily derived from these. He suggests that the underlying theme is that of 'innocence rescued', with the following as some of the prophetic texts and textual allusions:

Authorities at the trial: 'The kings of the earth set themselves, and the rulers take counsel together, against the Lord and his anointed,' from Psalm 2, 2;

Abuse and torture of Yeshua: 'I gave my back to the smiters, and my cheeks to those who pulled out the beard; I hid not my face from shame and spitting', from Isaiah 50, 6 and 'when they look on him whom they have pierced, they shall mourn for him', from Zechariah 12, 10;

Death among thieves: 'I (that is, the Lord) will divide him (his suffering servant) a portion with the great, and he shall divide the spoil with the strong; because he poured out his soul to death, and was numbered with the transgressors', from Isaiah 53, 12;

Jesus remains silent: 'He was oppressed, and he was afflicted, yet he opened not his mouth; like a lamb that is led to the slaughter, and like a sheep that before its shearers is dumb, so he opened not his mouth', from Isaiah 53, 7 and 'therefore I have set my face like flint, and I know that I shall not be put to shame', from Isaiah 50, 7;

Garments divided by lot: 'they divide my garments among them, and for raiment they cast lots', from Psalm 22, 18;

Darkness at noon: 'And on that day,' says the Lord God, 'I will make the sun go down at noon and darken the earth in broad daylight', from Amos 8, 9;

Gall and vinegar drink: 'They gave me poison for my food, and for my thirst they gave me vinegar to drink', from Psalm 69, 21;

Death cry: 'My God, my God, why has thou forsaken me?', from Psalm 22, 1.

It does certainly appear as if the writer of the source for this account, and probably also the account in Mark which is similar in many respects, was aware of and consciously used Old Testament texts. It is arguable to what extent this was done to make up the story in its entirety, or simply fill out details. It is also arguable that the writer was making a case that what he knew from sources, or believed had happened, was within the scope of what God had ordained. Hence the comment in the gospel of Peter that, 'they fulfilled all things and accomplished their sins upon on their own heads.' Rather than inventing evidence, the writer may have been trying to relate the evidence that he had to existing scripture. He appears to be stating that, though the wicked may appear to have had their way, it was still the fulfilment of prophecy and still God who was in control.

There are also many details in the gospel of Peter, whose beginning is missing, and in the gospel of Mark, which are hard to explain as simply deriving from Old Testament prophecy. These include the context of an insurrection, the place in the story of the character 'Bar-abbas', the 'betrayal' or handover involving Judas, actions by Joseph of Arimathea, the role of

Simon of Cyrene, the inscription placed on the cross and the young men in white or radiant robes at the tomb. Other details, such as scourging, torture and abuse, dividing up the victim's clothes, and the offer of vinegar to alleviate thirst might in any case have been customary practice with an execution by crucifixion. They would therefore have been elements in a crucifixion, and the fact that these elements can also be found in prophecy would be incidental.

Even so, Crossan makes a plausible case that a core part of the gospel stories could have been invented, using existing prophetic texts as a basis. So, how does this position square with his own beliefs as a Christian writer?

Like other intelligent people, who have considered the evidence and would still remain believers, Crossan's solution is to short-circuit the data and rely instead on an unproven and unprovable assertion. His evidence for the validity of Christianity – after all his careful research! – is the 'continuing presence of the risen Jesus and the abiding experience of the Spirit' with Jesus defined as 'the unmediated presence of the divine to the human'.

Unfortunately, as has been illustrated, the Jesus in the gospels is largely a fictional construction, with his characteristics borrowed from pagan myths and his story and biography adapted to suit the changing needs of an imperial religion, the *Roman* Catholic Church. The Jesus who was Yeshua, a Jewish masioch or would-be liberator, has been buried under this avalanche and his limited biography is now almost impossible to disentangle. Except, that is, we have some somewhat more reliable details about his brother James and the tradition he engendered, some evidence on other members of Yeshua's family, a good picture of the context in which the alleged events in the life of Yeshua took place and the almost miraculously preserved writings of another contemporaneous, parallel (or even identical) nationalistic group.

None of this gives the slightest support for Crossan's position. Those who believe that they feel the spirit have to link it in some objective way to Jesus/Yeshua, rather than to Buddha or some other force, if they are to maintain that it is a specifically 'Christian' experience. In addition, it cannot be argued that, if an experience is claimed to be good, it must necessarily be 'Christian'. Throughout history, Christians have acted no better than anyone else, a force as much for evil as for good. There have been wars against other religions, continuing persecution by one Christian group against another and murderous intolerance visited on unbelievers. As a record of an 'abiding presence', it is singularly unimpressive.

So, intuitively there is no link, just as historically there is no link. The quest to establish such a link has been one of the obsessions of the Roman Church, with the written record unashamedly edited, reconstructed and forged by Constantine's bishop and biographer Eusebius and others in the first few centuries of the Christian era.

Paul needed the link with Judaism, and its respectable pedigree provided by the Old Testament writings, to give authority and credibility to his created religion. This is why he desperately hung on to links with the Nazorean Jewish community under James long after a complete schism had become inevitable. It is why Luke, the author of Acts, did his best to paper over the cracks, forcing Simon Peter into the role of a mediating go-between – even though it is clear from other details in Paul's letters and Acts that Peter remained with James as an upholder of Jewish Law.

So how do writers *now* preserve the fiction of continuity from Yeshua and the people around him, including his brothers, to present day Christianity? They do this by a verbal trick, by describing the followers of James as 'Christian Jews' 'who had converted from Pharisaic Judaism to Christian Judaism'! (*In search of Paul* by J D Crossan and J L Reed).

The fallacy in this is that the immediate followers of Yeshua did not convert to anything. They remained as Jews, just as Yeshua was a Jew, and did not suddenly become something else when he was executed. Yeshua prayed at the temple and in the synagogues and he observed the Jewish Law, just as James did. There were no 'Christians' at all until years later when Paul, or someone like him, invented the term for a breakaway group that he had created (Acts 11, 26).

As Nazoreans, 'keepers of the Covenant', Yeshua and James and their followers may indeed have observed the Law more strictly than many of their fellow Jews. The actions of Yeshua and James suggest that they were like the Essenes, a parallel and most probably linked group, who were very much occupied with the question of maintaining temple purity. Yeshua threw out the money changers. James set himself up as an opposition High Priest. The Essenes withdrew entirely from temple worship. These actions recorded in different sources – the gospels, early accounts of James and the scrolls – may be variations on a theme of fundamentalism in ritual and belief.

James and his followers claimed that Yeshua was the expected Jewish messiah, their national liberator. This was a perfectly respectable position to take within Judaism, just as other groups of Jews supported or followed other individuals who had put themselves forward as messiahs at different times.

The Ebionites, or 'poor ones', the group succeeding as followers of James, maintained that the *only* difference between them and their fellow Jews was their belief in this particular messiah. Others continued to believe that the messiah would come later. Despite the differences on this particular question, Judaism was broad enough to contain the different sectors of opinion. They were after all still all Jews, bound by the same laws and the same religion.

But, by contrast, the differences between James and his followers and Paul were multiple and irreconcilable. Paul secretly wanted to abandon the entire Torah with the requirement for circumcision, purity laws and dietary restrictions. Paul transformed a Jewish messiah into a world-redeeming saviour. Borrowing from paganism, he converted Yeshua into a pagan cult figure who was half-man and half God. He constructed or adopted a pagan ritual, based on Mithraism, in which participants ate the body and blood of the sacrificed God.

The only Christian church was the one later created by Paul and his followers and, as Acts notes, the term 'Christian' was first used for one of the communities he had set up at Antioch. There simply were no 'Christian Jews' immediately following the time of Yeshua; the term is therefore an absolute misnomer. There were only Jews, Jewish followers of James, 'Nazoreans' who 'kept the covenant', an important and very influential group but one of many groups and sects fully within Judaism.

The bridge which Crossan seeks to make is, as much as the one that Paul sought to make and Eusebius and others later concocted, a false one. It cannot disguise the evidence of Christianity's roots as a humanly invented religion.

It is worth noting that another writer, Bart Ehrman (in *Misquoting Jesus*) creates similar confusion in treating the Ebionites as 'Jewish Christians', while conceding at another point that they were, like Yeshua, simply Jews. Ehrman describes how some editors eliminated direct references to Yeshua's father Joseph in Luke's gospel. Their aim was to counter the implication in the childhood stories in Luke that Yeshua was fully human, son of a human father rather than the 'Son of God', and therefore not divine. In the event, these changes did not achieve wide circulation and the version of the gospel available now frankly describes Joseph as Yeshua's father.

Ehrman characterises these theologically motivated, attempted changes as antiadoptionalist, that is against the position that Yeshua was not a preexisting divine being but a human who was adopted by God to have a special role. This rather implies, in the context, that the original text as now still preserved was 'adoptionalist', in other words the position of some early, variant Christians. What Ehrman does not see is that the original template for Mark, afterwards reflected in Matthew and Luke, was a description originating from Nazorean Jews, most probably followers of Yeshua. This was simple and straightforward in many respects. Yeshua is described as having a father and siblings, because he *had* a father and brothers and sisters. It may be that the tale was also in a sense politically motivated in maintaining that Yeshua had survived crucifixion and thus escaped from his enemies. But it was not a theological argument, simply a description of what happened and the situation as people close to Yeshua knew it.

Ehrman may well be right that it was antiadoptionalists who tried to make the changes. But he is wrong in supposing that the essential conflict was between adoptionalists and antiadoptionalists. Though the canonical gospels are all by Christian authors, they originate from Jewish sources because that is what the original sources were. They embody some of the Nazorean view and some of the discordance generated as a separate Christian theology evolved. In attempting to suppress the fact that Yeshua had a natural father, the antiadoptionalist editors were not in fact attacking an alternate Christian position but a record originally preserved and handed on by Nazorean Jews. Ehrman does not appear to recognise that, if the record is projected back far enough, a point is reached when there are no Christians at all! Around CE 40 – 45, a few years after the crucifixion, Paul/Saul had not yet set up his new 'ecclesia' at Antioch with its very different rituals and the followers of Yeshua remained fully within the Jewish fold.

It should be acknowledged that Ehrman, once a fundamentalist evangelical Christian believing in the 'inerrancy' of the bible, came to recognise that the bible was full of mistakes, inconsistencies and contradictions and deliberate falsification. He then brought this understanding, which had long been known to bible scholars, to a wider audience through his book *Misquoting Jesus*. His reason for rejecting Christianity, however, was his difficulty in reconciling belief in God with the evidence of human suffering. The errors and false propositions in the gospels that he uncovered, I would argue, would have been sufficient.

Two other writers, Freke and Gandy, promote a gnostic interpretation of Christianity in their book, *The Jesus Mysteries*. Like Crossan, they take the position with the sceptics that the gospel story is a mixture of myth and invention. They point to the myths of Egyptian and Greek godmen Osiris and Dionysus as templates for the story of Yeshua/Jesus and argue that many of the teachings of Christianity are similar to pagan teachings. They argue that the mystical, 'gnostic' form of Christianity, which was suppressed by the early Church, was the original form of the religion. Originally, as with paganism, there were 'inner' and 'outer' mysteries. The myth of the dying and resurrecting godman, the literal form of the story, comprised the outer shell, but there were inner shells of spiritual meaning that could be attained by initiates.

Christianity, as it disseminated, became detached from its inner mysteries so that a literalistic interpretation of the Jesus myth became prevalent – with what was intended or constructed as allegory now taken entirely literally. The process was completed when the gnostics were declared heretics and persecuted out of existence.

Freke and Gandy dismiss any evidence of a historical Yeshua/Jesus, such as references in Josephus and by the Roman historian Tacitus, as unreliable. They argue against the idea that the gospel story is a biography, on to which pagan elements have been grafted. Instead, they suggest that there is no historical Yeshua/Jesus at all, but that the story is a 'consciously crafted vehicle for encoded spiritual teachings created by Jewish gnostics'. They suggest that a group of Jews called Therapeutae, living near Alexandria, or some similar group, could have reworked the Osiris myth, substituting their own mythical hero-figure, Yeshua/Jesus, after the Old Testament prophet and leader Joshua from the book of Exodus.

Part of the motivation, they suggest, may have been to provide a form of consolation (in which death and defeat are turned to victory) for refugees flooding out from Judea after the disastrous Jewish uprising. But the theme failed to take hold with this displaced Jewish audience, while appealing greatly to the Gentile community. As promoted by Paul and his followers, Yeshua became a saviour not just for the Jews but for the whole of humanity.

It is certainly evident that there are pagan elements adapted within the Jesus/Yeshua story. But some parts of Freke and Gandy's arguments are tenuous. For example, they take pains to try to discredit historical evidence for the existence of Yeshua. Yet, at the same time, they put forward the theory of a Jewish community at Alexandria, or somewhere else, taking the Osiris myth and grafting on to it Yeshua as their own mythical hero. But they offer no evidence for this thesis at all (and there is none!); it is merely a supposition on their part.

The evidence for the existence of Yeshua by contrast comes not merely in the New Testament and in non-canonical gospels, imperfect as these records are, but in references by the Roman historian Tacitus and other contemporary writers. There are direct references in Josephus that have clearly been either altered in copying or inserted by later Christian editors. It may be that these editors changed existing copy to suit their views, rather than inventing it entirely. There are also some very revealing oblique references in Josephus and some further comments, assumed to have been added in a translation, that could also be original (see ch 9).

Freke and Gandy have also argued there are no grounds for believing that there ever was a Nazorean Jerusalem community, with James and other brothers of Jesus featuring strongly among its followers.

Again, the evidence for such a community is quite good, to the extent that Paul devotes considerable space in his letters trying to counter the Nazoreans' arguments for a strict interpretation of Jewish Law. Although Acts was written much later, it describes a community of followers of Yeshua within Judaism and outlines the conflict with Paul. Ebionite sources, such as the *Pseudoclementine Recognitions*, also maintain that the early followers of Yeshua under James were fully Jews, differing from other Jews only in their belief in Yeshua as the predicted Jewish messiah.

As evidence for their case, that the Jerusalem community never existed, Freke and Gandy point to the fact that when a prominent churchman Bishop Melito of Sardis went in search for it in CE 160, 'all' he found was a small group of Ebionites or 'poor men'. This is extraordinarily revealing because, of course, it completely negates rather than supports their view!

These authors fail to perceive, or they have forgotten, the crucial point that the Ebionities were the direct inheritors of the Jerusalem tradition; they venerated James and they adopted similar practices such as vegetarianism. Despite the upheaval of two Jewish revolts, and the banishment of Jews by the Romans following the second uprising, these genuine apostolic successors were back in Jerusalem! The Bishop's discovery was actually the best evidence there could have been for the original existence of the Jerusalem community and, at that time, its continuation.

Freke and Gandy call these Ebionities 'Jewish Christian gnostics', whereas they were in fact in a line of succession from Nazorean Judaism, which persisted locally after the 'Christian' sect had broken away to gain an increasing following among non-Jewish populations.

As already noted, early church sources give a considerable amount of information on James which demonstrates that he was the leader of the Nazorean community after Yeshua. It is also made clear in the gospel accounts, even as they have been subsequently moulded and edited, that James was one of the brothers of Yeshua. Eusebius also refers to James as 'the brother of our Lord' and 'the son of Joseph'. Later, as the associated doctrines of the divinity of 'Christ', his miraculous birth and the virginity of his mother Mary developed, the recorded family of Yeshua became a source of embarrassment. The details of the lives of these family members inconveniently gainsaid the developing orthodoxy. That was when authorities, such as Jerome, began to produce arguments that those described as the brothers of Yeshua were really only his 'cousins'.

Freke and Gandy, however, have an arguably even more difficult position to defend. They maintain that Yeshua never existed. Therefore he cannot have had brothers, cousins or for that matter a mother, father and disciples.

So they are forced by their argument to deny that Paul really meant what he said when he referred to James as the brother of the Lord. They ignore references in Paul's letters that distinguish the 'brothers' of Jesus from the apostles. They have to suggest that it is an accidental coincidence that the same character Simon nicknamed Petros (Greek) or Cephas (Aramaic) appears in equivalent roles in the gospels and Paul's letters.

A further weakness in Freke and Gandy's argument derives from the historical evidence (which they concede) that a Christian cult had become established in the first century during the fifties and early sixties, driven to a great extent by the efforts of Paul. But the period into which these authors postulate that the mythical Yeshua was retrojected was a mere twenty five years or so earlier than this. This would have been well within the living memory of members of the cult and other people who had been in Judea at the relevant time. So it would have been quite possible for witnesses to come forward to deny a story, if one had been invented.

Freke and Gandy, however, assume that the Yeshua in Paul's early letters such as the first letter to the Thessalonians (written around CE 50) was a mythical dying and resurrecting godman. This is even though Paul writes in these letters as if the death and resurrection of Yeshua were facts.

If Paul had simply grafted on to Judaism a pagan story, based on the myth of Osiris, then it is extraordinary that there is no reflection of this in the interactions between Paul and James and his followers recorded in Acts. James restated the laws that Gentile 'god fearers' should be required to follow in a letter to the communities that Paul was seeking to set up. When later it became apparent that Paul was teaching against the Torah and circumcision, Paul was summoned to Jerusalem and made to undergo a penance to indicate that he did accept Jewish Law. There is no indication amongst these concerns that Paul might also have been promoting a sacrilegious pagan teaching of a god sacrificed for mankind.

Paul certainly *was* doing something like this. But it would not have been so apparent to James and other members of the Jerusalem community because Paul was talking about Yeshua – and Yeshua was someone who had existed and was centrally important to this community.

It would moreover not have been evident that, on this point, Paul was teaching something so radically different from the Nazorean position. Paul preached a resurrected saviour. The Nazoreans maintained that their messiah was 'resurrected' and had been taken up directly into heaven by God like many other figures in Jewish legend, such as Elijah. What they were suggesting, as will become apparent, was that Yeshua surmounted death by *surviving his ordeal.* The ascension story, whatever other purpose it might have served, provided useful cover against the question which the Roman and Sadducee authorities might raise: where was Yeshua now?

If Yeshua had, on the other hand, never existed, then the Nazorean Jews would certainly have also picked up on this point in Paul's preaching and confronted Paul with this additional perversion of Judaism.

Paul could hardly have grafted a mythical Osiris figure on to Judaism unchallenged. But setting this aside for the moment, the next weakness comes when, according to Freke and Gandy, the story is given a historical context. This, they argue, happened around CE 70 when the gospel of Mark was written. It was however still only 34 years or so on from Yeshua's crucifixion. Despite the immense disruption and loss of life during the Jewish revolt, there would still have been some people, including first hand witnesses, who could have confirmed whether it had or had not happened.

Even assuming that a fiction could have taken hold so soon after the event, it still has to be explained why the Romans went on harassing and persecuting 'Sons of David' who they believed were related to Yeshua, including his brother Simon/Simeon and the grandsons of his brother Judas.

There are some strong points in Freke and Gandy's arguments including their case that the gnostics, persecuted out of existence by Catholic literalists, may have been the original Christians. The evidence suggests that the gnostic Christians did incorporate preexisting ideas and teachings.

But the point is that, pagan influences or not, the first Christians were themselves a breakaway from Judaism, from a Jewish movement or sect that had a real messiah – who had lived but whose life and character were then fictionalised and recreated. The gnostics formed an interesting group, which can now reinstated in its proper place in the development of Christianity – having at one stage been almost written out. But they were no more numbered among the original followers of

Yeshua than Paul's Antioch 'Christians'.

Like Crossan, Freke and Gandy are trying to build a bridge, not in this case to the original Yeshua and his followers (whom they try to demolish) but back to the pagan past. Their argument is that there is one philosophy, embodying the secrets of gnosis, behind pagan philosophies and Christianity, that by understanding the myth (the 'Christ within') the individual can be resurrected into his own immortal, divine entity.

The bridge, like Crossan's, is based on a verbal sophistry. 'Christ' is Greek, translated from masioch or messiah, an awaited Jewish national (and very much mortal) liberator. It does not translate from its immediate context to the past, to paganism or gnosticism, that predate events in the first century. Nor can it be related to future developments that happened after Nazorean leaders, including Yeshua, and their followers had been defeated, dispersed and obliterated – and which have no connection to them. Pagans certainly did not believe in a 'Jewish messiah within' and neither did the gnostics. Christianity thus remains what it always has been, a travesty of its Jewish origins. But, if the bridges so created by these scholars are false, then what remains of the gospel narrative?

Crossan maintains that the passion story was invented by interweaving Old Testament prophecy. Freke and Gandy contend that the quest for any real underlying biography is hopeless because Yeshua, they contend, is a mythical, invented character. Surprisingly, there is something left – and it is a coherent story – if all the accretions are stripped away.

For the purpose of this exercise, I am taking the story of Yeshua as primarily though not exclusively given in the gospels of Mark and Peter (see Appendix III). I will strip from it the anti-Jewish statements and rhetoric, clearly added on because Yeshua was himself Jewish and relied on the support of his Jewish followers. I will disregard sayings and quotations, on the grounds that it was common practice in telling stories at this time to give characters appropriate things to say. While I accept that a good case can be made (as Crossan has done) for a core of Jesus/Yeshua sayings, from multiply attested sources, I will disregard these too. This is because there is no way of knowing whether these came from Yeshua or someone else or from a common source, for example the collected wisdom of his followers.

I will leave out elements which could simply be Old Testament prophecy incorporated into the story. It should be borne in mind, as I have argued, that some prophecy may have been used by the gospel author as a means of explaining his source material. The author of John, for example, makes four successive, explicit references to existing scripture in explaining elements of the passion story (John 19, 24-37).

Yeshua, well versed in scripture, might have deliberately acted out some sayings to increase the dramatic impact of his actions. Mounting a donkey on the way to Jerusalem, would have made him the embodiment of Zechariah's prophecy that the 'triumphant and victorious' king of the Jews would come 'humble and riding on an ass' (Zechariah 9, 9). But this detail could equally have come from the gospel author, filling out his tale and adding credence to it by reference to ancient prophetic text. Matthew certainly seems to have done this. He has Yeshua riding into Jerusalem astride two animals, an ass *and* and a colt! In the original Hebrew of Zechariah there is a doublet, giving poetic emphasis by repetition: 'and riding upon an ass, even upon a colt the foal of an ass'. In the version in the Septuagint, a Greek translation for non-Hebrew speaking Jews, this was rendered as 'on an ass, and a young foal'. Matthew used this as his source and repeated the mistake.

I omit the incident in which the tables of the money changers are overturned, partly because it may have been derived from prophecy (as in John 2, 17) but chiefly because it appears to have been displaced. The temple police would surely have made an attempt to arrest the perpetrators, so sparking an immediate conflict, but in all the acounts Yeshua and his followers go on their way unmolested. While the synoptic authors have the incident taking place in passion week, in John's gospel it happens at a Passover celebration two years prior to this.

I retain the details of crucifixion itself, despite the argument that it might simply derive from Old Testament prophecy (psalm 22), because this is corroborated by other sources, including the Roman historian Tacitus and because this would have been a likely punishment inflicted by the Romans.

The offering of vinegar, arguably from psalm 69, I retain because there is a variation in the gospel of Peter indicating that Yeshua was either drugged or poisoned that needs to be explained. It could also have been customary, as an act of compassion, to offer crucifixion victims wine vinegar to quench their thirst.

This then is the stripped-down passion story:

A Jewish man named Yeshua was born at the end of the reign of the Roman client king Herod and crucified towards the end of the time that Pontius Pilate was procurator/prefect in Judea. He lived for a time in Galilee.

Descent from King David and thus a claim to the throne of Israel was attributed to him.

He had a cousin John, nicknamed 'the Baptist' who was arrested and executed by Herod Antipas, son of Herod and Roman-appointed ruler of Galilee. John had objected to Herod Antipas divorcing his wife in order to marry his niece who was also his brother's former wife. John baptised his followers in the river Jordan.

Yeshua preached and knew his scriptures. He was on friendly terms with and helped by Pharisees.

He had sisters and brothers, including James, Simon and Judas, as well as cousins, James and John. His followers had nicknames with aggressive or messianic overtones. His mother was called

Mary and his father was Clopas. He was most probably married.

It was reported to Yeshua that there had been a riot in Jerusalem in which the blood of his fellow Galileans had been spilled. Yeshua went with his brothers and followers from Galilee to Jerusalem, just prior to the Passover festival. Yeshua told his followers to arm themselves. His cousins, James and John, asked for high positions in Yeshua's forthcoming kingdom.

They stayed at a nearby village, Bethany. Yeshua was anointed with precious oil, a ceremony confirming a claim to kingship or religious leadership. Yeshua and some of his followers went to a safe house in Jerusalem to eat their Passover meal on the Wednesday before the Passover festival.

Yeshua was betrayed and taken prisoner by the collaborating Roman-appointed High Priest.

He temporised under questioning by Pilate, but was condemned just before Passover.

Another person, Simon of Cyrene, carried the heavy cross piece to the place of execution. This was a garden with a tomb, owned by Joseph of Arimathea, a supporter of Yeshua and member of the Sanhedrin.

Yeshua refused the customary offer of wine mixed with myrrh, to deaden pain. He was tied or nailed by the hands to the cross. Two or three hours afterwards, he was given vinegar or vinegar and 'gall' to drink, and slumped forward.

A Roman soldier came with the traditional club used to break the legs of victims and hasten death. Finding Yeshua apparently already dead, he thrust a spear into his side and blood and water flowed out.

Joseph of Arimathea asked Pilate for the body. Nicodemus and Joseph of Arimathea took the body to the tomb plus a large load of spices.

When some of the women followers went to attend to the body over a day later, they found it had gone but a man, a messenger in white, was there.

Some of Yeshua's followers went to Galilee where Yeshua had prearranged to meet them, but found someone else they did not recognise. Yeshua met with James and others of his supporters in the following weeks, but then disappears from the record.

There are some points where a choice has had to be made; for example, the timetable in John's gospel which would have the Passover meal on the Wednesday, rather than on the Thursday as in Mark, is more feasible. This would also explain why the meal was taken on a different day from the bulk of the community. Yeshua and his disciples were following a 52 week Essenic calendar which has Passover on a fixed day each year, a Wednesday.

It is clearly possible to quibble with the detail of what I have included, and I accept this. But the above synopsis does I suggest extract a general framework for the story that is not derivative from preexisting Old Testament text.

It should be noted that spirit appearances after the crucifixion are absent from the earliest record, the gospel of Mark minus the last twelve verses which were subsequently added. But references in non-canonical gospels, such as the gospel of Peter and the gospel of the Hebrews, are indicative of a flesh and blood man: helped from the tomb after his ordeal, handing his grave clothes to the servant of the High Priest. In conjunction with these, the appearances described in later gospel material can be seen as giving a miraculous gloss to claims which were physical and possible. The spirit tradition, like the eucharist, derive from what Paul and his followers were saying (Corinthians, I, 15).

Once the extraneous material has been removed, the most immediate and compelling feature of the narrative is its simplicity and directness. There are two essential themes.

The Christian tale is of a man who went meekly to his death, even invited it, for the cosmic purpose of saving mankind. The original version by contrast suggests that he went to Jerusalem, possibly with an army of followers, under cover of pilgrims going for the annual Passover celebration. His action was in response to an incident in which Jews had been taken prisoner by the Romans, possibly the temple funds massacre instigated by Pilate. The original is thus a story not of compliance, but one of resistance.

The Christian tale is that he was betrayed, executed and then miraculously brought back to life by God. The original Nazorean version, still embedded in the text, is that the execution was botched and/or interfered with *and that Yeshua survived!*

This latter theme, which I will consider first, needs to be related to the Roman practice of crucifixion. Nailed to a cross and simply left to hang, victims would very soon perish because of the additional effort needed to lift the chest each time to breathe. So the Romans used two additional modifications.

Where inflicting torture and pain was the prime objective, the victim was nailed to a cross with a crotch piece and simply left. With the upper torso supported, there would be no initial difficulty breathing and the victim would take maybe three, four or more days to die from the combined effects of thirst, starvation, exposure and wounds inflicted by being beaten and then nailed to the cross. This was the slow method.

When it was intended merely to fulfil a death sentence, combined possibly with a degree of public humiliation, the victim was attached to a cross with a small platform which enabled him to stand. When the moment came to complete the execution, a soldier came with a heavy club to break the victim's legs. Unable then to support the weight of his body, the victim would immediately have difficulty breathing and would die within about an hour from the effects of his traumatic injury, heart failure and shock.

This was the quick method which, it is apparent from the gospel narrative, was intended to be used in Yeshua's case. The reason was apparently to ensure that he was not left on the cross after sunset and at the start of the Sabbath, which was also that year the Passover day. But the crucial element, the breaking of Yeshua's legs, necessary to bring about the swift demise of the victim, did not happen, according to the text.

The execution was not completed; it was certainly botched.

Yeshua did *appear* to be dead. He had just been given a drink which caused him to slump in a comatose or death-like state. According to the gospel of Mark, the drink was simply vinegar. This is certainly puzzling because vinegar would have had a mildly stimulating effect.

Th administration of the potion, supposedly vinegar, did in fact produce or precede a lapse into death or unconsciousness. So, was it vinegar, or something else?

The gospel of Peter seems to provide the answer. It was not just vinegar but a mixture of vinegar and 'gall', some bitter-tasting substance, which was administered. The implication is that this was done to poison Yeshua, so that he would not be alive after sunset, the start of Passover and the Sabbath.

Confusingly this had come, according to this gospel, just *after* a decision not to break Yeshua's legs 'so that he might die in torments', thus prolonging the execution. This reference to breaking the victim's legs, confirmed by the description in John's gospel (supposedly from an eyewitness account), indicates that the quick method of crucifixion was being used for Yeshua and the other two victims. Since the victims had to be got down in this instance before sunset, there was a limit to how long Yeshua's despatch could be delayed, by withholding the leg-breaking coup de grace purely for the purpose of inflicting pain. So this element of the story, as it is placed in the gospel of Peter, is not wholly convincing.

The reason then given for the sudden reversal of this plan, resulting in a decision to apply poison, was an unnatural darkness over the land. The executioners, Jewish not Roman in this gospel's account, were worried that the sun might already have set with Yeshua still alive on the cross. Appearing also in the synoptic gospels, though not in John, the detail of the sudden and unnatural darkness in the middle of the day appears to have been introduced to show fulfilment of Old Testament prophecy (Amos 8, 9) and so is therefore omitted from my summary.

Could the administration of a mixture of vinegar and gall likewise have been taken from an Old Testament source, psalm 69, 'They gave me poison for food, and for my thirst they gave me vinegar to drink.'? Quite possibly, although in the gospel of Peter it was poison and vinegar both in a drink.

This still leaves unresolved the motivation behind the decision (in Peter and John) not to break Yeshua's legs, given the imperative to complete the execution and get the body down from the cross before sunset. Against the evidence of poison or a drug in the gospel of Peter, however, the sequence in the canonical gospels begins to make sense.

It is not just vinegar, but vinegar laced with 'gall', possibly a commonly available substance like opium or mandrake, that was administered to the victim on the cross. This had, as the gospels describe it, an immediate effect. Yeshua either died or lapsed into deep unconsciousness.

The author of the gospel of Peter knows of the detail that Yeshua's legs were not broken, either from other gospels, or from an original passion source. He also has, either from some other source or the original passion story, the information that a mixture of vinegar and a drug, a bitter tasting substance, was administered to Yeshua on the cross. He struggles to reconcile these two pieces of information, and in doing so may have placed them in the wrong sequence. In Peter, the decision is made not to break Yeshua's legs and then a poison or drug is administered. In the canonical gospels, the drink is administered before there is any question of breaking the victim's legs and Yeshua slumps on the cross in a deathlike state. Then (gospel of John), the soldiers come round to break the victims legs, but desist in Yeshua's case, finding him apparently already dead.

There would appear to be some source behind all this that goes back beyond Christian commentators to the Nazoreans, the original followers of Yeshua. What this source may have been saying is that Yeshua was deliberately drugged to make it look as if he were dead.

Conspiracy? Are there any other details to support this?

There is actually a surprising amount of circumstantial detail in the text that isn't sourced in prophecy – and that cannot be accounted for as later add-ons by Christian editors, as these details go counter to the Christian case.

There is, for example the detail that someone else (Simon of Cyrene) offered or was recruited to carry the heavy crucifixion cross piece to the place of execution. This would have had the very useful benefit of helping to conserve Yeshua's strength for the ordeal ahead. It must be remembered also that Yeshua would have been about 42 years old, a man used to physical labour and walking long distances, perhaps at the height of his powers. With his legs unbroken, there is a strong likelihood that he would have easily survived the period of three or four hours when he was on the cross.

Another point is that it is related that Yeshua had earlier refused the customary offer of wine mixed with myrrh, as an anodyne to deaden pain before execution. Why is this small detail included? The explanation I suggest is that Yeshua wanted to avoid drowsiness and remain fully conscious, so as later to be able to take the potion of drugged vinegar that would immediately simulate death. Or, alternatively, that is what the writer of the original source *wants us* to deduce.

If there were a conspiracy, in an attempt to save Yeshua, then some provision beyond hope would been included in the plan to prevent the Roman soldier with the crucifragium from breaking Yeshua's legs – which would have certainly resulted in his death. The gospels agree in describing the place of crucifixion as

Golgotha. John describes this as a Hebrew name: 'which is called in Hebrew Golgotha', meaning 'the place of a skull'. Mark and Matthew follow in providing the same description, 'Golgotha' and the same meaning in Greek, 'the place of a skull'. Luke just gives the place name, 'Golgotha'. However, John's gospel also provides the apparently contradictory information that Yeshua was crucified, not in a public place, but in a private garden where Joseph of Arimathea had an as-yet unused family tomb. The other gospels agree on the detail of the unused tomb.

The problem is that 'Golgotha', or 'glgth' (because written Hebrew lacks vowels), does not mean 'place of the skull'. In Hebrew, the word for skull is 'gulgoleth' or 'glglth'! Nor does the word relate, on the assumption that the author of John was mistaken, to the Aramaic which has 'gulgalta' for skull. What 'glgth' does appear to signify is 'gol' 'geth' or 'stonepress'. This is something that would have been at home in a garden, as a means of extracting oil from seeds or plants. It might have been a garden's colloquial name.

If Yeshua were, as suggested in John's gospel, executed in a private garden, why was that? And how was it arranged?

Did the Romans agree to this with Yeshua's Pharisee supporters, who argued that crucifixion in a public place might have led to some kind of demonstration? It must be remembered that this was at Passover, with the city's population swollen by many tens or even hundreds of thousands and perhaps only 1500 Roman troops available at most. The Romans might have had reason to agree – and Yeshua's supporters an ulterior motivation in making such a request. With a crucifixion taking place at a public place of execution, there would have been little opportunity to influence the course of events. In a private garden, on the other hand, it might have been possible to exert some sort of control.

The crucial moment would have been when the soldier came with the crucifragium to execute the coup de grace. At that point, he was confronted with the victim slumped forward, apparently already dead. Moreover, there may well have been a group between him and the cross, arguing that it would be disrespectful to break the legs of a corpse. As John's gospel relates, the soldier did thrust a spear, perhaps through a throng of supporters, into Yeshua's side. If this is speculation, it does at least explain one fact on which all the accounts agree. The necessary act of breaking the victim's legs, to complete the execution, was not carried out.

John's gospel goes on to relate that, from the spear wound, blood and water came out. The author takes the trouble to state that his source was an eyewitness and affirms that what he saw is true. The object may have been to counter the Docetists who were arguing in the second century CE that Yeshua was pure spirit and that his physical body, and therefore the crucifixion, was an illusion.

He bled, so he was real. The bleeding would indicate that he had circulation and was still alive. Or it could, as perhaps the author intended, suggest that the spear had pierced the heart, spilling a little blood and watery fluid that had gathered in the heart's outer membrane. In which case, had Yeshua survived to that point, the spear thrust would have been fatal.

There is further evidence, none of which can be seen to be derived from prophecy, which suggests that at the very least Yeshua's was an irregular and flawed execution. Despite the fact that handling a corpse would have been regarded as highly polluting, an especial risk just before Passover, and despite the fact that this was very much women's work, Nicodemus and Joseph of Arimathea who were members of the Sanhedrin and secret supporters of Yeshua, took this upon themselves. Joseph even went to Pilate and asked for the body. Why? Why go to such lengths just to prepare a dead body for burial?

The two took with them to the tomb a huge quantity, about 100 lbs weight, of burial herbs and spices. It would have required a very large sack, so heavy that it probably had to be carried on the back of a donkey. Why such an excessive amount of material? Is the source, in this case for John's gospel, trying to tell us something else, that other items may have been concealed with the spices?

What would have been needed, for a man perhaps still barely alive, were ointments and dressings for wounds, water, food and clothes.

Joseph of Arimathea, 'a respected member of the Council (Sanhedrin)' is mentioned in Mark as the person who asked Pilate for Yeshua's body. There is, however, a problem with this Joseph's role in the story, in that Roman law provided an entitlement for a close family member to come and take away the body, but no right for someone not related. If would have been imperative for a relative to come forward quickly to collect the body, both to ensure proper burial and, if as I have suggested Yeshua were still alive, attempt revival.

In the absence of someone entitled to take the body, the Romans might well have dumped it on the communal rubbish tip outside the city to be devoured as carrion. Why would Yeshua's family have taken the risk? Why would they have let a comparative stranger go forward when there were available close relatives such as his mother Mary, aunt Salome, brother James and other brothers?

The answer I think is the simplest, that Joseph *was* a close relative, outranking in seniority other male family members. This explains why he was entitled to ask for the body and why no one else did.

Yeshua's father (named Clopas, I have argued) would have been the most senior relative. But by the time of the crucifixion he is no longer mentioned and can be presumed to have died.

The Joseph who claimed the body was I suggest Mary Magdalene's father and the father-in-law of Yeshua. He may have been described as such in an original source. But, in the edited version of the gospel we have, this information was altered in order to obscure the relationship between Yeshua and Mary Magdalene. As has been seen, original names were often deliberately or accidentally mistranslated. In this case, the Hebrew original Joseph 'father of Mary', written without vowels as Ysf 'ab Mryh', became corrupted to Joseph from 'Arimathea', a place which did exist as Aramathaim at the time.

It could be seen as a difficulty that Yeshua should have had, as his father-in-law, someone who was a prominent Pharisee. But Yeshua is described in the gospels as dining with, and being on friendly terms with, Pharisees. He was even assisted by Pharisees in escaping from Herod Antipas. So, in spite of the ritual denunciations of Pharisees at other points in the gospels, the relationship is possible (see also Apprendix I).

Mark, the earliest of the canonical gospels, makes no mention of Joseph, the supposed husband of Mary. Taken with evidence that Yeshua's mother Mary was in fact married to someone called Clopas, this suggests that Joseph as the husband of Mary was a later invention. The purpose may partly have been to draw attention away from the normal family in which Yeshua was brought up, with brothers and sisters who were also the children of his father Clopas/Alphaeus. It also helped disguise the role of Joseph 'of Arimathea' which would have pointed up Mary Magdalene as the wife of Yeshua.

Nicodemus and Joseph of Arimathea are marked out by their conduct as possibly providing immediate help and resources for Yeshua, if he were still alive after the crucifixion. Is there any evidence of other helpers staying within the tomb to carry out intensive first aid? The answer is that there is. Mark's gospel describes the three significant women in Yeshua's life – his wife/partner Mary Magdalene, mother Mary and aunt Salome – later going to the tomb, finding it open and Yeshua gone. The women find a young man there dressed in a white robe, 'sitting on the right side'. This person is very much a human helper, who gives a very precise message for Simon Peter and the disciples to go to Galilee as prearranged to meet Yeshua.

In the later synoptic gospels, Matthew and Luke, the young man is transformed into an extraterrestrial being, clad in dazzling raiment, an angel or heavenly messenger. In the non-canonical gospel of Peter, there is a graphic description of three men coming out of the tomb, 'two of them sustaining the other'. Yeshua's helpers, concealed within the tomb, would have been drawn from his own Nazorean or Essene supporters in Jerusalem.

It is worth noting that *nowhere* in any of the gospels or any other source is it suggested that Yeshua was nailed through the feet to the cross, something the Romans might well have done as a precaution against rescue, had they intended to use the slow method and leave him to die of exposure over a long period. As it happened, it was necessary to get the body down before the onset of sunset, marking the start of a new day which was both the Sabbath and the day of the Passover.

The gospel of Peter has 'the Jews' removing nails from Yeshua's hands, after he had been taken down from the cross. In John's gospel, Thomas refused to believe that Yeshua was alive 'unless I see in his hands the print of the nails, and place my finger in the mark of the nails, and place my hand in his side'. According to the story, Thomas later met with Yeshua who showed him his hands and invited him to place his fingers in the nail marks and in the wound in his side. No mention here also of nail wounds in Yeshua's feet.

Omission is in no sense proof, but it is significant that nothing is said in any of these sources to suggest that Yeshua was nailed through his ankles or feet. Had this happened, it would have greatly reduced Yeshua's chances of survival. He would, even had he survived, been unable to walk about afterwards. He would almost certainly have been crippled for life.

Again, the original source is giving information suggesting that Yeshua could have, might have, in fact *did* survive.

The gospels are also agreed that Yeshua was beaten, a practice that could be both a punishment and a means of extracting information during interrogation. Paul claims to have suffered in this way several times and Acts describes one incident when, under the magistrates at Philippi, Paul was beaten with rods.

As part of the punishment, a person condemned to crucifixion was sometimes scourged with a leather whip knotted with pieces of metal. This inflicted such damage that the victim could be brought to the point of death, unable even to stand or walk to the place of execution. So the scourging was usually carried out, for the convenience of the executioners, at the crucifixion site.

Though the gospels do not agree in detail, the message appears to be that Pilate was minded to release Yeshua but was pressured into changing his mind. The beating inflicted at the praetorium under interrogation (Luke 23, 22) may thus have been more akin to the treatment received by Paul, and not the heavy scourging that would have directly threatened Yeshua's life.

There is then a wealth of detail given, not derived from prophecy and running counter to the Christian story, suggesting that Yeshua might have survived or did survive his crucifixion. This is likely to have been one of the themes of the original passion narrative, told not by later Christian editors and censors but by someone or some people who would have been part of Yeshua's following.

It is then a Nazorean story. But can it be believed any more than later Christian myth?

It is most definitely a very clever piece of propaganda. The Romans have crucified the Nazoreans' leader but now the Nazoreans are saying that he survived the ordeal! There is no body. So this piece of counter information is hard to deny. And, since the Nazoreans are now claiming that Yeshua, like Elijah and other figures in Jewish legend, has been taken directly up into heaven, it is something that the Romans won't ever be able to disprove.

It is, or rather was, certainly a good way of snatching a verbal victory from what was probably a physical defeat.

The story also appears to serve other purposes. 'Don't go looking for Yeshua,' is the message. 'He's in heaven'. This is certainly a useful cover, if in fact Yeshua is by this time actually living somewhere in exile.

Another vital point is that Yeshua was treated by his supporters as, and was convicted by the Romans as, the king of the Jewish people. The Romans were well aware of the principle of monarchical succession, as practised not long before by the Jewish Maccabean kings and sometimes by their own emperors. Vespasian was, for example, succeeded by his sons Titus and then Domitian. What the Nazoreans' story is in effect saying is, 'Don't go after possible successors. Our leader, Yeshua, has gone to heaven and we are awaiting his miraculous return.'

Of course, the Romans did eventually go after Yeshua's successors, as 'Sons of David'. But the story of his resurrection, direct 'ascension' into heaven and awaited return may have bought some of them a little time.

So, one of the themes of the residual passion story, after extraneous and added material has been removed, is that of survival. It goes counter to the Christian myth, and the intentions of later Christian editors of the text, and so I suggest is part of the original message. Whether true or a piece of ingenious Nazorean propaganda is now difficult to determine, a matter of judgement.

The other crucial theme is that of resistance, and it provides possible explanations as to why Yeshua went to Jerusalem and how he ended up in Roman hands. The Christian myth has it that Yeshua went in order to be crucified, a sacrifice of the god-man (in line with the Osiris-Dionysus myth) to atone for the sins of the world. The act of deliberate surrender is there in the gospel story line, though not in the residual version (above) which has been deduced. Yeshua supposedly took pains to antagonise the chief priests, so that he would be arrested. According to Mark, he predicted in quite precise terms his death and resurrection, though his disciples implausibly simply ignored this (Mark 10 32-35). They went on, as if nothing had been said, the reason being I suggest is that no such thing was said!

He took his followers, gathered them on the Mount of Olives, overlooking the city – and then meekly allowed himself to be handed over, 'betrayed' by one his own key disciples. This explanation is not only improbable, and at odds with actual history and Jewish context, but clearly derivative from Christian preoccupations and pagan myth.

There is however an underlying story. As with the survival motif, it is not a product of prophecy and not something that later Christian writers would have put in. On the contrary, this original tale has clearly been gutted by the censors so that only a few isolated references remain.

One reference occurs in Luke's gospel, during a description, interspersed with parables and other teachings, of Yeshua's journey from Galilee through towns and villages towards Jerusalem. As Luke (13, 1) has it, 'there were some present at that very time who told him (Yeshua) of the Galileans whose blood Pilate had mingled with their sacrifices'. Yeshua then continued on on his way with his followers. Because he was already on the way, it could not apparently have been this information that spurred Yeshua to go to Jerusalem.

However, Luke's description of the sequence of the journey is to say the least confusing. Yeshua sets out and is almost immediately half way in 'a village of the Samaritans' (Luke 9, 53). Next, he is with Martha and Mary, who lived in Bethany a mile or so from Jerusalem (Luke 10, 38). Then, he is told of the Roman massacre (Luke 13, 1). But Yeshua and his followers cannot be as close to Jerusalem as Bethany because, a little later (Luke 13, 31), Pharisees warn Yeshua that Herod the Tetrarch (Herod Antipas) was seeking to kill him. So, they were presumably on Herod's patch. This must have been in Galilee, rather than further south in Perea since, a few parables later, Yeshua is still only 'passing along between Samaria and Galilee' (Luke 17, 11). He hasn't even reached the point where he was supposed to have been at the outset in chapter 9! Finally, Yeshua arrives in Jericho (Luke 19, 1), reaches Bethany (again) and Jerusalem (Luke 19, 28-45).

The curious fact is that there is a proper sequence, which makes perfect sense, from the point at which Yeshua is told of the temple funds massacre, if it is assumed that this was in Galilee. The first two references, in chapters 9 and 10, before this are thus out of sequence. The references after this provide a coherent description of a purposeful journey. Yeshua sets out (Luke 13, 1), is still in Galilee a little further on (Luke 13, 31), is then between Samaria and Galilee (Luke 17, 11), reaches Jericho (Luke 19, 1), then Bethany (Luke 19, 29) and finally Jerusalem (Luke 19, 45).

The author of Luke's gospel apparently did not know, or did not want us to know, that Mary and Martha's parental home was in Bethany. He did not know, or did not want us to know, that Yeshua was told of the Roman massacre while he was in Galilee and at the beginning of his journey. The reason of course is that this would have indicated that Yeshua was responding with a march on Jerusalem which, however it ended, would have been seen as a military gesture. The author or editor of Luke, I suggest, added two incidents, which could have happened at another time, to the story that he already had. He then placed them in time before Yeshua set out on his journey, in order to mask Yeshua's intent.

It is a more reasonable proposition, given the clear and coherent sequence which follows, that Yeshua set out to Jerusalem as a result of hearing the news about his fellow Galileans, whose blood Pilate had spilled. It is certainly more reasonable than believing in the Christian-fabricated idea that Yeshua went with the set purpose of being crucified as some form of atonement (to a vengeful deity) for the general misdoings of mankind. How Yeshua might have responded verbally to news of the massacre is forever lost. But he may well have indicated that he intended to do something about this latest Roman atrocity and the prisoners who were taken and still held captive

If such a response were ever there, it would certainly have been cut out. The Christian gospel writers and editors were after all seeking to promote a figure appealing to the Gentile world, a saviour for mankind, and not a flesh-and-blood, Jewish liberator or messiah who would have been very much concerned about the fate of his fellow Galileans. Such people, in a relatively small community, were almost certainly also among his relatives and friends.

What the censor put in, precisely to fill the gap, was a homily about the Galileans who perished being no worse than anyone else and the importance of being ready in case one's own time came. The insertion of extraneous material was a means, in editing documents that had to be laboriously copied by hand, of reducing the amount of work. If an altered page could be kept to the same length, then only one page had to be rewritten.

The next reference to the incident appears later on, after Yeshua has been captured. According to Mark, 'among the rebels in prison, who had committed murder in the insurrection, there was a man called Barabbas' (Mark 15, 7). Now the point of this story, and indeed the reason why it was retained, was to blacken still further the reputation of 'the Jews'. Offered the choice of having Barabbas, described in Matthew as a 'notorious' prisoner and in John's gospel as a robber or bandit, or Yeshua released, the people chose the former. In this way, in the Christian writer's view, they heaped iniquity upon themselves. Luke has the same detail as Mark, but with the added detail that the insurrection was started in the city.

Clearly, there is some confusion here, perhaps some deliberate muddying of the water. The reason Barabbas was in prison was that he had taken part in a protest or uprising against the Romans. So, the suggestion that he was a robber, in John, is there in translation to serve as a distraction. The Greek word 'lestai' used in the text can be translated as robber or bandit, but it was also the term that the Romans themselves dismissively applied to militant Jewish nationalists. Barabbas was, if he was anything at all, one of the sicarii assassins or a zealot.

There is no historical support for the suggestion in the gospels that there may have been a custom whereby one prisoner was released at Passover. It is also unlikely that the Romans would ever have entered into such an ongoing arrangement.

The crowds are described as demanding the release of Barabbas instead of Yeshua (Jesus), improbably turning against the man they had supported in their thousands. But the name ascribed to the prisoner they really wanted, though familiar to us, was not a personal name at all. It was simply a description, bar-abbas, meaning 'son of the master'. In ancient Syriac (Aramaic) versions of the gospel of Matthew, the name is given fully as Jesus Barabbas, or in other words 'Jesus (that is, Yeshua) son of the master'.

This sheds more than a little light on what may have been the situation. I have suggested one possibility, that Yeshua's father, social or biological, also had a reputation as a teacher of scripture. The crowds were therefore actually demanding Yeshua's release, the son of this also learned father. That is certainly more plausible. It might explain why Pilate, faced with a population in Jerusalem hugely inflated at the time of Passover, a very angry crowd and only a small garrison of Roman soldiers to help him, acceded to demands including the staging of the crucifixion of Yeshua in a private place.

Another possibility is based on the evidence that Yeshua married and had sons, one of whom could have been named Yeshua after him (but not Jesus which is a later Greek rendering of this name). The son, Yeshua bar-abbas, took part in the demonstration over the misappropriation of temple funds and was taken prisoner by the Romans.

After hearing about the protest and its outcome, Yeshua and his followers moved south towards Jerusalem. I have argued that this follows on from the information that the massacre of demonstrators had taken place and, it can be presumed, was in response to it.

Yeshua had with him his cousins, James and John, engaged in unseemly manoeuvres to secure prominent places for themselves in the independent Jewish kingdom, after the expected victory over the Romans. He had armed followers, among them his fiery commander Simon, nicknamed Peter, who swung his sword and cut off the ear of the High Priest's servant.

There is no doubt that a confrontation was expected. There also seems little doubt that the Romans could have been overwhelmed. They had about one cohort of 500 men actually in Jerusalem and possibly up to 1000 more in the area, if they could be got back to the city in time. The population of Jerusalem had already vastly increased by the arrival of Passover pilgrims. Swilling around in the multitude were militant nationalists who could be counted on to join the column of Yeshua's supporters mingling unobtrusively among the pilgrims as they went south.

Thirty years later, there was such a revolt. The Roman garrison, with the sole exception of the commander, was massacred.

So how did this earlier, potentially decisive and promising confrontation apparently fizzle out? There was no great battle (had there been, the Jewish historian Josephus would have recorded it). The Nazorean's leader, Yeshua, was taken and crucified and his followers dispersed.

The gospel accounts are agreed that Yeshua was betrayed by someone called Judas. They are also agreed, though the details vary, that the Jewish authorities (the chief priests and the scribes and the elders) were at one in plotting his downfall and initiating his arrest. The reason appears to have been that Yeshua behaving like a messianic figure, someone who could or would try to overthrow Roman rule. He was also becoming increasingly popular. They feared this challenge would cause the Romans to react and 'come and destroy both our holy place and our nation'. They were prepared, in the words given to the High Priest Caiaphas, to sacrifice Yeshua so that 'one man should die for the people and the whole nation should not perish'. (John 11, 47-53).

There may have been other reasons too. The Sadducee chief priests must also have perceived Yeshua as a threat to their authority and livelihood. They had become wealthy through their control of sacrifices and money changing at the temple. In attacking this system, Yeshua directly challenged them.

The process under which Yeshua was tried by the Jewish authorities was, as many have pointed out, severely deficient on almost every count. Under Jewish law, an accused person could not be tried in secrecy or at night. The charges had to be laid against him first, rather than sought through interrogation. He was not obliged to say anything and could not in any case be convicted solely on the basis of his own admission. There had to be witnesses against him, whose testimony was convincing and in agreement. In the case of a capital offence, a day had to elapse between the proceedings and the sentence, to allow time for the judges to reflect and give further opportunity for witnesses to come forward for the defence. No one could be tried, convicted and executed in one day.

On all of these points, the proceedings against Yeshua were at fault. The case should have been dismissed out of hand because the witnesses failed to convince or agree. The judges however decided, according to the gospel account, that Yeshua was claiming to be, or posing as, the Son of God and that this was blasphemous. He was taken before the Romans because at that time only they had the authority to carry out a death sentence.

However, this was done on the basis of a different charge which had not previously been examined. It was contended that

Yeshua was claiming the kingship of Israel and was therefore, in relation to the Roman authorities, guilty of treason.

It is possible that reported deficiencies in the trial process may result from the fact that the gospel authors were not Jews and so not familiar with Jewish law and custom. They may also have been motivated to emphasise Jewish injustice and procedural weakness.

The gospel writers were certainly operating in a context where it served them best not to criticise the Romans but rather to blame the Jews. In the story, this happens in several ways. The Jewish authorities as a whole indict and convict Yeshua. His betrayer is a man, Judas, whose name has the same derivation as 'Jew', someone from the kingdom of Judah. The crowd, the Jewish people, are then made to demand Yeshua's crucifixion, spurning the offer of his release in favour of a `notorious' criminal Barabbas. Pilate is portrayed as sympathetic to and reluctant to condemn Yeshua.

There are however many details in the gospel evidence which indicate that this is not entirely valid. The investigating council, convened at dead of night, is most unlikely to have been anything like a full Sanhedrin. It would have contained a disproportionate number of the Sadducee priests, since they were most threatened and since it was their High Priest who had instigated the action. Luke (23, 51) points to the absence of one possible Pharisee member, Joseph of Arimathea. Thus it may not have been the Jewish authorities, properly constituted, but rather a Sadducee faction that acted against Yeshua. This could well explain many of the reported flaws in procedure. These happened because a group, intent on eliminating Yeshua, hijacked the judicial process.

The argument that the collaborating Sadducees were the instigators fits with evidence of Pharisees being on friendly terms with or assisting Yeshua. It also accords with the picture presented, as the gospel narrative progresses. It is the chief priests (present and former Sadducee High Priests) who bring charges against Yeshua, whom Pilate suspects as having acted out of envy and who try to stir up the crowd to demand Yeshua's crucifixion (Mark 15, 3-11).

It is possible, I have argued, that the character of Judas Iscariot was invented precisely for the purpose of having a typecast betrayer. The real Judas Sicarios, portrayed as a sicarii assassin, was one of Yeshua's brothers. Yeshua's father, also in the messianic line, would have been referred to with some deference. So the crowds shouting for 'Jesus Barabbas' could in fact have been demanding the release of Yeshua, 'son of the master'! This detail, a fragment of the original source story, has been incorporated but with its meaning turned and deflected.

The situation which this points to is more realistic and convincing. Only some Jews, largely collaborating Sadducees, act against Yeshua. Ordinary people remain as his supporters and he remains a popular figure.

Far from acting as they had apparently intended, before Passover (Mark 14, 2), Yeshua's enemies had actually brought about a confrontation on the eve of the celebrations, when Jerusalem's population had already doubled through an influx of pilgrims. Pilate was effectively trapped in the city with only a cohort of troops and with many miles, not in effective Roman control, between him and his palace at Caesarea. Self-preservation, rather than sympathy, might have motivated him to wish to release Yeshua.

But he was trapped also by the cunning suggestion that, if he released the man regarded as a Jewish king, he would not be 'Caesar's friend'. As he had over the issue of the standards embossed with the head of the Roman emperor, Pilate bent under pressure. He gave way. He sanctioned the execution. It is at this point, with Pilate in a weak position, that prominent Pharisees came in to exert some influence.

Pilate had by this time no choice but to go ahead with the

crucifixion. But he would not have been able to enforce it, with so few troops, had the situation turned ugly. He would have been facing a riot, possibly a full-scale insurrection.

Neither he, nor the Pharisees, nor even the Sadducee High Priest's faction wanted that. Pilate allowed the execution to take place, most unusually, in a private garden. He let the body be taken down early. For whatever reason, the legs of the victim were not broken.

Pilate was certainly a man under pressure from all sides. The execution that did take place was, if the gospel accounts and the sources behind them are to be believed, deeply flawed. I have argued that the twin themes of the original, and probable Nazorean, account behind the later gospel stories were resistance and survival. This much is the truth of the gospels.

Whether Yeshua survived crucifixion, even for a short time, or whether this was simply a clever piece of zealot propaganda may never be known.

From that moment on, Yeshua disappeared as an effective player from the political scene. If he survived the crucifixion, as the evidence suggests that he might have, then either he died later from his wounds or went into exile, never to return.

His Nazorean followers suggested and maybe believed that Yeshua would come back. This translated into the later Christian belief in the gospels that Jesus/Yeshua would in the immediate future stage a 'second coming'. I believe there was a difference. The Nazoreans were expecting a flesh and blood man, whereas Christians expected a returning god made in the flesh of man.

In neither case, was the expectation fulfilled. But, in the case of the historical Yeshua as opposed to the mythical Christian Jesus, it needs to be remembered that the man was only one link in the chain, one part of the movement.

Yeshua took on the mantle of religious authority and kingship from John the Baptist. This would then have passed on to his successors, as indeed happened with the Maccabeans. His brother James certainly did take on a role of popular religious leader, with thousands of followers, opposed to the official and popularly much despised leadership of a collaborating Sadducee priesthood under Roman patronage.

But there was also continuing political resistance during this time period, the thirty years following the march south to Jerusalem which had ended apparently ignominiously in the loss of the Nazoreans' leader.

As history is recorded by the Jewish turncoat general Josephus, Yeshua gets scarcely an authentic mention. The various incidents, in the period leading up to the first great Jewish revolt, appear disconnected from each other and the culminating rebellion *and* from the circumstances surrounding Yeshua's lifetime, of which we have only badly refracted commentary in the Christian gospels.

So is the account by Josephus an accurate portrayal and, if not, how did it come about? What if anything does it tell us about the place of Yeshua and his followers in the conflicts of his time?

Chapter 9: Making history

At this point, it is possible to answer some of the questions first raised at the end of chapter 3. Yeshua did not act alone but was part of a Jewish messianic movement. His own resistance was both religious and political, culminating in a march on Jerusalem, which ended with his capture and execution. This move may have been prompted by a Roman massacre of people protesting against the misappropriation of temple funds.

The assault on the Roman garrison, expected by at least some of his followers, did not happen. Yeshua was captured by the Sadducee High Priest's officers, subjected to a highly irregular judicial procedure and handed over to the Romans.

The Roman governor Pilate was disinclined to sanction the execution of a popular figure in circumstances that could have led to the Roman garrison being overrun. But he was pressured into conducting a crucifixion, where not all the elements were entirely under his control.

That the core Nazorean message was that Yeshua then survived and escaped was not something that could be portrayed as a Roman success, rather a matter for considerable embarrassment. It can be argued that this was what led Josephus to maintain a diplomatic silence on the issue.

It can also be argued, as will be seen, that Josephus did not want to draw attention to the linkages in a chain of messianic succession from John the Baptist through Yeshua to other family members.

Yeshua's religious leadership passed to his brothers James and then Simon or Simeon. But what of the aspirations to kingship? Josephus kept silent on this for many good reasons, just as he failed likewise to describe the circumstances of Yeshua's rebellion and death.

As described in Acts, the crucifixion of Yeshua did not lead to the dissolution of the Nazorean movement. New members were recruited, pooling their possessions. The message these Jewish followers proclaimed was that Yeshua was alive (in other words had survived crucifixion) and had been taken up, like Elijah and others before him, straight into heaven.

The High Priest and his followers attempted to suppress the promulgation of this message, without success. But then a move was made to purge members of the movement, beginning with the trial and execution of Stephen. As Acts notes, the chief figures in the movement had begun to devote themselves to prayer and preaching, leaving day to day administration to others. This may explain why, after the death of Stephen, the High Priest's police enforcers including Saul went after the members of the 'ecclesia', the Jerusalem church, while leaving its religious leadership alone.

A little later in the narrative, the action suggests that this distinction was not quite so clear cut. Herod, presumably Herod Agrippa I who was Roman-appointed king of Judea, executed Yeshua's cousin James, one of the 'sons of thunder', and arrested Simon, known as 'the Outlaw' and also nicknamed 'the Rock' (Peter).

It would appear that the Rome appointed authorities directed their efforts with some success against militant activists within the Nazorean movement. But attempts to disrupt the growth of the movement and its increasing popularity failed. This in turn made it difficult to deal with its spiritual leadership, which had popular support, and which was not apparently conducting any overt political resistance. For this reason, Yeshua's brother James remained as religious head of the Nazorean movement for twenty five years, following the crucifixion.

The existence and development of this movement, including the role of James, is documented in Acts and in other sources. So it is strange that the historian of this period, Josephus, records next to nothing on the life of Yeshua or James or, indeed, militant messianic nationalism which was an evident force in the first century and a major dynamic of the Jewish rebellion. I have suggested that what happened with Yeshua may have been such an embarrassment to the Romans, for whom Josephus was writing, that the historian deemed it best to keep silent.

But this may only be part of the explanation. For the rest, it is necessary to consider the circumstances of Josephus' own life and the situation in which he was writing.

Born in CE 37, just after the crucifixion of Yeshua, Josephus was a member of a privileged Jewish family with links through his mother's side to the Maccabeans. He was educated in a rabbinic school in Jerusalem, developing expertise in Jewish law and Greek literature. He claims to have spent time in his youth studying with all the main schools of Jewish religious thought: Sadducee, Pharisee and Essene and finally three years in the desert with a character given the pseudonym 'Banus'.

This person was described as spiritual, ascetic, vegetarian and, like Yeshua's brother James, a celibate who engaged in the practice of cold bathing.

Having run the gamut of these philosophies, Josephus chose to become a Pharisee priest.

A few years later, he took it upon himself to go to Rome to intercede on behalf of fellow priests, arrested on what Josephus describes as a 'trivial' charge. This may have been to do with the issue of the privacy of temple proceedings. King Agrippa II had built a room in his palace overlooking the temple in Jerusalem, in response to which the priests had built a wall blocking his view and incidentally also that of a Roman guard post.

Josephus made some valuable contacts in Rome, including Poppea, wife of the Roman Emperor Nero, which helped in securing the release of his friends. He then returned to Jerusalem two years later in CE 66, when war threatened between the Jews and Rome.

Josephus was a Pharisee and not one of the collaborating

High Priest's party, nor apparently a militant messianic nationalist. He can be placed among a substantial section of Jews who also wanted freedom, but were wary of conflict. In Rome, he would have been able to see at first hand Roman supremacy in terms of men, resources, equipment and training. He was therefore especially well placed to argue the case, after the conflict had started, that further struggle was futile and his countrymen should come to terms. For taking this view, Josephus was threatened by his compatriots and accused of collusion with the Romans.

Relations between the Jews and their Roman masters were tense and there had been a number of occasions when disregard of Jewish customs and sensibilities might have sparked a full-scale conflict. The Roman Governor Pilate was involved in some of these, revolving around issues such as the presence of Roman standards, embossed with images of the Emperor, in the temple at Jerusalem and the use or misuse of temple funds. Perhaps most provocative of all was the Emperor Caligula's decision to order a statue of himself as the Roman god Zeus to be placed in the temple. What saved the situation at this point was some adroit delaying tactics by the Syrian legate, and then the timely death of the Emperor himself.

It was one of Pilate's successors as governor, Gessius Florus who, as Josephus described it, was chiefly responsible for provoking the Jewish population into open revolt. Florus accepted bribes, failed to act impartially in resolving disputes and appropriated money from the temple treasury. When he demanded that those who had so protested be handed over, Jewish leaders pointed out that it might be hard to identify individuals and that such action could lead to further trouble. Florus' response was to unleash his soldiers in a series of brutal massacres of civilians.

While Josephus seems anxious to portray Florus as the insti-gator of conflict, he mentions later that annual taxes to the

Romans were overdue. With the crisis teetering on the brink of outright rebellion, King Agrippa II intervened to persuade Jewish leaders to collect the 40 talents demanded. To give an idea of the amount involved, a single talent was worth 60,000 drachmas and this alone would have have paid the subsistence wages of more than 100 labourers for a year. The burden of taxation was considerable and, not surprisingly, widely resented.

Florus eventually withdrew to Caesarea while the tax was being collected. King Agrippa, who had been attempting to mediate, also left Jerusalem.

The account of the Jewish uprising provided by the captured turncoat Josephus is not always entirely transparent; it has to be remembered that this was provided primarily for the purpose of demonstrating to subject peoples the futility of resistance. The impact of recent Roman mismanagement and atrocities may well have triggered the conflict. But there were also root causes of dissatisfaction that can be traced back several years.

One of these was the assassination of the popular Nazorean leader James, four years before in CE 62. This was followed by a period of civil unrest during which insurgents, described by Josephus as sicarii, captured members of the former High Priest Ananias' staff to exchange for their members taken prisoner.

The taxes demanded by the Romans are also implied as a causative factor. Josephus may not have wanted to stress this, for fear of drawing comparisons with an earlier tax revolt by the zealot leader Judas the Galilean. In the war which was about to start, Josephus would become one of the commanders on the Jewish side. Though he later went over to the Romans and became their spokesman, he might have wanted to avoid emphasising and possibly being identified with the militant nationalism behind the conflict.

The massacres by Florus, it would seem, eventually prompted some lower order priestly officials in the temple to refuse to make the daily sacrifices on behalf of Rome and the Emperor

Nero. Such offerings, though a necessary accommodation with Roman authority, had long been seen by fundamentalists as polluting the temple.

A heated debate followed in which Herodians and followers of the High Priest argued for resuming the sacrifices on the grounds that failing to do so would make war inevitable. They sent delegations to Florus and also to Agrippa II, great-grandson of Herod and ruler of Galilee, demanding reinforcements for the city to quash any revolt. Agrippa did indeed send a large number of cavalry, after which fighting broke out between the rebels and loyalist forces.

If not planned in advance, the uprising must have been coordinated to a substantial degree. A force under Menahem, described by Josephus variously as zealots or sicarii, assaulted the rock fortress at Masada, overwhelmed the Roman garrison and plundered the Roman armoury. With these newly acquired weapons, they then entered Jerusalem and joined with other insurgents to press the attack on forces loyal to the Romans.

Menahem, described by Josephus as a son of the earlier tax rebel Judas the Galilean, was no ordinary rebel but entered Jerusalem 'like a king' and went into the temple 'decked in kingly robes'. His forces pushed back the Romans further, allowing only Agrippa's troops to come out under an amnesty, and captured and killed the former High Priest Ananias.

But then Menahem was himself killed and this led to some of his supporters returning to Masada. Under Eleazar, son of Jairus, they successfully defended the fortress long after the uprising was effectively over and Jerusalem had been retaken by the Romans.

The situation in the meantime for the remaining Roman defenders, encircled by other rebel forces in Jerusalem, was hopeless. A surrender was negotiated under which the Romans would give up their weapons and equipment in return for safe passage out of the city. But once the troops had come out and laid down their arms, they were treacherously massacred. The insurgents spared just the Roman commander of the garrison, Metilius, on the promise that he would undergo circumcision and become a convert to Judaism.

The Roman response to this major setback was to send a force of many thousands of troops under Cestius Gallus from its regional headquarters in Syria. Meeting little resistance on the way to Jerusalem, the Romans were then caught outside the city in a pincer attack.

Regrouping, the troops forced their way through the outskirts and besieged the city.

According to Josephus, the Roman force then inexplicably retreated, at the very point of victory. However, it may be that, with lines of communications stretched and food in short supply with winter approaching, the Romans were not equipped to carry out a long siege. They had also lost a lot of baggage, including possibly such vital items as siege engines, in the earlier fighting on the way to Jerusalem.

The retreating army was harried, disrupted and successfully ambushed at a mountain pass, Beth Horon, suffering very substantial losses. Cestius was forced to abandon most of his equipment in favour of ignominious flight. For the rebels, this was a very substantial victory; they had all but wiped out an entire Roman legion.

Josephus, or rather Joseph son of Matthias as he was then known, was one of the influential citizens in Jerusalem. He had argued initially for coming to terms and as a result was accused of collusion and forced for his own safety to go into hiding in Jerusalem. By his own account, he emerged from hiding, following the death of Menahem and the defeat of the twelfth legion sent from Syria under Cestius Gallus. With a full-scale war with Rome now inevitable, preparations were made to organise the defence of Jerusalem and other parts of the country.

Rather than military prowess, the appointments made

reflected the realities of political and religious power. The former High Priest Ananus was given joint control of Jerusalem and Josephus himself assigned to take on the defence of the northern province of Galilee. It would appear that those who argued for accommodation at least initially had a share of power.

This was not, however, a situation that lasted long.

In Galilee, John son of Levi, from Gischala, among others, gathered forces against Josephus and sought to have him relieved of his post – on the grounds that he was colluding with the Romans.

In Jerusalem, Eleazar, son of Simon, fresh from the victory over Cestius and flush with captured money, supplies and other goods, gained support as a popular leader. Then, later, as the Romans advanced and rebel forces fled to Jerusalem, civil war broke out between forces loyal to Ananus on the one hand and more militant nationalists on the other. These latter consisted of the supporters of Eleazar, John and his fighters who had retreated from Gischala in Galilee plus a force of Idumeans they had invited into the city. In the ensuing conflict, Ananus was killed and his body tossed out over the city wall.

In Galilee, Josephus, having survived attempts to displace him, had set about training an army and fortifying the major towns and cities. However, this proved no match for the considerable force that the Emperor Nero had assembled under his general Flavius Vespasian. Some smaller towns and villages were quickly overrun and Josephus' own army fled without offering to fight. At this point, Josephus sent a letter by messenger to Jerusalem to the effect that the cause was lost and that the Jewish authorities should seek to come to terms.

Josephus was then surrounded and besieged by the Roman forces at Jotapata. When the Romans were about to take the town, he proposed that he and other leading citizens should try to escape. According to his own account, Josephus was persuaded by the people of the town to stay.

After the town had fallen, Josephus and a small group of companions hid for two days in a cellar or cave. When they were discovered, the group resolved to commit suicide, in true zealot fashion, rather than be killed or sold into slavery by the Romans. Josephus, perhaps with some confidence of being spared if captured, argued against such a course. Accused of cowardice, and faced with the prospect of being run through with a sword if he demurred, he went along with the plan – but he managed to memorise the lots which determined the sequence in which individuals would be killed. The idea was that the man drawing the first lot would have his throat cut by the second, who in turn would have his throat cut by the third in line, and so on. A similar plan was carried out at Masada where several hundred rebels, holding out long after the war had ended elsewhere, committed mass suicide rather than be taken by the Romans.

Josephus must have noted and taken the lot, possibly as at Masada a broken pottery shard, which held one of the two last numbers.

He then managed to persuade the last survivor to surrender with him and was captured and taken before Vespasian. The Roman general intended to send his important and valuable prisoner to Nero. But Josephus ingeniously declared that Vespasian himself would soon become Emperor, which it appears encouraged the general to hold Josephus for a while to see how the situation would turn out.

Nero was subsequently deposed and, two years on, Vespasian took over the office of Emperor with the help of his own loyal troops. In the meantime, Josephus had proved his usefulness in interviewing Jewish prisoners and deserters. He was even deployed, during the siege of Jerusalem, to go round the walls calling on the Jewish defenders to surrender. The fulfilment of the prophecy that Vespasian would become Emperor further enhanced Josephus' standing in Roman eyes. He was given his freedom and, as was the custom, took on the family name of his benefactor. The transition from being a Jewish commander of rebellious forces against Rome was thus completed. Joseph, son of Matthias, became Flavius Josephus.

After the war, Josephus was given Roman citizenship, a pension, the house in Rome in which Vespasian had lived as a private citizen and estates in Jerusalem, which he never visited, fearing quite justifiably for his own safety. He was commissioned to write a history of the war, in which he was implicitly or explicitly given the task of justifying Roman actions and demonstrating to other subject peoples the futility of resistance.

Josephus ably carried out this undertaking, publishing his account in CE 75, five years after the war had ended with the fall of Jerusalem. The first edition was in Aramaic but then a Greek translation was produced to make it more accessible, since Greek was the common language of the Roman Empire. Josephus then embarked on an ambitious history of the Jewish people, *Jewish Antiquities,* published much later in CE 93, some parts of which provide varying accounts of events described in the earlier *Jewish War.*

Two subsequent shorter works were inspired by criticism. His *Vita* (Life) was designed to counteract the suggestion, which was potentially damaging in view of his delicate position in relation to Rome, that he was really the instigator of the revolt in Galilee. This came from Justus of Tiberias, one of Josephus' opponents in Galilee, who also survived the war and who wrote an alternative account which is no longer extant.

Josephus' *Vita* also included useful biographical details about his earlier life and his life following the war. His final publication, *Contra Apionem,* was devoted to defending Judaism against anti-Semitic attacks made by an Alexandrian writer, Apion, and a number of other authors.

There are deficiencies in Josephus' work, many of which can be attributed to the fact that this was someone writing over 19 centuries ago, much nearer to the dawn of civilisation and certainly to the beginning of literacy, and with it the production and dissemination of written accounts. As a historian, he did not have the tools that are now available and he was operating to different standards and conventions.

It was, for example, common among writers at the time to put into the mouths of key characters discursive speeches. These were certainly not what the characters had said but what they might, in the opinion of the author, have said in the circumstances in which they were placed. This may add to the dramatic quality of the narrative, but provides detail that cannot be relied on.

The text is often hard to follow, with frequent digressions to deal with other contemporaneous events and detailed descriptions that were sometimes not even relevant to the story's development. It is also possible that, even in the original writing, literal mistakes crept in. Books were then produced by the laborious procedure of writing them out, using scribes paid by the line. It would have been difficult for the author to go back and correct mistakes, assuming even that he recognised them, and probably no one was employed to check for errors.

The original manuscripts would not have lasted for long. Copies were made decades or centuries later, for someone wanting the book or for the convenience of having something less fragile to read, and ultimately these replaced the originals. Mistakes were introduced in copying. Sometimes these would have been accidental when, for example, a marginal explanatory note made by a reader was incorporated into the text. Sometimes, as will be suggested, the copyists wanted to put their own gloss on Josephus' account.

Even by the standards of the time, Josephus did not and could not have produced an impartial record. He was writing to please the Romans, justify their actions and deter further revolts by subject peoples. As a captured Jewish general, in a war in which there had been atrocities on both sides, he was in a precarious position and he could not have stepped too far out of line.

Josephus' account is coloured by his own character. Undoubtedly learned and a good organiser, he also had a huge opinion of himself and appears at times highly credulous, adding conjecture and fanciful detail to the description of events. He was also a survivor, as can be seen by the means by which he escaped a suicide pact and the way in which he managed to ingratiate himself with Vespasian. If these events are a guide, self-preservation would have come some way before any consideration of providing an exact historical record.

It is certainly a difficulty that, in the *Jewish War*, Josephus is not only the narrator but also one of the main characters in the drama – and we do not have another account to provide a check on what he says.

Even so, the works by Josephus provide a unique record of contemporary events, providing a lot of insight and a huge amount of detail. For the second major Jewish uprising sixty years later, there was unfortunately no one like Josephus to record it. So, the information available for this later revolt is sparse even though there were just as many important characters involved, events took place over a similar time period and the historical significance of what happened was arguably just as great.

Antiquities and the *Jewish War* do, therefore, provide a very useful record despite their deficiencies. In addition, though Josephus may have written for his patrons and his audience and coloured his accounts, he might not have been able to get away with glaring discrepancies, especially with what had happened in the very recent past. If he tampered at all with this, then it would have had to be done (and I suggest it was done) very subtly. The problem, both for those seeking historical evidence for Christianity and those seeking to make a critique of the origins of Christianity, is that there is either nothing or next to nothing on the subject, depending on one's viewpoint, in the writings of Josephus.

There are two references to Pontius Pilate, who was procurator or prefect at the time, in the *Jewish War*. These relate to Pilate's maladroit handling of the issue over Roman standards in Jerusalem and the protest over the misuse of temple funds to build an aqueduct. The event which brought Pilate's rule in Judea to a close, the massacre of Samaritans at Mount Gerizim, is dealt with only in the later work, *Antiquities*.

In this work there are two references to Jesus (Yeshua), one fairly substantial and the second in passing in reference to James, Yeshua's brother. But most scholars agree that the first of these, at least, is an insertion made by a later Christian writer:

About this time there lived Jesus, a wise man, if indeed one ought to call him a man. For he was one who wrought surprising feats and was a teacher of such people as accept the truth gladly. He won over many Jews and many of the Greeks. He was the messiah. When Pilate, upon hearing him accused by men of the highest standing amongst us, had condemned him to be crucified, those who had in the first place come to love him did not give up their affection for him. On the third day he appeared to them restored to life, for the prophets of God had prophesied these and countless other marvellous things about him. And the tribe of the Christians, so called after him, has still to this day not disappeared.

There are a number of reasons for thinking that this is a later insertion. The piece does not entirely follow the style of Josephus. It breaks the continuity of text, dealing with a series of riots and protests, which would follow on quite naturally without the passage relating to Yeshua. The passage begins with the phrase 'About this time' which, if original, would make the introduction to the next paragraph, 'About the same time', a clumsy repetition.

Most seriously, it contains the flat statement 'He was the

messiah' which Josephus could hardly have made as a Pharisee priest. Nor, for that matter, as a newly enrolled Roman citizen, depending for his position and his life on Roman favour, could he have appeared to support a group regarded as a nuisance and actively persecuted by successive Emperors.

The early church authority Origen twice explicitly stated, around CE 280, that Josephus did not believe that Jesus (Yeshua) was the Christ. He was, however, familiar with a passage, which has since disappeared from Josephus' work, to the effect that it was the death of James that led to the disaster of the failed revolt and the destruction of Jerusalem and the temple by the Romans. So it would seem that the reference to Jesus, quoted above, was a later insertion: had it been present at the time Origen wrote, he would have known about it. He could not, in the knowledge of the text as it is set out above, have asserted that Josephus did not believe that Jesus (Yeshua) was the Christ.

The passage is first quoted in the early fourth century by Constantine's bishop Eusebius who quite unashamedly admitted to rewriting history, leaving out what he considered unfit and including only that which reflected to the credit of Christianity and the Roman church.

There is a narrow time gap during which the forged passage could have been inserted and it is possible that the arch propagandist and manipulator Eusebius did it himself. There are several references which make it appear that the text was written by a Jewish commentator, rather than a Christian interpolator, for example that Jesus was a 'wise man' who 'wrought surprising feats'. However, the reference to 'the tribe' of Christians indicates that it might have been Eusebius who introduced such comments, ostensibly in the manner of Josephus. Other writers prior to Eusebius, Pliny and Trajan, did not use the word tribe or race (in Latin, 'tribus') with reference to Christians, but Eusebius – in quoting these sources – did! So it may have been his word which he then put into the mouth of Josephus.

It is possible that the reference further on in *Antiquities* in relation to James was also inserted to provide apparent historical evidence for the life of Jesus (Yeshua). The passage in question refers to the High Priest at the time, Ananus, the man later appointed by moderates to take charge of Jerusalem during the revolt but then subsequently overthrown and killed by zealots. Taking advantage of a temporary power vacuum, with the Roman procurator dead and his replacement not yet in post, Ananus had James arrested and stoned to death. The passage reads:

> The younger Ananus who, as we have said, had been appointed to the high priesthood, was rash in his temper and unusually daring. He followed the school of the Sadducees, who are indeed more heartless than any of the other Jews, as I have already explained, when they sit in judgement. Possessed of such a character, Ananus thought he had a favourable opportunity because Festus was dead and Albinus still on the way. And so he convened the judges of the Sanhedrin, and brought before them a man named James, the brother of Jesus who was called the Christ, and certain others. He accused them of having transgressed the law and delivered them up to be stoned.

There is evidence from the gospels, one of Paul's letters, Acts and early church sources that James was indeed one of the brothers of Yeshua. If this reference to Jesus was inserted, perhaps initially as a note in the margin which was later then incorporated into the text, then as far as the relationship with James was concerned the editor was adding what he believed to have been true, and what I have suggested on the evidence was probably true. It must be pointed out, however, that Christian editors did as far as possible seek to diminish the role of the brothers of Yeshua, including James who was even called 'James the less' in Mark's gospel! So, if the phrase 'the brother of Jesus who was called the Christ' was inserted, then it is indicative of a degree of desperation to find – or provide – any evidence anywhere in Josephus to give belief in the world redeemer Jesus a historical basis.

The part of the phrase 'who was called the Christ' is, interestingly, less emphatic than the earlier, clearly inserted statement 'He was the messiah'. It indicates a degree of distance, offering the alternative possibility that Josephus did actually write this particular passage or at least a version of it that may have then been modified.

The belief that Josephus did have something to say about 'Jesus Christ', that he did indeed provide confirmation for the story independent of the gospels, provided a compelling motivation for medieval monks and earlier scribes to preserve his works. The works of many other writers of this period are lost, known if at all through quotes and references given by subsequent authors. Josephus, by contrast, fared much better. His works were carefully and studiously copied over the centuries by Christian monks, in the sure conviction that they were preserving a vital part of the Christian record. It is ironic that forgeries perpetrated and added in by Eusebius, or someone like him, may thus have helped to preserve a unique historical commentary on first century Palestine that might otherwise have been lost.

While there is apparently complete silence on the subject of Yeshua in the *Jewish War* and just two references in *Antiquities*, the most significant of which is patently a Christian addition, this is as it happens not quite the end of the matter.

Josephus claims to have written his first version of the *Jewish War* in Aramaic, for distribution to Jews in Palestine and Babylonia. It is quite probable this happened following the imperative to get the message across to those who might consider resisting Roman rule. This was then translated, and quite possibly extensively rewritten in Greek, the language of empire, to provide a version for the Romans themselves and the wider world.

The Aramaic version does not survive. But another version of the *Jewish War* does exist, translated into Old Russian around the year CE 1200, which has a number of differences from the generally available Greek version. It is clear, from the construction of the language and style, that alterations were neither written in Old Russian and then inserted into a translation of the Greek text, nor were they the result of translation from the early, Aramaic text. It appears that the Old Russian text as a whole is a translation from Greek. In which case the differences, including a number of references (not by name) to John the Baptist and Yeshua, arise from another Greek version of the *Jewish War* that was made quite early on. There is more on John the Baptist than in the gospels or in the short reference in *Antiquities*. There is also a short account of the activities of the followers of Yeshua, either Nazoreans or early Christians.

For present purposes, the focus is on the main passage below relating to Yeshua:

At that time also a man came forward, — if even it is fitting to call him a man [simply]. His nature as well as his form were a man's; but his showing forth was more than [that] of a man. His works, that is to say, were godly, and he wrought wonder-deeds amazing and full of power. Therefore it is not possible for me to call him a man [simply]. But again, looking at the existence he shared with all, I would also not call him an angel. And all that he wrought through some kind of invisible power, he wrought by word and command.

Some said of him, that our first Lawgiver has risen from the dead and shows forth many cures and arts. But others supposed [less definitely] that he is sent by God. Now he opposed himself in much to the Law and did not observe the Sabbath according to ancestral custom. Yet, on the other hand, he did nothing reprehensible nor any crime; but by word solely he effected everything.

And many from the folk followed him and received his teachings. And many souls became wavering, supposing that thereby the Jewish tribes would set themselves free from the Roman hands.

Now it was his custom often to stop on the Mount of Olives facing the city. And there also he avouched his cures to the people. And there gathered themselves to him of servants a hundred and fifty, but of the folk a multitude.

But when they saw his power, that he accomplished everything that he would by word, they urged him that he should enter the city and cut down the Roman soldiers and Pilate and rule over us. But that one scorned it.

And thereafter, when knowledge of it came to the Jewish leaders, they gathered together with the High-priest and spake: 'We are powerless and weak to withstand the Romans. But as withal the bow is bent, we will go and tell Pilate what we have heard, and we will be without distress, lest if he hear it from others, we be robbed of our substance and ourselves be put to the sword and our children ruined.' And they went and told it to Pilate.

And he sent and had many of the people cut down. And he had that wonder-doer brought up. And when he had instituted a trial concerning him, he perceived that he is a doer of good, but not an evildoer, nor a revolutionary, nor one who aimed at power, and set him free. He had, you should know, healed his dying wife.

And he went to his accustomed place and wrought his accustomed works. And as again more folk gathered themselves together round him, then did he win glory through his works more than all.

The teachers of the Law were [therefore] envenomed with envy and gave thirty talents to Pilate, in order that he should put him to death. And he, after he had taken [the money], gave them consent that they should themselves carry out their purpose.

And they took him and crucified him according to the ancestral law.

There has been considerable scholarly controversy over the authorship of this passage and the others relating to John the Baptist and the early followers of Yeshua. There are enough similarities in language and form to indicate that these all came from the same hand. But whose?

It is hardly likely to have been Josephus himself, writing a second Greek version, of which we have no account, for another audience. He was not, as has been pointed out, a covert Christian and he would not, in his precarious position of favour with the Romans, have done anything to put himself at risk. So he would not, in the terms of the passage above, have expressed admiring appreciation of Yeshua's uniqueness or superhuman powers. Yeshua's descendants, 'Sons of David' and followers, were sought out and persecuted under successive Roman Emperors while Josephus was living as an honoured guest in Rome!

The Romans did not always distinguish between Messianism which was virulently nationalist and the Christian form which was world embracing, obedient and benign. So Josephus could not and would not have risked associating himself with a messianic cult, that could at that time have been seen as a threat to Rome.

In addition to which Christianity had, largely through the circumstances of its break with James and Yeshua's other followers, become strongly anti-Jewish. This can be seen in the Slavonic *Jewish War* passage quoted above where it is the Jews who crucify Yeshua (as in the gospel of Peter) and not the Romans. Pilate is here made out to be quite a sympathetic character who tries, acquits and even frees Yeshua! It is only then, after receiving a bribe of thirty talents from the 'teachers of the Law' (presumably the High Priest and his Sadducee followers), that he consents to them taking and killing Yeshua. This has the hallmarks of a Christian interpretation, rather than an authentic account in Josephus' hand.

The evidence certainly is conflicting as to how the Slavonic *Jewish War* arose. There is a reflection of the forged passage in *Antiquities*, for which Eusebius may have been responsible, in the use of the term 'Jewish tribes'. However, by the time that Eusebius was organising new versions of the gospels, a more definite view of Yeshua as divine and 'Son of God' had evolved which is not reflected in the uncertain terms expressed in the Slavonic passage. Taking the passage at face value, it is not something that Eusebius, given the doctrine that he was promoting, would have contrived.

When it comes to describing what happened following the crucifixion of Yeshua, the author expresses himself in an even greater uncertainty:

> And it was said that after he was put to death, yea after burial in the grave, he was not found. Some then assert that he is risen; but others, that he has been stolen by his friends. I, however, do not know which speak more correctly. For a dead man cannot rise of himself – though possibly with the help of another righteous man; unless it will be an angel or another of the heavenly authorities, or God himself appears as a man and accomplishes what he will, – both walks with men and falls, and lies down and rises up, as it is according to his will. But others said that it was not possible to steal him, because they had put guards all round his grave, – thirty Romans, but a thousand Jews.

This gives the impression of an attempt at impartiality, of a struggle to come to terms with conflicting evidence and opinions.

It is hard to believe that someone, later in the Christian tradition, would have had the discipline and subtlety to invent such a travesty of received dogma, purely to project back into Josephus evidence for the origins of Christianity. In doing so, the author would also have had to be astute enough to write without giving away his knowledge of the canonical gospels, which he would at that time have been familiar with.

It is interesting that this piece of text, as well as being uncertain about the possibility of resurrection, also includes the rumour that the 'friends' of Yeshua (his immediate followers and family) had stolen the body. Again, this indicates that the piece was not of late Christian origin but possibly written by someone who was sympathetic, though not actually a Christian himself.

There is also in a passage on the early Christians a suggestion of the framework, though highly condensed, of the Acts of the Apostles:

Again Claudius sent his authorities to those states – Cuspius Fadus and Tiberius Alexander, both of whom kept the people in peace, not allowing them to depart in anything from the pure laws.

But if anyone diverged from the word of the Law, plaint was brought before the teachers of the Law. Often they expelled him and sent him to the Emperor's presence.

And at the time of these two many had been discovered as servants of the previously described wonder-doer; and as they spake to the people about their teacher, – that he is living, although he is dead, and that he will free you from your servitude, – many from the folk gave ear to the above-named and took upon themselves their precept, – not because of their reputation; they were indeed of the humbler sort some just cobblers, others sandal-makers, others artisans.

And [yet] as marvellous signs they accomplished in truth what they would.

But when those noble governors saw the misleading of the people, they deliberated with the scribes to seize and put them to death, for fear lest the little be not little if it have ended in the great. But they shrank back and were alarmed over the signs, saying: 'In the plain course such wonders do not occur. But if they do not issue from the counsel of God, they will quickly be convicted.' And they gave them [the Christians] authority to act as they would.

But afterwards, becoming pestered by them, they had them sent away, some to the Emperor, but others to Antioch, others again to distant lands, – for the testing of the matter.

But Claudius removed the two governors, [and] sent Cumanus.

Instead of approximately 25 years in Acts, this description is compressed into the four years in which there were two Roman Governors, Fadus and Tiberius Alexander, from CE 44 to 48. It includes a variant account of the advice which the Pharisee leader Gamaliel gave when Simon (Peter) and other followers were brought before the Sanhedrin, 'for if this plan or undertaking is of men it will fail; but if it is of God you will not be able to overthrow them.'

The question arises as to whether these two sources, Acts and the passage in the Slavonic *Jewish War*, depend on common information, the sense of what the Jewish authorities ruled in relation to Nazorean followers of Yeshua who were brought before them, or whether one is secondary to the other.

It is possible that the information about Yeshua and his followers and John the Baptist in the Greek original of the Slavonic *Jewish War* was compiled by someone in the second century when Acts was available. This would not, however, explain the wide divergences from the canonical gospel accounts and the lack even of any evidence that the author was aware of them.

Another, more convincing possibility is that this material was inserted into the *Jewish War*, around CE 90, before most of the gospels (apart from Mark) and Acts were written or were in wide circulation. Josephus is no longer heard of from this time, and can be presumed to have died.

The author of the material would have been aware of stories circulating about John the Baptist and Jesus and decided to incorporate them in a free-wheeling version of Josephus. He was able to give the less flattering version of the suicide pact at Jotapata, only hinted at in the widely available version, in which Josephus memorised the lots so as to escape death while his fellow fighters perished.

While he felt free to cast aspersions on Josephus with impunity, he was not so confident at the time to write directly naming Yeshua or John the Baptist, though it is very clear from content and context about whom he was writing.

Neither a Jew, nor a convinced Christian, it is likely that the writer was someone versed in the pagan gnostic tradition, from which early Christianity borrowed. He suggested, for example, that John the Baptist had access to the gnostic inner mysteries, but which John would not reveal to those hostile to him:

And there rose up in anger Simon, an Essæan by extraction, a scribe, and he spake: 'We read every day the divine books. But thou, only now come from the forest like a wild animal, – thou darest in sooth to teach us and to mislead the people with thy reprobate words.' And he rushed forward to do him bodily violence. But he, rebuking them, spake: 'I will not disclose to you the mystery which dwelleth in you, for ye have not desired it. Thereby an untold calamity is come upon you, and because of yourselves.'

The writer included in his story the thirty pieces of silver (talents) which in the gospels story was offered to Judas to betray

Yeshua but is here accepted by Pilate to authorise the execution of Yeshua – after Pilate had acquitted and freed him! But this detail, like so many others in the gospel tradition, is probably a borrowed item from pre-Christian tradition. Under Athenian law, Socrates might at his trial have escaped death by paying a fine but offered only a trivial sum. His friends, though to no avail, offered to pay thirty pieces of silver on his behalf.

Taken together, the references to John, to Yeshua and to Yeshua's followers, either Nazorean or later Christian, would form a gospel in their own right. So it would seem that someone decided early on that the Greek version of Josephus' *Jewish War* was deficient and added elements of a gospel account that he had available in making a freely adapted copy. Though not from the pen of Josephus, the equivocal expressions in relation to Yeshua would, according to this analysis, be entirely genuine contemporary comment from someone who was interested in, sympathetic to but not wholly convinced by the new movement.

The account follows other gospels in vilifying Jews who were given the blame for the execution of Yeshua. But it differs remarkably in one respect. John the Baptist is quoted as saying that 'God hath sent me, that I may show you the way of the Law, wherein ye may free yourselves from many holders of power.' John promises that, once the people have ceased from 'evil works' they will be given a ruler who would set them free. They would get, not just a spiritual leader, but someone who would actively overthrow oppressive rule.

That person, as in the canonical gospels, is presumably Yeshua/Jesus.

Although the 'wonder doer' Yeshua decides, despite being urged on by his followers, against trying to take Jerusalem it is clear from these statements attributed to John that there is a revolutionary agenda. Freedom 'from many holders of power'? The holders of power at the time were indeed many: the Romans, Herodian kings and princes and Sadducee high priests. Yeshua and his cousin John are here clearly cast as messianic liberators.

In sum, what there is in the Slavonic version of the *Jewish War* is not something written by Josephus himself, or another Jewish source, or a Christian commentator in the mould of Paul and his followers. It was written by a Gentile familiar with and sympathetic to an early 'gospel' account, which he used in freely amending the Greek original before this was later translated into Old Russian. The amended Greek version, like the first version in Aramaic to which Josephus refers, fell to dust or was destroyed and is no longer available, leaving just the Old Russian translation.

There were then perhaps different reasons for the insertions made in the Slavonic *Jewish War*. But though originating earlier, they have much the same status as references to Yeshua in *Antiquities*, forged and inserted around the time of Eusebius. They are forgeries, in the sense of not being written by Josephus, and they were added later. Which it would seem leaves the situation back at square one, with Josephus having had apparently nothing or next to nothing to say about messianic Jewish nationalists or early Christians – despite the fact that there is evidence that both of these were influential during the first century.

I have referred to the favoured though precarious position in which Josephus found himself, enjoying the Roman Emperor's patronage though formerly commanding Jewish forces in Galilee during the revolt. Like Ananus in Jerusalem, Josephus was apparently reluctantly drawn into the conflict, well aware of the awesome power of Rome and the likely eventual outcome, and hoping for some form of armistice. More militant nationalists in Galilee, including John of Gischala, accused him of collusion with Rome in an attempt to get him replaced and also tried to assassinate him.

After the war, some of his enemies tried a different tack, representing him to the Roman authorities as one of those responsible for stirring up the conflict. In the province of Cyrenaica around CE 72, a captured sicarii leader Jonathan tried to save himself – according to Josephus – by bringing charges of subversion against Josephus and other prominent Jews, alleging specifically that Josephus had provided arms and money for the movement. Jonathan was taken to Rome and brought before Vespasian where Vespasian conducted an inquiry, ruled against Jonathan and exonerated those accused.

The outcome was that Jonathan was first tortured and then burnt alive. One of a number of incidents of casual cruelty throughout the war and its aftermath, it is made more shocking by Josephus' attitude, that Jonathan simply got what he deserved. It was a fate, however, or something like it, that Josephus could well have suffered, had Jonathan been believed.

A lot later, around CE 93, Josephus experienced a similar attack from another quarter, Justus of Tiberias, one of his erstwhile nationalist rivals and enemies in Galilee, who represented him as an instigator of revolt in Galilee. This plainly put Josephus at risk, given that his former patrons Vespasian and his son Titan were dead and Domitian was now directing purges against Christians and Jewish messianic 'Sons of David'. In response, Josephus wrote an account of his life, *Vita*, chiefly a justification of his military command in Galilee in which he portrayed himself as on a mission to get the militants to lay down their arms!

Josephus did write one more book, *Contra Apionem*, defending Judaism, but his publisher Ephaphroditus, was executed in CE 95. Given that no more is heard of Josephus after this, it may be that in the end his enemies prevailed and Josephus perished under Domitian too.

The attacks on Josephus do show the very real danger he faced by any degree of association with the messianic movement. This would have sufficient for him both to play down his role and that of the messianic militants – as he clearly did when his later account of his military command in *Vita* is compared with that in the *Jewish War*. It has to be remembered also that, by his account, he had predicted to Vespasian that he would become Emperor, and ruler of the whole human race. Having done that, he would hardly have wanted to draw attention to the 'star' prophecy in Jewish messianic ideology, based on the Book of Numbers prediction that 'a Star would rise from Jacob, a Sceptre to rule the world'.

It is only towards the end of the *Jewish War* that Josephus gives some intimation of this, suggesting that: '(the Jews') chief inducement to go to war was an equivocal oracle also found in their sacred writings, announcing that at that time a man from their country would become monarch of the whole world.' But he hastened to add that, while many Jewish scholars thought that it applied to them, the oracle in fact pointed to the accession of Vespasian, who was proclaimed Emperor by his troops in Judea!

The star prophecy, or rather the religious conviction behind it, thus provided a predisposition to revolt. But what actually and immediately provoked the insurrection was the callous repression, as Josephus described it, under the Roman procurator Gessius Florus.

It is evident, from Josephus' own description of his life and events as they unfolded, that he was really one of the 'moderate' party who saw the war as doomed to end in disaster and entertained the hope, perhaps the faint hope, that some sort of truce could be arranged. He had a privileged background, he was well educated and he had been to Rome, where he made some significant contacts.

It was because Vespasian knew about him and had a use for him, that Josephus was taken on board instead of being summarily executed, as might otherwise have been his fate. On the other hand, Josephus was a Jew, and he been commander of the province, Galilee, that harboured some of the most militant nationalists. In his youth, he admits to having explored the main three religious approaches of Pharisees, Sadducees and Essenes and then spending three years in the desert with an ascetic, 'Banus' before deciding to become a Pharisee priest.

It must be wondered whether this character 'Banus' was someone in the mould of James or perhaps the Dead Sea scroll author of the Habakkuk commentary – fundamentalist, uncompromising and fiercely concerned to maintain the purity of Jewish faith. Such people could have provided the religious focus for the various nationalist movements that actually took up arms in the uprising.

If Josephus had flirted with a more fundamental brand of Judaism, it would have given his accusers grounds for attacking him. It would have been something that he really did have to worry about in his dealings with the Romans. Ironically, it would have also given him the broader credentials needed in the first place for taking on the tricky command of that hotbed of militants, Galilee. With an establishment background and links with the religious nationalists, Josephus could well have been the obvious choice.

What is very interesting is that Josephus' description of the various philosophies in Judaism parallels the evidence he gives for his own search for enlightenment. In the *Jewish War*, he lists and describes followers of only three main schools of thought: Pharisees, Sadducees and Essenes. But this comes just after his description of the Galilean Judas who founded a sect of his own. Based on the principle of accepting no master except God, Judas urged his fellow Jews not to pay taxes to the Romans. In *Antiquities*, Josephus expands this further, describing this Judas as the founder of an 'intrusive' fourth philosophy identical with that of the Pharisees except for their overriding passion for liberty. Josephus describes the movement as gaining an abundance of followers and links it to the rebellion provoked by the repression under Gessius Florus.

It would seem, on the surface, that the movement under Banus that Josephus flirted with had something to do with the freedom-loving alternative fourth philosophy. Even if, as his writings suggest, he had later repudiated this approach, it provided good reason for circumspection.

Certainly, the evidence is that Josephus was circumspect, to the point of omitting awkward details, blurring others and, as will be seen, doing a cut and paste job on some of the factual evidence.

Analysis of the supposed references to Jesus/Yeshua has indeed shown these to have been forged or insertions of another author's text. Josephus was not and could not have been that open. But does this mean there is nothing in Josephus that relates to the messianic movement or movements of which Yeshua and his brothers were a part?

Yeshua, if the gospels are to be given any credence, did have an impact. James as leader of the Nazoreans built up a formidable following. The newly emerged Christians presented a challenge to these original Jewish followers of Yeshua that was not insignificant or without wider impact. Josephus, part of the inner circle of power, given the vital command of Galilee in the war, was well placed to know all the key people in Jewish society and how they related to each other. It is simply not conceivable that lack of knowledge is the reason for gaps in his reporting.

Though disguised, the information can surprisingly be found – but not if one is looking for the fictionalised, romanticised, distorted and manipulated gospel accounts or indeed for the fiery anti-Roman fundamentalist rhetoric of some of the Dead Sea scrolls. Josephus did not have, and his writings were not manipulated to fit in with, the gospel agenda. And he was not writing from the position of Qumran fundamentalists who ranted against the Roman occupiers, against fornication, riches and pollution of the temple.

The scrolls that were left in caves by the Dead Sea, an unedited and undisturbed time capsule for almost nineteen centuries, at least provide an authentic voice of first century messianism. Josephus' account is authentic too, but coming from someone who had become part of a cautious establishment and who later was an apologetic for Rome.

Insertions were later made, to provide evidence for Christianity, and the books copied and retained by Christian monks because it was believed that Josephus could or should provide such evidence. But it would seem that the bulk of the material originally written by Josephus was not slanted by later copyists or edited like the gospel accounts. His books would have appeared to have been to do with Jewish history and not much else.

In the *Jewish War*, written and published just after the uprising, Josephus studiously avoided references to the Jewish messiahs who might have appeared as the genuine article. There was thus nothing to counter his slavish reference to Vespasian as fulfilling the Old Testament star prophecy. Two major incidents during Pilate's rule as procurator appear in both the *Jewish War* and *Antiquities*, the posting of the 'idolatrous' standards in Jerusalem and the quelling of the temple funds protest. The culminating mishap, when Pilate crushed a movement under a Samaritan messianic figure, only appears in the later work. Fifteen years or so on, it would seem that Josephus felt that it was safe enough to mention this.

There appears to be nothing in either work relating to the rise of the Jewish messiah Yeshua and his claim to kingship apart, that is, from the forged notice posted in *Antiquities* around the time of Constantine's bishop, Eusebius.

But, disregarding this, there is an extraordinary piece of text in *Antiquities*, sandwiched between the descriptions of Pilate's soldiers clubbing panic-stricken demonstrators in Jerusalem and his heavily-armed infantry slaughtering the followers of the Samaritan Taheb at Mount Gerizim. Just where there should have been a description of Yeshua's capture, trial and execution,

Josephus chooses to digress with a long and gossipy tale about a woman deceived into having sex followed by a shorter story, oddly linked to the first, about the theft of funds collected for the temple in Jerusalem.

In outline, the first story deals with a woman named Paulina of noble Roman descent married to Saturninus. Another character Decius Mundus, having fallen in love with Paulina, tried to bribe her first with gifts and then with a large sum of money to go to bed with him.

He was rejected, and on the point of dejectedly trying to starve himself to death, when his female servant Ida offered to help him accomplish his objective for money.

Ida bribed priests at the temple of Isis, where Paulina worshipped. One of them went to her with the tale that the god Anubis had fallen for her and wished her to come to the temple at night and share his bed. Paulina agreed and even told her husband.

At the temple, Decius pretended to be the god and as a result he and Paulina spent the night together.

When next Decius met her he could not, however, resist gloating about his successful impersonation and the fact that ultimately he had got her for nothing (or, rather, next to nothing having paid a bribe via Ida). Paulina, realising the deception, rent her garments in dismay (a Jewish gesture, surprisingly) and told her husband. He then reported the matter to the Emperor Tiberius. The Emperor decided to crucify the priests and Ida, but for Decius Mundus the sentence was merely exile. Tiberius razed the temple and had the statue of Isis cast into the Tiber.

With its obvious implausibilities, this has to be a folk tale rather than something Josephus expected in all its aspects to be taken seriously. But why has he included it? The answer seems to be provided by unsettling parallels on many levels with the Christian myth, too many to be purely coincidental.

The jackal-headed god of the underworld, Anubis, was for

example identified by early gnostic Christians with Yeshua. But, the story suggests, the identification of a mortal with the god is merely a pretence. The unison of a god with a mortal woman is the Christian nativity theme even to the detail of the husband, having been told, feeling honoured at the prospect!

The pretender, Decius Mundus, is based on Decius Mus, a famous, legendary Roman war hero. He was a soldier who in battle sacrificed himself in to appease the gods, thus dying for the benefit of the many – in the same way that Caiaphas speaks of Yeshua in John's gospel. Like the figure of gospel creation, Jesus, Decius claims in the story to be a god and he makes public his resolution to die. Like Jesus/Yeshua, Decius appears on the third day (after two days). But his purpose was quite contrary to that of Jesus/Yeshua who proclaimed thereby his divinity. Decius' objective was to tell Paulinus that he had been pretending to be Anubis; that he was not after all, a god.

The outcome, as in the case of Yeshua, is crucifixion. But Decius escapes into exile, as indeed I have earlier suggested that Yeshua may have.

When the *Jewish War* was written, the Christians were just one of many developing sects. Fifteen years on, the Nazoreans were dispersed and depleted, and Christianity had grown sufficiently to be in a position ultimately to push them aside. Josephus, however, was aware of what had been happening and could not, I suggest, resist a brilliant if malicious parody in *Antiquities*, mixing up and splaying out the myths of the gospel story.

How much of a parody it was is revealed by the content of the second, shorter story.

In this, a woman also of great dignity and high birth, Fulvia, was conned by a man portraying himself as a Jewish rabbi. In carrying out his deception, he was aided by three confederates. Still a Roman, though now a Jewish proselyte or god fearer, the woman was urged to part with goods and money for the temple in Jerusalem. But, instead of passing the gifts on, the men used them for their own expenses.

The woman's husband, who again just happened to be an acquaintance of the Emperor, reported the matter to Tiberius and as a result the whole of the Jewish community was deported from Rome.

Josephus wants to make absolutely sure that his readers understand that the two stories are linked. In each case the victim is a woman of high birth, betrayed by a priest or priests, and the husband knows the Emperor and reports the matter. Tiberias exacts punishments, including in both cases a sentence of banishment. To make quite sure the point is not lost, he calls the husband in each case by the same name, Saturnicus! So Paulina is Fulvia and Fulvia is Paulina, perhaps even Fulvia Paulina.

And it becomes a lot clearer that this is another wicked parody of the activities of the Christians, just a few years further on in time. Josephus is making a mocking attack on Paul. What could be clearer from the story's introduction?

There was a certain Jew, a complete scoundrel, who had fled his own country because he was accused of transgressing certain laws and feared punishment on this account. Just at this time he was a resident of Rome and played the part of an interpreter of the Mosaic law and its wisdom.

It's an almost exact précis of Paul's position as described in the Acts of the Apostles and, as in Acts, Paul is on a mission, ostensibly to collect money for Jews in Jerusalem. Josephus maliciously repeats rumours that Paul had been using some of the money for himself, something that Paul himself appears to have been acutely aware of (Corinthians I, 9, 3-12).

The use of Paulina for the gullible lady of high birth makes the parody almost perfect. Josephus is perhaps implying that the misogynist self-obsessed Paul who advocates and chooses chastity (though why can't he have a wife, Paul complains in Corinthians) is a bit of a woman.

On one level, these stories provide reasons why Tiberias chose to persecute priests at the temple of Isis and expel Jews from Rome, in the latter case presumably to eliminate their proselytising of Roman citizens. But these events happened some years before the point in the narrative in which the stories are placed, precisely the moment when Josephus should be giving an account of how Pilate dealt with Yeshua. He doesn't do that. What he does do is poke some fun at Christian accounts, which he knows to be false and based on pagan mythology, and also at Paul, their chief perpetrator.

Josephus delivered an acerbic parody, dismissing the Christian birth myths. But would he have been any less harsh in discussing Jewish messianism, had he felt safe enough to deal with it in his text?

It will be seen that he was almost as dismissive of the real Jewish messiahs. The evidence is there, though Josephus has broken it up in order that this messianism should not be seen as an underlying force in the Jewish rebellion.

In his role as a propagandist for the Romans, Josephus tended to adopt the language of his masters. The term for robbers or bandits, 'lestes', could mean just that, groups of individuals outside the law carrying out criminal acts for gain. But the Romans also applied the term liberally to their opponents, national insurrectionists prepared to use force, as did Josephus. Thus Josephus described the rebel Hezekiah, killed by Herod who was at that time administrator in Galilee, as a 'bandit' chief. Hezekiah had a son Judas who was one of three who started uprisings, on the death of Herod in BCE 4, as rival claimants for the throne of Israel. So Hezekiah must also have been a nationalist with an agenda, possibly claiming kingship on the basis of descent and possibly one of the last of the Maccabeans.

In general terms, Josephus described the nationalists who

took part in the Jewish revolt as 'zealots.' It was a popular uprising, partly at least in response to the harshness of Roman rule, notwithstanding Josephus' efforts to describe 'the people' as having been misled by militants. For this reason, it was probably a broad coalition with the common purposes of defeating the Romans and eliminating the Sadducee elite, especially the families which had provided the High Priests and chief priests who cooperated with Rome.

The religious dimension was demonstrated by a determination not to compromise fundamental Jewish belief in any way, which meant opposing admission of foreigners to the temple or sacrifices made on their behalf. It was the action of lower order priests in stopping sacrifices on behalf of Rome and the Emperor that, as Josephus described it, initiated the revolt. Political and religious self-determination were, for the Jews, inextricably intertwined. This made it harder for themselves during periods of subjugation and hard also for their rulers, forever faced with claims for autonomy in religious observance which also subtly undermined political control.

To an extent, 'zealot' was a term of self-designation, echoing the zeal of the Maccabees who refused to accept their religion being outlawed by King Antiochus and who actually succeeded in overthrowing foreign rule.

In describing his 'fourth philosophy', like that of the Pharisees in every respect except for a 'passion for liberty that is almost unconquerable', Josephus may have been trying to denote the religious fundamentalism which was a driving force behind the zealots in the war. He ascribes the initiation of this approach to a rabbi, Judas the Galilean, who advocated refusal to pay taxes to Rome under the slogan 'No Lord but God' and who had a Pharisee co-conspirator 'Saddok'. This was in CE 6, at the time of a census undertaken under the Syrian legate Quirinius, for the purpose of providing a basis for exacting taxation.

The more militant anti-Roman, nationalistic, religiously

fervent Dead Sea scroll authors, whom some have identified as Essenes and an offshoot of the Sadducees, might also in their passion for freedom have been ascribed as adherents of Josephus' 'intrusive' fourth philosophy. Not all of the Essenes were members of a peaceable, ascetic sect, withdrawn from the world as the historian described them. One, at least, 'John the Essene' was chosen to be commander for the West Judea region in the war against Rome and was killed in battle. Josephus describes the Essenes as enduring torture and death, rather than compromise their principles, in a similar fashion to the zealot members of his fourth philosophy (see p 187).

Followers of James, 'Nazoreans' or 'keepers of the covenant' who believed that the messiah had already come, were also uncompromising in their beliefs. Were they too adherents of this philosophy, given that they were conforming Pharisee Jews, except for their belief in that one of their number had been the awaited messiah? Followers of the fourth way were, according to Josephus, similar in every respect to the Pharisees, except for their unquenchable thirst for liberty. As I have pointed out, the Nazoreans and the Dead Sea scroll writers were closely linked in their organisation, self designation and beliefs. It may be that what there is here is one group, described in alternative ways by different people at different times.

Josephus was not explicit as to who he was referring to in describing his fourth philosophy. But what he was, I believe, trying to do was point up a fanatical religious fundamentalism in which believers were quite prepared to die, or kill, for their beliefs.

Josephus also uses another term, sicarii, to describe opponents of the Romans. This was a Roman term which Josephus adopts and it was applied to those who used their curved daggers (sicae) to strike down their victims, often mingling in crowds and then melting away in the ensuing confusion.

The term is a label, a convenient one, for describing a method of attack and, it would seem on the evidence, to denote a quite specific group. As with the word 'Essene', this is probably not a label that the group would have applied to themselves.

The sicarii were militant followers of people with aspirations to kingship, members of a messianic line in which the mantle was passed from brother to brother and father to son.

They make their first appearance in the *Jewish War* as 'bandits', in the period from about CE 51 when Felix became governor or procurator, using their curved daggers to assassinate opponents. One of their victims was Jonathan, a former High Priest.

In *Antiquities*, Josephus described a simmering conflict at this time between the 'high priests, on the one hand, and the priests and the leaders of the populace of Jerusalem', manifested in stone throwing and mutual abuse. Since former high priests retained their title, this was a dispute involving the Sadducee families or faction from which the high priests came. Against them may well have been the supporters of James, brother of Yeshua, who according to Josephus was shortly afterwards stoned to death at the behest of the High Priest Ananus.

In the countryside, the sicarii are described as plundering and setting fire to villages. After the death of James, coincidentally or consequentially, the sicarii stepped up their activities, kidnapping staff from the household of Ananias, a wealthy and influential former High Priest, in order to establish a basis for exchange with their own followers taken prisoner.

At the outbreak of the Jewish revolt, perhaps finally provoked by atrocities committed by governor Gessius Florus, nationalist Jews captured the Roman fortress atop the sheer rocky outcrop at Masada, killing the garrison and plundering the armoury. The rebels are described as being led by Menahem, 'son of Judas the Galilean, the very clever rabbi who in the time of Quirinius had once reproached the Jews for submitting to the Romans after serving God alone'. Menahem then took his forces 'like a king' to join the fight in Jerusalem where he entered the temple to worship, 'decked in kingly robes'. He was then killed, apparently as a result of infighting among the rebel forces, and his commander Eleazar, son of Jairus, then went back to the stronghold at Masada.

These forces, later identified as sicarii, established dominance over the surrounding area and then extended their control to a wider area including eastern Judea. In this, they were helped by Simon son of Gioras, a prominent leader in the initial battle with Roman troops under Cestius Gallus. Simon had subsequently turned his attention to relieving 'the rich' of their possessions. Confronted by the forces of the former High Priest Ananus, he then retreated to join the sicarii at Masada.

Simon, like Menahem, had aspirations. Building on his military successes, he grew stronger, gathering an army which included 'many respectable citizens who obeyed him like a king'. After joining battle with Eleazar's zealots outside Jerusalem, he was invited into the city to counter the growing despotism of John of Gishala, Josephus' former enemy who had fled from Galilee to Jerusalem. Once in the city, Simon became involved as leader of a competing faction, in an often three-cornered fight, even as the Romans were approaching the city walls. His opponents were John of Gishala's supporters and zealots under Eleazar, son of Simon.

In a bizarre episode at the very end of the conflict, having failed in an attempt to tunnel out of the city now occupied by the Romans, Simon appeared out of the ground where the temple had stood. He was 'dressed in several short white capes with a crimson cape fastened over them'. This was, according to Josephus, a ruse intended to frighten the Romans. More likely, it would have been a last gesture, a claim to messianic leadership, by a man who then knew that the game was up.

It is certainly difficult to sort the truth from the chaff in reading Josephus. There is no other authority to check against;

his work provides the only surviving account of the Jewish uprising, not merely as interpretation of history but as a record of the sequence of events. Furthermore, Josephus was not an eyewitness to what happened during the siege of Jerusalem. After his capture by the Romans, he had to rely on evidence provided by prisoners and deserters, including colourful and unlikely tales of deeds in battle – which he duly recorded. Josephus was credulous, faithfully recounting as fact such details as a Roman catapult stone striking a man's head and carrying it on more than six hundred yards.

Joseph digressed, he elaborated and he employed the convention of the time, putting suitable speeches into the mouths of participants, not what was said, but what might have been said in the circumstances.

Not only is there no independent check available, but many of those who might have been able to provide corroboration, or otherwise, were killed in the mass slaughter during and following the battle for Jerusalem. To some extent, Josephus could give his version of history without fear of contradiction. His own past and role in the conflict did, however, leave him open to attacks intended to undermine his credibility and standing. Justus of Tiberias later provided an alternative account of the conduct of the war, unfortunately since lost, which put Josephus in a less than flattering light and portrayed him as an instigator of the revolt. This is exactly the reverse of what Josephus himself indicated, that he was reluctantly in charge, hoping ultimately to be in a position to minimise the damage and sue for terms.

Undoubtedly, creating and conveying his own version of events is just what Josephus did. He had an agenda, a large part of which was to please the Romans and ensure his own survival. He painted a generally favourable picture of Roman conduct in the conflict and he underlined the message, that rebellion was futile.

Accepting all of this, Josephus' testimony does give a picture of first century messianic opposition that is better than anything available in the canonical gospels, transmuted as they have been from an ideology of resistance to a passive, pro-Roman doctrine of world redemption by belief alone.

Josephus doesn't spell it out. But he makes it clear, by his description of a man entering Jerusalem and the temple with the dress and demeanour of a king, that Menahem was a messianic contender. He links Menahem as the son of Judas, who led a tax revolt against Rome in CE 6. He describes Judas as the instigator of a 'fourth philosophy' which put freedom above all else but which, by virtue of its uncompromising zeal, created division and created 'the ruin of our (ie the Jewish) cause' (*Antiquities*, book XVIII, opening).

Josephus described two other sons of Judas, James and Simon who, presumably because of their revolutionary activities, were crucified under the Roman governor Tiberias Alexander around CE 47.

Menahem, killed later (CE 66 or 67) in the early stages of the Jewish revolt, had a follower Eleazar whom Josephus describes interestingly as also 'related' to Menahem and as a descendant of Judas. This Eleazar, son of Jairus, subsequently led the nationalist, sicarii forces at Masada. These held off the Romans for a further three years and then, when defeat was imminent, committed mass suicide rather than surrender.

If Menahem claimed to be a king, then it would have been by descent and it means that his brothers and his father before him, in their rebellions, would likely have been making just the same claim. What Josephus is patchily presenting, and not at all explicitly, is a messianic movement based on succession, similar to the Maccabees. It was, in fact, a monarchy.

Since no one came forward to step into Menahem's shoes, it may be that he was the last of the brothers in the line of succession. Eleazar retreated to Masada to consolidate, and perhaps protect royal children who could later stake a claim. Simon son of Gioras, who acted just as autocratically as Menahem and operated as an ally of the sicarii, may have had ambitions on his own account. Or he may have been acting as a custodian, on behalf of the children of Menahem or the children of Menahem's brothers, so that they could later inherit the throne.

The sicarii, as a group interested in establishing a non-Herodian Jewish man, a descendant of David, on the throne of Israel, had supporters but they were also opposed. Under Menahem, they joined with a revolt against the chief priests and the sacrifices made on behalf of the Emperor and Rome. But then Menahem was killed, according to Josephus by the very same forces he had gone in to support.

Under Simon son of Gioras, the sicarii were involved in a clash with Ananus, one of the chief priests and a former High Priest, who had been appointed after the initial stages of the revolt to help organise resistance in Jerusalem. Simon joined up with the sicarii at Masada and from there embarked on the conquest of Idumea. This brought him into conflict with zealot forces under Eleazar, son of Simon, based in Jerusalem.

The initial rebellion focussed specifically on the Roman occupiers; it was inflamed almost certainly by the punitive actions of the governor Gessius Florus. Once the Romans were defeated, attention shifted to those who were seen as collaborators. The former High Priest Ananias and his brother Hezekiah were killed, it would appear by Menahem's men.

Although a setback, this did not quite signal the end of the power of the Sadducee elite. With Ananas in joint charge in Jerusalem, priestly families maintained a continuing power base. But this was eroded as the conflict gained momentum. After the death of Ananus, the zealots under Eleazar set about eliminating all the prominent men of the priestly families.

The messianic line that Josephus describes, not overtly but by nods and winks, was not accepted by everyone, certainly not by the chief priests and the 'moderate party' and also not by John of Gischala who had his own designs on power. It was based at the time on Menahem and his 'sicarii' forces operating from the captured stronghold of Masada.

Like the zealot leader Eleazar son of Simon, Simon son of Gioras had been involved in battles to defeat the forces of Cestius Gallus sent against them after the Roman garrison at Jerusalem had been massacred. Simon allied himself with the sicarii at Masada but, once Menahem was dead, was not accepted by Eleazar. This could simply have been because the two men had competing ambitions. Another explanation, which also makes sense, is that Simon had identified himself with the sicarii forces of Menahem, whose claim to kingship Eleazar did not accept.

Eleazar son of Simon is first mentioned in the *Jewish War* as coming back to Jerusalem with his victorious zealot forces and the spoils of victory after the defeat of Cestius at Beth Horon. Simon son of Gioras is noted as harrying Cestius at the same pass on his initial approach to Jerusalem. This was about two months after the uprising in the city in which the Roman garrison was defeated and slaughtered.

It would have taken time to raise an army sufficient to defeat Cestius, which suggests that forces must have been in preparation and in training at least at the time that Menahem conducted his attack on Masada, if not for months beforehand. It would also have required a substantial body of trained fighters to defeat both the Roman garrison in Jerusalem and the reinforcements that King Agrippa sent in.

When Menahem entered the city like a king, he must have believed that support was available for him to consolidate his claim. It would seem that he had miscalculated and not all the rebels wanted him as king.

There is, then, evidence of a messianic movement, that Josephus only refers to indirectly and indeed whose very existence he is not keen to point up. It brought forth 'messiahs' who were sons or brothers of previous 'messiahs' who, had they been allowed to rule, would have been kings of Israel. They were not accepted by all, which is unsurprising. There were, for example, three separate messianic contenders claiming kingship in different parts of Israel after Herod's death. Even the Maccabees, who 150 years previously had successfully wrested back the kingship, came from a fairly minor priestly line – and they then had to fight to establish dominance over the whole of Palestine.

So it was not the provenance of any particular claim that was really critical. After many centuries, and several mass deportations, the line of descent from King David had become tenuous, lost in the mists of time. What mattered was not so much the validity of the claim of a new 'son of David' to take the throne of Israel, but his ability to make it stick. In this respect, Menahem and his brothers and his father before him failed.

But did someone called Yeshua also make a failed attempt? The problem now seems to be compounded by the fact that a messianic movement can be discerned in the pages of Josephus, over the same time period in which the gospel Yeshua and his followers lived, also with roots in Galilee and also active in Jerusalem. The Judas-Menahem movement, with its ruthless sicarii followers, seems to leave no room for a parallel movement, operating in the same places and at precisely the same period.

That is just not credible. But what is credible is certainly *very* unsettling, especially for anyone still clinging to the romantic, gospel story. There are a number of curious discrepancies in Josephus' account and these, together with some startling evidence from the gospels themselves, speak of a much fuller story, one that is violent and dark.

For the journey back to the real, first century Palestine, the dualism of the twenty-first century mind needs to be left behind.

Good and evil? There are simply no white knights, no good guys in this story.

The Romans, Herodians, Sadducee high priests and chief priests, bandits, zealots, Eleazar ben Simon, Simon of Gischala, Menahem, Eleazar ben Jair, even Josephus himself and most importantly the sicarii, all had blood on their hands.

Chapter 10: Family of zealots

Corrupt and inept, and maybe welcoming an insurrection as a distraction from his own shortcomings, the Roman procurator Gessius Florus managed at a stroke to unite a wide cross section of the Jewish population in opposition. According to Josephus, Florus went to Jerusalem, when he should have been dealing with riots between Jews and Greeks in Caesarea, in order to extort money. However, the subsequent description of what actually happened suggests that Florus' chief motivation was to secure the handover of troublemakers he believed were being harboured in the city. When the community's leaders refused, he ordered his troops to sack an area known as the Upper Market. Several thousand civilians were killed in this collective punishment and, while the massacre was going on, Florus had other citizens seized and executed.

This happened in May of CE 66. The revolt started a few months later in August, during which interval there would have been time to organise and bring together a fighting force. Josephus describes the actual outbreak of war as instigated by lower order priests, refusing to make the customary daily sacrifices in the temple on behalf on Rome and the Emperor, no doubt with the memory of the brutality of Florus and his soldiers fresh in their minds.

There followed a battle involving stone throwing and hand-to-hand fighting between the chief priests plus 'the peace-loving section of the populace', supported by 2,000 cavalry called in from King Agrippa, on the one hand and the insurgents on the other.

The balance was then tipped by very large numbers of sicarii entering the city under the cover of a Feast of Wood Gathering, when it was customary for people to bring in offerings of fuel for the temple altar fire. It is unclear precisely what these forces were and it is not indicated who led them.

By the time that Menahem arrived with his own small army, described on this one occasion as 'zealot' but subsequently as 'sicarii', the conflict was already virtually resolved. The rebels had first taken the temple, the fortress Antonia and the lower city. They had then driven Agrippa's men and the Romans out of the upper city, confining them to Herod's Palace and three adjacent towers on the old city wall.

On arrival, Menahem took charge of the siege, seizing the palace and forcing the Romans to retreat to the three remaining towers. But he is then reported as being killed as a result of an attack instigated by the Temple Captain and deputy High Priest Eleazar, son of Ananias, a former High Priest.

This is certainly very confusing. The Temple Captain Eleazar had earlier been described as the immediate instigator of the conflict, through his action in persuading lower order priests to suspend temple sacrifices for foreigners. Ostensibly on the rebel side, he then rather surprisingly attacked Menahem. It is feasible that he was motivated by the fact that his own father Ananias, on the pro Roman side, had just been killed by rebels, presumably Menahem's followers.

One of the reasons it is difficult to sort out what is happening is that Josephus fails to say who the leaders of the revolt were in the early stages. So, after the subsequent rout of the Roman twelfth legion, he reports that 'those who had pursued Cestius' returned to Jerusalem. He then describes the generals that 'they' chose with the brief to administer and defend different regions, anticipating correctly that the Emperor Nero would send a bigger army in an effort to retake the territory.

Josephus had two good reasons for not being more forthcoming. One was that the leaders were known to him and, at the time he wrote *Jewish War*, some may still have been alive. He did not want through his writing to betray them to the Romans. The second reason is that he himself was appointed as one of the generals by these very same leaders! By drawing attention to them, he might also have drawn attention to his own zealot credentials. This was a sensitive matter, in view of his later status as a captured Jewish commander and his new role as spokesman and apologist for the Romans.

Eleazar son of Ananias was I suggest in part a proxy for these unnamed instigators of the struggle. Given his background, he would have been an unlikely rebel leader and he was indeed (as Josephus describes in his later work *Antiquities*) the focus for sicarii attacks in the two-year period prior to the rebellion. Members of his own and his father's staff were captured and taken hostage in order to be exchanged for rebel prisoners.

Having been written in as Menahem's nemesis, Eleazar shortly disappears from the story. The lower temple priests may have taken his advice, or suspended the sacrifices on their own initiative. But they would not themselves have provided him with a sufficient fighting force against the Romans and King Agrippa's troops. Eleazar's final act, as described, was to allow out the beleaguered Romans under a truce under which they would surrender their weapons and other equipment for their lives. But instead of keeping his promise, Eleazar had the defenceless Romans massacred.

It would certainly have been convenient to blame the Temple Captain for this especially if, as seems likely, he had subsequently perished in the pogrom which the zealots initiated against the chief priests and their families. The massacre of the garrison would have rankled with the Romans long after the event. They would certainly have been interested, had Josephus mentioned anyone still living who was responsible.

So, by not naming them, Josephus protected the instigators of the revolt. One of them may have been Eleazar son of Simon, a zealot leader of one faction who played a prominent part in internal infighting and then the defence of Jerusalem once Vespasian's army reached the city.

This Eleazar is first identified as having in his possession the money and other loot taken from Cestius 'together with vast public funds', when the victorious Jewish forces returned to Jerusalem early in December 66. He must have been someone of considerable importance, even though Josephus states that he was not put in charge of affairs because of his dictatorial tendencies. Instead, a former High Priest Ananus was appointed together with Joseph, son of Gorion, who thereafter gets no mention.

Eleazar son of Simon appears on the scene, when his namesake Eleazar the Temple Captain, son of a former High Priest, and as I will suggest his stand-in, disappears. Eleazar is described by Josephus as gradually gaining power in Jerusalem, because he has control of funds and because of his 'trickery'.

It is difficult to know what to make of this, given that Josephus devoted a considerable amount of space in the *Jewish War* to an account of his command in Galilee and its conquest by Vespasian. When the last town is finally taken and John of Gischala and his retreating army arrive at Jerusalem, it is November 67, and the story is picked up at that point even though eleven months have elapsed. Hardly anything is said of what has been happening in Jerusalem in the intervening period. It has to be presumed that this is the period in which Eleazar is 'gradually' becoming dominant by virtue of his funds and his trickery.

From that moment onwards, however, a conflict is described between on the one hand John of Gischala and Eleazar son of Simon, in alliance for the most part, against the forces of Ananus.

Why, it must wondered, did this struggle take so long to develop? How also did Ananus get such a position of power, given the record of his family of high priests against the opposition line represented by Yeshua and his followers? This, it will be remembered, included James whose summary trial and execution Ananus is described as presiding over.

The answer is partly that Ananus was not appointed as a ruler, but as an administrator. The existing High Priest Matthias, certainly a ruler of sorts, was present at the time, although completely sidelined. He remains in the storyline unmentioned, and apparently without any role, until later deposed when the zealots under Eleazar themselves decided to chose the High Priest from a minor priestly lineage, by lot.

The leaders of the fighting forces I suggest were not necessarily equipped and probably not motivated to deal with day-to-day matters. Ananus was chosen because as a former High Priest he had experience of running the city, which was the job of the High Priest selected either by the Romans or one of the Herodian kings.

Someone was needed to deal with crime and custody, tax, education, water supply, the minting of new coinage, rebuilding and strengthening defensive walls, securing supplies. The initial choice of Ananus reflects possibly an initial sinking of differences, brought on by the widespread revulsion at the indiscriminate massacres initiated by Gessius Florus. The chief priests had refused to hand over any rebels or scapegoats and the consequent suffering was shared, creating if only for a time a common cause against the Romans.

The difficulty with this analysis is that Ananus, when High Priest, is supposed to have ordered the execution of James. By all accounts, James was a very popular figure. So, if Ananus was implicated, it is scarcely credible that he could have been chosen as a leader in Jerusalem after the revolt.

It is, however, possible that the account in *Antiquities* implicating Ananus was misconstrued and then misrepresented in copying. It may instead have been another former High Priest, Ananias, who presided over the downfall of James. In Acts (24, 1), he is described as interrogating Paul/Saul in pursuit of the 'sect of the Nazarenes'. Josephus portrays him as a man of great wealth and influence who was the object of sicarii attacks, around CE 62 in the build up to the Jewish revolt. When the Roman garrison in Jerusalem was overwhelmed, Ananias and his brother Hezekiah were immediately sought out and killed.

Ananias, although not High Priest at the time, appears to have been an inquisitor and persecutor of messianic nationalists. This would explain both why he was killed and why it happened so swiftly once the Romans were gone. There were plenty of people seeking his death and no one was left to offer protection.

But Ananus was spared and went on to become the chief adminstrator in Jerusalem. The followers of James, said to number many thousands, could have exacted vengeance had Ananus indeed been responsible for their leader's death. They could at the least have made it difficult for him to become a ruler in Jerusalem. They did I suggest take swift revenge – but it was on the wealthy and corrupt former High Priest Ananias.

This gives even greater clarity to the description in the *Habakkuk* scroll of the Wicked Priest who 'forsook God and the precepts for the sake of riches' but who was 'delivered into the hands of his enemies' who then 'took vengeance upon his body of flesh'.

While the writer of the Habakkuk commentary could have directed his veiled attack on either one of the two High Priests, the time frame in the case of Ananus is more limited. Josephus reports that Vespasian took control of the Dead Sea region in June of CE 68, when it is likely that the Romans overran and destroyed the settlement at Qumran. This idea is supported by archaeo-logical investigation of the site. The latest Jewish coins found in the destruction layer were put into circulation in March of CE 68, while Roman coins in the reconstruction layer above date to CE 67/68. The pesher was thus likely to have been written at some time in the months leading up to the Roman attack in June CE 68.

Ananias was killed at the outset of the revolt in September CE 66 while Ananus died around February of CE 68, according to the chronology of the *Jewish War*. For the scroll author, these were both fairly recent events. But, if the reference to the demise of the Wicked Priest applies to the first of these events, then he would have had more time to receive the news, reflect and write his commentary.

It is possible, of course, that the scrolls were deposited some years later, though it then has to be surmised where they might have been kept for safety during the Roman occupation. The period immediately prior to the final assault on Jerusalem, when many thousands were killed and whole communities destroyed, provides the best context, not least because it explains why the scrolls were left and forgotten. The people who used the scrolls were annihilated; the knowledge of where they were was lost.

In *Antiquities*, there is a description of 'a man named James the brother of Jesus', who was stoned to death on the orders of a court convened by Ananus. It appears that later Christian editors may have added the words 'who was called the Christ', perhaps first as an assumption in a marginal note which was then incorporated in the text when the book was copied. This James, however, also fits well as the brother of Jesus the son of Damneus, mentioned in the text a few lines later. There is agreement between early Christian sources (Clement and Hegesippus quoted by Eusebius) and the *Pseudoclementine Recognitions* that the Nazorean James was thrown down from the temple, breaking one or both of his legs, possibly pelted with stones and then beaten with a club. This may or may not have led to his death immediately: in *Recognitions* James survives at least for a while, still limping weeks later, after the attack.

The point is that these descriptions do not suggest a formal process of trial and execution but are indicative of a spontaneous, opportunistic and chaotic assault. The early Church sources were, in the second century, using an account they had in common with the Ebionites but amalgamating it with what they thought was an account of the death of James, Nazorean leader and brother of the gospel Jesus, written by

Josephus at the end of the first century.

So James may have been killed later than CE 62, the time when Ananus was High Priest. His death thus could then have been (as suggested in versions of Josephus no longer extant) a more immediate factor which precipitated the conflict with Rome.

Josephus, as has been noted, is not specific about the rebel leaders who appointed generals to command different areas, following the defeat of Cestius Gallus. He claims that 'they' chose not to appoint Eleazar son of Simon because of his 'dictatorial tendencies'. But it may have been Eleazar, or a zealot leader like him, who appointed Josephus to take command of Galilee.

Eleazar, whose forces were based in the temple, is likely to have been in Jerusalem much earlier than the point at which he is first mentioned. He was opposed to Simon son of Gioras who was allied with the sicarii at Masada. So it is reasonable to assume that he would have been opposed to Menahem also.

Could it have been in reality this Eleazar, rather than the son of the former High Priest, who secured the overthrow of Menahem and subsequently slaughtered the Romans after they had surrendered? If it was Eleazar son of Simon who killed the sicarii leader Menahem, this would explain why Simon son of Gioras subsequently launched an attack on him.

By substituting in this Eleazar's place, his namesake who was the Temple Captain and son of the former High Priest, Josephus would cleverly have achieved several objectives. He would first of all have covered the tracks of those really responsible for the massacre of the Roman garrison. He would also have continued to obscure, as he does elsewhere, who were the real leaders of the revolt in the initial stages. These were activists, no doubt zealots and certainly not members of the Sadducee establishment! If 'they' had appointed Josephus, the Romans might have had good reason to regard Josephus in much the same light.

In the text of the *Jewish War* as written, just as one Eleazar fades from the picture, another slips seamlessly in. There is no further mention of Eleazar, Temple Captain and son of a former High Priest, after the massacre of the Roman soldiers. It is likely that he died, most probably in the subsequent slaughter by the zealots of the Sadducee elite. But the point at which this Eleazar disappears from the text is also the point at which Eleazar son of Simon must have been operating.

The main objective, it should be emphasised, in all this would have been to blame Eleazar son of Ananias for the treacherous massacre of the Roman garrison instead of Eleazar son of Simon who, I have suggested, actually instigated it. The Temple Captain Eleazar might, as I have argued elsewhere (see *Censored Messiah*) have been the nemesis of Menahem as Josephus reports it, though as a consequence of the initial fighting and while in actuality remaining on the pro-Roman side. It was either the establishment Eleazar acting against the rebels, or possibly the rival nationalist Eleazar son of Simon. But it was not an establishment Eleazar, improbably acting on the rebels' side.

Josephus wants the militant zealot leader Eleazar kept out of the picture from the early stages of the revolt. So he substitutes a member of the collaborating Sadducee chief priests' party, also called Eleazar, someone safe to blame. As he has written his history of the war, Josephus is despatched to Galilee when the extreme zealot Eleazar son of Simon appears on the scene. In this way the historian avoids guilt by association, certainly any suggestion (whether true or not) that Eleazar son of Simon had any hand in his appointment.

Josephus' anxiety about his position was certainly not exaggerated. He was appointed by the successful zealot commanders (whom he choses not to name) from the battle with Cestius Gallus and he had a zealot past, as an acolyte of the ascetic 'Banus'. When he was given command of Galilee, this was a province which at that stage had not revolted. It was Josephus who persuaded the people of Tiberias to demolish the palace of the former ruler of Galilee Herod the Tetrarch (Antipas), ostensibly because it was decorated with pagan images of animals, but in reality because it was a symbol of Roman and Herodian power.

The Jerusalem council, presumably the civil administration under Ananus rather than the Sanhedrin, attempted to recall Josephus from his command. This has similarities with action taken against Simon son of Gioras, who was expelled from Acrabata by Ananus and went to join the sicarii forces at Masada.

So Josephus' enemy, Justus of Tiberias, had some ammunition to hand for suggesting that Josephus may have been the real revolutionary. After the war, each historian, for fear of the Romans, blamed the other. Justus, it should be noted, eventually defected to King Agrippa II, who later shielded him when Vespasian demanded his execution. Though Justus was imprisoned by Agrippa, he was also employed for a time as his secretary.

Early church sources Eusebius and Origen both record that Josephus asserted that the catastrophe which struck the Jews, culminating in the destruction of Jerusalem, was God's vengeance for the death of James. But no such statement can be found in the versions of Josephus' works that are available now. The orthodox Christian doctrine was that the fall of Jerusalem and the destruction of the temple came about as a result of Jesus' (Yeshua's) death. So it may be that this reference to James was subsequently edited out in order to make Josephus consistent with the Christian perspective.

Josephus certainly reports a step-up in the activity of the sicarii following the death of James. The first mention of them is during the rule of procurator Felix (CE 53-60), when they assassinated the former High Priest Jonathan. They continued to pick off their chosen victims and, after James had been killed in CE 62 or later, began to take hostages to exchange for their own followers taken prisoner. This suggests a considerable escalation of conflict as well as increasing boldness and confidence on the part of the sicarii themselves.

Josephus records, in language that is very revealing, bitter civil strife towards the end of Felix's time as procurator, around CE 59:

> There now was enkindled mutual enmity and class warfare between the high priests, on the one hand, and the priests and the leaders of the populace of Jerusalem on the other. Each of the factions formed and collected for itself a band of the most reckless revolutionaries and acted as their leader. And when they clashed, they used abusive language and pelted each other with stones.

This passage in *Antiquities* echoes the outbreak of fighting at the outset of the revolt a few years later, recorded in the *Jewish War*, when the two sides exchanged a barrage of stones, thrown by sling or by hand.The difference is that the chief priests/high priests are now linked with the 'peace-loving section of the populace' while the insurgents are clearly the bad guys!

Josephus is, in this earlier work, unsparing in his scathing condemnation of all the groups of rebels, however described. In one passage he characterised the sicarii, who began 'this lawlessness and this barbarity to kinsmen' and who 'left no word unspoken, no deed untried, to insult and destroy the object of their foul plots'. He then described John of Gischala who 'not only put to death all advocates of just and profitable courses, treating such as his most bitter foes among the citizens, but by his public actions he subjected his country to countless woes.' Then there was Simon son of Gioras whose followers 'thought it a proof of brilliance to savage their own kith and kin'. The Idumeans, called in by the zealots as reinforcements against Ananus, he described as 'disgusting people' who 'butchered the high priests so that no trace of divine worship should be left'. The zealots 'gave themselves this title in view of their zeal for what was good, either mocking their victims, brutes that they were, or regarding the greatest evils as good!'

Josephus has by contrast only good words for Ananus, as 'a man of the soundest judgement who might have saved the city if he had escaped the hands of the plotters'. Thus Josephus put himself firmly in the place of those reluctantly drawn into the conflict, who would have sought an accommodation – an armistice on reasonable terms – neglecting such matters as the fact that it was Ananus who had sought to recall him from his command!

In his description in *Antiquities* of the situation before the war, he is perhaps presenting a more realistic picture of his sympathies. The high priests/chief priests were not the leaders of the people but acting *against* the leaders of the people. And who were these leaders of the people? Again, there are no names. Perhaps they were the same people who were the unnamed leaders who defeated Cestius and divided up the country, giving Josephus command in Galilee.

James, as the evidence in Acts and the *Pseudoclementine Recognitions* suggests, was a major force with thousands of devoted Nazorean followers. Many Jews fought in the war, and some of the Nazoreans must have too. So is it possible that there was a militant faction, supporting James' religious perspective but also prepared to take up arms? 'Zealous' for the law like James, but prepared to 'come out' like the followers of Mattathias, the first of the Maccabees?

Followers of the 'fourth philosophy', like the Pharisees in every respect except for their unquenchable passion for liberty, parallel the Nazoreans, like the Pharisees except for the belief that one of their leaders was the awaited messiah.

There is a case that this is where the messianic movement of the followers of Yeshua and James has its place in the history of the conflict, among those who tipped the balance against the forces of the Romans and King Agrippa and among those who fought and defeated Cestius Gallus, under leaders unnamed. Not pointed out by Josephus because, for all the reasons earlier described, it would have been too dangerous both for Josephus himself and any survivors in the royal line.

There are, however, some strange discrepancies in the story of the 'other' Messianic line involving Menahem that need to be dealt with and there are questions arising that need to be answered. How come there are two contemporaneous messianic movements, followers of Yeshua and James and followers of Judas and Menahem, both originating from exactly the same area, Galilee? Such a duplication of effort and resources not only seems unlikely but it should have engendered (since these would have been rival claims) some conflict. What, if anything, do the gospel story line and the accounts by Josephus offer in the way of evidence?

Another brother of Yeshua, Simon or Simeon was next in line after James and, according to early sources, was elected after him as leader of the Nazorean community. But he does not appear to have played any active part in the Jewish revolt. The early church tradition is that the community evacuated to Pella, one of the Decapolis cities, north of Jerusalem and across the river Jordan. So, while Menahem was making a claim to the kingship in Jerusalem, Simon it must be presumed was quietly looking after his followers, about sixty miles away.

While Josephus can be forgiven where his sources for past events are insufficient, he cannot be excused for any lack of precision about his contemporaries. Josephus was an important player in Judean society, sufficient for him to have been made commander of the forces in Galilee. Menahem was a claimant to the throne able to raise a small army of sicarii, capture Masada, enter Jerusalem and take charge of the siege of the remaining Romans and King Agrippa's troops. There would have been a relatively small circle of people at the time with power and influence, all known to each other.

Yet Josephus provides in his *Jewish War* information about Menahem's origins that certainly cannot be accurate. He relates that Menahem was the 'son of Judas the Galilean, the very clever rabbi who in the time of Quirinius had once reproached the Jews for submitting to the Romans after serving God alone.' The Roman governor of Syria Quirinius had been charged with the task of conducting a census for the purpose of collecting taxes. This was in the areas of Judea, Samaria and Idumea which had come under direct Roman administration following the banishment of Herod's son Archelaus.

Judas urged his fellow Jews not to register in the census and so avoid paying taxes to the Romans.

Not only did the attempted tax rebellion fail but, as Acts records, Judas was killed in the process. If he fathered any children, this would therefore have been at or before the time of the census undertaken in CE 6. As a son of this tax rebel Judas, Menahem sixty years later is likely to have been in his eighties. He would have been far too old to have led a force up the sheer rock face to take the stronghold at Masada!

Given the time span involved, and given the tendency for people to have their children young in those days, it is far more likely that Menahem, if related, was a grandson or great grandson of Judas. Why didn't Josephus say so?

In *Antiquities*, almost in passing, Josephus mentions two other supposed sons of Judas the Galilean, James and Simon, brought up for trial and crucified under the procurator Tiberias Alexander, around CE 46 or 47. Again, this is such a long time after the census rebellion that it seems unlikely that James and Simon were sons of that Judas, assuming even that they were related to him.

Menahem's behaviour, in entering Jerusalem like a king and going into the temple dressed in kingly robes, indicates that it was a monarchical line, with each in succession making a claim to the crown of David. But, if so, why did James and Simon wait forty years or so after their father Judas' failed attempt? What had they been doing in the meantime?

Eleazar son of Jairus, who had been Menahem's general, slipped away when his leader was killed and became the 'autocrat' of Masada, where he held out against the Romans long after the conflict had ended elsewhere. Josephus interestingly describes Eleazar also as a 'descendant' of Judas the Galilean and as 'related' to Menahem. Not merely interesting, these relationships are, I believe, highly significant.

If many of these names – Judas, James, Simon, Eleazar and Jairus - seem oddly familiar, it is because you will almost certainly, even before tackling this book, have already come across them. They are the names of characters who make up some of the basic building blocks of the gospel story.

It could just be coincidence that the names of Judas the Galilean and his descendants/relatives are also the names for three brothers of Yeshua, a close friend of Yeshua who was the brother of Mary of Bethany, and thus arguably also his brother-in-law, and finally the father of someone Yeshua miraculously revived from the dead. Judas, James, Simon, Eleazar and Jairus!

But if it is a coincidence, it is a very, very big one. Could the explanation be that the gospel writers rehashed history in making legend, borrowing extensively from the works of Josephus? The author of Luke's gospel and Acts did on the evidence borrow some characters from Josephus to fill out and embroider his text.

There is, however, good independent evidence for the existence and life of James, the brother of Yeshua. In addition, the note about the crucifixion of the brothers James and Simon appears only in *Antiquities*, written many years after the gospel of Mark. So the author of the earliest of the synoptic gospels, Mark, could not have borrowed and recycled these characters from Josephus.

The gospel character Eleazar appears not only in John's

gospel but in an early version of Mark's gospel known as Secret Mark, quoted in a letter by the second century writer Clement of Alexandria. The authenticity of the letter and the quote are however, it should be noted, a matter of scholarly dispute.

As I will show, the story of Lazarus is also refracted in other gospel tales. So here too, the gospel account is prior to and therefore independent of Josephus. It certainly appears as if something else is going on besides copying and beyond pure coincidence.

The key to the puzzle may well lie in the gospel character Judas, one of the brothers of Yeshua and possibly not entirely distinct from Judas Iscariot (sicarios), the betrayer/assassin. In the gospel lists, this brother of Yeshua is variously described as Judas or a variant of this name, 'Thaddeus', as in Mark's gospel. Matthew has in the place of Judas, 'Lebbaeus who was surnamed Thaddeus'. A second or third century document, the *Apostolic Constitutions*, makes the link explicit in referring to 'Thaddeus also called Lebbaeus and surnamed Judas the Zealot'.

Luke in writing his gospel and the Acts of the Apostles dropped the title Thaddeus in favour of Judas (brother) of James, while the *Epistula Apostolorum* refers to Judas Zelotes in its list precisely where Luke has Judas (brother) of James.

John (14, 22) goes out of his way to point out that the brother Judas is not the same person as the betrayer Judas. Is he protesting too much? In describing the betrayal (handing over) of Jesus, he refers to Judas (6, 71 and 13, 26) as [ ] 'of Simon'. The Greek reads literally 'Judas [ ] of Simon of Iscariot'. New Testament translators usually render these references as 'Judas, the son of Simon Iscariot'.

Now this would be odd because there is no character 'Simon Iscariot' anywhere else, and because the appellation 'Iscariot' is applied in all other references to Judas himself. Given that Greek construction can involve a qualifying phrase within a description, a more probable rendering is 'Judas Iscariot [ ] of

Simon'. This would leave just two questions: the nature of the unspecified relationship between the two and the identity of Simon.

The author of John consistently refers to Yeshua's commander Simon as 'Simon Peter', and in the case of both pieces of text, there are references to Simon Peter close at hand. So the Simon related to Judas Iscariot does not appear to be the same person as Simon Peter. It is someone whose identity is not defined, it may be because the author or the original source expected the reader already to know who Simon was.

The four probable and possible candidates as brothers of Yeshua – James, Simon, Judas and Matthew – have largely been written out of John's gospel. But these characters would have been there in the minds of readers, familiar with the earlier gospels. So there is a case that the person described as related to Judas Iscariot was Simon, one of Yeshua's younger brothers.

What then was the relationship between the two? Given that he held the responsible position of group treasurer, Judas is not likely to have been the son of Simon. In any case, early church authorities describe Simon as having remained celibate. Judas Iscariot may instead have been Simon's brother.

Rather than 'Judas, son of Simon Iscariot', the text thus reads better and makes more sense as 'Judas Iscariot, brother of Simon' – and by extension this person is also the brother of James and Yeshua. The two Judases are then the same.

The betrayer and the betrayal of Yeshua would, by this reading, have been invented so that 'Jews' could be held responsible for the Gentile saviour's death. Acts early on describes an election to replace Judas, odd since there was no need for there to be precisely twelve close followers of Yeshua. This was a Christian fiction, borrowing from the reality of the genuine Nazorean/Essene council of twelve. If, in this case, the life – and death – of Judas the betrayer were a fiction, then there would have been no need for an election to replace him.

Eisenman (*James, the brother of Jesus*) suggests that the story in Acts (1, 15-26) is a garbled version of the election of James to replace Yeshua as leader of the Nazorean community in Jerusalem. He further argues that Stephen, a powerful character who arrives almost fully fledged without prior mention in the gospels, is a fictional surrogate for James. The story of his martyrdom is thus the story of the hounding to death of James, also described in the *Pseudoclementine Recognitions.* There are indeed parallels between this story (see pps 131-133 above) and the version in Acts (6, 7-15), indicating that the two texts may have been working from a common source. Why the story of James' death needed to be disguised in Acts is simple: the involvement in it of Paul, the founder of the Christian Church, could not be admitted.

Two points are case fairly clear from the evidence. The first is that the character Judas, the brother of James and of Yeshua, and Thaddeus are one and the same. The second is that Judas, from his nickname or nicknames, was known to be a warlike character, a rebel, one of the zealots or sicarii.

The analysis can be taken on a little further with a reference in the *Second Apocalypse of James*, a third of fourth century gnostic source from Nag Hammadi, which refers to the main disciple of James as a 'relative', naming him as 'Theuda'. This piece of evidence bring the gospel story right up against the narrative of Josephus, not as copied material but as overlapping testimony.

Immediately before the notice about the crucified brothers James and Simon in *Antiquities*, there is a story about an 'imposter' Theudas who persuaded people to follow him to the river Jordan with their possessions. Theudas promised them the waters would part to allow them across. But, before this could happen, Roman cavalry sent by the procurator Fadus fell upon the crowd. Many were killed and Theudas was captured and summarily beheaded.

Neither this story, nor the account about James and Simon,

appear in the earlier work *Jewish War*, suggesting that Josephus only felt that it was politic or safe enough to include these episodes after a lapse of many years. Why was the material so potentially explosive? My suggestion is the obvious one, that Theudas is a variation of Thaddeus or Theuda and that therefore the 'imposter' was none other than Judas, one of the brothers of Yeshua!

That Theudas and his followers went to the Jordan with their possessions suggests that they were fleeing from Roman persecution, attempting to get to safe territory. Theudas/Judas (zealot or sicarios) was one more rebel leader who fought and lost, one more in a monarchical line, staking a claim to the kingship.

The jigsaw is beginning to fall into place, though with profound implications. One of the brothers of Yeshua, Judas, has found a place as one of the implacable zealots, who challenged Rome and lost, according to Josephus during the procuratorship of Fadus, around CE 45 or 46. Next mentioned in the narrative, a year or two later, two more claimants to the throne, James and Simon, stepped up and were tried and crucified. These successive challenges would appear to have been from quite different messianic lines, both as it happened based in Galilee. Yet it hardly seems likely that these events, coming hot on the heels of one another, were unconnected.

There were, I suggest, linked and in a way that resolves the difficulties presented by the time gaps involved in the rebellions by Judas the Galilean, James and Simon and Menahem. The latter three, James, Simon and Menahem, were indeed all brothers. But, instead of being sons of Judas the Galilean as Josephus describes, they were sons of another Judas from Galilee, the brother of Yeshua, also known as Thaddeus or Theuda! And this was the Theudas whom Josephus describes as trying to escape with his followers across the Jordan, before being cut down by the Romans. It is even recorded that

Menahem had another brother named Judas, the fourth in the family, who quite possibly took his name from his father.

The pieces now really do begin to fit into place. It was common at that time for certain names to be kept in families, passed down from generation to generation. The gospel Judas, one of Yeshua's brothers, could well have named two of his sons after his brothers, James and Simon. It is recorded that these brothers, who were leaders of the Nazorean community in Jerusalem, remained celibate. So they themselves would not have been able to pass on their own names.

The two sons may incidentally, like the third son Menahem, have been distant descendants of the Judas who initiated a tax revolt in CE 6 but not his sons as indicated by Josephus.

If the line of descent was really Davidic, then it must have gone back in time. Yeshua, and for that matter John the Baptist, may not have been the first to be have been conscious of having a right to the throne of Israel and in some way staked a claim.

Cleophas/Alphaeus, the father of Yeshua, appears not to have been among them. This may have been because he predeceased John, a more direct claimant.

So far, clear explanations have been found for three of the 'coincidences' involving names (those of Judas, Simon and James). There remains in the list of characters in Josephus with resonance in the gospels, Eleazar son of Jairus, also described as a descendant of Judas the Galilean and a relative of Menahem.

In the story in John's gospel, Lazarus, brother of Mary of Bethany, fell gravely ill only to be miraculously brought back to life by Yeshua. The gospels describe Yeshua as being very close to Martha, Mary and Lazarus. I have suggested that this was because Mary (who also doubled as Mary Magdalene) was married to Yeshua. Lazarus was consequently Yeshua's brother in law and would therefore, to use Josephus' wording, have been a 'relative' of Menahem. This is because Menahem was, I have deduced, the son of Yeshua's brother Judas/Thaddeus.

I suggested previously (in *Censored Messiah*) that the 'raising' of Lazarus may, in its origins, have a story about the testing of a drug such as mandrake or opium. The drug was then later used to give the impression of death, so that Yeshua could be taken alive from the cross. But there are also indications that the death of Lazarus was symbolic, in a baptism and initiation ritual in which, according to Secret Mark, Yeshua taught Lazarus, gnostic style, the 'mystery of the Kingdom of God'. This might explain why Thomas in John's gospel, on hearing that Lazarus was dead, expressed the desire to (symbolically) 'die with him'.

The gospel writers collected stories which had become changed in retelling, such that it was possible for two variations of the same tale to be retold as separate events. A good example of this is provided by the tales of the feeding of the five thousand and feeding of the four thousand in Mark, which are so similar in many details that they must have related to the same event. The same, I suggest, would apply to the story told in the synoptic gospels, almost certainly first originating in Mark, in which Yeshua brings the daughter of Jairus, one of the rulers of a synagogue, back to life.

This is no quirky coincidence but a thoroughly understandable consequence of the ways stories were told and retold before being copied down. The raising of the 'daughter' of Jairus parallels the raising of Lazarus and is, in fact, another version of the same event. Someone who was 'ben' or 'bar' Jairus, the son of Jairus, became as the story was passed on 'bat' Jairus, his daughter rather than his son. In John's gospel, the parallel version is retold as well as the story of Lazarus, just like the alternate versions of the feeding of the five thousand and four thousand in Mark. But, in the parallel version of the story of Lazarus in John, it is the *son* of an official who is saved by Yeshua at the point of death.

At one point, it is the son of someone not named and, at another, the daughter of someone named as Jairus. At another, it is simply Lazarus who was 'raised'. But Josephus describes someone who was called Eleazar who became a sicarii commander and who was the son of Jairus.

The elements of a story have clearly been pulled apart. But they can be compellingly and convincingly recombined. The brothers and companions of Yeshua often had ferocious and aggressive nicknames, linking them to the resistance movements, 'zealots' and 'sicarii'. So it would be not at all surprising if one very close to Yeshua, the brother of Mary and Martha and also I have argued his brother-in-law, should have become a prominent sicarii leader.

Since written Hebrew and Aramaic lack vowels, 'Lazarus' and 'Eleazar' represent exactly the same name. And the Lazarus or Eleazar who was 'raised' by Yeshua was I suggest the same person (an offspring of Jairus) as the sicarii commander Eleazar, son of Jairus, described by Josephus! This same person was Yeshua's brother-in-law. And, as such, this person was indeed related to Yeshua's brother Judas (the zealot) or Thaddeus, who was I have argued the rebel leader Theudas – the real father of Menahem. Eleazar (Lazarus) is thus also 'related' to Menahem, just as Josephus describes.

In the initial battle with the Romans in Jerusalem, Eleazar was one of Menahem's men. When his leader was killed, Eleazar returned to take command of Masada. He held out here for several years before perishing with over 900 other defenders, men, women and children, in an act of mass suicide when the Romans were about to break through.

One of the poignant finds during excavations at Masada was a group of eleven inscribed pieces of broken pottery (ostraca). Josephus describes how the men first killed their wives and children and were in turn slain by a group of ten chosen to be the executioners of the rest. Finally, these ten drew lots to decide who would kill the others and then himself.

The inscribed pottery sherds may well have been the lots they used. One was simply inscribed with the name of the commander, 'Ben Jair'.

It is worth noting that the suicide pact at Masada was not entirely complete. Josephus records that an old woman, five small children and a woman 'who was related to Eleazar' escaped by hiding underground. Possibly, it was intended that they should not be killed. The woman, described as related to Eleazar, would thereby also have been related to Menahem. Could it be that, among these small children, there were heirs to the messianic line, whom it was hoped the Romans would unknowingly allow to survive?

There is so much direct and circumstantial evidence, and so much that falls into place once the identifications are made, that I am confident that Menahem, James and Simon were sons of Judas/Theudas and part of Yeshua's messianic line. This provides a much more likely and more plausible key to events than the myths which, in the gospels, have been written over history.

For some of the other remaining elements in the puzzle, however, there is so little evidence left that the only options are to speculate or keep the imagination in check and draw no conclusions. The actions of gospel censors and the self-censor Josephus, combined with the lack of other records, make it impossible to determine for sure who the significant people were, how they related to each other, what their objectives were and quite often simply what really did happen.

Josephus, I have suggested, knew precisely who Menahem was, and who for that matter the rebels James and Simon were, but chose deliberately not to tell us. He must have known more about Eleazar son of Jairus too. In letting us think they were all primarily descendants of the tax rebel Judas, he obscured their connection to Theudas/Judas and the messianic Davidic line of James and Yeshua. What was his motivation?

Hardly a simple act of forgetfulness, he didn't say anything at all about Theudas and James and Simon in the *Jewish War*, written and published just after the revolt. He only referred to them, and then only in passing, years later in *Antiquities*.

Josephus also failed to mention in his *Jewish War* the Samaritan messianic contender, the Taheb, who was crushed by Pilate's cavalry at Mount Gerizim. He said nothing in this book about Simon, 'with a reputation for religious scrupulousness' who had the audacity to denounce King Agrippa as unclean. But, like Theudas, these characters did get a later mention in *Antiquities*.

Clearly, there was something that Josephus was worried about which, in some instances, became less pressing with the passage of time.

This something, I have already argued, was that he did not want to draw attention to a genuine messianic movement behind the conflict. If recognised, it could detract from the oracle he had adapted and applied to Vespasian and it might possibly draw attention to his own zealot connections. Such as they were, it must be added! Josephus, as well as being a resourceful self-interested survivor, was a well-educated, well-off, snobbish member of the Pharisee establishment, exhibiting ill-concealed contempt for his enemies, the lower classes and those he called 'bandits' and, variously, 'sicarii' and 'zealots'.

Josephus, to his credit, did use his position with the Romans after the fall of Jerusalem to secure the release of his brother, fifty friends and a number of women and children lined up for deportation and enslavement. He also asked for three of his friends he saw being crucified to be reprieved and taken down, though only one of them survived.

In his *Jewish War*, he deliberately neglected to name the leaders in the early stages of the revolt who defeated Cestius Gallus. Possibly, this was because some of them were his friends and some were still alive.

He obscured the messianic link back from Menahem through James and Simon to Judas/Thaddeus partly because at the time he was writing *both* his major works, *Jewish War* and *Antiquities*, the descendants of Judas/Thaddeus, the brother of Yeshua, were still alive and very much at risk from Roman retribution. Early church sources report that Judas had children. Two of his descendants, named in some accounts as Zoker and James, were rounded up and interrogated under Emperor Domitian (CE 81 – 96) on the charge of being 'of the family of David'. But they were released when it was found that they were merely labourers, believing in a spiritual kingdom, adjudged not to be a threat to Rome.

However, a few years later another Emperor Trajan continued with the persecution of the 'Sons of David' and arrested and crucified among others Simon bar Cleophas, Nazorean leader and brother of Yeshua, who would by then have been very old. Eusebius reports that, in this purge, the descendants of Judas were also executed. So it seems that, under fresh scrutiny, Zoker and James were considered to be too much of a risk, and were killed.

The drive to eliminate the descendants of David was in fact begun by Vespasian, Josephus' patron, after the capture of Jerusalem. This was, as reported by Eusebius quoting Hegesippus, a persecution visited on Jews. The newly formed 'Christian' community, created by Paul and still in its infancy was based outside Judea and not affected – and it had in fact split from the Nazorean Jewish community under James.

Vespasian was certainly aware of the messianic roots of the Jewish rebellion and the unrest that happened both beforehand and afterwards; all the more reason that Josephus had to be careful in what he reported.

There are no reliable direct references to Yeshua in Josephus, though there is in *Antiquities* what appears to be a wicked parody of the Christian birth story and Paul's alleged misuse of funds intended for the Nazoreans. As for the story of Yeshua's march to Jerusalem, which did not in the event ignite a rebellion, there are curious parallels with the tale of the 'Egyptian' false prophet which appears with only minor variation in both the *Jewish War* and *Antiquities*. Early versions of the gospel of Mark, and the source for the passion story in both Peter and Mark, are believed to have been written before Josephus' account of the *Jewish War*. This appears to rule out the possibility that the writer of Mark simply quarried Josephus to provide details for the passion narrative. The Egyptian story could not therefore have provided a template for the gospel account.

Like Yeshua, the Egyptian took a large band of followers to the Mount of Olives, overlooking Jerusalem. His objective was to enter the city, overwhelm the garrison and seize power – not what Yeshua is credited with intending but certainly what his followers, James and John the sons of Zebedee, believed he was about. As in Yeshua's case, the plan was thwarted and his followers were scattered. The Egyptian escaped. Yeshua may also have evaded the Romans though in his case, having been captured or handed over, by surviving crucifixion.

The parallels are not perfect and the episode happened, according to Josephus, while Felix was procurator about CE 55. According to Matthew's gospel, Yeshua spent some of his childhood in Egypt and may have thereby acquired the nickname, 'The Egyptian'. Josephus sometimes uses pseudonyms when he wants to avoid revealing who a character really is. In this case, as in others already discussed, he may have been concealing or obscuring something to do with a messianic counterclaim to Rome. Could it be that he transferred the tale of Yeshua, suitably amended for Roman consumption, from the time of Pilate to that of Festus, twenty years later on? It is debatable whether he would have risked or could have got away with this, given that it was fairly recent history for Roman readers of his *Jewish War*.

The author of Luke's gospel and of the Acts of the Apostles was also concerned, though for different reasons, to minimise the

Jewish messianic militancy of the movement of Yeshua and his brothers. This is why he attempted, not entirely successfully, to play down the rift between Saul/Paul and James and cast Simon (Peter) in an unlikely mediating role. It is also why he ended his account in Acts with Saul/Paul in Rome, a few years before the death of James.

Writing his gospel towards the end of the first century, and Acts thirty or so years later around CE 130, the author of Luke had the advantage of other written accounts to draw on, but suffered the disadvantage of being distant in time from the actual events. He had no eyewitness accounts and no reliable oral tradition. Acts in particular is a hotch potch of embroidered fable, interspersed probably with some solid facts.

But when writing Acts, the author did have available to him the works of Josephus which he drew from.

In one crucial passage, Simon (Peter) and other apostles were brought before the Sanhedrin for preaching about Yeshua (Jesus), having already been told not to do so. The basis for the original injunction, as expressed by the High Priest (possibly Jonathan), was fear of Roman retribution bringing 'this man's blood upon us'.

The Pharisee leader Gamaliel advised the council to release the men and keep away from them on the grounds that 'if this plan or if this undertaking is of men, it will fail; but if it is of God, you will not be able to overthrow them. You might even be found opposing God!' He cited two previous rebellions which had failed, by Theudas and then afterwards by Judas the Galilean 'in the days of the census'.

What is interesting is that the author of Acts has Gamaliel lump together the actions of Simon Peter and the others with other rebellions against Rome which Josephus had recorded. So, in the picture presented in Acts, Simon and the other Nazoreans were to be seen in this way, as militant Jewish rebels. The fear of a reaction from the Roman authorities, attributed to the High

Priest, provides further confirmation. This mirrors the view attributed to the previous High Priest Caiaphas in John's gospel in respect of Yeshua, 'it is expedient for you that one man should die for the people, and that the whole nation should not perish.'

The people the Romans were really intent on tracking down were those who saw themselves as messianic contenders, as 'Sons of David', and their supporters. That is what Judas the Galilean and Theudas were, and therefore what Simon Peter and his followers were in being bracketed with them.

However, the author of Acts did not get his history right, which he surely should have done given that he had Josephus as a source. In Gamaliel's speech, the incident involving Theudas is put far back in the past before the tax uprising by Judas the Galilean in CE 6. Yet, according to Josephus, Theudas was crushed under procurator Fadus around CE 46, forty years afterwards. Furthermore, the timing of Acts suggests that Simon Peter's arrest took place in CE 40. Gamaliel, when speaking at this time, could not have referred to the defeat of Theudas which which was still to take place six years later!

Why did the author of Acts make such an elementary mistake?

My first conclusion (in *Censored Messiah*) was based on the fact that, unlike the other synoptic gospel authors, Mark and Matthew, the author who wrote both Acts and Luke's gospel did not have 'Thaddeus' in his list of apostles. Instead, he had Judas (brother) of James, though elsewhere the names Thaddeus and Judas are identified as relating to the same person. I suggested that he could not relate the revolt by Theudas, described by Josephus, to anything from his own sources for the forties, because the name meant nothing to him. So he put the event, on the lips of Gamaliel, into a time unspecified in the distant past.

On subsequent reflection, this has to be too charitable an explanation. The list of Apostles provided by the author of Luke is virtually identical with those of Mark, which he would have had to hand, and Matthew. He follows Matthew in swapping the positions of Andrew with James and John, and follows Mark for the position of Matthew and Thomas. But the names are all the same, *except* for the one difference that he has Judas (brother) of James in place of Thaddeus in the earlier gospels. Judas is displaced one position in his list from the position occupied by Thaddeus in the other two gospels.

Since the author of Luke used Mark and possibly Matthew as sources, and could see as well as we do now, this one striking difference in names, the explanation must be that he recognised 'Thaddeus' as 'Judas'. He decided to put the version of the name which was clearer for readers in his own gospel (see table of Apostles lists on p 45) and at the same time he eliminated 'Thaddeus' from the record.

So why, then, in Acts did he put Theudas (alias Theuda and Thaddeus) into the distant past when his source, *Antiquities*, was quite clear when Theudas' failed uprising happened? If the event as described by Josephus had no resonance with anything that the author of Acts knew about, then there should have been no reason for altering its chronological position so drastically. If, on the other hand, there was something that happened around CE 46 that the author of Acts did not want highlighted, then that provides a possible motivation.

The author of Acts knew that Thaddeus, Theudas and Judas were one and the same. I suggest that he also knew of the uprising and subsequent massacre of Theudas/Judas and his followers by the Romans, as they fled with their possessions and tried unsuccessfully to cross the Jordan. Judas's anti-Roman militancy, for which he no doubt deservedly earned the nickname 'Judas Zelotes' or 'Judas the Zealot', was not something that the gospel writers wanted attention drawn to. They were fashioning a messiah for the wider world, someone obedient, and pro-Roman, severed from his Jewish roots. And this person, since the very existence of his brothers could hardly be denied, had to have brothers who were marginalised and passive. The author of Acts not only shut his eyes to the activities of Yeshua's rebellious younger brother but actively created a diversion: the failed revolt by 'Theudas' was firmly placed, on the lips of Gamaliel to a moment in the distant past. This is even though the author would have known, from reading Josephus if not from other sources, that this revolt happened a few years after the crucifixion and during the time frame of Acts, when Simon Peter and the others were active.

Paul may, as I have suggested earlier, have been referring to this period of rebellion and consequent Roman repression in his first letter to the Thessalonians. He rejoiced in the calamity because he saw the victims as his opponents. However, one of the main objectives of Acts by contrast was to minimise the split between Paul and the Nazoreans so as to connect the Roman Church with its origins. So the identity of 'Theudas' and the timing of his rebellion were deliberately misrepresented and obscured.

But how could Judas, and then in turn his sons, have staged rebellions claiming the throne of David when there were others in line with a possibly better claim, in particular Simon/Simeon son of Clopas/Cleophas? This Simon, it will be recalled, did take over the leadership of the Nazorean community in Jerusalem, and carried on (presumably elsewhere) after the city had been destroyed, until his execution under Trajan around CE 98. But he was not, and neither was James before him, exercising a political leadership which amounted to kingship. For that, they would both have been killed much earlier on.

James and Simon were acting as religious leaders of their community, which was numbered in thousands – a large slice of the adult population of Jerusalem. The stories relating to James in early church sources suggest that he was taking on the role of supplicant before God for the people, in opposition to the officially sanctioned Sadducee High Priests.

In a sense, James was stepping into a vacuum because the

High Priest, appointed by the Roman client King of Galilee Agrippa II and before that by other client kings or the Romans directly, was often held in little public esteem. However, the High Priest, or perhaps more precisely the class of chief priests from which this office was derived, did exert real power by virtue of Roman patronage. This included dealing with criminal cases, though not capital offences.

But the source of power was at this time only patronage. As has been seen, once the Jewish revolt got under way, two people – Joseph son of Gorion and Ananus – were chosen as joint administrators in Jerusalem, leaving the then current High Priest Matthias on the side lines. In the absence of the Romans, he had become superfluous. James however had generated so much antagonism among the Sadducee priests' cabal that he was killed, without the sanction of the Roman authorities when (or arguably because) there was no procurator currently in place. He was then, and Simon after him, acting as an unacknowledged High Priest for the people or at least the Nazorean people.

The division of supreme responsibility between two offices had originated early in Israel's history, with the kingship passing along a Davidic line and the office of High Priest confined to those in particular priestly lineages. However, the line of succession to the kingship became blurred after centuries during which foreign conquerors dispersed large sections of the population. The most traumatic upheaval occurred in 587 BCE when the Babylonian King Nebuchadnezzar conquered Judah and forced the ruling and artisan classes into exile.

The Davidic succession was effectively suppressed and ultimately client kings substituted. Likewise, the office of High Priest became a gift bestowed by foreign powers on priestly lineages of their own choosing.

The claim to the leadership of the people came to be linked with a messianic tradition in which a 'messiah' (literally from the Hebrew 'masioch', meaning anointed) would come forward, ideally from the line of David, to set free the Jewish people. There were two strands in the expectation of the way that this would happen, either some act of divine intervention as predicted by the prophet Daniel or alternatively an active act of deliverance by a mighty 'son of David', as expected in the Songs of Solomon. Roles and expectations were thus complex, and tempered by the realities of power. When there seemed no possibility of securing freedom from foreign domination, the expectation that God would finally deliver would have provided some consolation. In a perverse way too, the sufferings of Israel at the hands of others was often attributed to punishment by God for the people's wrongdoing. So when, and only when, the nation became pure, could it shake off the shackles of oppression.

Another dimension was added by the fact that there had been a comparatively short period during which the kingship of Israel was restored under the Hasmoneans, also known as Maccabees after Judas nicknamed Maccabeus (Judas the hammer). It was brought to an end by the Romans and King Herod. During the time that Yeshua lived, this was not history or folk tale but, for the elderly at least, something that had taken place in living memory. The last of the Hasmoneans, John Hyrcanus II, had been murdered on the orders of Herod as recently as BCE 30.

The Hasmoneans conducted a successful guerilla campaign against Syrian Greek or Seleucid rule to establish an independent Israel. Crucially, under two brothers Jonathan and Simon and then Simon's son, the first John Hyrcanus, the offices of King and High Priest were combined. Coming from a minor priestly line, and with the succession to David lost in the mists of time, the Hasmoneans most probably had no strong genealogical claim to either office.

But this combination of the two roles in relatively recent history was something that put the Nazorean leadership in a more precarious position. It was insolence enough that James should by his actions have presented an apparent challenge to the High Priest chosen by the Roman client-king Agrippa II. That rebel messiahs had in the recent past claimed the roles of ruler *and* High Priest would only have added to suspicion. And then there was the fact of James' brother or half-brother, Yeshua, executed by Pilate as 'King of the Jews'. It is astonishing, a tribute certainly both to James' popularity and his tenacity, that he survived as long as he did.

That he did continue leading the Nazoreans for twenty five years after the crucifixion of Yeshua suggests that he made no overt political challenge, that his leadership was essentially religious and that his role was to defend the fundamentals of Judaism from those, like Paul, who wanted to undermine or transform it. James was a zealot in that he was zealous for the law and for it to be observed in all its details, as must have been Simon after him.

It may be that this presents a picture that is closer to the teaching of Yeshua than the intended thrust of the sayings collected, modified and restructured in his name in the years after his execution, and incorporated in the gospels. Yeshua taught the twin Pharisaic principles of loving God and one's neighbour, which go back to books of the Old Testament. He was a practising Jew. He said that he came only for 'the lost sheep of the House of Israel', therefore not for Samaritans and Gentiles. He was strict on divorce. He advocated, like James, that the Jewish law be respected, not in parts but in its entirety. What was said by Yeshua, or maybe not even Yeshua but his followers after him, was moulded and edited. Yet the censors did not entirely eliminate what was essentially a fundamentalist formulation of Judaism. Seen in context, Yeshua must also have been a religious zealot.

Unlike James, however, he may have taken steps towards an armed rebellion. The gospel accounts indicate that he was betrayed and then seized by the High Priest's officers before being handed over to the Romans. Traces of information still in the gospels link the march on Jerusalem to another event at the end of Pilate's rule, the suppression of a protest in which people were killed and prisoners taken.

Josephus did not directly report the seizure and execution of Yeshua. But, if it were linked to the temple funds protest, then it was in a sense covered as part of this story. The historian may have left out the detail of the executed messianic `bandit' for a number of reasons. In his role as propagandist, he had a brief to portray the Romans in a positive light and this was not a particularly flattering episode. Pilate had been pressured into conducting an execution that was flawed. This led to ingenious claims, a source of considerable annoyance, that the Nazorean leader had survived, becoming a messiah waiting in the wings to offer liberation.

Above all, the story of Yeshua, properly told, would have established a link with later messianic contenders including Menahem and with the roots of the Jewish rebellion. This was something, I have argued, that Josephus simply had to suppress.

Yeshua, if a claimant for the kingship as Pilate acknowledged, was not in many ways a satisfactory one. He did not become King of the Jews, even for a day. He did not fight a major battle with the Romans. He did not alter the balance of power in any significant respect.

This lack of success may have made it easier for his brothers James and Simon after him to continue for some time as religious leaders, without being taken out sooner as a potential political challenge. The manner in which the Nazoreans successfully manipulated Yeshua's execution did however provide a highly effective propaganda weapon: there was no body and their leader, they claimed, had come back from the dead and was going to liberate them.

Representing in part a religious challenge and in part a political challenge to the authorities, Yeshua came somewhere between James and Simon and the active, militant messianists who were sought out in a great persecution carried out by Saul/Paul and other agents of the High Priest following the crucifixion. As Acts (8, 1) noted, the apostles, meaning primarily James and the other brothers and cousins of Yeshua, were left alone. Whether or not this is an embroidery, the fact remains that James and Simon did survive for years afterwards. They managed to keep their claims to religious leadership, and keep clear of trouble.

If my analysis is correct, one brother, Judas, did not. He betrayed the cause by drawing down the wrath of the Romans on it. He was forced to flee with his followers but was captured and killed by the Romans, before being able to cross the Jordan to safety. He was nicknamed 'the Zealot' and may also have been the basis for another character called Judas known as 'sicarios', 'the assassin'.

It might have been possible for one branch of the movement to carry the religious leadership, while another exercised claims to kingship. There would then theoretically have been no cause for disagreement. But the activities of Judas/Thaddeus jeopardised safety and would have been seen by some as a problem.

Judas could have had precedence as a brother of Yeshua, if he were older than James and Simon. Many in the early Church held the belief that Yeshua did in fact have a brother Judas who was his twin and who would therefore have been older than the other brothers. This was Judas Thomas or Didymus, from respectively the Aramaic and the Greek words for twin. It may even be that the doubting apostle Thomas, described in John's gospel as Thomas who was called Didymus, was yet another incarnation of Jesus' brother Judas. Taking the point further, it is possible that Bartholomew, who may also have doubled as Nathanael, was 'bar Thauma' rather than 'bar Talmai', and so one of the the sons of Thomas/Judas.

Once Judas was dead, however, the succession might well

have been in doubt. No sons of Yeshua are recorded as coming forward to claim the kingdom. So, in their absence, should the succcession have rested with Judas' sons or with Yeshua's remaining brothers, James and Simon?

Rivalry between close kin for the throne of Israel was by no means an exceptional circumstance. A relatively recent precedent had been set by the Maccabeans whose power had waned as two brothers, Aristobulus and Hyrcanus, engaged in bitter conflict. The fight was taken up by Aristobulus' son Antigonus against his uncle Hyrcanus. Antigonus became both King and High Priest with Parthian help until Herod, backed by the Romans, intervened.

When Yeshua expressed his claim seventy years or so later, these events were almost in living memory. Judas/Theudas, 'the twin', may subsequently have been the source of division among the brothers. In taking up arms against the Romans and failing, he brought retribution against the nationalist militants.

When it came to the next generation of the Nazorean movement, represented by James, Simon and Menahem, who were the sons of Judas, the possibility of conflict was enhanced. Indeed, the rivalry between these 'Sons of David' and the old order mirrors that between Antigonus and Hyrcanus less than a century before. The crucial difference, of course, is that while the Hasmoneans operated an open kingship, the dynasty of the Nazoreans was submerged and repressed.

Josephus records that Menahem's claim to the kingship was not universally accepted. His nemesis may not have been Eleazar, a former High Priest's son, but Eleazar son of Simon, whom Josephus for good reason did not want to feature in the early stages of the revolt as a key player in Jerusalem.

Eleazar son of Simon did in fact represent a wider zealot cause, while the sicarii as portrayed by Josephus generally took part as the assassins, shock troops and bodyguards for the kingship contenders. Eleazar was not only opposed to Menahem, as I have deduced, but also as Josephus records to Simon son of Gioras. The latter, it will be remembered, went down to Masada, allied himself with the sicarii there, and then established a wider power base by taking Idumean territory in eastern and southern Judea. He was joined by a number of prisoners freed from Jerusalem; perhaps some of these were the comrades whose release sicarii hostage takers had sought in the period prior to the war.

Simon next engaged in himself in open conflict with Eleazar's forces. However these, as a result of the continuing internal strife within Jerusalem, were pushed with John of Gischala's men back to the temple area. At which point, Simon was invited in to the city as a counterbalance to John and the zealots though soon, as Josephus notes, proving as despotic as these others before him.

The situation was complex in that it appears that there were some who would not, as with previous messianic claimants, have accepted the claims to kingship of Yeshua's Davidic line. There may also have been a degree of rivalry between claimants within the same line, as happened with the Maccabeans, reflecting differing approaches and possibly beliefs. James and Simon, brothers of Yeshua, represented a religious zealotry which provided sustenance to a wider zealot cause. In this wider cause, some of their Nazorean followers would have almost certainly have participated, joining in the war effort. They also provided religious leadership for their own followers within Judaism, the Nazorean community.

Judas/Thaddeus/Theudas and his descendants were, I suggest, with their followers part of an activist tradition engaged in battle with the Romans and their Sadducee stooges, long before the Jewish revolt. They appear in the pages of Josephus among those the historian describes as sicarii. Although part of the same family, they appear to have followed a different approach from that of James and Simon/Simeon.

Just as Judas had children and grandchildren, as early church sources confirm, so probably did Yeshua, who was married as has been deduced to Mary of Bethany/Mary Magdalene. Even more so than Yeshua's deliberately marginalised brothers and sisters, any reference to these would have been suppressed in the gospels. Jesus Barabbas, the 'bandit' imprisoned after a demonstration or uprising may have been Yeshua's son (hence Bar-abbas or 'son of the master'). So too may have been Judas 'called Barsabbas', who was foremost among those sent with a letter from James containing the decisions relating to Gentile god fearers after the Jerusalem Council (Acts 15, 23).

This could well be the same person as 'Joseph called Barsabbas' who failed in an election by lot to replace Judas Iscariot (Acts 1, 23) but who may then, as Jude or Judas, have become the leader of the Nazoreans after Simon, as reported by Eusebius and Epiphanius.

This would fit with the idea of a primarily religious messianic leadership expressed definitely through James and Simon, equivocally through Yeshua who may have tried to lead a rebellion and then again through Jude or Judas, alias Joseph called Barsabbas or 'son of the master'. It was a leadership which could not however contain the differences which led to internal conflict during the rebellion against Rome. Indeed, it may have provided the seeds for discord by generating, within its messianic line, alternative contenders for the throne.

There were also alliances, cross-cutting and overlapping, which bound the rebels together. At the outset of the war with Rome, the wanton massacres instigated by Gessius Florus may even have caused many of the traditionally pro-Roman moderates (under Ananus) to embrace a coalition. So, here was a case of moderates and zealots fighting on the same side.

The activists, although depicted as split by Josephus, were not always irrevocably divided. Despite the differences between sicarii and zealot forces, Josephus records that two sons of Jairus, Simon and Judas, distinguished themselves on the zealot side against the Romans in the final battle for Jerusalem. It seems likely that these were brothers of the sicarii leader Eleazar, son of Jairus.

Josephus also records that, when faced with the enemy actually at the gates of Jerusalem, the rival factions of Simon son of Gioras, Eleazar son of Simon and John of Gischala, agreed to sink their differences. In the final death throes of the rebellion, internal divisions must have appeared less pressing than the overwhelming threat presented by the Romans.

Church tradition has it that the Nazorean Jerusalem community fled to the Decapolis town of Pella prior to the war. Certainly, since Simon or Simeon son of Cleophas survived the war to continue as Nazorean leader, this is a very reasonable possibility. A high proportion of the adult males who stayed were killed either through civil conflict, disease and starvation or the battle with the Romans. Those who remained at the end were either executed, transported as slaves or taken to face death in the arena.

But those who went to Pella, or some similar place of safety, were probably women and children and some of the older men including Simeon/Simon. The royal line was effectively safeguarded, just as it was for a time further south at the fortress of Masada. The younger zealot supporters of Yeshua and James may well have stayed behind in Jerusalem to fight and die with their fellow Jews.

Those who stayed could well have included Yeshua's fiery commander Simon Peter (nicknamed 'the Rock' or 'the Outlaw') who, arguably in the pages of Josephus, had the confidence to confront and secure a ransom from King Agrippa I.

In the gospel story line, it was Simon who took a swing with his sword, when Yeshua was being arrested or handed over, and sliced off the ear of the High Priest's slave. It is difficult to imagine such a character going meekly off to Pella, allowing fellow zealots to fight in his stead, unless perhaps debarred by age. He most probably stayed.

Simon, I have suggested, may have been caught and executed in the later stages of the siege of Jerusalem when the desperate defenders made forays to break through the enemy lines in search of food. The bored Roman soldiers amused themselves by crucifying their victims in different positions, and that is how Simon ended up crucified upside down, though outside Jerusalem and not in Rome as church tradition suggests.

To complete the puzzle, I have suggested, must involve some speculation, as there is so much detail missing. There were many Nazoreans and so some of them must have fought in the battle for Jerusalem. Some may also have been among the leaders. Simon Peter, I suggest may have been there, though perhaps by then too old to be one of the key commanders. That would have been left to the next generation, among them possibly his own sons. He was, as Acts records, married and therefore likely to have had children.

The fiercest and most uncompromising leader in the revolt, Eleazar, is described by Josephus as a son of Simon, though there is no indication as to who this might have been. It could have been someone whom Josephus otherwise neglected to mention. Among the characters that he does mention, however, is the Simon 'with a reputation for religious scrupulousness' who confronted King Agrippa. This Simon fits both in terms of context and time as possibly the father of the zealot leader in the Jewish uprising, Eleazar. He may also have been the Simon who was Yeshua's right hand man, nicknamed 'the Rock' in the gospels.

Simon's other nickname, 'bariona' from the Aramaic for outlaw, suggests another possibility. Eleazar's rival Simon is described as 'bar Gioras' or son of Gioras. This name may well derive from the Hebrew root grs, meaning to cast out or expel. So the sicarii leader Simon is being described as a son of 'the outcast' or outlaw, and is therefore another possible candidate as a son of Simon Peter.

It does appear that the conflict between Simon bar Gioras and Eleazar son of Simon represented a division in the messianic movement between claimants and lines of succession which were in some way related. This would certainly explain the force of the accusation, made by Josephus, that Simon bar Gioras' followers 'thought it a proof of brilliance to savage their own kith and kin'.

It is hard after so long, and after a degree of deliberate obfuscation, to delineate the relationships involved. But the general outline of a schism in the family of messianic claimants is certainly apparent in the history of the time, as Josephus describes it. The conflict between the sicarii forces of Menahem and of Simon son of Gioras on the one hand and the wider zealot coalition led by Eleazar, son of Simon, on the other parallels the divide between the militant followers of Yeshua who were pursued by Saul and the 'apostles' were left alone. It parallels the divide between Judas 'the betrayer' and 'sicarios' and the other loyal apostles or disciples/brothers. It parallels and intersects with the divide between the active Judas/Thaddeus 'Zelotes' and the passive James who prayed and prayed for his people until his knees became thick and callused as a camel's. It is expressed, I have suggested, in the person of Theudas, who was also Theuda or Thaddeus, brother of Yeshua and James, who provoked the Romans and jeopardised and thus betrayed 'the cause'.

And, for all the opprobrium that Josephus in his books heaped liberally and even-handedly on the various factions, this was ultimately the cause of most Jews and Josephus himself too. Liberation. It was not a practical objective for Josephus who had seen for himself in Rome the might of the Roman Empire and the resources it could muster. For the sicarii who held Masada under Eleazar, son of Jairus, practicality was not even remotely a consideration. They at the end died by their own hands rather than submit as slaves to Rome.

There were, I have suggested, no good guys whatsoever in

this complex story: each faction matched the atrocities of its enemies with horrors of its own. So, when Eleazar's men took Simon son of Gioras' wife hostage, Simon captured and tortured anyone he could get hold of, even the elderly outside the city gathering firewood, and he sent some people back with their hands cut off as a terrifying message to the others.

Eleazar and his zealots massacred the chief priests and their families. John of Gischala tried to murder Josephus in Galilee. Josephus for his part was brutal in dealing with his enemies; in one instance he flogged a delegation he had invited in on the pretence of peace talks 'till he had torn their flesh to ribbons'.

The Romans casually crucified anyone they captured. The rebels killed their Roman prisoners without compunction, after they had surrendered on a guarantee of safe conduct.

Such were the realities of conflict at that time. Messiahs who came forward preaching liberation and freedom for the Jewish people were inevitably promoting a struggle that would involve extreme suffering and violence. The religious leaders who taught a religion that was rigid in all its details, uncompromising and exclusive were also embracing a violent prospectus. Foreigners were excluded; foreign rulers were to be excluded. It was inevitable that there would be conflict.

It was possible to take a position that encompassed the yearning for freedom though without setting a course for confrontation. There were those who looked for divine deliverance, in the manner of the prophet Daniel, or who were prepared to wait for the power of the Romans to crumble as had many other previous empires. That may have been the consolation of the Nazoreans, under James and Simon, who appeared to believe in a spiritual kingdom on earth that could perhaps be made to work alongside the realities of political submission.

Others like Judas took a more proactive stance and this acted to undermine those who adopted a wait-and-see approach.

Atrocities committed under the procurator Gessius Florus and his recent predecessors must also have brought the conflict closer.

Random collective punishment, such as the mass slaughter of civilians in Jerusalem initiated by Florus, would have made it harder for moderate counsel to prevail. What argument would there have been for delay? Only, I would suggest, the need to organise, build up funds, make alliances and stockpile arms and armour. When the daily sacrifices to Rome were finally symbolically suspended, that had been done.

Like other messiahs, Yeshua had preached liberation, though in a subtle way and for a time at least avoiding confrontation. But he too had his band of armed supporters; he marched on Jerusalem, was captured and executed by the Romans.

There was, just as with Menahem, a tension between the message preached and the actions that had to be accomplished to achieve deliverance. Menahem, it will be recalled, went into Jerusalem 'like a king' when the battle was all but over and the remnants of the Roman force and King Agrippa's cavalry confined to Herod's Palace. At which point, Josephus makes a revealing comment. Menahem was killed, even though he was 'not violent', a surprising aside given that Josephus depicts almost everybody else in the most bloodthirsty of terms!

But, even though he was 'not violent', Menahem had a 'train of armed zealots' (elsewhere described as sicarii). Like Yeshua, he needed protection and he needed, if necessary, force to achieve his ends. The message and the means were distinct, the same message and ultimately the same means as his predecessor Yeshua.

In religious terms, Yeshua was a fully-observing, zealous Jew who read the Torah and went to the temple. He preached against fornication and impurity, if the gospels are read carefully, in the manner of the religiously strict community of 'the poor' at Qumran.

Divorce, whatever the position had come to be, he argued was unacceptable. If a man or woman divorced someone and then remarried, they were committing adultery. Even looking at a woman lustfully was sinful, a form of adultery.

Riches provided an insurmountable barrier. The only means to enter the kingdom of God was to give it all up, distribute it to the 'poor'. This could have meant the poor in the community as a whole. Or it could have meant the poor who were Yeshua's followers, giving up and pooling their possessions in a form of organisation that parallels precisely that of the 'poor' at Qumran.

As for the third 'net of Belial', 'impurity', Yeshua took what was actually an even tougher line. It was not so much ritual observance that mattered, but what came from within, evil ideas and thoughts. Purity required controlling these, much harder to achieve than washing hands at the appropriate time or using the right vessels for cooking.

He was also prepared to take tough, practical action, throwing out the money changers and the traders he regarded as defiling the temple.

Christians may be aghast at my suggestion that Yeshua was religiously a zealot and practically too in terms of what he and his followers did. How, they may wonder, could their Son of God be this?

But I have shown that Yeshua was not a world-redeemer, but a Jewish messiah for the Jews. Christians do not even follow Yeshua's teaching even as it has been modified and transmuted in the gospels. They do practice divorce. They do not share their possessions. They do not obviously behave any better than others, in terms of harbouring evil thoughts. They have been responsible over the years for their share, or possibly more than their share, of the world's atrocities, committed against unbelievers, people of other faiths, or Christians with slightly varying beliefs.

For the Nazorean Jews, Yeshua's real followers who had

known him, he was an important figure, with perhaps added significance in that the story of his 'miraculous' recovery from death provided useful propaganda against the Romans. Here was a messiah who was out of reach of the Romans and who one day might return to deliver them.

But he was only one of a number of different messiahs, one of a number in a particular line of succession of 'Sons of David'. In practical terms what mattered was who was able to give the Jews freedom. Yeshua was equally important as, but not more important than, John the Baptist, James, Simon and Judas and Hezekiah, executed by Herod, and his son Judas who conducted a rebellion and claimed the kingship when Herod died.

The focus is only on Yeshua because Christians have appropriated him, his biography and even the historical setting! But though he was not *the* important messiah, he was an important Jewish messiah.

His supposed humble origins, son of a mere carpenter, are a fiction compounded to distract from the fact of his real Jewish origins. Yeshua's story came out of a period of very real, very violent turmoil leading to a bitter, uncompromising war in which there was vengeance and destruction on all sides. It is no surprise that the picture of the real Yeshua that emerges, of Jesus the Zealot, reflects the times in which he lived.

Chapter 11: Myth and method

The analysis of the way the tales in the New Testament have been put together is to me a fascinating subject in itself, quite aside from any theological argument. Indeed, the same applies to non-canonical sources relating to the same period. I have kept this chapter to last, because I wanted to keep separate the exposition of methods of analysis, which admittedly sometimes provide startling results, from any debate about the likely validity of the conclusions.

So, I must state at the outset that I am not claiming absolute proof in any of the examples which follow. What I am suggesting is twofold. Firstly, in every case there are very good reasons for believing that the picture presented by the text as it is now is not complete or accurate. Secondly, in every case I contend that the explanation derived from my analysis makes more sense than a reading of the text as complete and literally true.

Of course, it is bound to be the case that the probability of such explanation actually being right will vary, even though arguably more probable that a straight reading of the text. To give a sense of what I mean, that is of the parameters involved, here are two instances that provide guidelines:

In the first instance, I think on the evidence that the disciple named Simon the Cananite, as conveyed in Mark, was not so named. Rather, I give a high probability to the explanation that he *was* nicknamed Simon the Zealot (from the Aramaic 'Cana'), as in Luke. This would explain why the author of Mark was loth to give a proper translation, and it fits in with a lot of other evidence.

Secondly, I also think that it highly unlikely Simon Peter was crucified upside down because he requested it, as described in the non-canonical *Acts of Peter*. I have provided a reason how he came to be crucified upside down that would explain why this detail was falsified. But this comes from an intuitive association with other textual material, and so has a *relatively* low probability of being true. That is despite the solid contention that it is a better explanation than taking the text as given, and notwithstanding my personal assessment of it!

I will spare the reader the tedium of entering such qualifications case by case. There is little disagreement that the gospels, and other such material relating to time of Yeshua, are the result of a long process involving compilation, comparison, copying, recopying and editing. That is why, in the manuscripts now available, there are sometimes scores of variations of the same piece of text. Accidental mistakes will have been introduced and sometimes marginal notes incorporated in copying. Embellishments will have been made to account for apparent discrepancies, or to fill in gaps, or simply to make a good story out of a sparse account. In addition to which, writers and historians in the early part of the first millennium, such as Josephus and doubtless the gospel authors themselves, were quite comfortable with a convention of putting words into the mouths of their characters. It made the narrative more interesting. It was at the time (and conceivable could still be) justified, providing the fictitiously attributed words merely reflected the evidence available of what had actually happened.

The *Pseudoclementine Recognitions* and *Homilies*, Ebionite in origin, demonstrate many of these points. The travels of Clement as described are almost certainly fictitious. So may be Clement himself. His quest for and rediscovery of his long-lost family helps the story hang together; it is a literary device. There is not a shred of a chance that the long discourses put into the mouth of Simon Peter were ever spoken by Yeshua's disciple. They represent the philosophical and theological speculation of the work's anonymous author, and possibly reflect that of a real group who existed in the second or third century CE. Contained within these very lengthy works, however, are details which indicate how these successor followers of Yeshua, and possibly how the first followers of Yeshua, may have viewed their leader and the emerging Christian Church. Just separating out such material is one task; evaluating it is then another.

There is considerable evidence that the gospels, as well as containing embroidery for the purposes of story telling, were also censored and edited over a period of time. The objective was always primarily to present a picture of Yeshua that was in accordance with the developing theology of the Christian church. That such a picture might not be historically accurate is indicated in a variety of ways. One is the context, that is what is known from a variety of sources of Jewish society at the time into which a historical Yeshua would have had to fit. Then there is the good evidence from the gospel material itself including Acts, supported by non-canonical sources, of a clash of interests and values between the immediate followers of Yeshua and the founders of a breakaway Christian sect. Since the gospels became the property of Christians, as opposed to Nazorean or Ebionite Jews, it can be expected that the story will have been moulded to fit their views rather than those of their opponents. Finally, there is independent evidence as to what sort of people the successors to Yeshua were, his brothers and other followers, what they did and what was their religious philosophy. This, it should be noted, is despite the effort to censor them as well and more latterly to misrepresent these circumcised Torah-following Jews as 'really' Christians or 'Jewish Christians' or even 'Christian Jews'!

Many changes, either to oral tradition or to source texts, were made to turn a Jewish Yeshua into a Christian Jesus. Identifying such changes and trying to tease out what was the original story have been two of the central concerns of this book. The process did not of course stop at this point. Ehrman (*Misquoting Jesus*) identifies early changes that were made with the objective of reaffirming orthodox Christian theology against alternative

Christian perspectives (adoptionalist, docetic and separationist). What his framework lacks however is a focus on first base, the examination of evidence for the Jewish Yeshua/Jesus and how this has been altered.

With all this is mind, it has been possible to attempt to make some sense of the contradictions, inconsistencies, oddities, impossibilities and sometimes simply baffling passages in the gospel texts.

One factor that is very apparent is the large number of points at which, either directly or by implication, the gospels contradict themselves. Since it is known that the material was being edited (the early gospel compiler Eusebius cheerfully admits as much!), and since the purpose was to project a developing Christian view, comparison of variant texts should give an indication of which was original and which later added. As Maccoby (*The Myth Maker*) has suggested, where a passage goes against the grain of the narrative, and the case that is being made, then there can be some confidence that it is original. The point of course is that censorship and editing will have achieved a general effect but, without wholesale and extremely careful rewriting, fragments indicating the original intent will have been left in. It is also unlikely that an editor would introduce new elements that contradict the case that he is trying to make.

Internal inconsistency

I propose to give two examples of the way of the way in which internal contradiction provides the evidence of a position that has been altered.

The first of these concerns the family of Yeshua, more particularly his brothers. These presented a problem for later gospel editors, when a doctrine of the perpetual virginity of Yeshua's mother Mary had been developed. Quite simply, if Mary went on to have more children she could not have remained a virgin – quite aside from the fact that she could not have been a virgin, having had even one child! Furthermore, this was a Jewish family which remained Jewish. So Yeshua had to be separated from them, as a saviour for the Gentile world, or they had to be discounted.

But Yeshua's brothers could hardly be written out, as their existence was very well-known. Since they were unavoidably there, something from a literary point of view had to be done with them. In the gospels, they are given bit parts and are shown as trying to obstruct Yeshua's ministry. This is illustrated in the story in Mark when his family, his mother and brothers, embarrassed at the fuss Yeshua was making, came to take him home. Whereupon Yeshua claimed that henceforth those who listened to him were now his mother and brothers, thereby denying his own family:

Then he went home; and the crowd came together again, so that they could not even eat. And when his friends heard it, they went out to seize him, for they said, 'He is beside himself.' And the scribes who came down from Jerusalem said, 'He is possessed by Beelzebul, and by the prince of demons he casts out demons.'...

And his mother and his brothers came; and standing outside they sent to him and called him. And a crowd was sitting about him; and they said to him, 'Your mother and your brothers are outside, asking for you.' And he replied, 'Who are my mother and my brothers?' And looking around on those who sat about him, he said, 'Here are my mother and my brothers! Whoever does the will of God is my brother, and sister, and mother.'
(Mark 3, 20-35)

It is a nice story, coming just after Mark's list of the twelve appointed 'to preach and have authority to cast out demons'. This is, as it happens, a very interesting juxtaposition. A little bit of disentangling the obfuscation (see ch 2) shows that the list of apostles included certainly one and most probably two brothers of Yeshua (James and Thaddeus/Judas), quite possibly a third (Simon/Simeon) and just maybe even a fourth (Matthew/Levi). James, and after him Simeon, went on to lead the Jerusalem Nazoreans. This is hardly carping from the sidelines, more like being part of the same messianic enterprise!

The central place of Yeshua's brothers, which goes against the grain, is I suggest original. The story of the petty-minded interference by his brothers is I suggest fictional, later in origin and placed in the text with a purpose.

That purpose was of course to diminish their role and cast them as uncomprehending Jews who failed to recognise, or even actively opposed, Yeshua's cosmic mission.

My second example concerns Yeshua's relationship with the Pharisees, who were the dominant force in Judaism at the time and had a majority on the Sanhedrin. In the earliest of the canonical gospels, Mark, the Pharisees are portrayed as testing Yeshua and trying to catch him out on points of doctrine. They are abetted in this by the legal interpreters of the Law, the scribes, whose members were often Pharisees themselves. There are several such instances described involving the Pharisees (Mark 7, 5; 8, 11; 10, 2; 12, 13) and only one relating to the Sadducees (Mark 12, 18). This sole instance relates to the Sadducee belief that there is no resurrection into an afterlife. So, it would seem, just on this basis, that the Pharisees are Yeshua's primary opponents and enemies. But when it comes to those who actually plot to kill Yeshua, and deliver him up to the Romans, it is the chief priests who are central (Mark 14, 1, 10, 43, 53, 60, 63; 15, 1, 10-11, 31). Pharisees as such do not get even a single mention! So, who are the 'chief priests'? The chief priests and the High Priest are from the collaborating Sadducees, traditionally opposed to the Pharisees, and they are the ones depicted as trying to harm Yeshua.

Who then are really Yeshua's enemies? What the author or editor of Mark is trying to show is Yeshua rejecting mainstream Judaism and formulating a new approach appealing to the Gentile population of the Roman world. It is a portrayal that is easy to achieve in set-piece theological confrontations. But, in describing the detail of what may have happened to Yeshua, this comes up against the likely historical realities. The Sadducee High Priest and his faction had power, conferred by the Romans – and Yeshua stood opposed to this power.

The gospels do certainly describe 'the chief priests, with the elders and scribes, and the whole council' (Mark 15, 1), bringing Yeshua to trial, condemning him and then handing him over to the Romans. The Pharisees (rendered as 'elders' and 'scribes') on the council (Sanhedrin) can thus be presumed to have acquiesced. On the other hand, when Yeshua is before the Roman governor Pilate, the Sadducees, in the guises of chief priests, are the prime movers. It is they who bring many charges against Yeshua, it is they who Pilate suspects of having delivered Yeshua up out of envy and it is they in the story who stir up the crowd to demand the release of a surrogate (Bar-abbas) instead of Yeshua:

And the chief priests accused him of many things. And Pilate again asked him, 'Have you no answer to make? See how many charges they bring against you.' But Jesus made no further answer, so that Pilate wondered.

Now at the feast he used to release for them one prisoner whom they asked. And among the rebels in prison who had committed murder in the insurrection, there was a man called Barabbas. And the crowd came up and began to ask Pilate to do as he was wont to do for them. And he answered them, 'Do you want for me to release for you the King of the Jews?' For he perceived that it was out of envy that the chief priests had delivered him up. But the chief priests stirred up the crowd to

have him release for them Barabbas instead.
(Mark 15, 3-11).

What these passages suggest is that Yeshua was opposed by the collaborating Sadducees. But the author or editor of Mark also describes doctrinal conflict between Yeshua and the Pharisees. Which portrayal is correct? On the principle already elaborated, the passage which goes against the grain is probably nearer the truth: Yeshua was in opposition to the Sadducees but probably not the Pharisees.

The same sort of internal inconsistency is seen in even starker form in the gospel of Luke which, like Matthew, includes a denunciation of Pharisees for (among other things) laziness, hypocrisy and neglecting justice. But Luke also describes three occasions (Luke 8, 36; 11, 37; 14, 1) when Yeshua dines with Pharisees, not something he would surely have been accustomed to do with his sworn enemies. Luke also notes Pharisees coming to warn Yeshua of an imminent attack by Herod Antipas, the Rome-appointed ruler of Galilee who had already killed John the Baptist. This kindly intervention, as reported, may have saved Yeshua's life. Luke also has Joseph of Arimathea, a member of the Sanhedrin (Council) who opposed the handover of Yeshua, seeking and preparing Yeshua's body for burial after the crucifixion.

Joseph was assisted by Nicodemus, a prominent Pharisee who held secret, night-time conversations with Yeshua and had opposed the moves to arrest him (John 3, 2; 19, 39; 7, 45-52).

As in the case of the analysis of Mark's gospel, the passages that show Yeshua on friendly terms with and cooperating with Pharisees are more believable, and more likely original, than those that show them as his enemies. The passages that go against the tenor of the gospel writer's argument have survived the censor and are more likely to be part of the original record.

Disparities between sources

Internal analysis of texts is limited by the fact that, when a change has been made, the original text will often have been discarded. In the examples above, alterations have been deduced from the fact that fragments of the original survive that go against the main thrust of the text and the writer's intentions. If only the original manuscripts were still available for comparison!

But there are instances where the first version, or a near approximation to the first version, is still there – under our very noses! It is just a case of recognising the original and the copy.

The four canonical gospels are independently written, though drawing on some common sources. The authors of Luke and Mathew in particular extensively used the earlier gospel Mark, which was available to them, as one of their sources. There are passages which have so much in common with Mark, word for word in sections, that these later versions can only be copies. But they are not always exact copies. And in this case, the original still exists for comparison, in the form of the text in Mark. Making comparisons between versions in Mark, as against Luke or Matthew, provides fascinating insight into the minds and motivations of the gospel editors. For the first exposition in this section on the 'angry Jesus', or rather the 'angry messiah', I draw from analysis in Bart Ehrman's *Misquoting Jesus* as well as my earlier book, *Censored Messiah*.

The Angry Jesus

The writer of Mark portrays Yeshua as someone with all-too human emotions, prone to irritation, petulance and outbursts of anger.

To take the story of the man with the withered hand, Mark reports that before healing him, Yeshua looked around 'with anger' at those who were watching him. His opponents were trying to catch him out for apparently breaking the Law by healing someone on the Sabbath (Mark 3, 1-6). Luke has the same story, borrowed almost word for word, except that the reference to Yeshua's anger is omitted (Luke 6, 6-11). Matthew also follows Mark closely, again word for word in places, but also omits the reference to anger (Matthew 12, 10-14).

In another story, the disciples told people off for bringing forward their children. Yeshua responded to this action by his disciples with indignation (Mark 10, 13-15). The other synoptics repeat the tale, following Mark's wording, while losing Yeshua's angry reaction (Luke 18, 15-17; Matthew 19, 13-15).

The story of the fig tree appears to be much the same in Matthew and Mark. Yeshua was hungry, found the tree without fruit, cursed it and it withered. However, it is only in Mark that it is made explicit that Yeshua had actually cursed the tree (Mark 11, 12-14, 20-25). As an aside, it is worth noting that the variations in Mark and Matthew illustrate one of the processes by which 'miracles' develop when stories are retold. In Mark, Yeshua cursed the tree and the next day his disciples passing the same way noticed that it had withered. In Matthew, Yeshua admonished the tree and it rolled up and died immediately (Matthew 21, 18-22)! Quite possibly, in an oral, pre-Mark version, there was an even longer period between cursing and the tree's demise, something within the bounds of coincidence and in line with a natural explanation. If the tree bore no fruit when it should have, then maybe it was already diseased. Had copyists decided at some point that Matthew's gospel was good enough, and had remaining copies of Mark then been destroyed, there would now only be available Matthew's description of an instant miracle.

Luke omits altogether the story of Yeshua's petulant response to finding the fig tree without fruit. He may have felt that, for all its dramatic quality and ennobling though discordant conclusion (faith can move mountains), the detail did not reflect well on Yeshua's character.

Sandwiched in the middle of the fig tree parable in Mark, there is the story of the cleansing of the temple (Mark 11, 15-17).

Yeshua is described in Mark as having taken three violent actions: he drove out those who bought and sold, he overturned the tables of the money changers and the seats of those who sold pigeons for sacrifice and he barred people from carrying anything through the temple. The other synoptics tell the same story, with Mark evidently as their source and using the same wording. But Matthew omits to mention that Yeshua barred people from carrying goods through the temple (Matthew 21, 12-13). Luke omits both this and any mention of tables of the money changers and seats of the pigeon sellers being overturned (Luke 19, 45-46).

So here again, Luke and Matthew have diminished the 'angry' aspect of Yeshua's character. But they did not and perhaps could not have not eliminated it entirely in this story because, without some action on the part of Yeshua, the text would not have made sense. It was a pivotal moment. It was, according to both Mark and Luke, because of this climactic confrontation in the temple that the 'chief priests and the scribes ... sought a way to destroy him' (Mark 11, 18). Whether or not the event did take place as described is another issue (see ch 8).

The final example in this section, from *Misquoting Jesus,* is interesting in that it shows how text came to be changed and also how, almost inevitably, traces were left which make it possible to reconstruct what was probably originally intended. Early on in Mark's gospel, there is a story of a leper coming to Jesus and being cured. The text given below is from the New Testament Revised Standard version:

> And a leper came to him beseeching him, and kneeling said to him, 'If you will, you can make me clean.' Moved with pity, he stretched out his hand and touched him, and said to him, 'I will; be clean.' And immediately the leprosy left him, and he was made clean. And he sternly charged him, and sent him away at once, and said to him, 'See that you say nothing to

any one; but go, show yourself to the priest, and offer for your cleansing what Moses commanded, for a proof to the people.' (Mark 1, 40-44)

There would seem on the surface to be nothing problematic, the story illustrating Yeshua's healing powers and compassionate nature. However, the versions in Matthew and Luke, once again for the most part word-for-word copies, have some interesting omissions (Matthew 8, 1-4; Luke 5, 12-15). They both omit the phrase 'Moved with pity' and neither do they say anything about Yeshua rebuking the leper and sending him away.

Why would these later gospels writers eliminate the reference to Yeshua being moved by pity? They otherwise have no problems about portraying a compassionate Yeshua and, in all the other examples found, what they seek to remove are references to Yeshua being irritable and angry.

The answer would seem to be that the Greek manuscript which was used for the New Testament translation was not original in respect of this particular detail. In a variant version of Mark, supported in a number of manuscripts, the text has the phrase 'Becoming angry' instead of 'Moved with pity.' So here the text reads, 'Becoming angry, he stretched out his hand and touched him, and said to him, "I will; be clean."

This at least is consistent with the tone of the passage as a whole in which, in literal translation from the Greek, Yeshua rebuked the leper severely and 'cast him out'. As Ehrman points out, when there are two conflicting versions in different manuscripts, the one which conflicts with prevailing theology, and so is seen as 'more difficult', is more likely to have been the original. This is because it provides an explanation for the existence of the other version: scribes could not understand why Yeshua was being described as angry in the context, assumed that a mistake must earlier have been made and so in copying changed the text to what they believed must or ought to have been the original. The explanation, it should be noted, does not work the other way round. Faced with an original Greek version which fitted with received theology, there would have been absolutely no motivation for changing the text to something which did not fit and apparently made no sense! Furthermore, there is in this case added confirmation elsewhere in the texts in Matthew and Luke which are derivative from Mark. Both gospel authors consistently omitted references to Yeshua being angry, in copying from Mark, and in this case they omitted the description of Yeshua severely rebuking the leper and casting him out. So it is highly probable that the omission they made in the earlier part of the passage was from the version of Mark which had Yeshua 'Becoming angry' instead of 'Moved with pity'. They simply cut out another reference to an angry messiah.

What are here being examined, as in the earlier instances, are identified changes made by writers at the end of the first or at the beginning of the second century, from an earlier mid to late first century document. It is of course possible that both the imperfect copies (Matthew and Luke) and the source (Mark) have subsequently been substantially altered in further copying. But the consistency of the pattern of difference, and the consistency of the explanation for it, makes it hard to envisage that the picture of an angry messiah which emerges is a later invention or addition, rather than being original to Mark.

So why would the authors of Matthew and Luke have been so motivated to eliminate or modify the references which show Yeshua as being angry and moody – petulant and violent? The answer I suggest is that, by the time of these later gospels, Christianity had developed its theology to the point at which Yeshua was both a perfect man and a divine being, 'Son of God'. So there was no place for reprehensible reactions and human frailties. The angry Jesus was, so far as possible, expunged from these gospels.

Writing earlier, and basing his material on a source more

likely to have been linked with the Jewish followers of Yeshua, the author of Mark would have had no such problems. Yeshua, though chosen by God and, it was contended, taken up by God like Elijah, was human and could be angry. Moreover, in the mould of other would-be messiahs or Jewish liberators, he *would* have been angry, uncompromising, fearless and a warrior.

The fact that Yeshua was mortal, like the rest of us, is sufficient to explain why he was angry at times. There is no need to go to each individual instance and find a reason. In the case of the cursed fig tree, Yeshua might have angry because, as the story suggests, he was hungry and frustrated at finding the tree without fruit. Or he might have been angry because he was rehearsing in his mind the coming confrontation later in the day in the temple, and transferred his feelings to the tree. Or he might have been angry for some other undisclosed reason that the writer either forgot to relate or did not know. It is of no consequence: in general terms Yeshua expressed anger simply because he was human.

Those who feel that they have to explain away Yeshua's anger do, however, have a problem. Ehrman suggests that 'Jesus' evident anger erupts when someone doubts his willingness, ability, or divine authority to heal'. In other words, it is a form of divine irritation in the face of human doubt! Ehrman has travelled far to his discovery that the bible is not inerrant. But he still appears, like Crossan and Freke and Gandy (see ch 8), to have based his analysis on a preconception.

I have argued from textual analysis that Mark's angry messiah is more original and likely to be the picture presented in the text that the authors of Matthew and Luke had before them (and copied and altered) around CE 100. It is consistent with the warrior mode of many Jewish messianic would-be liberators from the time, as described for example in the pages of Josephus.

It is worth noting that there appears to have been at least one other earlier version of Mark (Secret Mark) and that Mark was using and almost certainly modifying an original source which was Nazorean in origin, that is from the followers of Yeshua. Tradition has it that this originated from Simon Peter, in the form of notes of his preaching recorded by John Mark. The original source, in the form of a putative Cross gospel or possibly prototype gospel of the Hebrews, told of the life and death of Yeshua.

The early Christian author of Mark was comfortable in describing the version, as he received it, of a thoroughly human Yeshua because that fitted with the theology of the time. But there were elements that he would have disguised. For example, the Nazoreans were messianic nationalists who like other Jews would at least have wished the Romans out. But the early Christians were in communities which followed (the Herodian) Paul's doctrine of obedience to temporal, Roman authority. So the description of an armed march on Jerusalem, following a failed demonstration resulting in deaths and the taking of prisoners, was scrambled, though not eliminated entirely. The author of Luke appears, as in other instances in his gospel and Acts, to have had access to some additional historical record (Luke 13, 1; 23, 18-19).

I have also suggested that the putative original Nazorean document, like contemporary Dead Sea anti-Roman commentaries, would not have mentioned by name key figures who would at the time have still been alive. There were two reasons: the risk to the person named, from appearing to be a messianic agitator, and the risk to the writer in being associated with the messianic movement.

This may also be why there is no reference to Yeshua's Pharisee supporter Nicodemus in the synoptic gospels. It may be why, in Secret Mark, the story of Lazarus (close follower and brother in law of Yeshua) is told, but Lazarus himself remains unnamed. There would have been less of a problem in naming the men, once they had died, and that could be the reason that they do feature openly in John's gospel.

As a final note, Yeshua is described as 'being angered' in Secret Mark, when Mary falls weeping at his feet over the death of her brother Lazarus. By the time John's gospel came to be published, anger was no longer seen as a suitable emotion for a supposedly divine being. So Yeshua is described instead as being 'deeply moved'.

These are by no means the only instances of text being altered, for use in later gospels, to create a picture of Yeshua more consistent with developing Christian theology. The story in Mark of the rich young man, who wanted to gain eternal life, carried with it the implication that Yeshua was not perfect (Mark 10, 17-22). In retelling the tale, Matthew shifted words around to eliminate Yeshua's rebuttal of the suggestion that he was good (Matthew 19, 16-22). But the dialogue, as a consequence, has lost a lot of its sense (see ch 6).

My second demonstration of the benefit of comparing an original story in Mark with a later version copied and subtly altered by a subsequent gospel writer comes, courtesy of Hyam Maccoby's *The Myth Maker: Paul and the Invention of Christianity*.

The friendly Scribe

As already noted, there is internal inconsistency in Mark and the other gospels over the way the Pharisees are depicted, denounced by Yeshua but often also shown as offering hospitality and actively helping him. There is also a passage in Mark which shows Yeshua in constructive dialogue with those otherwise portrayed as his critics. It comes just after the story of how he dealt with a conundrum posed by a Sadducee concerning relationships in an afterlife:

And one of the scribes came up and heard them disputing with one another, and seeing that he answered them well, asked him, 'Which commandment is the first of all?' Jesus answered, 'The first is, "Hear, O Israel: The Lord our God, the Lord is one; and you shall love the Lord your God with all your heart, and with all your soul, and with all your mind, and with all your strength." The second is this, "You shall love your neighbour as yourself." There is no other commandment greater than these.'

And the scribe said to him, 'You are right, Teacher; you have truly said that he is one, and there is no other but he; and to love him with all the heart, and with all the understanding, and with all the strength, and to love one's neighbour as oneself, is much more than whole burnt offerings and sacrifices.' And when Jesus saw that he answered wisely, he said to him, 'You are not far from the kingdom of God.' And after that no one dared to ask him any question.
(Mark 12, 28-34)

In this story, the exchange between Yeshua and the scribe (an interpreter of the Law, usually also a Pharisee) is courteous to the point of being friendly. The scribe appears motivated by admiration, noting how well Yeshua had responded to those testing him. He refers respectfully to Yeshua as teacher/master and he praises him for the answer to his question, adding a remark of his own to the effect that love is superior to sacrifices. Yeshua responds positively, applauding the scribe for his understanding.

This story is not only inconsistent with other accounts in Mark of Pharisees and scribes setting out to entrap Yeshua, it is also at odds with the version of the same story given later in Matthew:

But when the Pharisees heard that he had silenced the Sadducees, they came together. And one of them, a lawyer [that is, scribe], asked him a question, to test him, 'Teacher, which is the great commandment in the Law?' And he said to

him, 'You shall love the Lord your God with all your heart, and with all your soul, and with all your mind. This is the great and first commandment. And a second is like it, "You shall love your neighbour as yourself." On these two commandments depend all the Law and the prophets.'
(Matthew 22, 34-40)

In this second version, the author of Matthew has written out any element of friendliness. The Pharisees plot together and select a legal expert, a scribe, to ask a question 'to test him', that is to try and catch him out. There is no praise of Yeshua and no corresponding warm reply.

The earlier version in Mark, which the author of Matthew had before him and rewrote, is at least nearer in time to an accurate rendering of events. It is also likely to be more authentic against the general effort to portray Yeshua in a hostile relationship with Pharisees, belied in the gospel narrative however by numerous instances of positive interaction and support. The friendly scribe, like the angry Jesus, is much nearer to the truth.

Cuts and patches

So far, I have looked at changes which were either inadvertently or deliberately introduced when the gospels were copied in the process of their dissemination. An expanding Christian community would have needed more copies of the gospels for its members and old texts which were wearing out would have needed to be replaced. The new gospels of Luke and Matthew can in part be seen as a response to this demand. Their authors incorporated other material they had, and modified as they saw fit the Markian text. The outcome was a considerable degree of variation between manuscripts of the same texts, variation between versions in later gospels and Mark, and internal inconsistencies in a single text. In the latter case, this has to be explained by analysis when there is no original version or when possibly the author was creatively rewriting an oral tradition.

Following the Council of Nicea in CE 325, the Emperor Constantine appointed his bishop Eusebius to produce 50 new copies of the gospels, at the time an immense task, to be distributed among all the churches. Old copies would have been recalled and destroyed. New doctrines agreed at the Council, such as the divinity of Yeshua, would have been systematically incorporated; indeed Eusebius admits to have included only what he saw as reflecting well on the Church and excluded whatever did not! From that moment onwards, there was a prevailing orthodoxy, since there were many texts which were for the most part exact copies. From that moment also, the process of flux and change was substantially fossilised into the form dictated by the manuscripts that Eusebius chose to use and the variations that he had decided. It would be hard from then on for anyone to make a change that would stick. With the later advent of the printing press, the texts were almost literally cast in stone, widely disseminated in identical form. They were unchallenged, until scholars began to examine the early manuscripts.

Before the age of printing, and before Eusebius' colossal enterprise in replicating 50 handwritten copies, there would have been far fewer texts. At this much earlier time, it might well have been a practical proposition to look at a text and decide to change it. The outcome could well in some instances have been that the changed text, copied and recopied as old manuscripts wore out or further copies were needed, became the orthodox or indeed the only version.

Changing just a part of a manuscript would have been a different proposition from introducing variations when a document came to be rewritten in its entirety. In the case of scrolls, papyrus was glued together to make one continuous sheet which was then rolled from one wooden roller to another. This made alterations difficult. If the aim were to preserve a perfectly-presented document, then the only option would have been to copy out the whole document – even for just a single change. This would have been very costly, laborious, and possibly a wasted effort, if another error or undesired feature were then spotted and the whole process had to be started again.

In practice, the method for small changes appeared to have been carefully to scratch the ink from the surface of the offending part and then write new text over it. There is evidence in some surviving fragments that this practice was adopted with the Dead Sea scrolls. Cutting out small portions and glueing new text back in might also have been a feasible option. Either way, an alteration would have been achieved with just a tiny fraction of the time and expense of copying out the whole manuscript.

Lengthy alterations would almost certainly have involved creating and glueing a new section in to the papyrus roll. However arduous, this might well have been less trying and time-consuming than scratching out and writing over scores of lines of text.

Some of the early first century Christian documents may, like those discovered in the Dead Sea caves, have been written as scrolls. But what has survived, at first in fragments, from the second century onwards are codices, books formed by stitching together papyrus or parchment pages.

The codex may have been preferred by Christian authors and editors, for a several reasons. It was less cumbersome to use, it was better adapted for writing on both sides, thereby reducing bulk and cost, and it facilitated making changes.

Providing an alteration did not require significant cuts or extra text, a perfect looking codex could be preserved just by copying out the one page affected. However, even that may have involved considerable effort. So, for small changes, it is likely that the same procedures will have been used for the codex manuscripts as were used for scrolls: overwriting and cut and pasting.

The manuscripts that we have are for the most part copies of copies of copies. So the scrapes and patches, if they were once there, are now no longer visible. The alterations have to be deduced. Bearing in mind the provisos given at the start of this chapter, I will shortly offer some examples.

The additions of large amounts of text could have been accommodated in a scroll by cutting the scroll and glueing in the new section. In a codex, however, this would have caused a knock on effect, with displaced text running on to the next page, and then the next and so on. Either that or a 'loose leaf' could have been inserted, leaving the original flow of narrative disrupted and disjointed.

One, albeit rather drastic solution, would have been to cut out and remove text of the same extent, so discarding something regarded as less essential. Or it could have been that this was the whole purpose of the exercise, to remove something no longer conforming to the currently accepted cannon or currently accepted view of Yeshua. This points to the way major deletions would have been accomplished, as with small cuts, by inserting an equivalent amount of new material.

Large insertions made many years after the original material was written can be easy to spot. This is because, try as he may, the later editor will be using a different style and range of vocabulary. There is also likely to be some dislocation in the flow of text, at the points at which the new meets the old.

These telling signs are all encountered with the final 12 verses of the gospel of Mark, which are generally accepted by scholars as not part of the original text. The gospel ended with the women (Mary Magdalene, Yeshua's mother Mary and his aunt Salome) going to the tomb and finding a messenger telling them that Yeshua had 'risen' and gone to Galilee. Early manuscripts do not contain any additional verses and this is supported by quotes of Mark in early sources.

Moreover, the verses which have been added by later scribes contain vocabulary not used elsewhere in Mark and there are stylistic differences. The transition is clumsy, with a reference introducing Mary Magdalene 'from whom he had cast out seven demons' as if she were a new character, when in fact she had been named a few lines before in the main text.

The added 12 verses list appearances of Yeshua, provide instructions for his disciples in preaching the gospel and describe signs that will distinguish believers. Some of these are bizarre, to the point of being foolhardy: for example, the ability to handle venomous snakes or drink poison without ill-effect. Having given his final instructions, Yeshua is taken up by God to heaven.

Why were these lines added? It would seem to fill out the story, which did otherwise end rather abruptly, from the gospel editor's early Christian perspective. There would also seem to have been a motivation to counter, with spirit appearances, the impression in the original text of a recovered flesh-and-blood Yeshua, having to make a journey, 'going' ahead of the others to Galilee.

For similar reasons of style, provenance and vocabulary, most scholars think that the story of the woman taken in adultery in John's gospel also was a later addition. The story may have been present in another textual source or in oral tradition. It could have been incorporated as a loose leaf in a codex, or it may have been introduced to replace deleted material, possibly an earlier version of the same story (see p 359 below).

It provides a view of Yeshua flexible with regard to Jewish Law, in contrast with a more rigid Torah-abiding Yeshua in places in earlier gospels (eg Mark 9, 43-48). It also provides another example of 'Pharisees' attempting to entrap him.

Smaller changes made to eliminate what was regarded as offending material are often difficult to spot, if only because there is no substantial body of the new text available for comparisons of style and vocabulary. There may be many such changes in the gospels that will continue to remain undetected.

Some of the alterations will nevertheless stand out, contrasting not only with the piece of text it can be deduced has been removed but with the surrounding context. My first example of cut and paste, with the usual proviso that the reconstruction is simply more probable as original, comes in the story of the wedding in Cana.

Jesus, the wedding guest – rude or misconstrued?
The story of the wedding feast in which water was famously turned to wine (or offered to the guests when some were too drunk to know the difference!) comes very early in the gospel of John:

> On the third day there was a marriage at Cana in Galilee, and the mother of Jesus was there; Jesus also was invited to the marriage, with his disciples. When the wine gave out, the mother of Jesus said to him, 'They have no wine.' And Jesus said to her, 'O woman, what have you to do with me? My hour has not yet come.' His mother said to the servants, 'Do whatever he tells you.' Now six stone jars were there, for the Jewish rites of purification, each holding twenty to thirty gallons. Jesus said to them, 'Fill the jars with water.' And they filled them up to the brim. He said to them, 'Now draw some out and take it to the steward of the feast.' So they took it. When the steward of the feast tasted the water now become wine and did not know where it came from (though the servants who had drawn the water knew), the steward of the feast called the bridegroom and said to him, 'Every man serves the good wine first; and when men have drunk freely, then the poor wine; but you have kept the good wine until now.' This, the first of his signs, Jesus did at Cana in Galilee, and manifested his glory; and his disciples believed in him.
>
> After this he went down to Capernaum, with his mother and his brothers and his disciples; and there they stayed for a few days.
> (John 2, 1-12)

Yeshua's retort to his mother, especially in the context, appears as incredibly rude, a bizarre and discordant note. She merely points out that the wine has run out. He tells her sharply not to bother him. Moreover, the statement makes no sense. Yeshua's comment or realisation that his 'hour has not yet come' is reserved in John for occasions later when he was under real threat: at the Feast of the Tabernacles in Judea when his enemies ('the Jews' in John) sought to kill him (John 7, 6) and similarly when preaching in the temple (John 8, 20). Then finally, when Yeshua goes to Jerusalem at Passover, he realises or is made to realise that his hour has come (John 12, 23).

The comment is moreover contradicted by the surrounding text. Yeshua tells his mother not to bother him; by implication he is not going to do anything. But, following his reply, she tells the servants to follow Yeshua's instructions. So, it would seem that in an original reply which has been removed and substituted, Yeshua told his mother something different, that he was going to fix the problem. The reply in the story now is not authentic; it appears to have been borrowed from somewhere else.

Why was a substitution made?

The answer, I suggest, has to do with what the wedding in Cana was really about. There is a compelling weight of evidence that this was not just any old wedding, but Yeshua's own.

There is first the passive evidence, which would allow or suggest this. Yeshua would have been married and there is a case that he *was* married to Mary Magdalene (see ch 6). His marriage would likely have taken in his home territory, Galilee, and in his early adulthood, which is where and when in John's gospel the marriage took place.

There are also several pieces of strong, direct evidence from the text. Yeshua went to the wedding as part of a very large party, with his mother and his disciples and his brothers who afterwards went with him to Capernaum. This suggests that they were principle actors in the event, rather than merely guests at the wedding.

If a serious snag came up, the 'steward at the feast' or master of ceremonies would automatically consult whoever was responsible for the feast, that is the parents or parent of the bridegroom. In this instance, he went to Yeshua's mother. So she was the mother of the bridegroom and it was one of her children getting married. She then deferred to Yeshua, which indicates that it was in fact his marriage.

Furthermore, Yeshua fixed the problem and it must have been clear to the steward that he had (miraculously) done this and come up with some more wine. But a little later, the game is given away. The steward congratulates the person who resolved the issue of the lack of wine as … 'the bridegroom'! So Yeshua in this story is plainly the bridegroom.

A later editor cut out a reply by Yeshua to his mother which made it absolutely clear that he was the bridegroom. It could have been to the effect that 'I am the bridegroom, so I will deal with it'. Now the following line, 'His mother said to the servants, "Do whatever he tells you", follows perfectly smoothly and makes sense. It should be made clear that I am not suggesting that any of the dialogue actually took place (some of it *may* have, but it was common practice to put words in the mouths of characters to help along the narrative). What I am suggesting is that the sort of dialogue which I have deduced was in an earlier version of the story, and that this has been changed to the version we now have.

This example illustrates the difficulties involved in making changes so that the altered phrase or passage merges perfectly with pre-existing text. The editor or censor should also have cut or changed the reference to 'the bridegroom' but the story is to some extent a seamless whole. Should he then also have removed the references to Yeshua's mothers and the disciples and (by implication) his brothers being present, to Yeshua's mother's active role in the drama, to Yeshua resolving the problem? There would have been little or nothing left.

It is interesting to contemplate the origin of the piece of text that appears to have been inserted. The author of John makes use of the dramatic device of threefold repetition so that, for example, Simon Peter denies Yeshua three times. He is also made to affirm that he loves Yeshua three times, with Yeshua responding once 'feed my lambs' and twice 'feed (or tend) my sheep'. These responses make more sense in the Old Syriac (Sinaiticus Palimpsest) which has a progression from those needing most care to the whole of society - feed my lambs, feed my ewes, feed my sheep.

There are already two instances in the gospel where Yeshua is under threat and needs to be careful on the grounds that his 'hour has not yet come' (John 7, 6 and John 8, 20). This raises the possibility that the comment 'O woman, what have you to do with me? My hour has not yet come' was part of a threefold sequence including the other similar references in John.

I suggest that it could have been part of the original version the story of the woman taken in adultery (John 8, 1-11), a piece cut out and not wasted but used to fill a gap elsewhere. As already noted, the story appears to be insertion but what I suggest has been inserted is a remake of the original.

Unlike the description of the wedding at Cana, the comment by Yeshua is at home in this story. Yeshua was here at risk, as a result of the efforts of his enemies to entrap him. If he condoned stoning, then a capital charge could indeed be brought against him. This was because the Romans had taken the power to sanction the death penalty. On the other hand, if Yeshua allowed that the woman should be freed, then he was conceding that Roman Law had precedence and this might have diminished his authority.

Yeshua's possible comment to or about the woman ('O woman, what have you to do with me?) reflects the fact that he was not a witness to the alleged offence. Under the Law of Moses, executions by stoning could only take place outside of court procedure where the facts were agreed in detail by at least two witnesses and the offence was so heinous as to demand an immediate death penalty.

However, the story as presented does not make complete sense because the woman had been caught in the act and had already been condemned. Her accusers and sentencers, rather than Yeshua, might have been at risk from Roman retribution, had the woman then been executed without proper authority.

Several early manuscripts appear to recognise that the story is a variant text and an early Syrian text (*Disascalia Apostolorum*) discusses what may have been the original version. The woman, a sinner now guilty of crimes unspecified, is taken before Yeshua *after* the scribes and Pharisees have declined to give a judgement. Why would such an original version have been substituted? It is possible that it was because this original version indicated that Yeshua, rather than being a rebel against the Law, had some position of authority within Judaism – which indeed he might have had as leader of the Nazoreans. The people, before whom the woman was brought, passed her on to higher level, to Yeshua.

Certainly James, who was the Nazoreans' leader after Yeshhua, appeared to have an authority which extended beyond his own substantial body of followers. In the original story, therefore, Yeshua was the final arbiter; in the substituted version, this role had already been performed by others.

Now the whole comment, which I suggest was part of the original 'woman taken in adultery' story and subsequently used to fill a gap elsewhere, makes sense. Yeshua recognises the trap that has been set, the danger in which he has been placed. If he defers to Roman authority, then his position as a teacher/lawgiver is weakened. If he rules that the women be stoned, then he could be reported to the Romans and would be at risk of being regarded as an accessory. If, on the other hand, he rules that she should be set free, it might look as if he were disregarding Jewish Law.

So he disclaims jurisdiction, on the grounds that he is not a witness, with the comment 'O woman, what have you to do with me?' For good measure, he observes that the moment is not right for his final reckoning, 'My hour has not yet come'.

Note again, that I am not suggesting that Yeshua actually said any of this, and certainly not the latter comment. This was part of a literary device, a threefold repetition leading up to and giving added weight to a dramatic climax (John 12, 23). What I have sought to do is reconstruct an earlier version which may therefore be nearer to what an original story teller, closer in time and possibly even a contemporary, wanted to say about Yeshua.

Having denied jurisdiction (in the presumed original version), Yeshua completes the process (in the surviving version in John) by inviting the onlookers to judge the woman based on their own probity or otherwise in respect of the charge of adultery!

Why the writing in the sand? This fits with Yeshua being sought out wherever he happened to be and the woman brought before him for judgement. Though a court had not been constituted, it was still necessary to record the charge and the names of the witnesses. Without writing materials available, Yeshua wrote in the sand for this to be copied later.

The original version of the story was, I have suggested, dismembered and rewritten to disguise the fact that Yeshua was regarded as having some legal authority. One original piece was then used to fill a gap in the tale of the wedding at Cana. As to the motivation for changing this wedding story, the early Church (and for that matter the Church now) had problems with sexuality. Yeshua had to be a perfect man and Son of God, so it could not be contemplated that he did the ordinary human things, having sex and getting married. So he couldn't be allowed his own wedding. He could not be a bridegroom, and the remark which implied this was therefore written out of the story line. Among scraps cut from other parts of the codex, the gospel editor found a piece of replacement text which, though not at all relevant, provided a perfect fit!

A second example of cut and paste relates to a turning point, when Yeshua was told of a Roman massacre.

A march without motive?

One of the few points at which the gospel narrative intersects with the historical record occurs when Yeshua is told of some Galileans, Yeshua's fellow countrymen, 'whose blood Pilate had mingled with their sacrifices'. The Jewish historian Josephus describes a number of atrocities committed by Pilate. Considerations of sequence and timing suggest that the one most likely to correspond to the event described in Luke was the temple funds massacre. People gathered in Jerusalem to protest against the proposed use of Jewish temple funds to build an aqueduct. Pilate sent in his troops in disguise and the result was panic and a lot of causalities (see ch 3).

> There were some present at that very time who told him of the Galileans whose blood Pilate had mingled with their sacrifices. And he answered them, "Do you think that these Galileans were worse sinners than all the other Galileans, because they suffered thus? I tell you, No; but unless you repent you will all likewise perish. Or those eighteen upon whom the tower in Siloam fell and killed them, do you think that they were worse offenders than all the others who dwelt in Jerusalem? I tell you, No; but unless you repent you will all likewise perish".
> (Luke 13, 1-5)

There are other references to this protest or revolt and its consequences in Luke and the other canonical gospels. I have argued (ch 8) that the sequence for Yeshua's journey from Galilee to Jerusalem in Luke as presented is deliberately confused. It makes sense in space and time only from the moment when

Yeshua was told of the temple massacre, if this was in Galilee. Two prior references to incidents on the way to Jerusalem could not have taken place so early because they were located much too far south. If these are correctly sequenced, this would mean that Yeshua walked almost all the way to Jerusalem, then walked back to the beginning for no apparent reason and restarted his journey! It is a reasonable presumption that these incidents were added in to disguise the fact that the march from Galileee was a response to the Roman massacre.

At the point at which Yeshua has been arrested, Mark states that 'among the rebels in prison, who had committed murder in the insurrection, there was a man called Bar-abbas' (Mark 15, 7). The reference to 'the insurrection' suggests that the writer is confident that his readers know what he is talking about, one can presume because he had already referred to it. There is no prior reference to the insurrection in Mark, although it is there in Luke who used Mark as a source. It is therefore likely that there was such a reference in Mark, but at some later point it has been cut out.

Luke gives a description of Bar-abbas as 'a man who had been thrown into prison for an insurrection started in the city, and for murder' (Luke 23, 19). This advances understanding a little further by placing the revolt in Jerusalem. Matthew simply refers to Bar-abbas as 'a notorious prisoner' (Matthew 27, 16) and in John's gospel, he is described as a robber/bandit – the disparaging term the Romans used and Josephus also often used to describe messianic rebels, zealots and sicarii (John 18, 40).

The simplest and the most likely explanation for this detail is that the 'rebels' held in prison were there as a result of being taken during the protest or revolt which Yeshua had been informed about, before making his way to Jerusalem. There is no mistaking, either from the description in Josephus or what appear to be remnant references in the gospels, that it was a very major incident.

This is a lot of background to a simple, though significant

point. Yeshua's reaction to the news that his fellow Galileans have (perhaps once again) been butchered by the Romans is entirely inappropriate and wholly unlikely. Some anger, some scorn, might well have been appropriate from a warm-blooded 'angry' messiah, and it might well have there in Mark before the incident was cut out completely. Luke just eliminates Yeshua's reaction, substituting a homily with a mixed bag of mixed messages: everyone is mortal, death can come at any time, repent before it is too late, the Galileans were not necessarily any worse than anyone else because they suffered a horrible fate, on the other hand unless you repent you will suffer a horrible fate! I suggest that what was there in Mark, possibly even in the first version copied in Luke was a reaction which did express Yeshua's outrage – and indicate that he was going to do something about it.

I have argued earlier that Yeshua did in fact do something about it. He took a band of followers, some at least of them armed, to Jerusalem. The objective could have been, by threatening conflict, to force Pilate to back down (as Pilate had done over previous incidents) and free the prisoners. Some at least of Yeshua's followers, judging by the jockeying for position of the brothers James and John, were expecting a battle for liberation and the advent of the messianic kingdom.

The Romans did not as a rule keep prisoners. Those guilty of capital crimes would have been swiftly executed. Those found guilty of lesser offences would have been flogged and put to hard labour or released. But on this occasion they held their 'notorious' prisoners, including murderers.

The prisoners may have been held as potential bargaining counters, in the light of news of an alarming force of apparent insurgents gathered and on its way to Jerusalem. This analysis is at the very least more plausible than the reaction of Yeshua to the Roman massacre, as it is now described in Luke. That reaction I suggest was inserted to replace a version from an earlier story, which may once have been in Mark, which indicated (too clearly for the censor) Yeshua's intent. As in the previous case, an overly explicit piece of dialogue was cut out, and substituted with something else.

Misinterpretation

It is sometime unclear whether text has been deliberately swapped about, or simply misinterpreted when the original order and use of words in Greek lend themselves to alternative renderings in translation. In the example which follows, the likeliest explanation is that a passage in John's gospel has been misunderstood and mistranslated in the light of preconceptions at the time about the family of Yeshua and particularly the status of his mother Mary. Although this story has been examined earlier (ch 1), because of its importance in terms of method and analysis it is considered in more detail here.

The misplaced Mary
There is evidence that the author of John's gospel had an additional original source beyond the synoptics themselves (Mark, Luke and Matthew) and whatever material they relied on. Traditionally it is supposed, from the words at the end of the gospel, that this source was the long-lived 'disciple whom Jesus loved'.

All the gospels describe a number of women who went with Yeshua and his band of followers to Jerusalem. Luke does not name the women who 'stood at a distance' at the place of crucifixion. In Mark's gospel the scene is described as follows:

> There were also women looking on from afar, among whom were Mary Magdalene, and Mary the mother of James the younger (less) and of Joses, and Salome who, when he was in Galilee, followed him, and ministered to him;
> (Mark 15, 40)

The author of Matthew worked from this earlier gospel, quoting many passages with closely similar or identical wording. Here he follows Mark to the point of listing the third woman present, where he describes her differently:

> There were also many women there, looking on from afar, who had followed Jesus from Galilee, ministering to him; among whom were Mary Magdalene, and Mary the mother of James and Joseph, and the mother of the sons of Zebedee.
> (Matthew 27, 56)

The two Marys were, as would be expected from their place in the story, significant women in the life of Yeshua: the first his partner and the second his mother (and so also mother of James, the brother of Yeshua). The third woman named as present at the scene of the crucifixion should also be someone of significance. If Matthew is following Mark, as he has been for the rest of the passage, then he is adding further information. Salome is the wife of Zebedee and thus the mother of his sons, James and John.

At this point, it is not clear why the story teller has placed her there. James and John, 'sons of thunder', have been identified earlier in the narrative as recruits to the cause. But this would of itself scarcely have merited placing their mother at the centre of the action, at the cross, with the wife and the mother of Yeshua.

The author of John's gospel presents a picture which, as it is now translated from the Greek, does not seem to make sense:

> But standing by the cross of Jesus were his mother, and his mother's sister, Mary the wife of Clopas, and Mary Magdalene.
> (John 19, 25)

According to this, there are two sisters present, one the mother of Yeshua and the other his aunt, both called Mary. This is improbable, given that families did not then, as now, generate confusion by giving siblings the same forename. Furthermore, John's gospel is at odds with Mark and Matthew in that there is a new character, the wife of Clopas, in place of Salome.

The fourth century Catholic theologian Jerome nevertheless used this reading of the passage in John to put forward a theory which cut Yeshua from his natural family. Comparing this text with the parallel passages in Mark and Matthew, he proposed that 'Mary of Clopas' was the same person as Mary the mother of James and Joses. Since James was elsewhere identified as the son of Alphaeus, this Mary had to be married to Alphaeus. Since this Mary was described as the sister of Yeshua's mother, it also meant that James and the others described as brothers were really only Yeshua's cousins. Stripped of her other children, Yeshua's mother could – since in the case of Yeshua it was supposed to be God who impregnated her – be regarded as having remained a virgin.

The theory appeared to gain weight later when it was recognised that Clopas and Alphaeus, listed as the father of James in the gospels, are both derivations from the Aramaic name Chalphai.

Strained arguments have however been introduced to make Mary, a wife and mother, into a virgin. The authors of Matthew and Luke relied on a mistranslation of a prophecy by Isaiah that a young woman would bear a son who would rescue Israel. In their version of the Old Testament, translated from Hebrew into Greek, the young woman became a 'virgin' and this was then incorporated into the nativity stories.

Jerome's interpretation of the passage in John introduces further strains beyond the implausibility of having two sisters both called Mary and the difficulty of supposed cousins being frankly described as brothers in the gospels and other sources. In John's gospel, Yeshua's mother is present at the cross, as would be expected as one of the most significant women in his life. But if the wife of Clopas/Alphaeus is the sister of Yeshua's mother and also the mother of James and Joses, then it is she who is present instead of Yeshua's mother at the cross in the descriptions in Mark and Matthew. This is inconsistent to say the least. It is not likely that Yeshua's mother would have been missing from the scene in these gospels, especially when she is described as present in John.

An examination of the Greek text of John 19, 25, as literally written, shows that the translation usually made is in error and the cause of all the difficulties:

But there had stood beside the cross of Jesus the mother of him and the sister of the mother of him, Mary the wife of Clopas, and Mary Magdalene.

In the Greek used in the gospels, qualifying words are often placed later in sequence, leaving the reader to make a sensible judgement as to what they refer. In another later list (John 21, 2), Yeshua appears to his disciples:

There were together Simon Peter and Thomas the one called the twin and Nathanael the one from Cana of Galilee and the (sons) of Zebedee and others of the disciples of him two.

The word 'two', displaced to last position in the sentence, could be taken to apply in several contexts. But 'others of the two disciples' makes no sense. Using it as 'the two (sons) of Zebedee' makes sense, although 'two' is not used in other references to the sons of Zebedee and it leaves the phrase 'others of the disciples' incomplete. The best reading is therefore as 'two others of the disciples' which makes sense and gives a sentence which is coherent.

The same logic needs to be applied to the description of the women standing by the cross (see above) where there is, if anything, an easier decision to make. The phrase 'Mary the wife of Cleophas' comes after the second of two references to 'the mother of him', where it has been placed for convenience and which I suggest it qualifies. The reading this produces is better because it is more coherent and fits with other evidence:

> But standing by the cross of Jesus were his mother, Mary the wife of Clopas, and his mother's sister, and Mary Magdalene.

This now makes sense. Gone is the improbability of two sisters, both named Mary. The same three women are present as in the gospels of Mark and Matthew. Salome is now also there in John and the mother of Yeshua, and also of James and Joses/Joseph, is reinstated in the two synoptic gospels.

There is now also a reason for the third woman in the accounts in Mark and Matthew to be present at or near the cross. Salome, mother of the sons of Zebedee, appears in John as the sister of Yeshua's mother. As Yehua's aunt, though ranking third in importance after his wife and mother, she may well have been a significant person in his life.

As well as allowing Mary to have had other children beside Yeshua, this makes Clopas her husband rather than Joseph. This would accord with the portrayal of Joseph as rather a shadowy figure, not even mentioned in the earliest of the gospels, Mark. He is introduced in the nativity stories in Matthew and Luke, but then disappears in the passion narrative. Commentators have presumed that this is because he may by this time have died. An alternative explanation, supported by the evidence outlined above, is that he never was the husband of Mary but was introduced to distract from the real family of Yeshua involving a mother, father (Clopas) and brothers and sisters.

It has been argued that the versions of the women present at the cross in Mark and Matthew could be taken to indicate that one of the two Marys present was the daughter of James and mother of Joses. Both versions have the same format in the Greek wording. In Matthew, the full description is 'Mary Magdalene and Mary the of James and Joseph mother and the mother of the sons of Zebedeee'. The argument is threefold, that 'mother' only qualifies 'Joseph', that there is a word omitted in describing the relationship between Mary and James and that the word omitted is 'daughter'. The Old Syriac version in the Sinaiticus Palimpsest describes the women at the cross in Matthew as 'Mary Magdalene and Mary the daughter of James and mother of Joseph and the mother of the children of Zebedee'.

There are strong reasons for believing that the interpretation from the Greek is mistaken. In the first place, James and Joses or Joseph appear as the first part of the description of four of the brothers of Yeshua in both Mark (6, 3) and Matthew (13, 55). Having described the brothers in full, the narrator in each gospel apparently felt no need to do so again. The mother was then subsequently defined in relationship to two brothers, as mother of James and Joses/Joseph (Mark 15, 40 and Matthew 27, 56), or as mother of just one (James in Mark 16, 1 and Luke 24, 10 and Joses in Mark 15, 47) or evasively as 'the other Mary' (Matthew 27, 61 and 28, 1). It is clear from these descriptions that Mary was recognised as the mother of both James and Joses/Joseph. The interpretation that Mary was mother of Joses, but *daughter* of James, is a supposition not supported by this evidence.

Paul furthermore in his letters recognised James as a brother of Yeshua. Several early church authorities also described James as Yeshua's brother. He was thus another son of Mary, rather than her father. The description in John's gospel, properly interpreted, has the wife of Clopas as Yeshua's mother. Since it is considered that Clopas and Alphaeus are versions of the same name, this makes James the son of Alphaeus in the Apostles lists the same person described in John as the son of Mary and Clopas. This Mary matches the Mary described in Mark and Matthew as 'of James and Joseph mother' and therefore I suggest the mother not merely of Joses but James as well.

There is incidentally the same problem in interpreting both 'Mary [ ] of James' and 'Judas [ ] of James'. Early authorities depicted James as a lifelong celibate. He is likely therefore to have been the daughter of Mary and brother of Judas, rather than the parent of either or both of them.

Having deduced what the gospel descriptions of the women at the cross actually record, it remains to explain how they have come to be in their present form. I have suggested that the early gospel writers had little material to go on. There was the Nazorean claim in oral tradition, or possibly in written form, that Yeshua had survived crucifixion and had like Elijah been taken up to heaven. There were some sayings, transmitted orally and eventually written down. The author of Luke may have had access to some official Roman records.

There was very little else, in view of the fact that some years had passed since the crucifixion and a large part of the population had been killed or dispersed in the Jewish uprising. The gospel compilers were furthermore followers of Paul who had established a breakaway sect, advocating the abrogation of the Torah and in opposition to the Nazorean Jews. This could well have impeded the collection of source material.

But some key facts will have been well remembered, such as the warlike descriptions of Yeshua's followers described in chapter two, redolent of the struggles which were actually being conducted against the collaborating Sadducees and occupying Romans. It also seems probable that the gospel writers would have had access to the basic facts about the family of Yeshua. I suggest that when John's gospel was written, early in the second century, there may have been no problem about including straightforward information on Yeshua's mother, father and brothers individually and as a family.

Subsequently, a cult of Mary as a virgin and consort of God was developed. Yeshua was turned into Jesus, the product of a union between God and a mortal woman, following the precedent of myths which pagans themselves understood as allegories.

Yeshua's actual family as presented could have become an impediment to these new doctrines. So the gospels were re-examined. As a product of the way in which the Greek was written, the description of the women present at the cross in John's gospel *could* be taken to indicate that a sister of Mary was the father of those generally regarded as her children, though with all the difficulties, drawbacks and inconsistencies hitherto described. On this basis, the passage was retained.

References to Clopas in the synoptic gospels, now inconsistent with this reading, were written out or disguised. References to Mary, when being described in relation to her children were modified to exclude Yeshua in every instance. A nativity tale was introduced in which Mary was not even married but betrothed to a new man, safely described as Joseph, so that she could depicted as a virgin when God supposedly inseminated her.

Any direct references there may have been to Mary Magdalene as the wife of Yeshua were also eliminated.

What survives first and foremost is a not a record of three women present at the cross, which may or may not be true, but the story teller's perception of which three women were the most significant in Yeshua's life and therefore to be cast in place at this point in the drama. They were in order of listing in Mark and Matthew, and I suggest in order of precedence, his wife/partner Mary Magdalene, his mother Mary and his aunt Salome.

What survive too are the marks of the alterations, the text in John which read correctly gives the game away and a litany of brothers of Yeshua: James, Joses/Joseph, Simon and Judas.

It is hard to evaluate the extent to which misrepresentation was based on a misinterpretation arising from dogma or preconception, or was a wilful falsification.

I have argued here that an original presentation was not

altered, but rather misinterpreted, and that there may have been consequent changes to other parts of the gospel texts.

In creating scenes to add to the narrative there would, with little material available, have been plenty of scope. While some details may have had to be respected, a lot more embellishment could be added. The final way in which I want to suggest the record has been altered, in a manner which can often be identified, has to do with the interaction between the gospel compiler and his source material.

Embroidery and fact

I have suggested that it may be very difficult much later to reconstruct precisely what was said in a given situation, while retaining a good sense of what happened. Only the gist of the dialogue, fitting in with the action, may have survived. Writers of the period, when the gospels were created, adopted the convention of inventing speeches for their characters. The words were what might have been said in the circumstances rather what was said, the evidence for this being missing.

At the time the first gospels were written, there would have been little documentary material. What would have been most well remembered were actions and circumstances that stood out by being dramatic and unusual.

With little to go on, the gospel writers embroidered what they had in order to make a good story or to pad out the text. The outcome, largely invented, would of course have fitted with their preconceptions.

Another possibility, borne out by the examples below, is that the writers often knew the proper context of the prominent or remarkable circumstances they were recording. When this ran counter to the view that they were attempting to convey or believed, they suppressed the context (or the central fact) and substituted something of their own. This would have been a means of defusing potentially explosive orally-transmitted testimony which with time would lose its force, sharpness and finally identity against the abiding written text.

The last gasp of such tradition can be imagined with an old person telling his grandchildren what he had heard when a child from his own grandparent, a witness from the time. They counter that this does not agree with the received written word, a record by this time going back over 100 years. When that old person dies, the oral tradition, though with possibly greater provenance, is also obliterated. Though perhaps, not quite.... The embroidered text does sometimes bear signs of its origins.

I offer four examples, in the first of which I suggest a central fact has been retained and the context completely altered. In the second, both the central proposition and the context have been subtly changed. In the third, the context has been retained in surprising detail but something vital has been omitted from the central act to change its meaning. In the fourth, I suggest that both facts and context are largely accurate but incomplete.

My first example comes from the *Acts of Peter*, an extended tale of the often fabulous and fantastic deeds of Simon Peter in conflict with his adversary 'Simon Magus', similar in form to Acts and the *Pseudoclementines*. Like both the latter, there appears to have been a factual basis, though where fact ends and fiction begins is difficult to disentangle. The story tells of Simon Peter's return to Rome where his life is in danger, after meeting the risen Yeshua.

The execution of Simon Peter

As [Peter] went out of the gate he saw the Lord entering Rome, and when he saw him he said, 'Lord, where are you going? And the Lord said to him, 'I am coming to Rome to be crucified.' And Peter said to him, 'Lord, are you being crucified again?' He said to him, 'Yes, Peter, I am being crucified again.'... Then [Peter] returned to Rome rejoicing and giving praise to the Lord, because he said, 'I am being crucified'; since this was to happen to Peter. ...

When they had hanged him in the way which he had requested, [Peter] began to speak again, 'Men whose duty it is to hear, ... you must know the mystery of all nature, and the beginning of all things ... For the first man, whose likeness I have in my appearance, in falling head downward showed a manner of birth that was not so before ... He therefore, being drawn down, ... established the whole of this cosmic system, being hung up as an image of the calling, in which he showed what is on the right hand as on the left, and those on the left as on the right, and changed all the signs of their nature, so as to consider fair those things that were not fair and take those that were really evil to be good. ... You then, my beloved, ... must leave your former error ... You should come up to the cross of Christ, whom is the word stretched out, the one and only, of whom the Spirit says, "For what else is Christ but the word, the sound of God?" So that the word is this upright tree on which I am crucified; but the sound is the crosspiece, the nature of man; and the nail that holds the crosspiece to the upright in the middle is the conversion and repentance of man."

(*Acts of Peter*, chs 35, 38)

It is a clear that there was a motivation in compiling this story, besides neutralising a competing tradition. In the gospel stories, Simon Peter is finally left as a rather weak character, having denied Yeshua three times. But Peter is needed for the emerging Catholic Church as a bridge between its Nazorean Jewish origins and itself; Paul/Saul alone will not do as there is no direct link with Yeshua, only a claimed vision.

The Acts of the Apostles has Peter welcoming forbidden food, though this is somewhat vitiated by Paul's vitriolic attack on him in Galatians. The *Acts of Peter* take the process a stage further. Peter is placed centre stage in Rome, where he returns cheerfully to face martyrdom.

The question 'Lord, where are you going?' in John's gospel

(John 13, 36), preceding the three-times denial, is repeated but there is now a different answer. In John, Yeshua states that Peter cannot at that time go where he is going but will do so later, thus foreshadowing Peter's martyrdom. In the *Acts of Peter*, Yeshua's reply to the question is that he is going to be crucified again, this time in the person of Peter! So the prophecy in Acts is realised, the unfinished business in Acts is completed and Peter is rehabilitated to become the founding figure in the Catholic Church. It is all very neat and all, of course, fiction.

There is first of all no supporting evidence that Simon Peter was ever in Rome. Acts fails to mention this, even though the narrative is taken up to the point just before the death of James in CE 62. Going to Rome is an unlikely course of action for the fiery zealot commander Simon, 'the Rock' or 'the Outlaw', who had enough to do in Judea, keeping out of the hands of Roman governors and Herodian kings.

The Romans subjected tens of thousands of people to death by crucifixion, a cruel, degrading and often protractedly painful method of execution. The victims were those the Romans regarded as criminals, rebels or political agitators. It is a preposterous idea, bordering on the obscene, that the executioners might have entered into some form of civilised dialogue with the victim, as to how he might like to be tacked up. They had control, and they killed people how they liked.

Peter did not, of course, embark on a long philosophical discourse with bystanders as to the symbolism implied by his position, while nailed to a cross upside down. This, like other such long speeches, is pseudepigraphic, invented by the writer to illustrate his points. It cannot escape notice that the argument is rather strained; the writer has some difficulty in furnishing convincing theological explanation as to why (by divine decree!) Simon Peter had to meet such a peculiar and particular fate.

But there is an explanation, especially if this is seen as the crucial, remembered central fact and the rest as embellishment designed to distract from the real context in which this fact would have made sense.

Simon Peter didn't go to Rome. As the sword-wielding leader of Yeshua's forces – perhaps the man in Josephus with the courage to confront King Agrippa – he stayed behind and fought and died with his fellow Nazoreans. Josephus relates how, during the battle for Jerusalem, hundreds of defenders trying to break through enemy lines were captured and crucified by the Romans. The bored Roman soldiers amused themselves by nailing up their victims in a variety of postures – which rather more convincingly provides an explanation as to why Simon Peter came to be crucified upside down. He was captured and executed in this way.

The story could not be told as it was because Simon Peter could not be admitted to be as he was, as a militant, as an anti-Roman zealot. He had to be changed and the original tale defused in the process of creating the Christian myth.

The most dramatic fact, what would most likely be remembered, remains. But its meaning has been altered by the provision of a completely new and false context.

The second example of embroidery around a central fact comes from the gospel of Luke. Here, I suggest both the context and the central premise have been changed. Although the resulting narrative is plausible, there are indications of what may have been an earlier tradition.

The child Jesus stays in Jerusalem

The canonical gospel writers are largely silent about Yeshua's early life, perhaps because they lacked information and also because this was not their central concern. A host of other later writers sought to make up for this with fantastic tales of miracle working by the child Yeshua. There is just one story in Luke's gospel, in which the twelve year old Yeshua confounds his elders with his knowledge and understanding:

Now his parents went to Jerusalem every year at the feast of the Passover. And when he was twelve years old, they went up according to custom; and when the feast was ended, as they were returning, the boy Jesus stayed behind in Jerusalem. His parents did not know it, but supposing him to be in the company they went a day's journey, and they sought him among their kinsfolk and acquaintances; and when they did not find him, they returned to Jerusalem, seeking him. After three days they found him in the temple, sitting among the teachers, listening to them and asking them questions; and all who heard him were amazed at his understanding and his answers. And when they saw him they were astonished; and his mother said to him, 'Son, why have you treated us so? Behold, your father and I have been looking for you anxiously.' And he said to them, 'How is it that you sought me? Did you not know that I must be in my Father's house?' And they did not understand the saying which he spoke to them. And he went down with them and came to Nazareth, and was obedient to them; and his mother kept all these things in her heart. (Luke 2, 41-51)

Where, it must be wondered, were Yeshua's siblings at the time? They were either back in Galilee being looked after by relatives or travelling with their parents. Either way, this would have amplified the inconvenience, including possibly loss of income, caused by the three day delay. As the story relates it, Yeshua even as a 12 year old was being more than a little inconsiderate.

It is also surprising how Yeshua's talent for scriptural analysis had gone unnoticed thus far. It may be wondered where and from whom he got the knowledge to give the right answers.

It is worth noting that the Jewish historian Josephus has a similar story how he, as a fourteen year old, was so precocious that religious leaders came to him for advice. Luke was writing around 120 years after the event and there is no indication where he got the information. It is not in Mark or Matthew or any other earlier source. Could he, as he appears to in other instances, have borrowed from Josephus?

These considerations aside, the tale would stand up, apart that is from a story in both Mark and Matthew which is in direct contradiction. Yeshua appears in this story as a fully-fledged adult and attempts to preach in a synagogue in 'his own country':

> He went away from there and came to his own country; and his disciples followed him. And on the Sabbath he began to teach in the synagogue; and many who heard him were astonished, saying, 'Where did this man get all this? What is the wisdom given to him? What mighty works are wrought by his hands? Is not this the carpenter, the son of Mary and brother of James and Joses and Judas and Simon, and are not his sisters here with him. And they took offence at him.
> (Mark 6, 1-3)

The trouble is that Yeshua's prodigious talent had, according to Luke, been recognised as early as twelve – and there would have been plenty of time for it to have developed further. It is hardly feasible that it could or would have been kept a secret. Even the initial event, without any further exhibition of scriptural brilliance, would have been enough to cause a stir and mark Yeshua out.

Yeshua's disappearance, the halting of the journey home for three days, his parents' distressed return to search for him and the circumstances in which he was found would have made a memorable event, worth retelling. So that, when the talented Yeshua began to teach in the synagogue as an adult, it would have been unremarkable and unremarked.

But this is not how the earlier source Mark, as followed by Matthew, reports it. Yeshua's fellow countrymen are, on the contrary, astonished by his learning. Moreover, they do not even seem to recognise him, 'this man', wondering whether or not he can really be the carpenter/builder, brother of James and son of Mary. Luke retains the story, but it is significantly altered:

> And he came to Nazareth, where he had been brought up; and he went to the synagogue, as his custom was, on the Sabbath day. And he stood up to read; and there was given to him the book of the prophet Isaiah. He opened the book and found the place where it was written, 'The Spirit of the Lord is upon me, because he has anointed me to preach good news to the poor. He has sent me to proclaim relase to the captives and recovering of sight to the blind, to set at liberty those who are oppressed, to proclaim the acceptable year of the Lord.'
>
> And he closed the book, and gave it back to the attendant, and sat down; and the eyes of all in the synagogue were fixed on him. And he began to say to them, 'Today this scripture has been fulfilled in your hearing.' And all spoke well of him, and wondered at the gracious words which proceeded out of his mouth; and they said, 'Is not this Joseph's son?'
>
> (Luke 4, 16-22)

There is now a new context: Yeshua is according to Luke claiming himself as fulfilling the prophecy of Isaiah, coming among other things to restore the sight of the blind and release the oppressed. Gone is the wonderment at his learning because, if Luke's childhood tale is to be regarded as true, then by that time Yeshua's teaching talent will have become common knowledge. Gone also is the wondering uncertainty as to whether this really could be the person they once knew. Joseph has been restored to the story for the purpose of a straight question, which invites an answer. Because of his miraculous deeds, Yeshua cannot be Joseph's son 'as was supposed' (Luke 3, 23) but must therefore have been conceived by God.

A clever piece of rewriting, it must be conceded, but it is less authentic than the earlier version in Mark. The questions which the earlier version poses remain to be answered. If Yeshua had suddenly embarked on accomplished preaching and teaching as an adult, where indeed did he 'get all this'? If his audience were not sure that they recognised him, he must have been away for some time, long enough for his appearance to have changed. Where had he been?

This suddenly suggests a glimmer of an explanation. The missing years of Yeshua in the narrative, from child to adult, really were missing for the people who knew him in Galilee. Yeshua was somewhere else; he simply wasn't there.

At this point, some help is provided by what else is known about Yeshua from the canonical gospels and other early sources. He is described as a Nazarene or Nazorean, that is a member of a religious movement, 'keepers' of the covenant, which strictly upheld the Torah. It is known also that Yeshua's brother James went on to be leader of the expanding Jewish Nazorean community based in Jerusalem and that another brother Simon or Simeon took over afterwards.

The Nazoreans, as for example borne out in Acts, had an organisation with remarkable parallels with the people who lived at the same time at Qumran, and wrote the Dead Sea scrolls. Described as 'Essenes', these people described themselves in other ways, most often as 'the poor', like the Ebionites who succeeded the Nazoreans as followers of James. The coincidences are so great that it may be that 'the poor' at Jerusalem and Qumran were one and the same. They might alternatively have been loosely linked, with parallel messianic aims and organisation. It is also possible that the Jerusalem Nazoreans originated as an offshoot from Qumran, but became so successful that that it soon outgrew and eclipsed its source.

One of the ways in which the organisation recruited new members was by adopting young men who had reached the transition point to adulthood, at around 13 when boys celebrated their bar mitzvah. So Yeshua, who became a Nazarene, could have been adopted into the Essene/Nazorean community in Jerusalem – and that is where he would have acquired his scriptural learning. This would explain why, in Mark, those who had known him in childhood found it hard to recognise him again and were surprised by his knowledge and understanding. He had been away not for a day or so but for several years. He had been living in a Nazorean/Essene community, in or near Jerusalem.

The gospels indicate that Yeshua was seen as a son of David, that is as part of a line that claimed Davidic descent and thereby kingship over Israel. Other evidence also suggests that Yeshua and his brothers were part of a messianic movement.

Herod had ruthlessly eliminated Maccabean contenders, so it may be that this was another, separate line. Herod's sons and their descendants had been given control over Israel and so they and the Romans, who ruled Judea directly from CE 6 – 37, would have been a threat to Yeshua and his brothers. The decision to place them for a time in a closed and secretive community might thus have been influenced by concerns for their safety, as well as their religious and educational upbringing.

When Luke came to write his gospel, it was still remembered through oral tradition (and possibly even written testimony subsequently suppressed) that Yeshua had lived for several years in his youth in a community of keepers of the covenant, and had in that way become a Nazarene/Nazorean. But this version was something that Luke would have wanted to suppress, since the Nazoreans were fiercely Torah-abiding, messianic, nationalistic and undoubtedly Jewish. Luke and the other gospel writers, including Mark as edited, wanted instead to make Yeshua into a rebel against Judaism, a messiah for the Gentile world.

This childhood story is significant; it is the *only* one that Luke or for that matter any of the canonical gospel writers chose to give and it was chosen for a purpose. The dangerous knowledge about Yeshua's origins was defused by being modified and transformed. Instead of several years, Yeshua is depicted as staying just three days with the teachers in Jerusalem. He is not taken to be adopted into the Nazorean community, but absents himself from a family trip to celebrate the Passover. He does not gain his knowledge from his teachers or any teachers but displays it, God-given, instantly.

A related piece of potentially explosive information, that Yeshua like his brother James was a Nazorean, is similarly treated. The first stage occurs in Mark's gospel, which uses an account probably deriving from the immediate followers of Yeshua. In several places (Mark 1, 24; 10, 47; 14, 67 and 16, 6,), Yeshua is frankly described as Yeshua 'the Nazarene' though this is variously and incorrectly translated in different New Testament editions as 'Jesus of Nazareth'. There is no mention of any place called Nazareth in the Old Testament. Outside of the gospels and one reference in Acts, there is no record of any place of this name at the time that Yeshua lived. The Jewish historian Josephus lists all the towns and villages that were defended or fortified, when he was Governor of Galilee a few years afterwards, and Nazareth is not among them. Indeed, the place is nowhere mentioned in any of his writings.

There is only one reference in Mark's gospel, at the outset, which directly states that Yeshua came from Nazareth (Mark 1, 9). In view of several other references elsewhere in Mark, that Jesus was known as a Nazarene, this may well be a later insertion rather than part of Mark's source material. The word Nazarene which was applied to Yeshua was also used elsewhere to refer to the fundamentalist Jewish sect which had been troubling the Romans. Paul was accused of belonging to it, as 'a pestilent fellow, an agitator among the Jews throughout the world, and a ringleader of the sect of the Nazarenes' (Acts 24, 5). It is hardly likely that the word 'Nazarene' had a different meaning in Acts from that in the gospel of Mark.

The author of Matthew, who used Mark as a source, must have been aware of the problem, because he suggests that Yeshua lived in a *city* called Nazareth in order to fulfil biblical prophecy, 'He shall be called a Nazarene' (Greek, 'Nazoraios') (Matthew 2, 23). It is pretty thin as an explanation; there is no such prophecy anywhere in any of the books of the bible!

And, if 'Nazarene', was commonly understood to mean 'someone from Nazareth', why did Matthew have to invoke biblical prophecy to explain why Yeshua was described in this way? Presumably, it was because it was recognised that the explanation did not hold. The alternative being too awful to contemplate, that Yeshua was actually a Nazorean, a second line of argument had to be invoked. To bolster the assertion that 'Yeshua the Nazarene/Nazorean' meant 'Yeshua from Nazareth', an Old Testament prediction was retrospectively provided – the awaited messiah would live in Nazareth.

Subsequent Christian apologists have tried to argued that the base for the place name Nazareth is the Hebrew word 'nezer' meaning 'shoot' or 'branch', rather than 'nozri' meaning 'keeper', and that Yeshua's residence in such a place was therefore the fulfilment of a general prophecy that the Jewish messiah would be of Davidic descent, that is a branch of that lineage.

But it is stretching Old Testament statements (eg Isaiah 11, 1) beyond any reasonable limit to argue that these actually indicated that the future messiah would be a resident of Nazareth. It is also not without irony that a Jewish messianic explanation has here been sought to explain away a Christian conundrum.

The derivation of 'Nazorean', as the name applied to members of a religious movement, from the base 'nozri' corresponds well with a group which was, under James, extremely scrupulous in observing Jewish law, conscientious in keeping the covenant. But the name could also reflect 'nezer', as applied to a group which considered that it had inherited, in the line of

David, the mantle of kingship or religious leadership.

The fourth century writer Epiphanius, describes both James and Simon/Simeon bar Cleophas as Nazoreans. These were brothers of Yeshua and subsequent leaders of the community of his followers. It is reasonable to assume that this label would have applied to Yeshua also and that this explains why he was called the Nazarene/Nazorean in Mark and Matthew.

In the end, it comes down to an assessment, whether what I have argued is more plausible and probable than a literal reading of the tales recorded in Matthew and Luke. My explanation makes sense, which is not the same as saying that it is proof, while the effort by the later gospel writers and Christian commentators to explain away Yeshua's Nazorean origins makes no sense at all. My explanation also accords with the variant evidence from the earlier, and thefore probably more reliable, gospel of Mark.

My third example of the process of embroidery is taken from the Acts of the Apostles. It is an interesting case, where the context is probably largely accurate, but the central fact has, by process of omission, been significantly changed.

The trial of Ananias and Sapphira

Acts describes how the followers of Yeshua under James organised themselves, selling their possessions and pooling their resources, distributing the proceeds according to need. Paul's letters to the Galatians and Corinthians, which relate to roughly the same period, provide further detail: there was a ruling triumvirate of three comprising James, John and Cephas (Simon Peter) and a council of twelve. The Essenes (self-designated 'poor') at Qumran likewise pooled property and had a ruling council of twelve laymen and three priests. The parallels are so close that I have suggested that James and Yeshua's Nazoreans either grew out of an Essene community in Jerusalem, or were simply part of the same organisation.

The Essenes had a strict code with punishments, varying in severity, for breaking the rules. It appears that cheating among the Nazoreans was also not without consequences...

There was not a needy person among them, for as many as were possessors of lands or houses sold them, and brought the proceeds of what was sold and laid it at the apostles' feet; and distribution was made to each as had any need. ...

But a man named Ananias with his wife Sapphira sold a piece of property, and with his wife's knowledge he kept back some of the proceeds, and brought only a part and laid it at the apostles' feet. But Peter said, 'Ananias, why has Satan filled your heart to lie to the Holy Spirit and to keep back part of the proceeds of the land? While it remained unsold, did it not remain your own? And after it was sold, was it not at your disposal? How is it that you have contrived this deed in your heart? You have not lied to men but to God.'

When Ananias heard these words, he fell down and died. And great fear came upon all who heard it. The young men rose and wrapped him up and carried him out and buried him.

After an interval of about three hours his wife came in, not knowing what had happened. And Peter said to her, 'Tell me whether you sold the land for so much.' And she said, 'Yes, for so much.' But Peter said to her, 'How is it that you have agreed together to tempt the Spirit of the Lord? Hark, the feet of those that have buried your husband are at the door, and they will carry you out.' Immediately she fell down at his feet and died. When the young men came in they found her dead, and they carried her out and buried her beside her husband. And great fear came upon the whole church, and upon all who heard of these things.

(Acts 4, 34-35, 5 1-11)

This is certainly a dramatic tale, undoubtedly seen as worth recording by the compiler of Acts for its moral message: if you try to cheat God, you will be punished. The fate of Ananias and Sapphira was something that would have stood out and been remembered, passed on as oral recollection and then ultimately put into writing by the author of Acts.

But was it recorded as it actually happened, or even as it was remembered? As the story stands, there are two alternative explanations for the death of Ananias and Sapphira. They were struck down by God, taking time off from running the universe to wreak personal vengeance on these malefactors. Or they were each so overcome with their own guilt and shame, that they spontaneously died of it.

Either of these explanations stretches well beyond bursting point the bounds of credulity and credibility: the approach to such 'miracles' should be at least to see whether there is a more prosaic and possible theory.

The first point to make is that Ananias and Sapphira were each in turn facing a trial. The facts having been established (in a manner unspecified in the text), they were each questioned about their actions. Sapphira, more of an accomplice since her husband would have had control of the property, was given the better chance. She was given the opportunity to admit the land was sold for more, and presumably hand over the balance and so save herself. But she stuck to her story, and paid with her life.

If there was a trial, as with other cases of breaches of rules of the community, this implies that there would also have been a verdict and punishment. Ananias and Sapphira did not, I suggest, spontaneously die but they were executed. They were moreover killed either directly by Simon Peter, or at his behest.

The objection may be made that only the Romans could exact the death penalty. But this is to view the community of the Nazoreans as if it were part of the establishment rather than, at this stage at least, as an anti-establishment organisation with rules of its own. The Roman writ only ran so far, and the occupiers may well not have been so concerned when (as they might have seen it) extreme nationalist religious agitators fell out among themselves. The Essenes exacted the death penalty for some offences, according to their codes, and so might also have the Nazoreans, as a linked or even identical organisation. With either group, however, such an outcome might well have been a very rare occurrence. All the more reason, however, why it would have been remembered and passed down as an oral tradition. It would certainly have served as an object lesson, inspiring the 'great fear' which Acts describes among other members of the group.

It was a good story which could be used in Christian literature to put across a useful message. But the author (or subsequent editor) of Acts would not have wanted Simon Peter, who was to be adopted as the founding father of the Christian Church, depicted as someone who ran people through with his sword when they held back on the collection! So this element of the story was changed, and at the same time the dangerous and subversive message of the oral tradition was defused.

I am by no means the first to suggest that Simon Peter might have ordered or carried out the execution of Ananias and Sapphira. A fourth century bishop John Chrysostom (the golden-tongued) mentioned in passing that, if Paul could be called a reviler because of his approach to the Galatians, Simon Peter could, on account of the treatment of these two, be called a killer (homicide). Perhaps he drew his conclusion likewise from the evidence as it is now, or perhaps he had a version of Acts that is even more explicit.

If the conclusion in this instance as to what happened to Ananias and Sapphira, and Peter's part in it, is seen as shocking, it will be because of preconceptions ingrained through centuries of repetition of what is essentially Christian myth. The sword-wielding Simon Peter was in fact the church (ecclesia) militant.

He was part of the face of militant, nationalist messianism.

The death of two members of the community, who offended against its code, gives an idea of what really was entailed in being a zealot in first century Palestine.

My last example, on a lighter note, also involves Simon Peter. Here we have a story with details and context all essentially true. The story nevertheless fails to convey an accurate impression. Because of a number of crucial omissions, the significance of what is happening is lost.

I build a case, admittedly on circumstantial evidence, but the direction in which it points is interesting.

The unnamed mother-in-law

While the first significant action in John's gospel is the marriage at Cana, Yeshua begins in Mark by undertaking acts of healing. Four characters are introduced, the brothers Simon and Andrew and James and John, as disciples Yeshua recruited where they were fishing by the Sea of Galilee. Yeshua next goes into the synagogue at Capernaum with his disciples to preach, encountering and calming a man who is mentally disturbed:

> And they went into Capernaum; and immediately on the Sabbath he entered the synagogue and taught. And they were astonished at his teaching, for he taught them as one who had authority, and not as the scribes. And immediately there was in their synagogue a man with an unclean spirit; and he cried out, 'What have you to do with us, Jesus the Nazarene? Have you come to destroy us? I know who you are, the holy one of God.' But Jesus rebuked him, saying, 'Be silent, and come out of him!'
>
> And the unclean spirit, convulsing him and crying with a loud voice, came out of him. And they were all amazed, so that they questioned among themselves, saying, 'What is this? A new teaching! With authority he commands even the

unclean spirits, and they obey him.' And at once his fame spread everywhere throughout all the surrounding region of Galilee.

And immediately he left the synagogue, and entered the house of Simon and Andrew, with James and John. Now Simon's mother-in-law lay sick with a fever, and immediately they took hold of her. And he came and took her by the hand and lifted her up, and the fever left her; and she served them.

That evening, at sundown, they brought to him all who were sick or possessed with demons. And the whole city was gathered together about the door. And he healed many who were sick with various diseases, and cast out many demons; and he would not permit the demons to speak, because they knew him.

And in the morning, a great while before day, he rose and went out to a lonely place, and there he prayed. And Simon and those who were with him pursued him, and they found him and said to him, 'Every one is searching for you.'

And he said to them, 'Let us go on to the next towns, that I may preach there also; for that is why I came out.' And he went throughout all Galilee, preaching in their synagogues and casting out demons.

(Mark 1, 21-37)

It should be noted that Simon's mother-in-law is staying at his house, while ill, and not at her own home. This is presumably so that the daughter can care after her, while at the same time performing her own domestic duties.

The major omission in the story is the name of Simon's mother-in-law, despite the fact that she is a central character. Names were sometimes left out or changed when it might at the time have put someone at risk. But there is no suggestion here that this was a consideration. The gospel writers and editors sometimes omitted names when they wanted to avoid telling us something about Yeshua, his circumstances or family. This is a possibility.

Other points the story avoids telling is how Yeshua came to be there: where he had been and how he came by his knowledge of treatment and illness.

Yeshua was not there simply because he lived in Galilee. As the text makes clear later he had been away, so long that some people could hardly recognise him. As I have argued above (*The child Jesus stays in Jerusalem*), he went to stay with a community of the Nazoreans/Essenes in Jersualem with one of more of his brothers. That is where he gained his knowledge of the scriptures and quite possibly also of plants and herbal medicines. The members of the community would have shared out tasks, including caring for the sick and infirm. Quite plausibly, this is how Yeshua gained his knowledge and experience.

The encounter in the synagogue with a man possesssed with 'an unclean spirit' was not planned and prearranged. But the story then relates that Yeshua was immediately taken to the house of Simon Peter after the service, for the purpose of assisting Simon's mother-in-law. After she had been healed and the disturbed man in the temple calmed, the word spread and many of the physically and mentally ill people in the town were brought to him. This suggests that the healing of Simon's mother-in-law was a dramatic triumph; she must therefore have been suffering from a serious condition.

It is possible that James and John recognised Yeshua in the synagogue and, knowing that their friend and business partner's mother-in-law was sick, asked him to help. These fishermen were not merely, as Mark suggests, strangers picked up by the Sea of Galilee. James and John, the sons of Salome and Zebedee, were Yeshua's cousins and Simon and Andrew were their partners in a joint fishing enterprise (Luke 5, 10). Yeshua would have grown up with them. Despite the years of absence, they would have known who he was. Mark used the device of a lakeside encouter to introduce them into the story and perhaps also to avoid saying who in relation to Yeshua they really were.

Yeshua's arrival, after being away for many years, was certainly timely, indeed remarkably lucky for a woman who was very sick. Had it been left to chance or had it been arranged that Yeshua would be there?

The possibility that the encounter was prearranged is suggested by a comment later in the extract quoted above. Yeshua 'came out' from where he had been specifically to engage on a mission to preach and, it is clear from numerous examples in Mark and the other gospels, also to heal. The first incident in the temple may have been incidental, but the encounter at Simon's house appears to have been planned. Yeshua came out at least partly to heal, beginning with Simon's mother-in-law. I suggest that he may have been summoned from his seclusion in Jerusalem.

Yeshua's family knew that he was there and they would have made regular visits, especially for the Passover celebration in Jerusalem and possibly at times of other religious festivals. They would have known that he had special knowledge and healing skills. They may have asked Yeshua to help Simon's mother-in-law who was seriously ill.

On the surface information presented in the story, she was just the relative of people Yeshua was yet to meet. Even knowing the relationship between Yeshua and James and John, the link is still apparently tenuous. A woman who is the mother-in-law of a friend of a cousin does not present a very strong claim. But this is to accept the conventions that Mark has used, the ostensible random recruitment of followers, most of whom have turned out to be related to Yeshua in some way, chiefly as brothers and cousins.

Simon, after his 'call' by the lakeside, became in short order Yeshua's commander-in-chief, given 'the keys of the kingdom. It is not likely that Yeshua would have entrusted this position to someone he hardly knew or had only recently met. It is more likely that Simon Peter was also linked in, like James and Simon/Simeon and Judas, by ties of kinship.

In a family with a claim to kingship, or even property, there could be tension between brothers as potential rivals, as amply demonstrated by the Maccabeans. Relatives by marriage were often safer to trust because there were ties and a common interest but without the same threat from competition. Lazarus (Eleazar), the brother of Yeshua's wife/partner Mary Magdalene, would thus have been a good choice as a military leader for a family claiming the kingship of Israel. In fact, I have argued (ch 10) that he *did* become a zealot commander, the very one who held out against the Romans at Masada for years after the fall of Jerusalem. It would no surprise if the sword-wielding Simon Peter, Yeshua's commander, also proved to be a relative by marriage.

So who might Simon Peter's mother-in-law have been? The clue may be provided by the presence of James and John at Simon's house. When characters are placed in a particular gospel story it is usually because they have a significant role. The three women placed at the cross, for example, are the three significant women in Yeshua's life, mentioned (in Mark and Matthew) in order of precedence: his wife Mary Magdalene, his mother Mary and his aunt Salome.

James and John were not there because they had just been recruited by Yeshua and were sticking to him; that is a product of Mark's introductory fiction. They might have been there because they were the friends and business partners of Simon. Or they might also have been there as close relatives summoned to the bedside of a very sick and potentially dying woman. They were perhaps her sons.

This would mean that Simon had married their sister, in so doing becoming their brother-in-law. It would thus have provided the tie that cemented a business partnership.

If these cousins of Yeshua were sons of the sick woman, it

provides the compelling reason for Yeshua to have come all the way up from Judea in an effort to save her. She was also his close relative.

It explains why the author or editor of Mark chose not to name Simon's mother-in-law. Simon was being fashioned into the pivotal connection between the Nazorean Jewish Yeshua and the emerging Christian church. He was needed as a figurehead and so, unlike the brothers of Yeshua, could not be pushed to one side. But he was certainly not wanted as a reminder of Yeshua's family connections and position within the Jewish community, as a practising Jew.

Who was Simon's mother-in-law? She was, I have suggested, the mother of James and John. These were the men nicknamed 'Boanerges', or 'sons of thunder', whose father was Zebedee.

Simon Peter's mother-in-law was, I suggest, Salome.

Appendix I Joseph of Arimathea

Joseph of Arimathea appears in a key support role in the gospels. His function is to approach Pilate after the crucifixion and ask for the body of Yeshua to be interred in a rock tomb. In the earliest of the gospels, Mark, he is described as a 'respected' member of the Sanhedrin and a sympathiser 'who was also himself looking for the kingdom of God'

The other gospels add further details: that he was a disciple and wealthy (Matthew), that he did not consent to the Sanhedrin's condemnation of Yeshua (Luke) and that he was actually a secret disciple (John) 'for fear of the Jews'.

Matthew provides the information that the rock tomb belonged to Joseph. In John's gospel, it is revealed that the tomb was in a garden, and that this is where the crucifixion took place. In preparing the body, Joseph was helped by another supporter Nicodemus, bearing a very substantial quantity (a hundred pound's weight) of spices.

According to Mark and Matthew, Joseph then rolled a stone across the entrance of the tomb.

The difficulty with this account is that it does not explain why a member of Yeshua's family did not go and ask for the body, why indeed this task appears to have been left to a comparative stranger. Tradition and sentiment would also have demanded that the body be interred with other previously deceased family members. No explanation is given as to why the family departed from this norm. Even granting his secret allegiance, it is also difficult to believe that Joseph or Arimathea would as a stranger have yielded up his own family tomb.

The argument that Yeshua's family were all too afraid to ask for the body does not bear much scrutiny. According to Roman law, there was an entitlement for a close family member of an executed person to come and take away the body. So Yeshua's mother Mary, or his aunt Salome, or his father, or his father-in-law or his brother James or another brother could have sought for permission.

There was no right for a non-relative to have it. Should a non-relative ask for it, there was more chance that the body would be dumped or discarded, denying it proper burial. Still more pressing was the possibility that, after a very flawed execution procedure, Yeshua was still alive. If alive, after being scourged and nailed by the hands to a cross for three of four hours, it would have been essential to get Yeshua as quickly as possible into a safe and private place (the rock cave or tomb) where helpers could administer first aid. For that reason, the request had to carry as much weight as possible; it had to have come from a close family member.

So, how does this outsider, Joseph of Arimathea fit into the picture? Mark must have conjured up his character from somewhere. The name of the town, from which Joseph is supposed to have originated, does relate to a place that existed in biblical times: Ramathaian or Aramathaim, the birthplace of Samuel. There are possible sites for this ancient town at Beit Rima and Ramallah, both north of Jerusalem.

There is however no apparent reason, in terms of the construction and comprehension of the story, for the reader to be told the name of Joseph's home town. This is a little suspicious, especially given the tendency of the gospel writers to leave Aramaic or Hebrew names untranslated, or mistranslated as place names, where the original meaning conveyed an uncomfortable fact. Could there have been something about the original Aramaic or Hebrew description of Joseph, from the Nazorean account of the capture and execution of Yeshua, that Mark either failed to understand or deliberately misrepresented?

I suggest that there is a solution. By the time of the crucifixion, there is no longer any mention of Yeshua's father. He has disappeared from the scene and can be presumed to have died. In his absence, Yeshua's father-in-law or mother's father, would have been among the most senior members of the family. As such, they qualified for the task of dealing with the Romans and securing the body.

As it happens, both of these men had a daughter called Mary, one the mother and one the wife of Yeshua. If either or both were named Joseph, then they would have been referred to in relation to their daughters as Joseph father of Mary, Ysf ab Mryh. This represents closely in lettering and sound the name of the supposed stranger, Joseph of Arimathea, and provides the most convincing explanation as to where the name came from. It is a corruption of the original Hebrew, rendered into Greek. Joseph was described as the 'father of Mary (Mariah)'. He did not, unless by pure coincidence, come from Arimathea.

Once it is accepted that the original Joseph was not Joseph of Arimathea but the similarly sounding and written Joseph Ab Mariah, the story begins to make sense. Yeshua's wife Mary was it seems wealthy in her own right, one of the women who according to Luke provided for Yeshua and the apostles 'out of their means'. She could well have had a wealthy father who was a respected member of the Sanhedrin, able to afford a family tomb in its own garden.

Her father is therefore a prime candidate to fill the role of the elusive Joseph 'of Arimathea'. He would perhaps have been in his early fifties, still sharp enough and fit enough to organise and transport the material needed for Yeshua once in the tomb. He would most importantly have been a close family member, someone who could have asked for the body and, without offending tradition or sentiment, have provided the burial place.

The gospels do not state whether Joseph was a Pharisee or a Sadducee, only that he was a secret supporter of Yeshua. This carries the implication that he was, like Nicodemus, one of the Pharisees given that the gospels also attempt to portray these as Yeshua's implacable opponents. There would, in such circumstances, have been a need for discretion in lending support, as for example with the visits by Nicodemus to talk with Yeshua in secrecy and at night. But, as already discussed, there are counter indications of an original story line, perhaps closer to reality, indicating that Yeshua and his followers and the Pharisees were on reasonably good terms.

Yeshua, according to the gospels, spent a lot of time dining with Pharisees, as he would have with one of them as his father-in-law. From similar stories of the woman anointing Yeshua in gospels of Luke and John, it can be seen that Martha, the sister of his wife Mary, served at the table of the house of Simon, a Pharisee. There is also another story in Luke, where Martha berates his sister Mary for not helping at table.

Martha is thereby likely to have been a family member in Simon's house, adding to the argument that Yeshua was linked by family ties to Pharisees. It was incidentally most often the duty of the wife of the householder to prepare and serve the food. In Mark and Matthew, Simon is nicknamed 'the leper', quite possibly derived from the phrase 'jar maker'; which has the same written form 'grb' as 'leper' in Aramaic. The source could also have been a mistranslation into Greek of 'gbr', an Aramaic word which can mean 'husband'. The presumption which would fit with these details is that Simon was Martha's husband.

Yehua was given timely warning by Pharisees that Herod Antipas was seeking to kill him. In Mark, he spent time in civilised discourse with Pharisees. His teaching (such as the doctrine to love God and one's neighbour as oneself) accorded with Pharisaic principles.

Joseph, a wealthy and prominent member of the Sanhedrin and possibly also a Pharisee, was an appropriate father-in-law for a man, as the eldest of a number of brothers, carrying the mantle of the kingship of Israel. As a close relative, he would have had no need to be a 'secret disciple', nor would this have been an appropriate way to describe him. The element of secrecy was, I suggest, introduced in accordance with the propositions that Joseph was a Pharisee and not a relative and that the Pharisees and Yeshua were at odds.

There remains the possibility that it was the father of Yeshua's mother Mary who was called Joseph and thereby the source of the reference to 'Joseph of Arimathea'. He would in this case have been the man who provided the tomb and secured Yeshua's body. As an explanation, this fits just as well, in that this person was also a senior and close family member. It also accords with the possible resolution of another puzzle, the discordant genealogies in the gospels of Matthew and Luke. Both of these purport to be that of Yeshua's father Joseph and should therefore agree in great detail. But, in the generations going back to King David, they are in fact completely different.

There is a further, curious anomaly. The author of Matthew asserts that the generations follow a symmetrical structure, with fourteen from Abraham to David, another fourteen from David to the deportation to Babylon and then fourteen to the birth of Yeshua. However, he appears to have made an error, in that he only lists thirteen generations in the last of these sequences.

In the original Greek of Matthew's gospel, Joseph is described at the end of this genealogy as the 'husband' of Mary. But in the Aramaic version of the gospel used in the Eastern Church (the Peshitta) the word applied to Joseph in the genealogy is 'gbr', meaning 'protective male', and this can apply equally to a father as to a husband. Assuming that the gospel source did here mean father, the last part of the genealogy reads as 'Jacob the father of Joseph the *father* of Mary of whom Jesus was born'. It may be that the Greek author of Matthew misunderstood an original Aramaic source, which the Peshitta has correctly rendered.

The interpretation which makes Joseph the father of Mary adds one generation to the genealogy. It restores symmetry, bringing the total in the last sequence to fourteen. It allows Matthew to be correct in his assertion about the number of generations. It also resolves the larger problem of the genealogies that do not agree. The one in Luke is that of Mary's husband, while the genealogy in Matthew is that of Mary herself through her own father Joseph. Finally, it provides another possible candidate for Joseph ab Mariah as the source, when corrupted, for Joseph of Arimathea.

There is however a problem in assuming that it was this person, Yeshua's maternal grandfather, who secured the body. Yeshua is believed to have been born around BCE 6 and would have been 42 years old at the time of the crucifixion in CE 36. His mother Mary would have been around 58 and her father about 80 years old. It has then to be presumed that, at a very great age, this man took with Nicodemus a considerable weight of spices to the tomb and himself rolled a heavy stone across the entrance to the tomb. This is even assuming that he had survived to around the age of 80, at a time when life expectancy was low. It does seem unlikely that such a very old person would have taken on such an exacting role, when there were other, younger family members available to help.

A younger and presumably fitter and more active member of the succeeding generation provides a better fit for the character 'Joseph of Arimathea' and, in the case of Mary Magdalene's father, a reason why the original name may have been deliberately mistranslated. There would have been no problem with the father of Yeshua's mother Mary being correctly identified. There was nothing there to disturb the evolving Christian interpretation of Yeshua's family. But this was not so with Mary Magdalene, who doubled as the sister of Martha and the wife of Yeshua.

Describing the man who provided the tomb and secured the body as her father would have drawn attention to the fact that she, like him, was family. As everywhere in the gospels (including some non-canonical) depicted as his companion, she could only as a family member have also been his wife. But in the early Christian view, in which sex was seen as sinful, Yeshua was made into an asexual being. So he was denied the wife that he undoubtedly had.

I suggest therefore that the Joseph 'of Arimathea', who collected the body, was really the father of Yeshua's wife Mary; hence 'ab Mariah'. It may be that the maternal grandfather of Yeshua, as indicated by the resolution of the generations conundrum in Matthew, was also called Joseph. But he was not the same person as the influential Pharisee who secured the body of Yeshua and placed it in his own family tomb.

The Church in the early centuries was certainly aware of the fact that it should have been a close relative who demanded the body of Yeshua. It would seem that it was also sufficiently concerned about the explanation, which I have deduced, that it was Joseph, the father of Yeshua' wife/partner Mary, to offer an alternative. This was that Joseph of Arimathea was (as well as really being from Arimathea!) the uncle of Yeshua's mother Mary. This would still have meant a likely rather aged relative taking an unusually active role, when there were younger and more closely related family of Yeshua available. It is also an explanation without any foundation in the text.

The explanation which I have offered for the identity of Joseph by contrast fits facts, eliminates difficulties with the text and accords with the circumstantial evidence.

So was he from Arimathea? Only, assuming the derivation I have deduced is correct, and if at all, by a very unusual coincidence.

Appendix II Philip, the go-between

While others among the followers of Yeshua have Hebrew or Aramaic names, or names translated from an original into Greek, the name of Philip is Greek in origin. It derives from 'philos' 'hippos' and means 'lover of horses'. So, in this way and as will be seen in other ways, this disciple is marked out from the others. Among the twelve listed in the gospels he is one of a few who are not, on the evidence, related to Yeshua by blood or by marriage.

As such, Philip performs the role of a broker between Yeshua's kin-based group of supporters and another power base, designated in the gospels as 'Greeks' or 'Hellenists'.

Mark and the other synoptic gospels have little to say about Philip, other than to include him among the twelve. But the gospel of John, which describes itself as the witness of the long-lived disciple 'whom Yeshua loved' provides more information. Philip is described as being from Bethsaida on the eastern side of the Sea of Galilee. This was also where the brothers Andrew and Simon (Peter) came from. In a passage, obscure in its message and intention, Philip introduces Nathanael to Yeshua. Since this immediately precedes the wedding at Cana, which I have argued was Yeshua's own wedding, it may have had something to do with preparations for this event. The means of reckoning dates used at that time as so many days before or after a particular festival, opened the way for memory mishaps and misunderstanding. There was a need to make sure that a groom, travelling from afar, arrived in time. Philip I suggest performed that function, taking Yeshua to Galilee to meet Nathanael.

Yeshua surprised Nathanael by recognising him. Although back in his home territory, Yeshua had apparently been away for some time. This is why he may have had difficulty recognising some of the people who were part of his social network or related to him. Yeshua, I have suggested, had spent his formative years in a community of the Nazoreans in or near Jerusalem. Nathanael greeted Yeshua as 'Son of God', probably a later Christian gloss, and as 'King of Israel', at this point a rather hopeful assertion.

Philip also appears much later, in a crucial situation. This is when Yeshua, having made the long march from Galilee with his followers, is in Jerusalem at Passover. The move on the city was apparently in response to a Roman massacre of people protesting about the misuse of temple funds. Yeshua was informed of the incident in which the blood of his fellow Galileans had been spilled.

His followers, some certainly armed, were expecting a battle and anticipating victory over the Romans. His cousins James and John, aided by their scheming mother Salome, were jockeying for positions of power in the independent Jewish kingdom to come. As Nathanael had anticipated in his greeting years earlier, this is when Yeshua would or should have claimed his kingdom. With masses of militant zealots in the city, and potentially many more among the thousands of pilgrims swilling about the streets, it was a highly precarious and combustible situation. The Romans had a relatively small garrison of 500 men which could have been overwhelmed, though with massive bloodshed and the certainty of further retribution. There would have been some anxious to prevent a confrontation, especially among the Sadducee high priests and members of the Herodian family, both of whom benefited from Roman rule.

Yeshua, however, had gained so much popular support that the moderate leadership, the Pharisees who had a majority on the Sanhedrin or ruling council, felt powerless to do anything. In the words of John's gospel they said to one another 'You see that you can do nothing; look the world has gone after him'.

Next in the sequence of events, Philip brings to Yeshua some 'Greeks' at the Passover celebrations who were anxious to meet him. Why, and what they may have said, is not stated. But Yeshua is now immediately given to make a statement of his intent. He now avers, having previously twice or three times denied it, that finally 'his hour has come'. He expects to die, to be 'lifted up from the earth'.

The Christian interpretation of this is that the Greeks were simply seekers after enlightenment (from Greece), who wanted to meet Yeshua and learn from him. It is however a sort of meeting which would sit oddly in the context of an impending confrontation. Why would the narrator, perhaps the original narrator, have bothered with such a digression in the climactic build-up of events?

Furthermore, 'Greeks' did not usually in the gospel context mean specifically people from Greece, but members of the Greek-speaking Roman Empire, followers of Greek culture who were often non-Jewish. There were certainly people who fell into that category who would at that moment have wanted urgently to speak to Yeshua. They would have wanted to urge him to desist from what they would have perceived as a potentially ruinous confrontation.

Seen in this way, the sequence described in John makes sense. Yeshua is in the city with a large body of followers and has immense popular support. The Roman garrison looks threatened. The Pharisee majority on the Sanhedrin concedes that nothing can be done. A delegation of leading 'Greeks'/Hellenists approach him, asking him not to attack the Romans.

Their request has to be inferred because the question has been cut out. But the comment with which Yeshua 'answered them', makes clear what they were seeking to know. Yeshua's reply, 'The hour has come for the Son of Man to be glorified' indicated that he intended to stick to his course.

Of all people Agrippa, grandson of King Herod via his marriage to the Maccabean princess Mariamme, may have had most to lose in an uprising against Rome. At the very time that

Yeshua went to Jerusalem with his army of followers he was, as Josephus relates, actively engaged in conspiring to wrest power from Herod Antipas, Tetrarch of Galilee. Moreoever, he also had his eyes on Judea, currently ruled directly by the Romans through a procurator.

I suggest that Agrippa or his close associates may have been among the delegation of 'Greeks' who urgently sought and gained an audience with Yeshua in CE 36, when an attack on the Roman garrison in Jerusalem seemed imminent. Placed precisely in the text between the Pharisees' realisation of the gravity of the situation and Yeshua's declaration of his intentions, the meeting must have been to do with the crisis. The objective of the delegation of 'Greeks' was to prevent a calamitous pitched battle in Jerusalem.

Given that this did not happen, it appears that Philip's mediation was successful. It is interesting to observe that, after this, Agrippa's credit with the Romans was such that he rapidly progressed from being, as Josephus puts it, a private citizen to 'king of the entire kingdom of his forbears'. He gained, under successive emperors, control of first Galilee and then Judea and Samaria. Unlike Yeshua he did become, albeit on a client basis, King of Israel.

Another biblical source, the Acts of the Apostles, describes the activities of a character named Philip a few years later on, after the crucifixion of Yeshua. There is a strong case that this Philip is the same person as the one listed as one of the twelve disciples. This is more likely than there being two separate individuals, one of whom is active in the gospel period but not mentioned in Acts and the other appearing from nowhere in Acts though without a mention in the gospels. Moreover this Philip, despite his label as an evangelist in Acts, is operating in the same home territory as the disciples. As in the gospels, he takes on a preaching role. Also, as in the gospels, he is placed in an intermediary role, one of seven appointed to administer food distribution to those in need, a group which had become wider and more demanding than the Nazoreans' own immediate supporters.

This very probable identification of the two characters as one is important in furthering the understanding of Philip's identity and role. The Nazoreans under James, brother and successor to Yeshua, had an organisation which was well adapted to deal with a national emergency. There were many thousands of members, accountable to a ruling body of twelve and a key group of three priests, who strictly observed the Torah, shared their wealth and looked after those less fortunate among their number. In the CE 40s there was a devastating famine, described elsewhere in Acts and also by the historian Josephus. The Nazoreans shared food and other resources so that in this situation none of their members would have gone without.

But the rest of the community, especially those who were not Jews, might well have been less well prepared. As Acts describes it, 'the Hellenists murmured against the Hebrews because their widows were neglected in the daily distribution.' Regardless of any past differences, the Nazoreans generously widened the scope to provide what amounted to national relief. This could only have helped James, already a popular figure, a little later when there would be a clampdown on the Nazoreans, regarded (with justification) as harbourers of zealots who wanted the Romans out. Acts notes that the apostles, presumably meaning James and other key figures, were left out of this 'great persecution'.

Philip was appointed as one of seven to administer the food distribution. As with the story in John's gospel where he brings 'Greeks' to Yeshua, this suggests that he had a connection with the Hellenist, Greek-speaking community.

Later in Acts, Philip is described as preaching and healing in Samaria and then being instrumental in bringing about the conversion of the Queen of the Ethiopians' minister who was a 'eunuch'. As Eisenman points out (*The New Testament Code*) the story is historically implausible: there was no Ethiopian Queen at the time and no harems in the Ethiopian court and so therefore no eunuchs required to protect them.

It would seem that the Queen may have been Helen, who sent famine relief to Jerusalem. The garbled – and spiteful – story in Acts is then a reference to her sons Izates and Monobazus who converted to Judaism, and were circumcised, becoming 'eunuchs' in the eyes of early Pauline, anti-circumcision Christians.

Philip is arrogated here into the role of proselytiser, as he is in a passage just prior to this when he encounters in Samaria a character called Simon, a magician or sorcerer. Simon was successful in his calling it would seem since he 'amazed' the people with his magic. However, Simon and his followers are persuaded by Philip and are baptised converting, as Acts has it, to Christianity.

Simon then becomes a follower or companion of Philip. Next, Peter (that is Simon Peter) and John are despatched from Jerusalem to complete the process of conversion by the laying on of hands. When Simon perceives this as passing on the Holy Spirit, he offers money to possess the same power. But he is reproached by Peter for wanting to purchase with money what is essentially a gift of God.

The final reference to Philip in Acts, and one relevant to this tale, occurs just before the would-be apostle Paul (aka Saul) is summoned to Jerusalem to account before James for his activities in preaching against the Torah and against circumcision. Paul arrives and stays first with Philip, now residing in Caesarea.

Acts, it will be remembered, is essentially an adventure story, a romance, quarrying material from a variety of sources, adding some fiction to maintain the plot and fill in gaps, changing it all to suit the author's purposes and mixing it with a very few facts. The character of Simon the Magician is borrowed from tales circulating widely at this time. He is characteristically the adversary of Simon Peter, engaging in battles of magic or philosophical discourse.

Contained within similar Romantic tales from about the same period, the *Pseudoclementine Recognitions* and *Homilies*, are passages which reflect the beliefs of the successors to James' Nazorean followers, the Ebionites or 'poor ones'. In one section of *Homilies*, there is an extended debate between Simon Peter and Simon Magus, that is Simon the Magician, over the question whether the Magician's claim to be a true apostle is more or less valid, having only ever encountered Yeshua through a vision, than that of Peter who knew him in person.

The correspondence with Paul's situation is exact, in that Paul never met Yeshua and claimed to have received inspiration from him in a vision. The confrontation described in *Homilies* reflects the conflict between Paul and Simon Peter described in Paul's letter to the Galatians and in more muted form in Acts.

Undoubtedly, as many authorities agree, 'Simon Magus' is here a stand-in for Paul. Could that also be the case for the passage in Acts relating to Simon the Magician, at least as it was intended in the source from which it was borrowed?

As has been noted, Acts and the *Pseudoclementines* seem in part to be working from the same source or sources, emanating from a group closer in time and in its perspective to the Nazorean followers of James. The early Church for the most part succeeded in destroying the writings of the Ebionites, gospels which reflected more nearly the Judaism preached and practised by Yeshua and James.

If, in this borrowed and muddied passage in Acts, Simon the Magician is indeed a stand-in for Paul, then once again Philip appears in the role of broker, bringing in the Herodian Paul, 'Greek' at least in culture and language, who is seeking to join the apostles. It should be noted, however, that later in Acts it is Barnabus who performs the function of introducing Paul.

In the story, Simon the Magician/ Paul tries to buy what he cannot have with money. In a similar way, in the Letters, Paul is collecting money from Jewish communities in the diaspora in order, it would seem, to buy favour with the Nazorean leaders in Jerusalem. In his letter to the Galatians, Paul reproaches Peter (Cephas) whereas in the Nazorean version, which has apparently crept into Acts, Peter reprimands Paul, aka Simon Magus.

The context of Acts does provide for the possibility of Philip introducing Paul to the Nazoreans, via the story about 'Simon the Magician'. Paul is described in Acts as staying with Philip in Caesarea, and is therefore known to him.

The text of the gospels and Acts show Philip as a go-between, a broker between the Nazoreans and the Hellenised Herodians, a friend of Paul and a man with the connections quite possibly to try to arrange a peace deal when an assault on the Roman garrison in Jerusalem appears imminent. But this is limited information. We do not yet know what Philip's connection really is, whether he himself is a Gentile, a Herodian or a Jew and, if the latter, what sort of Jew.

Some of the characters in the gospels and Acts can also be found, as has been demonstrated, in the pages of the historian Josephus. The agenda of the gospels, to recreate Jewish characters as proto Christian apologists or apostles, means that the picture presented therein is highly distorted. Josephus too has own agenda, in large part to present himself in a favourable light to the Romans, refute his adversaries and maybe also to protect some of his erstwhile zealot colleagues who might still be at risk of retribution. So this also has to be borne in mind.

Even so, the historian's portrayal of characters is likely to be, and does certainly appear to be, more realistic than their depiction in Acts and the gospels. Saul, self-reinvented as Paul, can be found in Josephus as the Herodian Saul, whose frustrated ambitions and rejection by the Nazoreans led him to create his own sphere of influence. Ephaphroditus, Nero's secretary and Paul's keeper, performed the same role later in looking the defector Josephus and was publisher and patron for the books

Josephus wrote in the service of the Romans.

Philip entertained Paul at Caesarea and, it would appear from the Simon the Magician story, became his companion. So, if Paul is there in Josephus, Philip should be there also. What is needed to demonstrate the case is someone called Philip who fulfils all the requirements demonstrated in the gospels and Acts.

And there is indeed such a character, Philip son of Jacimus and grandson of Zamaris. This Philip was from what Josephus describes as a colony of 'Babylonian Jews' established by King Herod in hills east of the Sea of Galilee (not far from Bethsaida, where the gospel Philip is supposed to have originated). Herod's purpose was to establish a buffer zone between outside forces, specifically the Babylonians, and Jerusalem, the core of his kingdom. These colonists were not ordinary Jews in Israel but people whose ancestors had been exiled and who had in exile absorbed some of the ways of their hosts. They were loyal to the Herodians: Herod 'the Great' and then later Agrippa I and Agrippa II.

So this fits with Philip as someone who straddled two cultures and acted as a broker. He should also have been a person of substance, as indeed Philip Jacimus was. His grandfather and father before him had been placed in charge of the Babylonian Jewish community, governing the city of Bathyra.

Philip should have been, as in Acts, a compatriot of Paul. In Josephus' *Jewish War*, he is just that, fleeing Jerusalem with Saul and Saul's brother Costobar to join the Roman commander Cestius Gallus. He should have been, as I have deduced, on intimate terms with 'Greeks' who sought an audience with Yeshua when an assault on the Romans seemed imminent. Again, this is found to have been the case. Josephus describes Philip as a close friend of Agrippa I.

The apparent weakness in all this lies in the argument that the Herodians were the enemies of the Nazoreans. Agrippa II made Philip son of Jacimus the commander of his army, which he then sent to bolster the Roman garrison at the outset of the Jewish uprising in CE 66. Could someone with such credentials have acted as a go-between with the Nazorean zealots who opposed the occupation?

The answer appears to be that it is feasible, in a complex situation in which loyalties were often divided. There may have been less Jewish resentment towards Herodian rulers (Agrippa I and Agrippa II) from the branch which had links to the Maccabeans through Herod's wife Mariamme. Also, Agrippa I on becoming client King made strenuous efforts to court popular support by reducing taxes, paying for the ritual observances of the Nazoreans and appointing a more sympathetic High Priest. Josephus was himself, though appointed commander over Galilee in the revolt against Rome from CE 66-70, a personal friend of Agrippa II.

The point is that, while the Romans ruled through their military presence and the threat of further force, the client Herodians could only do so by measures which involved a degree of accommodation. If necessary, by gifts and bribes.

They were also Idumeans, a group which had in the past been forcibly converted to Judaism. They were thus part of the cultural context, not fully Jews in the eyes of many but nevertheless people who had something in common with their subjects. It was probably without any great enthusiasm that Agrippa II sent Philip in to support the beleaguered Roman troops in Jerusalem, at the outset of the revolt. This was precisely the sort of conflict that he and his father before him had worked hard to avert.

The outcome of this move is highly instructive. The rebels were able to encircle and close in on the defending Roman and Herodian forces. Surrounded and in a hopeless position, King Agrippa's soldiers sought an armistice and were allowed to surrender without harm. Josephus later related that Philip 'miraculously escaped', though he might well have been easy to identify as he came out, had the insurgents intended to kill him.

The Romans were treated differently. Allowed out on the pretext that they could go free, if they laid down their arms, they were then treacherously massacred.

Rumours and accusations then persisted that Philip was really on the side of the rebels, that he had even become their commander. When the war reached its climax, with the arrival of forces under Vespasian, Philip was denounced as having deliberately betrayed the Roman garrison on orders from King Agrippa. Vespasian advised the King to send Philip to render an account to Nero.

This he did. But Nero was preoccupied with matters in Rome and Philip came back without having seen the Emperor.

So Philip son of Jacimus survived. If he were on the side of the Herodians, he was not so anti-zealot that he could easily shake off an accusation of treason. He ran up against the problem of all go-betweens, of being distrusted by either side or even by both sides. He may well, given the evident parallels and links, have been transmuted into another character, the apostle Philip, by the Gentile Christian editors of the gospel stories.

Unlike other close followers of Yeshua, indeed I believe unlike all of the other disciples, Philip was not a part of Yeshua's extended family, his kin-based core of support. Could the man who acted as a go-between, who had a foot in two cultures, and who was a friend/companion of Saul, have joined Saul's breakaway Christian sect?

If he were also Philip son of Jacimus, then he would have had a lot to do as a leader in the Babylonian Jewish community, and then as commander of the army or more likely militia of Agrippa II. It is possible that he did join the small circle, including the Herodians Saul and Manaen, who set up a sect at Antioch which absorbed core parts of the Nazorean message into Mithraism. This included the idea of a Jewish Messiah (Greek – 'Christos') which is why this group, as Acts notes, 'were for the first time called Christians'.

It may be that the man who was not part of the family really did become an apostle. But it would have been for Saul, not James and the Nazoreans.

Appendix III The gospel of Peter

from translation by M R James

But of the Jews no man washed his hands, neither did Herod nor any one of his judges: and whereas they would not wash, Pilate rose up. And then Herod the king commanded that the Lord should be taken into their hands, saying unto them, 'All that I commanded you to do to him, do.'

Now there stood there Joseph the friend of Pilate and of the Lord, and he, knowing that they were about to crucify him, came unto Pilate and begged the body of Jesus for burial. And Pilate sending unto Herod, begged his body. And Herod said, 'Brother Pilate, even if none had begged for him, we should have buried him, since also the Sabbath is dawning; for it is written in the law that the sun should not set upon one that has been slain.'

And he delivered him unto the people before the first day of their Feast of Unleavened Bread. And they having taken the Lord pushed him as they ran, and said, 'Let us hale (drag along forcibly) the Son of God, now that we have authority over him.' And they put on him a purple robe, and made him sit upon the seat of judgement, saying, 'Give righteous judgement, thou King of Israel.' And one of them brought a crown of thorns and set it upon the Lord's head; and others stood and did spit in his eyes, and others buffeted his cheeks; and others did prick him with a reed, and some of them scourged him, saying, 'With this honour let us honour the son of God.'

And they brought two malefactors, and crucified the Lord between them. But he kept silence, as one feeling no pain. And when they set the cross upright, they wrote thereon: This is the King of Israel. And they laid his garments before him, and divided them among themselves and cast lots for them. But one of those malefactors reproached them, saying, 'We have thus suffered for the evils which we have done; but this man who has become the saviour of men, wherein has he injured you?' And they were angry with him, and commanded that his legs should not be broken, that so he might die in torment.

Now it was noon, and darkness prevailed over all Judea: and they were troubled and in an agony lest the sun should have set, while he yet lived: for it is written for them that the sun should not set upon him that has been slain. And one of them said, 'Give ye him to drink gall with vinegar.' And they mingled it and gave him to drink. And they fulfilled all things and accomplished their sins upon their own heads. And many went about with lamps, supposing that it was night: and some fell. And the Lord cried out aloud saying, 'My power, my power, thou hast forsaken me.' And when he had so said, he was taken up.

And in the same hour was the veil of the temple of Jerusalem rent in two.

And then they plucked the nails from the hands of the Lord and laid him upon the earth: and the whole earth was shaken, and there came a great fear on all.

Then the sun shone, and it was found to be the ninth hour. And the Jews rejoiced, and gave his body unto Joseph to bury it, because he had beheld all the good things which he did. And he took the Lord and washed him and wrapped him in linen and brought him unto his own sepulchre, which is called the Garden of Joseph.

Then the Jews and the elders and the priests, when they perceived how great evil they had done themselves, began to lament and to say, 'Woe unto our sins: the judgement and the end of Jerusalem is drawn nigh.'

But I with my fellows was in grief, and we were wounded in our minds and would have hid ourselves; for we were sought after by them as malefactors, and as thinking to set the temple on fire. And beside all these things we were fasting, and we sat mourning and weeping night and day until the Sabbath.

But the scribes and Pharisees and elders gathered one with another, for they had heard that all the people were murmuring and beating their breasts, saying, 'If these very great signs have come to pass at his death, behold how righteous he was.' And the elders were afraid and came unto Pilate, entreating him and saying, 'Give us soldiers that we may watch his sepulchre for three days, lest his disciples come and steal him away and the people suppose that he is risen from the dead, and do us hurt.' And Pilate gave them Petronius the centurion with soldiers to watch the sepulchre; and the elders and scribes came with them to the tomb, and when they had rolled a great stone they that were there, together with the centurion and the soldiers, set it upon the door of the tomb; and plastered thereon seven seals; and they pitched a tent there and kept watch.

And early in the morning as the Sabbath dawned, there came a multitude from Jerusalem and the region roundabout to see the sepulchre that had been sealed.

Now in the night whereon the Lord's day dawned, as the soldiers were keeping guard two by two in every watch, there came a great sound in the heaven, and they saw the heavens opened and two men descend thence, shining with a great light, and drawing near unto the sepulchre. And that stone which had been set on the door rolled away of itself and went back to the side, and the sepulchre was opened and both of the young men entered in. When therefore those soldiers saw that, they woke the centurion and the elders (for they also were there keeping watch); and while they were yet telling them the things which they had seen, they saw again three men come out of the sepulchre, and two of them sustaining the other, and a cross following after them. And of the two they saw that their heads reached unto heaven, but of him that was led by them they saw that it reached beyond the heavens. And they heard a voice out of the heavens saying, 'Have you preached to them that sleep? And an answer was heard from the cross, saying, 'Yes.'

Those men therefore took counsel one with another to go and report these things to Pilate. And while they yet thought thereabout, again the heavens were opened and a man descended and entered into the tomb. And they that were with the centurion when they saw that, hastened to go by night unto Pilate and left the sepulchre whereon they were keeping watch, and told all that they had seen, and were in great agony, saying, 'Of a truth he was the son of God.'

Pilate answered and said, 'I am clear from the blood of the son of God, but thus it seemed good unto you.' Then all they came and besought him and exhorted him to charge the centurion and the soldiers to tell nothing of that they had seen. 'For,' they said, 'it is expedient for us to incur the greatest sin before God, rather than to fall into the hands of the people of the Jews and be stoned.' Pilate therefore charged the centurion and the soldiers that they should say nothing.

Now early on the Lord's day Mary Magdalene, a disciple of the Lord (who, having not performed at the sepulchre of the Lord those things which women are accustomed to do unto them that die and are beloved of them, was afraid because of the Jews, for they were inflamed with anger) took women friends with her and came to the tomb where he was laid. And they feared lest the Jews should see them, and said, 'Even if we were not able to weep and lament him on that day whereon he was crucified, yet let us now do so at his tomb. But who will roll away for us the stone also that is set upon the door of the tomb, that we may enter in and sit beside him and perform that which is due? For the stone was great, and we fear lest any man see us. And if we cannot do so, yet let us cast down at the door these things which we bring for a memorial of him, and we will weep and lament until we come to our house.'

And they went and found the sepulchre open. And they drew near and looked in there, and saw there a young man sitting in the midst of the sepulchre, of a fair countenance and clad in very bright raiment, who said to them, 'Why have you come? Whom do you seek ? Not him that was crucified? He is risen and is departed; but if you do not believe it, look in and see the place where he lay, that he is not here: for he is risen and is departed thither whence he was sent.' Then the women were frightened and fled.

Now it was the last day of Unleavened Bread, and many were coming forth of the city and returning unto their own homes because the feast was at an end. But we, the twelve disciples of the Lord, were weeping and were in sorrow, and each one being grieved for that which had befallen departed unto his own house. But I, Simon Peter, and Andrew my brother, took our nets and went unto the sea: and there was with us Levi the son of Alphaeus, whom the Lord ...

Appendix IV Herodian Family tree

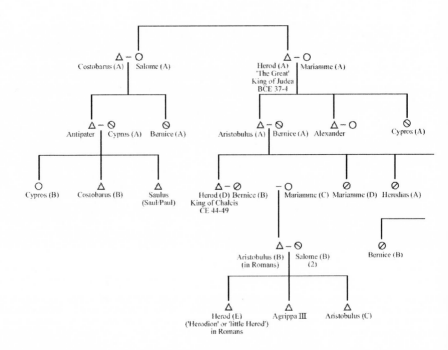

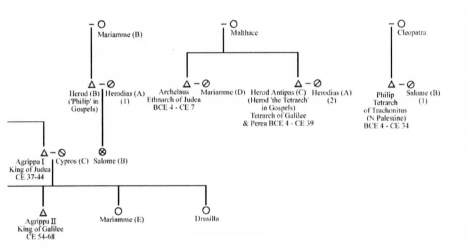

```
         ─ ○                         ─ ○                              ─ ○
        Mariamme (B)                Malthace                         Cleopatra

    △ ─ ⊘            ⊗          △ ─ ⊘       △ ─ ⊘              △ ─ ⊘
  Herod (B)  Herodias (A)   Archelaus  Mariamme (D)  Herod Antipas (C)  Herodias (A)   Philip    Salome (B)
 ('Philip' in    (1)        Ethnarch of Judea        (Herod 'the Tetrarch'    (2)      Tetrarch     (1)
  Gospels)                   BCE 4 - CE 7               in Gospels)                  of Trachonitus
                                                      Tetrarch of Galilee            (N Palestine)
                                                      & Perea BCE 4 - CE 39          BCE 4 - CE 34

   △ ─ ⊘      ⊗
Agrippa I  Cypros (C)  Salome (B)
King of Judea
CE 37-44

    △              ○              ○
 Agrippa II    Mariamme (E)      Drusilla
King of Galilee
 CE 54-68
```

(A) - (E) denotes different characters with same name

(1) - (2) order of marriage involving same character

⊗ cousin marriage

⊘ uncle-niece marriage

Appendix V Sadducee family of High Priests

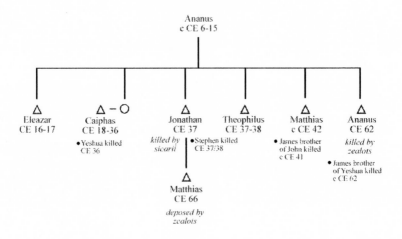

Ananus
c CE 6-15

Eleazar CE 16-17	Caiphas CE 18-36	Jonathan CE 37	Theophilus CE 37-38	Matthias c CE 42	Ananus CE 62

Eleazar
CE 16-17

Caiphas
CE 18-36
• Yeshua killed CE 36

Jonathan
CE 37
killed by sicarii

Theophilus
CE 37-38
• Stephen killed CE 37/38

Matthias
c CE 42
• James brother of John killed c CE 41

Ananus
CE 62
killed by zealots
• James brother of Yeshua killed c CE 62

Matthias
CE 66
deposed by zealots

Appendix VI Family of Lazarus

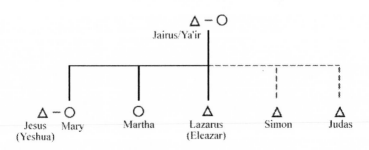

Jairus/Ya'ir

Jesus (Yeshua) — Mary   Martha   Lazarus (Eleazar)   Simon   Judas

Appendix VII
Messianic Family Tree

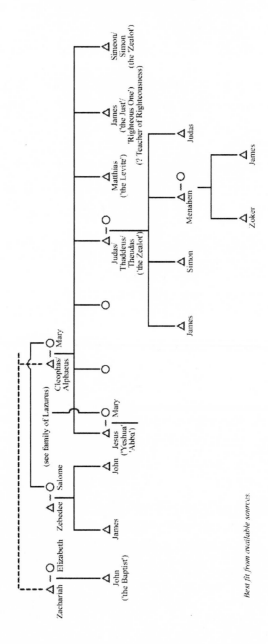

Best fit from available sources.

Appendix VIII Dramatis Personae

The list below comprises some of the key characters described in the text. It should be noted that there were fewer first names in the first century CE. People were also placed by reference to their family, as 'son of' or 'daughter of' someone. Some names like Eleazar (Lazarus), Shimon (Simon), Yeshua (Jesus), Yohannan (John) and Mariamme (Mary) were fairly common.

Agrippa I	grandson of Herod, King of Judea, CE 37-44, aka Herod Agrippa
Agrippa II	great-grandson of Herod, King of Galilee, CE 54-68
Alphaeus	variant of Clopas (qv)/Cleophas
Ananus	High Priest, CE 62, administrator in Jerusalem after Jewish uprising, killed by Idumeans
Ananias	High Priest, CE 46-52, killed by zealots in Jewish uprising
Andrew	brother of Simon (Peter)
Barabbas	imprisoned after insurrection in Jerusalem, release demanded by crowds (gospels), Aramaic – 'son of the master', in some sources 'Jesus Barabbas', possibly standing for Yeshua or son of Yeshua
Bartholomew	follower of Yeshua, one of the twelve disciples in

gospels, possibly Nathanael in John's gospel, from 'bar talmai' or 'bar thauma'

Cephas   see Simon (Peter)

Clopas   husband of Mary and father of James, Simon, Judas/Thaddeus, Joseph/Joses, and possibly Matthew/Levi (variant – Alphaeus)

Ephaphroditus member of Nero's court, patron and publisher for Josephus, custodian/supporter of Saul/Paul

Eleazar   Temple Captain, son of High Priest Ananias, cast

ben Ananias by Josephus as fighting on zealot side

Eleazar   zealot leader, prominent in Jewish uprising
ben Simon

Eleazar   sicarii leader, defended Masada, arguably also
ben Jair   gospel 'Lazarus'

Eleazar   supporter of Yeshua, brother of Mary and
(Lazarus)   Martha, Yeshua's brother-in-law

Herod   Roman-appointed King of Judea, BCE 37-4
'the Great'

Herod   see Agrippa I
Agrippa

Herod   son of Herod, Tetrarch of Galilee and Perea,
Antipas   BCE 4 – CE 39

Herod of Chalcis	grandson of Herod, King of Chalcis, CE 44-49
Herodias	divorced her husband (and uncle) Herod (Philip in the gospels) to marry another uncle, Herod Antipas
Hezekiah	bandit/messianic contender executed by Herod
Hezekiah	brother of Ananias (qv)
James	brother of Yeshua and his successor as leader of Nazoreans (Yacob)
James	son of Zebedee and Salome, cousin of Yeshua and brother of John, executed at behest of Agrippa I
James	crucified with his brother Simon by order of Governor Tiberias Alexander c CE 47, identified by Josephus as son of Judas the Galilean
James	grandson of Judas, who was brother of Yeshua, executed under purge by Trajan c CE 100
Jesus	Jewish messianic leader crucified by the Romans (English version of the Greek 'Iesous' which is in turn a transliteration of the Hebrew 'Yeshua')
Judas	one of three messianic figures conducting uprisings on death of Herod, BCE 4, son of Hezekiah who was executed by Herod

Judas	also known as 'Thaddeus' and 'Theuda', brother of Yeshua, grandfather of Zoker and James, arguably also the militant nationalist 'Theudas' killed by the Romans, arguably also father of James, Simon and Menahem, possibly in another guise Judas Iscariot
Judas the Galilean	leader of nationalist sect/tax rebel, led insurrection in CE 7 at time of census for tax purposes
Judas Iscariot	Nazoreans' bursar or treasurer when Yeshua leader, nickname – from 'sicarios', possibly doubling as Yeshua's brother Judas
John of Gishala	rebel leader opposed to Josephus, later leader of faction during Jewish uprising
John 'the Baptist'	son of Zachariah and Elizabeth (relative of Mary the mother of Yeshua), messianic claimant
John	son of Zebedee and Salome, brother of James, cousin of Yeshua
Joseph	in gospels, husband of Mary and father of Yeshua
Joseph 'of Arimathea'	asked Pilate for body of Yeshua, depicted in gospels as secret supporter
Josephus	born Yosef ben Matthias, commander of Galilee in Jewish uprising, defected to Romans becoming their propagandist/historian

Lazarus	see Eleazar (Lazarus)
Levi	son of Alphaeus, supporter/brother of Yeshua, possibly to be identified with disciple Matthew, qv
Mariamme	Maccabean princess, daughter of Alexander II, wife of Herod, executed by Herod, origin Greek from the Hebrew 'Miryam', rendered as 'Mary' in English
Mariamme	daughter of High Priest Boethus, wife of Herod
Martha	sister of Mary and Lazarus
Mary	wife of Clopas, mother of James, Simon, Judas (Thaddeus) and Joseph/Joses, and so also of Yeshua
Mary	sister of Martha and Lazarus, identified also as Mary Magdalene and as consort/wife of Yeshua
Mary Magdalene	see Mary above
Matthew	tax collector, in the gospel story, possibly to be identified with Levi son of Alphaeus (qv)
Menahem	Messianic (sicarii) leader in Jewish uprising, claiming kingship, identified as son of Judas the Galilean by Josephus
Nathanael	one of the twelve disciples, see Bartholomew

Nero	Roman Emperor CE 54-68
Paul	founder of breakaway 'Christian' sect in Acts, formerly Saul (qv)
Philip	son of Herod, Tetrarch of Trachonitus, BCE 4 – CE 34
Philip	supporter of Yeshua, one of the twelve disciples in the gospels
Philip	son of Jacimus, commander of Agrippa II's army, possibly source for character Philip in gospels and Acts
Salome	sister of Mary who was Yeshua's mother
Salome	daughter of Herodias, in the gospel story danced before Herod Antipas to secure a favour – the head of John the Baptist
Simon	appointed as Yeshua's chief minister, arguably also Simon 'with a reputation for religious scrupulousness' who confronted King Agrippa I, nicknamed 'the Rock', Petros in Greek, Cephas in Aramaic
Simon	crucified with his brother James by order of Governor Tiberias Alexander c CE 47, identified by Josephus as son of Judas the Galilean
Simon bar Gioras	leader in Jewish uprising, allied with Eleazar ben Jair and the sicarii

Simon /Simeon	brother of Yeshua and successor to James as leader of the Nazoreans, crucified by Emperor Trajan around CE 100
Theudas	rebel against the Romans, captured and executed while trying to escape with his supporters across the Jordan, around CE 46
Thomas	supporter of Yeshua, one of the twelve disciples in the gospels
Trajan	Roman Emperor, CE 98 – 117
Vespasian	Roman Emperor, CE 69 – 79
Yeshua	Jewish messianic leader crucified by the Romans (see Jesus)
Zoker	grandson of Judas, who was brother of Yeshua, executed under purge by Trajan c CE 100

References

Atwill J & Braunheim S, *Redating the radiocarbon dating of the Dead Sea Scrolls*, Dead Sea Discoveries, vol 11, no 2, 2004

Baigent M & Leigh R, *The Dead Sea Scrolls Deception*, Arrow Books, 2006

Book of the Maccabees, East and West Library, no author, 1949

Cresswell P A, *Censored Messiah*, O Books, 2004

Crossan J D, *The Birth of Christianity*, T & T Clark, Edinburgh, 1998

Crossan J D, *The Historical Jesus*, T & T Clark, Edinburgh, 1991

De Vaux R, *Archaeology and the Dead Sea Scrolls*, Oxford University Press, 1973

Ehrman B D, *Lost Scriptures*, Oxford University Press, 2003

Ehrman B D, *Misquoting Jesus*, Harper Collins, 2007

Eisenman R & Wise M, *The Dead Sea Scrolls Uncovered*, Element Books, 1992

Eisenman R, *Paul as Herodian*, Institute for Jewish-Christian Origins, 1996

Eisenman R, *James, the Brother of Jesus*, Faber & Faber, London 1997

Eisenman R, *The New Testament Code*, Watkins Publishing, 2006

Feldman L H (trans), *Jewish Antiquities*, Harvard University Press, 1965

Freke T & Gandy P, *The Jesus Mysteries*, Harper Collins, 1999

Garrow A, *The Gospel of Matthew's Dependence on the Didache*, T & T, 2004, (see also website www.didache-garrow.info)

Goldberg G J (comp), *A Chronology of the First Jewish Revolt against Rome*, 2000

Goldberg G J (comp), *Causes of the War against the Romans*, 2000

James M R (trans), *The Gospel of Peter*

Joyce D, *The Jesus Scroll*, Angus & Robertson, 1973

Maccoby H, *The Myth Maker*, Weidenfeld & Nicholson, 1986

Noth M, *The History of Israel*, Adam & Charles Black, 1960

Pagels E, *The Gnostic Gospels*, Weidenfeld & Nicholson, 1980

Porter J R, *The Lost Bible*, Duncan Baird, 2001

Roberts A & Donaldson J, *The Ante-Nicene Fathers*, Eerdmans, 1995 (for *Pseudoclementine Recognitions* and *Homilies*)

Schonfield H J, *The Passover Plot*, Hutchinson, London, 1965

Silberman N A, *The Hidden Scrolls*, BCA, 1995

Stirling J (ed), *The Bible, Revised Standard Version*, W M Collins

Thackeray H ST J (trans), *The Life*, Harvard University Press 1926

Thackeray H ST J (trans), *Against Apion*, Harvard University Press, 1926

Vermes G, *The Complete Dead Sea Scrolls in English*, Penguin Books, 1965

Williamson G A, (trans), *The Jewish War*, Penguin Books, 1981

Wilson E J & Kiraz G A, *The Old Syriac Gospels*, Georgias Press, 2003

Yadin Y, *Masada*, Weidenfeld & Nicholson, 1966

BOOKS

O is a symbol of the world, of oneness and unity. In different
cultures it also means the "eye," symbolizing knowledge and
insight. We aim to publish books that are accessible, constructive
and that challenge accepted opinion, both that of academia and
the "moral majority."

Our books are available in all good English language
bookstores worldwide. If you don't see the book on the shelves
ask the bookstore to order it for you, quoting the ISBN number
and title. Alternatively you can order online (all major online
retail sites carry our titles) or contact the distributor in the
relevant country, listed on the copyright page.

See our website **www.o-books.net** for a full list of over 500
titles, growing by 100 a year.

And tune in to myspiritradio.com for our book review radio show,
hosted by June-Elleni Laine, where you can listen to the authors
discussing their books.

MySpiritRadio